MOUS
Excel 2000
Exam Prep

Elizabeth Eisner Reding
Tara Lynn O'Keefe

The Coriolis Group, LLC
14455 N. Hayden Road, Suite 220
Scottsdale, Arizona 85260

480/483-0192
FAX 480/483-0193
http://www.coriolis.com

ISBN: 1-57610-480-X

President, CEO
Keith Weiskamp

Publisher
Steve Sayre

Acquisitions Editor
Jeff Kellum

Marketing Manager
Cynthia Caldwell

Product Managers
Sharon Sanchez McCarson
Rebecca VanEsselstine

Production Editors
Kim Eoff
Jennifer Goguen

Editorial Assistant
Hilary Long

Cover Design
Jesse Dunn

Layout Design
Joseph Lee
April Nielsen

CD-ROM Developer
Robert Clarfield

CORIOLIS

14455 North Hayden Road • Suite 220 • Scottsdale, Arizona 85260

Coriolis: The Smartest Way To Get Certified™

To help you reach your goals, we've listened to readers like you, and we've designed our entire product line around you and the way you like to study, learn, and master challenging subjects.

In addition to our highly popular *Exam Cram* and *Exam Prep* books, we offer several other products to help you pass certification exams. Our *Practice Tests* and *Flash Cards* are designed to make your studying fun and productive. Our *Audio Reviews* have received rave reviews from our customers— and they're the perfect way to make the most of your drive time!

The newest way to get certified is the *Exam Cram Personal Trainer* —a highly interactive, personalized self-study course based on the best-selling *Exam Cram* series. It's the first certification-specific product to completely link a customizable learning tool, exclusive *Exam Cram* content, and multiple testing techniques so you can study what, how, and when you want.

Exam Cram Insider —a biweekly newsletter containing the latest in certification news, study tips, and announcements from Certification Insider Press—gives you an ongoing look at the hottest certification programs. (To subscribe, send an email to **eci@coriolis.com** and type "subscribe insider" in the body of the email.) We also sponsor the Certified Crammer Society and the Coriolis Help Center—two other resources that will help you get certified even faster!

Help us continue to provide the very best certification study materials possible. Write us or email us at **cipq@coriolis.com** and let us know how our books have helped you study. Tell us about new features that you'd like us to add. Send us a story about how we've helped you; if we use it in one of our books, we'll send you an official Coriolis shirt!

Good luck with your certification exam and your career. Thank you for allowing us to help you achieve your goals.

Keith Weiskamp
President and CEO

Preface

Welcome to *MOUS Excel 2000 Exam Prep.* This highly visual book offers users a comprehensive hands-on introduction to Microsoft Excel 2000 and also serves as an excellent reference for future use.

▶ Organization and Coverage

This text contains sixteen units that cover basic to advanced Excel skills. In these units, you learn how to build, edit, and format worksheets and charts, work with formulas and functions, publish workbooks to the Web, automate worksheet tasks, use lists and analyze list data, use PivotTables, exchange data with other programs, and program with Excel.

▶ About this Approach

What makes this approach so effective at teaching software skills? It's quite simple. Each skill is presented on two facing pages, with the step-by-step instructions on the left page, and large screen illustrations on the right. You can focus on a single skill without having to turn the page. This unique design makes information extremely accessible and easy to absorb, and provides a great reference for after the course is over.

Each lesson, or "information display," contains the following elements:

Each 2-page spread focuses on a single skill.

Clear step-by-step directions explain how to complete the specific task. When you follow the numbered steps, you quickly learn how each procedure is performed and what the results will be.

Concise text that introduces the basic principles discussed in the lesson. Procedures are easier to learn when concepts fit into a framework.

Hints as well as trouble-shooting advice, right where you need it — next to the step itself.

Clues to Use boxes provide concise information that either expands on one component of the major lesson skill or describes an independent task that is in some way related to the major lesson skill.

Every lesson features large-size, two-color representations of what your screen should look like after completing the numbered steps.

Quickly accessible summaries of key terms, toolbar buttons, or

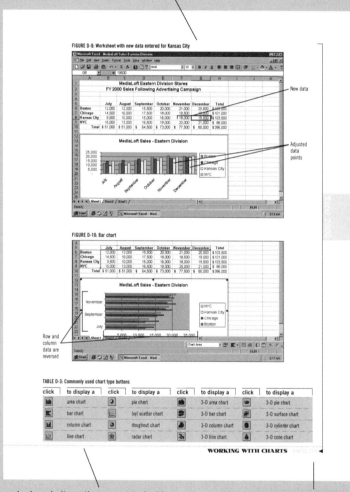

FIGURE D-9: Worksheet with new data entered for Kansas City

New data

Adjusted data points

FIGURE D-10: Bar chart

Row and column data are reversed

TABLE D-3: Commonly used chart type buttons

click	to display a	click	to display a	click	to display a	click	to display a
	area chart		pie chart		3-D area chart		3-D pie chart
	bar chart		(xy) scatter chart		3-D bar chart		3-D surface chart
	column chart		doughnut chart		3-D column chart		3-D cylinder chart
	line chart		radar chart		3-D line chart		3-D cone chart

WORKING WITH CHARTS

Features

The two-page lesson format featured in this book provides the new user with a powerful learning experience. Additionally, this book contains the following features:

▶ **MOUS Certification Coverage**
Each unit opener has a ⌊MOUS⌋ next to it to indicate where Microsoft Office User Specialist (MOUS) skills are covered. This book thoroughly prepares you to learn the skills needed to pass the Excel Core and Expert 2000 exams.

▶ **End of Unit Material**
Each unit concludes with a Concepts Review that tests your understanding of what you learned in the unit. The Concepts Review is followed by a Skills Review, which provides you with additional hands-on practice of the skills. The Visual Workshops that follow the Skills Review helps you develop critical thinking skills. You are shown completed Web pages or screens and are asked to recreate them from scratch.

keyboard alternatives connected with the lesson material. You can refer easily to this information when working on Your own projects at a later time.

The page numbers are designed like a road map. Excel indicates the Excel section, D indicates the fourth unit, and 9 indicates the page within the unit.

Contents

Preface   IV
Features   V

Getting Started with Excel 2000   EXCEL A-1
Defining Spreadsheet Software ....EXCEL A-2
Starting Excel 2000 ....EXCEL A-4
Viewing the Excel Window ....EXCEL A-6
  Personalized toolbars and menus in Excel 2000............EXCEL A-7
Opening and Saving a Workbook..................................EXCEL A-8
Entering Labels and Values ....EXCEL A-10
  Navigating a worksheet ....EXCEL A-11
Previewing and Printing a Worksheet ....EXCEL A-12
  Using Zoom in Print Preview ....EXCEL A-12
Getting Help ....EXCEL A-14
  Changing the Office Assistant ....EXCEL A-14
Closing a Workbook and Exiting Excel ....EXCEL A-16
Concepts Review ....EXCEL A-18
Skills Review ....EXCEL A-20
Visual Workshop ....EXCEL A-22

Building and Editing Worksheets   EXCEL B-1
Planning and Designing a Worksheet ....EXCEL B-2
Editing Cell Entries and Working with Ranges ....EXCEL B-4
  Using range names in a workbook ....EXCEL B-5
Entering Formulas ....EXCEL B-6
  Order of precedence in Excel formulas.......................EXCEL B-7
Introducing Excel Functions......................................EXCEL B-8
  Using the MIN and MAX functions ....EXCEL B-9
Copying and Moving Cell Entries ....EXCEL B-10
  Using the Office Clipboard ....EXCEL B-11
Understanding Relative and Absolute Cell References ....EXCEL B-12
  Using a mixed reference...EXCEL B-12
Copying Formulas with Relative Cell References ....EXCEL B-14
  Filling cells with sequential text or values ....EXCEL B-14
Copying Formulas with Absolute Cell References ....EXCEL B-16
  Copying and moving using named ranges....................EXCEL B-17
Naming and Moving a Sheet ....EXCEL B-18
  Moving and copying worksheets ....EXCEL B-19
Concepts Review ....EXCEL B-20
Skills Review ....EXCEL B-21
Visual Workshop ....EXCEL B-22

Formatting a Worksheet — EXCEL C-1

Formatting Values .... EXCEL C-2
Using the Format Painter .... EXCEL C-3
Using Fonts and Font Sizes .... EXCEL C-4
Using the Formatting toolbar to change fonts and font sizes .... EXCEL C-4
Changing Attributes and Alignment of Labels .... EXCEL C-6
Using AutoFormat .... EXCEL C-7
Adjusting Column Widths .... EXCEL C-8
Specifying row height .... EXCEL C-8
Inserting and Deleting Rows and Columns .... EXCEL C-10
Using dummy columns and rows .... EXCEL C-11
Applying Colors, Patterns, and Borders .... EXCEL C-12
Using color to organize a worksheet .... EXCEL C-12
Using Conditional Formatting .... EXCEL C-14
Deleting conditional formatting .... EXCEL C-15
Checking Spelling .... EXCEL C-16
Modifying the spell checker .... EXCEL C-16
Concepts Review .... EXCEL C-18
Skills Review .... EXCEL C-19
Visual Workshop .... EXCEL C-21

Working with Charts — EXCEL D-1

Planning and Designing a Chart .... EXCEL D-2
Creating a Chart .... EXCEL D-4
Moving and Resizing a Chart .... EXCEL D-6
Identifying chart objects .... EXCEL D-7
Editing a Chart .... EXCEL D-8
Rotating a chart .... EXCEL D-8
Formatting a Chart .... EXCEL D-10
Enhancing a Chart .... EXCEL D-12
Changing text font and alignment in charts .... EXCEL D-12
Annotating and Drawing on a Chart .... EXCEL D-14
Exploding a pie slice .... EXCEL D-15
Previewing and Printing a Chart .... EXCEL D-16
Using the Page Setup dialog box for a chart .... EXCEL D-16
Concepts Review .... EXCEL D-18
Skills Review .... EXCEL D-20
Visual Workshop .... EXCEL D-22

Working with Formulas and Functions — EXCEL E-1

Creating a Formula with Several Operators .... EXCEL E-2
*Using Paste Special to paste formulas and values
and to perform calculations* .... EXCEL E-3
Using Names in a Formula .... EXCEL E-4
Producing a list of names .... EXCEL E-5
Generating Multiple Totals with AutoSum .... EXCEL E-6
Quick calculations with AutoCalculate .... EXCEL E-7
Using Dates in Calculations .... EXCEL E-8

Using date functions...EXCEL E-8

Custom number and date formats...............................EXCEL E-9

Building a Conditional Formula with the IF Function ....EXCEL E-10

Inserting and deleting selected cells ....EXCEL E-11

Using Statistical Functions ....EXCEL E-12

Using the Formula Palette to enter and edit formulas...............EXCEL E-13

Calculating Payments with the PMT Function ....EXCEL E-14

Calculating future value with the FV function ....EXCEL E-15

Displaying and Printing Formula Contents................................EXCEL E-16

*Setting margins and alignment when printing
part of a worksheet*...EXCEL E-17

Concepts Review ....EXCEL E-18

Skills Review ....EXCEL E-19

Visual Workshop ....EXCEL E-21

Managing Workbooks and Preparing Them for the Web

EXCEL F-1

Freezing Columns and Rows..EXCEL F-2

Splitting the worksheet into multiple panes ....EXCEL F-3

Inserting and Deleting Worksheets...EXCEL F-4

Specifying headers and footers ....EXCEL F-5

Consolidating Data with 3-D References ....EXCEL F-6

Consolidating data from different workbooks using linking ....EXCEL F-7

Hiding and Protecting Worksheet Areas ....EXCEL F-8

Changing workbook properties..EXCEL F-9

Saving Custom Views of a Worksheet ....EXCEL F-10

Using a workspace ....EXCEL F-11

Controlling Page Breaks and Page Numbering ....EXCEL F-12

Using Page Break Preview ....EXCEL F-13

Creating a Hyperlink between Excel Files ....EXCEL F-14

Using hyperlinks to navigate large worksheets...........................EXCEL F-14

Inserting a picture ....EXCEL F-15

Saving an Excel file as an HTML Document ....EXCEL F-16

Send a workbook via e-mail..EXCEL F-17

Concepts Review ....EXCEL F-18

Skills Review ....EXCEL F-19

Visual Workshop ....EXCEL F-21

Automating Worksheet Tasks

EXCEL G-1

Planning a Macro ....EXCEL G-2

Macros and viruses ....EXCEL G-3

Recording a Macro ....EXCEL G-4

Using Templates to Create a Workbook ....EXCEL G-5

Running a Macro .... EXCEL G-6

Editing a Macro .... EXCEL G-8

   Adding comments to code .... EXCEL G-9

Using Shortcut Keys with Macros .... EXCEL G-10

Using the Personal Macro Workbook .... EXCEL G-12

   Working with the Personal Macro Workbook ...... EXCEL G-13

Adding a Macro as a Menu Item .... EXCEL G-14

Creating a Toolbar for Macros .... EXCEL G-16

Concepts Review .... EXCEL G-18

Skills Review .... EXCEL G-20

Visual Workshop .... EXCEL G-22

Using Lists   EXCEL H-1

Planning a List .... EXCEL H-2

   Lists versus databases .... EXCEL H-3

Creating a List .... EXCEL H-4

   Maintaining the quality of information in a list ..... EXCEL H-5

Adding Records with the Data Form .... EXCEL H-6

Finding Records .... EXCEL H-8

   Using wildcards to fine-tune your search .... EXCEL H-9

Deleting Records .... EXCEL H-10

   Advantage of deleting records from the worksheet .. EXCEL H-11

Sorting a List by One Field .... EXCEL H-12

   Rotating and indenting to improve label appearance .. EXCEL H-13

Sorting a List by Multiple Fields .... EXCEL H-14

   Specifying a custom sort order .... EXCEL H-15

Printing a List .... EXCEL H-16

   Setting a print area .... EXCEL H-17

Concepts Review .... EXCEL H-18

Skills Review .... EXCEL H-19

Visual Workshop .... EXCEL H-24

Analyzing List Data   EXCEL I-1

Retrieving Records with AutoFilter .... EXCEL I-2

Creating a Custom Filter .... EXCEL I-4

   And and Or logical conditions .... EXCEL I-5

Filtering a List with Advanced Filter .... EXCEL I-6

   Understanding the criteria range .... EXCEL I-7

Extracting List Data .... EXCEL I-8

   Understanding the criteria range and the copy-to location .. EXCEL I-9

Creating Subtotals Using Grouping and Outlines .. EXCEL I-10

   Show or hide details in an Excel outline .... EXCEL I-11

Looking Up Values in a List .... EXCEL I-12

   Using the HLOOKUP function .... EXCEL I-13

Summarizing List Data .... EXCEL I-14

Using Data Validation for List Entries...EXCEL I-16
Concepts Review ....EXCEL I-18
Skills Review ....EXCEL I-19
Visual Workshop ....EXCEL I-21

Enhancing Charts and Worksheets — EXCEL J-1

Selecting a Custom Chart Type ....EXCEL J-2
   Creating a custom chart type ....EXCEL J-3
Customizing a Data Series..EXCEL J-4
   Removing, inserting, and formatting legends...............................EXCEL J-5
Formatting a Chart Axis ....EXCEL J-6
Adding a Data Table to a Chart ....EXCEL J-8
Rotating a Chart...EXCEL J-10
Enhancing a Chart with WordArt..EXCEL J-12
Rotating Text ....EXCEL J-14
   Rotating chart labels..EXCEL J-15
Mapping Data ....EXCEL J-16
Concepts Review ....EXCEL J-18
Skills Review..EXCEL J-20
Visual Workshop ....EXCEL J-22

Using a What-If Analysis — EXCEL K-1

Defining a What-If Analysis ....EXCEL K-2
Tracking a What-If Analysis with Scenario Manager ....EXCEL K-4
   Merging scenarios ....EXCEL K-4
Generating a Scenario Summary ....EXCEL K-6
   Using Report Manager..EXCEL K-7
Projecting Figures Using a Data Table ....EXCEL K-8
Creating a Two-Input Data Table...EXCEL K-10
Using Goal Seek..EXCEL K-12
Setting Up a Complex What-If Analysis with Solver.....................EXCEL K-14
Running Solver and Generating an Answer Report ....EXCEL K-16
Concepts Review ....EXCEL K-18
Skills Review ....EXCEL K-19
Visual Workshop ....EXCEL K-22

Summarizing Data with PivotTables — EXCEL L-1

Planning and Designing a PivotTable Report ....EXCEL L-2
Creating a PivotTable Report ....EXCEL L-4
Changing the Summary Function of a PivotTable Report ....EXCEL L-6
Analyzing Three-Dimensional Data..EXCEL L-8
Updating a PivotTable Report..EXCEL L-10
   Maintaining original table data...EXCEL L-11
Changing the Structure and Format of a PivotTable Report ......EXCEL L-12
Creating a PivotChart Report ....EXCEL L-14
Using the GETPIVOTDATA Function ....EXCEL L-16
Concepts Review ....EXCEL L-18
Skills Review ....EXCEL L-19

Visual Workshop ....EXCEL L-22

Exchanging Data with Other Programs EXCEL M-1

Planning a Data Exchange ....EXCEL M-2
Importing a Text File ....EXCEL M-4
   Other ways to import text files ....EXCEL M-5
Importing a Database Table ....EXCEL M-6
   Exporting Excel data ....EXCEL M-7
Inserting a Graphic File in a Worksheet ....EXCEL M-8
   Importing data from HTML files ....EXCEL M-9
Embedding a Worksheet ....EXCEL M-10
Linking a Worksheet to Another Program ....EXCEL M-12
   Managing links ....EXCEL M-13
Embedding an Excel Chart into a PowerPoint Slide.......EXCEL M-14
Converting a List to an Access Table ....EXCEL M-16
Concepts Review...EXCEL M-18
Skills Review ....EXCEL M-19
Visual Workshop...EXCEL M-22

Sharing Excel Files and Incorporating
Web Information   EXCEL N-1

Sharing Excel Files...EXCEL N-2
Setting Up a Shared Workbook ....EXCEL N-4
Tracking Changes in a Shared Workbook ....EXCEL N-6
   Merging workbooks ....EXCEL N-7
Applying and Removing Passwords ....EXCEL N-8
   Removing passwords ....EXCEL N-9
Creating an Interactive Worksheet for an
Intranet or the Web...EXCEL N-10
   Managing HTML files on an intranet or Web site ......EXCEL N-11
Creating an Interactive PivotTable for an
Intranet or the Web...EXCEL N-12
   Adding fields to a PivotTable list using the Web browser..........EXCEL N-13
Creating Hyperlinks between Excel Files and the Web ....EXCEL N-14
   Using hyperlinks to navigate large worksheets..........EXCEL N-15
Running Queries to Retrieve Data on the Web ....EXCEL N-16
   Finding stock symbols ....EXCEL N-16
   Creating a new query to retrieve Web page data.......EXCEL N-17
Concepts Review..EXCEL N-18
Skills Review ....EXCEL N-19
Visual Workshop ....EXCEL N-21

Gaining Control over Your Work   EXCEL O-1

Finding Files ....EXCEL O-2
   File properties..EXCEL O-3
Auditing a Worksheet ....EXCEL O-4
   Circular references ....EXCEL O-5
   Hiding and displaying toolbars ....EXCEL O-5
Outlining a Worksheet ....EXCEL O-6

Controlling Worksheet Calculations ....EXCEL O-8
Creating Custom AutoFill Lists ....EXCEL O-10
Customizing Excel ....EXCEL O-12
Adding a Comment to a Cell ....EXCEL O-14
 Preview and print multiple worksheets ....EXCEL O-15
Saving a Workbook as a Template ....EXCEL O-16
 Storing, applying, and modifying templates ....EXCEL O-17
Concepts Review ....EXCEL O-18
Skills Review ....EXCEL O-20
Visual Workshop ....EXCEL O-22

Programming with Excel   EXCEL P-1
Viewing VBA Code ....EXCEL P-2
 Understanding the Visual Basic Editor ....EXCEL P-3
Analyzing VBA Code ....EXCEL P-4
Writing VBA Code ....EXCEL P-6
 Entering code ....EXCEL P-7
Adding a Conditional Statement ....EXCEL P-8
Prompting the User for Data ....EXCEL P-10
Debugging a Macro ....EXCEL P-12
Creating a Main Procedure ....EXCEL P-14
Running a Main Procedure ....EXCEL P-16
Concepts Review ....EXCEL P-18
Skills Review ....EXCEL P-19
Visual Workshop ....EXCEL P-22

Excel Glossary   1
Index   7

Getting
Started with Excel 2000

Objectives

▶ **Define spreadsheet software**
▶ **Start Excel 2000**
▶ **View the Excel window**
⌊MOUS⌉ ▶ **Open and save a workbook**
⌊MOUS⌉ ▶ **Enter labels and values**
⌊MOUS⌉ ▶ **Preview and print a worksheet**
⌊MOUS⌉ ▶ **Get Help**
▶ **Close a workbook and exit Excel**

In this unit, you will learn how to start Microsoft Excel 2000 and use different elements of the Excel window. You will also learn how to open and save existing files, enter data in a worksheet, and use the extensive Help system. Scenario▶ Jim Fernandez is the office manager at MediaLoft, a nationwide chain of bookstore cafés selling books, CDs, and videos. MediaLoft cafés also sell coffee and pastries to customers. Jim uses Excel to analyze a worksheet that summarizes budget information for the MediaLoft Café in the New York City store.

Defining Spreadsheet Software

Microsoft Excel is an electronic spreadsheet program that runs on Windows computers. You use an **electronic spreadsheet** to perform numeric calculations rapidly and accurately. See Table A-1 for common ways spreadsheets are used in business. The electronic spreadsheet that you produce when using Excel is also referred to as a **worksheet**. Scenario Excel helps Jim produce professional-looking documents that can be updated automatically so they always have accurate information. Figure A-1 shows a budget worksheet that Jim created using pencil and paper, while Figure A-2 shows the same worksheet Jim created using Excel.

The advantages of using Excel include:

 ### Enter data quickly and accurately

With Excel, you can enter information faster and more accurately than when using the pencil-and-paper method. For example, in the MediaLoft NYC Café budget, certain expenses such as rent, cleaning supplies, and products supplied on a yearly plan (coffee, creamers, sweeteners) remain constant for the year. You can copy the expenses that don't change from quarter to quarter, and then use Excel to calculate Total Expenses and Net Income for each quarter by simply supplying the data and formulas.

 ### Recalculate data easily

Fixing typing errors or updating data using Excel is easy, and the results of a changed entry are recalculated automatically. For example, if you receive updated expense figures for Quarter 4, you simply enter the new numbers and Excel recalculates the worksheet.

 ### Perform a what-if analysis

One of the most powerful decision-making features of Excel is the ability to change data and then quickly view the recalculated results. Anytime you use a worksheet to answer the question "what if," you are performing a **what-if analysis**. For instance, if the advertising budget for a quarter is increased to $3,600, you can enter the new figure into the worksheet and immediately see the impact on the overall budget.

 ### Change the appearance of information

Excel provides powerful features for enhancing a spreadsheet so that information is visually appealing and easy to understand. You can use boldface type and shade text headings or numbers to add emphasis to key data in the worksheet.

 ### Create charts

Excel makes it easy to create charts based on information in a worksheet. With Excel, charts are automatically updated as data changes. The worksheet in Figure A-2 includes a pie chart that graphically shows the distribution of the MediaLoft NYC Café's budget expenses for the year 2000.

 ### Share information with other users

Because everyone at MediaLoft is now using Microsoft Office, it's easy to share worksheet data among colleagues. For example, you can complete the MediaLoft budget that your manager started creating in Excel. Simply access the files you need or want to share through the network or from a disk, and then make any changes or additions.

 ### Create new worksheets from existing ones quickly

It's easy to take an existing Excel worksheet and quickly modify it to create a new one. When you are ready to create next year's budget, you can open the file for this year's budget, save it with a new file name, and use the existing data as a starting point.

FIGURE A-1: Traditional paper worksheet

MediaLoft NYC Café Budget					
	Qtr1	Qtr 2	Qtr 3	Qtr 4	Total
Net Sales	48,000	76,000	64,000	80,000	268,000
Expenses					
Salary	13,000	13,000	13,000	13,000	52,000
Rent	3,500	3,500	3,500	3,500	14,000
Advertising	3,600	8,000	16,000	20,000	47,600
Cleaners	1,500	1,500	1,500	1,500	6,000
Pastries	2,500	2,500	2,500	2,500	10,000
Milk/Cream	1,000	1,000	1,000	1,000	4,000
Coffee/Tea	4,250	4,250	4,250	4,250	17,000
Sweeteners	300	300	300	300	1,200
Total Expenses	29,650	34,050	42,050	46,050	151,800
Net Income	18,350	41,950	21,950	33,950	116,200

FIGURE A-2: Excel worksheet

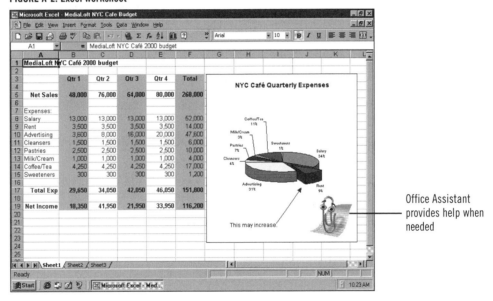

Office Assistant provides help when needed

TABLE A-1: Common business uses for spreadsheets

spreadsheets are used to:	by:
Maintain values	Calculating numbers1
Represent values visually	Creating charts based on worksheet figures
Create consecutively numbered pages using multiple workbook sheets	Printing reports containing workbook sheets
Organize data	Sorting data in ascending or descending order
Analyze data	Creating data summaries and short-lists using PivotTables or AutoFilters
Create what-if data scenarios	Using variable values to investigate and sample different outcomes

Excel 2000

GETTING STARTED WITH EXCEL 2000 EXCEL A-3 ◄

Excel 2000

Starting Excel 2000

To start any Windows program, you use the Start button on the taskbar. A slightly different procedure might be required for computers on a network and those that use Windows-enhancing utilities. If you need assistance, ask your instructor or technical support person. Scenario▶ Jim is ready to begin work on the budget for the MediaLoft Café in New York City. He begins by starting Excel.

Steps 123 4

1. **Point to the Start button** [Start] **on the taskbar**
   The Start button is on the left side of the taskbar and is used to start programs on your computer.

2. **Click** [Start]
   Microsoft Excel is located in the Programs group, which is at the top of the Start menu, as shown in Figure A-3.

Trouble?
If you don't see the Microsoft Excel icon, consult your instructor or technical support person.

3. **Point to Programs**
   All the programs on your computer, including Microsoft Excel, are listed in this area of the Start menu. See Figure A-4. Your program list might look different depending on the programs installed on your computer.

4. **Click the Microsoft Excel program icon on the Programs menu**
   Excel opens and a blank worksheet appears. In the next lesson, you will familiarize yourself with the elements of the Excel worksheet window.

FIGURE A-3: Start menu

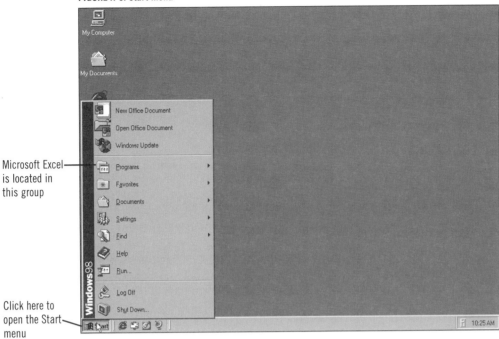

Microsoft Excel is located in this group

Click here to open the Start menu

FIGURE A-4: Programs list

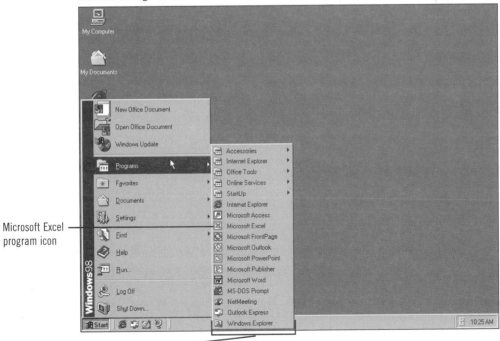

Microsoft Excel program icon

Your list of programs might vary

Viewing the Excel Window

When you start Excel, the **worksheet window** appears on your screen. The worksheet window includes the tools that enable you to create and work with worksheets. [Scenario] Jim needs to familiarize himself with the Excel worksheet window and its elements before he starts working with the budget worksheet. Compare the descriptions below to Figure A-5.

Trouble?

If your worksheet does not fill the screen as shown in Figure A-5, click the Maximize button in the worksheet window.

The **worksheet window** contains a grid of columns and rows. Columns are labeled alphabetically (A, B, C, etc.) and rows are labeled numerically (1, 2, 3, etc.). The worksheet window displays only a tiny fraction of the whole worksheet, which has a total of 256 columns and 65,536 rows. The intersection of a column and a row is a **cell**. Cells can contain text, numbers, formulas, or a combination of all three. Every cell has its own unique location or **cell address**, which is identified by the coordinates of the intersecting column and row. For example, the cell address of the cell in the upper-left corner of a worksheet is A1.

The **cell pointer** is a dark rectangle that highlights or outlines the cell you are working in. This cell is called the **active cell**. In Figure A-5, the cell pointer is located at A1, so A1 is the active cell. To activate a different cell, just click any other cell or press the arrow keys on your keyboard to move the cell pointer elsewhere.

The **title bar** displays the program name (Microsoft Excel) and the file name of the open worksheet (in this case the default filename, Book1). As shown in Figure A-5, the title bar also contains a control menu box, a Close button, and resizing buttons, which are common to all Windows programs.

The **menu bar** contains menus from which you choose Excel commands. As with all Windows programs, you can choose a menu command by clicking it with the mouse or by pressing [Alt] plus the underlined letter in the menu name. When you click a menu, a short list of commonly used commands may appear at first; you can wait or click the double arrows at the bottom of the menu to see expanded menus.

The **name box** displays the active cell address. In Figure A-5, "A1" appears in the name box, indicating that A1 is the active cell.

The **formula bar** allows you to enter or edit data in the worksheet.

The **toolbars** contain buttons for frequently used Excel commands. The **Standard toolbar** is located just below the left edge of the menu bar and contains buttons that affect operations within the worksheet. The **Formatting toolbar**—to the right of the Standard toolbar—contains buttons that change the worksheet's appearance. Each button contains a graphic representation of its function. For instance, the face of the Printing button contains a printer. To choose a button, simply click it with the left mouse button. Not all the buttons on the Standard and Formatting toolbars are visible on the screen. To view other toolbar buttons, click the More Buttons button [»] at the right end of each toolbar to display a list of additional buttons. Throughout the lessons in this book, you will need to remember to click the More Buttons button if a button you are instructed to click is not visible on your screen. When you use a button from the More Buttons list, Excel adds it to your visible toolbar. That's why each user's toolbars look unique. Be sure to read the Clues to Use in this lesson to learn more about working with Excel's toolbars.

Sheet tabs below the worksheet grid let you keep your work in collections called **workbooks**. Each workbook contains three worksheets by default and can contain a maximum of 255 sheets. **Sheet tabs** can be given meaningful names. **Sheet tab scrolling buttons** help you move from one sheet to another.

The **status bar** is located at the bottom of the Excel window. The left side of the status bar provides a brief description of the active command or task in progress. The right side of the status bar shows the status of important keys such as [Caps Lock] and [Num Lock].

FIGURE A-5: Excel worksheet window elements

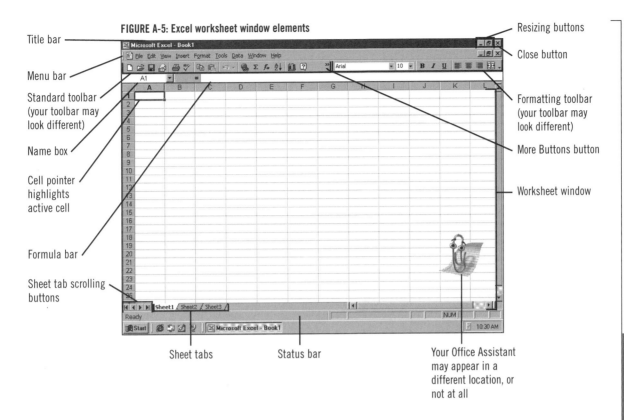

Title bar

Menu bar

Standard toolbar
(your toolbar may
look different)

Name box

Cell pointer
highlights
active cell

Formula bar

Sheet tab scrolling
buttons

Resizing buttons

Close button

Formatting toolbar
(your toolbar may
look different)

More Buttons button

Worksheet window

Sheet tabs   Status bar

Your Office Assistant
may appear in a
different location, or
not at all

CLUES TO USE

Personalized toolbars and menus in Excel 2000

Excel toolbars and menus modify themselves to your working style. The Standard and Formatting toolbars you see when you first start Excel include the most frequently used buttons. To locate a button not visible on a toolbar, click the **More Buttons button** ʺ on that toolbar to see the list of additional toolbar buttons. As you work, Excel promotes the buttons you use to the visible toolbars, and demotes the buttons you don't use to the More Buttons list. Similarly, Excel menus adjust to your work habits, so that the commands you use most often automatically appear on the shortened menus. Click the double arrow at the bottom of a menu to view additional menu commands. You can return toolbars and menus to their default settings by clicking Reset my usage data on the Options tab of the Customize dialog box, as shown in Figure A-6. Resetting your usage data erases changes made automatically to your menus and toolbars. It does not affect the options you customize.

FIGURE A-6: Customize dialog box

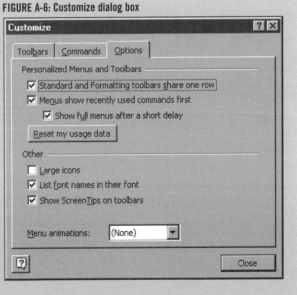

Excel 2000

Opening and Saving a Workbook

Sometimes it's more efficient to create a new worksheet by modifying one that already exists. This saves you from having to retype information that can be reused from previous work. Throughout this book, you will create new worksheets by opening a file from your Project Disk, using the Save As command to create a copy of the file with a new name, and then modifying the new file by following the lesson steps. Use the Save command to store changes made to an existing file. It is a good idea to save your work every 15 minutes or before printing. Saving the files with new names keeps your original Project Disk files intact, in case you have to start the lesson over again or you wish to repeat an exercise. Scenario > Jim wants to complete the New York City MediaLoft Café budget that a member of the accounting staff has been working on. Jim opens the budget workbook and then uses the Save As command to create a copy with a new name.

1. Insert your Project Disk in the appropriate disk drive

2. Click the **Open button** 🖻 on the Standard toolbar
   The Open dialog box opens. See Figure A-7.

3. Click the **Look in list arrow**, then click the **drive that contains your Project Disk**
   A list of the files on your Project Disk appears in the Open dialog box.

QuickTip

You could also double-click the filename in the Open dialog box to open the file.

4. Click the file **EX A-1**, then click **Open**
   The file EX A-1 opens.

5. Click **File** on the menu bar, then click **Save As**
   The Save As dialog box opens with the drive containing your Project Disk displayed in the Save in list box. You should save all your files to your Project Disk, unless instructed otherwise.

QuickTip

You can click 🖫 or use the shortcut key [Ctrl][S] to save a workbook using the same filename.

6. In the File name text box, select the current file name (if necessary), type **MediaLoft Café Budget**, as shown in Figure A-8, then click **Save**
   Both the Save As dialog box and the file EX A-1 close, and a duplicate file named MediaLoft Café Budget opens, as shown in Figure A-9. The Office Assistant may or may not appear on your screen. As you will learn, toolbars and menus change as you work with Excel. It is a good idea to return toolbars and menus to their default settings when you begin these lessons.

7. Click **Tools** on the menu bar, click **Customize,** make sure the Options tab in the Customize dialog box is displayed, click **Reset my usage data** to restore the default settings, click **Yes** in the alert box or dialog balloon, then click **Close**

FIGURE A-7: Open dialog box

Click to display a list of available drives and folders

Your folder may differ

Your files and folders display here

The selected filename will appear here

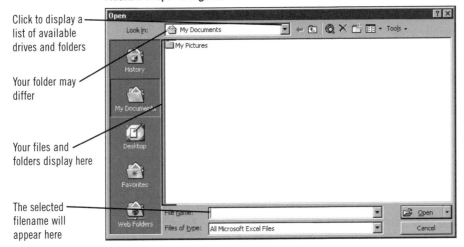

FIGURE A-8: Save As dialog box

Current drive or folder (yours may differ)

Your list of files might be different

Type the new filename here

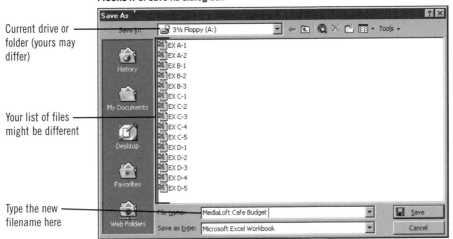

FIGURE A-9: MediaLoft Café Budget workbook

Because toolbars adapt as you work, your toolbars may not match the figures

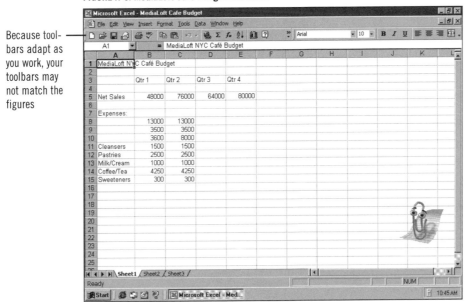

Entering Labels and Values

Excel 2000

Labels are used to identify the data in the rows and columns of a worksheet. They also make your worksheet more readable and understandable. You should try to enter all labels in your worksheet before entering the data. Labels can contain text and numerical information not used in calculations, such as dates, times, or addresses. Labels are left-aligned by default. **Values**, which include numbers, formulas, and functions, are used in calculations. Excel recognizes an entry as a value when it is a number or begins with special symbols: +, -, =, @, #, or $. All values are right-aligned by default. When a cell contains both text and numbers it is not a valid formula; Excel recognizes the entry as a label. Scenario➤ Jim needs to enter labels identifying the rest of the expense categories, and the values for Qtr 3 and Qtr 4 into the MediaLoft Café Budget worksheet.

Steps

1. **Click cell A8 to make it the active cell**
   Notice that the cell address A8 appears in the name box. As you work, the mouse pointer has a variety of appearances, depending on where it is and what Excel is doing. Table A-2 lists and identifies some mouse pointers. The labels in cells A1:A15 identify the expenses.

2. **Type Salary, as shown in Figure A-10, then click the Enter button ☑ on the formula bar**
   The label is entered in cell A8 and its contents display in the formula bar. You can also confirm a cell entry by pressing [Enter], pressing [Tab], or by pressing one of the arrow keys on the keyboard. If a label does not fit in a cell, Excel displays the remaining characters in the next cell to the right as long as it is empty. Otherwise, the label is **truncated**, or cut off.

   Trouble?
   If you notice a mistake in a cell entry after it has been confirmed, double-click the cell, use [Backspace] or [Delete] to make your corrections, then press [Enter]. You can also click Edit on the menu bar, point to Clear, then click Contents to remove a cell's contents.

3. **Click cell A9, type Rent, press [Enter] to complete the entry and move the cell pointer to cell A10, type Advertising in cell A10, then press [Enter]**
   The remaining expense values have to be added to the worksheet.

4. **Click cell D8, press and hold the left mouse button, drag the ✛ pointer to cell E8 then down to cell E15, then release the mouse button**
   Two or more selected cells is called a **range**. The active cell is still cell D8, the cells in the range are shaded in purple. Since entries often cover multiple columns and rows, selecting a range makes working with data entry easier.

5. **Type 13000, press [Enter], type 3500 in cell D9, press [Enter], type 16000 in cell D10, press [Enter], type 1500 in cell D11, press [Enter], type 2500 in cell D12, press [Enter], type 1000 in cell D13, press [Enter], type 4250 in cell D14, press [Enter], type 300 in cell D15, then press [Enter]**
   All the values in the Qtr 3 column have been added. The cell pointer is now in cell E8.

   QuickTip
   To enter a number that will not be used as part of a calculation, such as a telephone number, type an apostrophe (') before the number.

6. **Using Figure A-11 as a guide, type the remaining values for cells E8 through E15**
   Before confirming a cell entry you can click the Cancel button on the formula bar or press [Esc] to cancel or delete the entry.

7. **Type your name in cell A17, then click the Save button 🖫 on the Standard toolbar**
   Your name identifies the worksheet as yours when it is printed.

TABLE A-2: Commonly used pointers

name	pointer	use to
Normal or Cross	✛	Select a cell or range; indicates Ready mode
I-beam	I	Edit contents of formula bar
Select	▷	Select objects and commands

FIGURE A-10: Worksheet with initial label entered

Name box —

Cancel button —

Enter button —

Formula bar —

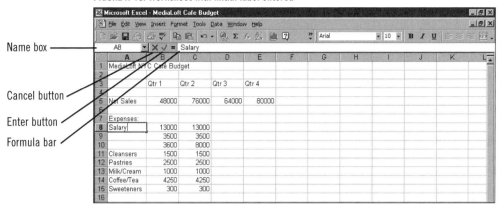

FIGURE A-11: Worksheet with new labels and values

Type these values —

Labels entered —

Values entered —

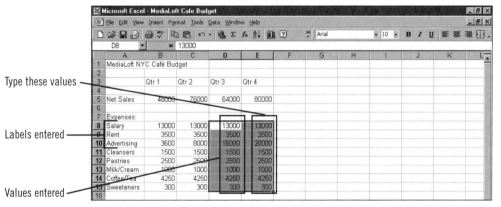

Navigating a worksheet

With over a million cells available to you, it is important to know how to move around, or **navigate**, a worksheet. You can use the arrow keys on the keyboard ([↑], [↓], [←], [→]) to move a cell or two at a time, or [Page Up] or [Page Down] to move a screenful at a time. To move a screen to the left press [Alt] [Page Up]; to move a screen to the right press [Alt] [Page Down]. You can also simply use your mouse pointer to click the desired cell. If the desired cell is not visible in the worksheet window, use the scroll bars or the Go To command to move the location into view. To return to the first active cell in a worksheet, click cell A1, or press [Ctrl][Home].

Previewing and Printing a Worksheet

Excel 2000

When a worksheet is completed, you may want to print it to have a paper copy to reference, file, or give to others. You can also print a worksheet that is not complete to review your work when you are not at a computer. Before you print a worksheet, you should save any changes. That way, if anything happens to the file as it is being sent to the printer, you will have your latest work saved to your disk. Then you should preview it to make sure it will fit on a page the way you want. When you preview a worksheet, you see a copy of the worksheet exactly as it will appear on paper. Table A-3 provides additional printing tips. **Scenario** Jim is finished entering the labels and values into the MediaLoft Café budget. Since he already saved his changes, he previews and prints a copy of the worksheet to review on the way home.

Steps

1. **Make sure the printer is on and contains paper**
   If a file is sent to print and the printer is off, an error message appears.

Trouble?

If ▣ is not visible on your Standard toolbar, click the More Buttons button ⠿ to view additional toolbar buttons.

2. **Click the Print Preview button** ▣ **on the Standard toolbar**
   A miniature version of the worksheet appears on the screen, as shown in Figure A-13. If there were more than one page, you could click the Next button or the Previous button to move between pages. You can also enlarge the image by clicking the Zoom button.

3. **Click Print**
   The Print dialog box opens, as shown in Figure A-14. To print, you could also click File on the menu bar, then click Print Preview.

4. **Make sure that the Active Sheet(s) option button is selected and that 1 appears in the Number of copies text box**
   Adjusting the value in the Number of copies text box enables you to print multiple copies. You could also print the selected range, the values you just entered, by clicking the Selection option button.

5. **Click OK**
   The Printing dialog box appears briefly while the file is sent to the printer. Note that the dialog box contains a Cancel button. You can use it to cancel the print job provided you can catch it before the file is sent to the printer.

Using Zoom in Print Preview

When you are in the Print Preview window, you can enlarge the image by clicking the Zoom button. You can also position the mouse pointer over a specific part of the worksheet page, then click it to view that section of the page. Figure A-12 shows a magnified section of a document. While the image is zoomed in, use the scroll bars to view different sections of the page.

FIGURE A-12: Enlarging the preview using Zoom

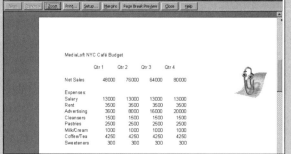

FIGURE A-13: Print Preview screen

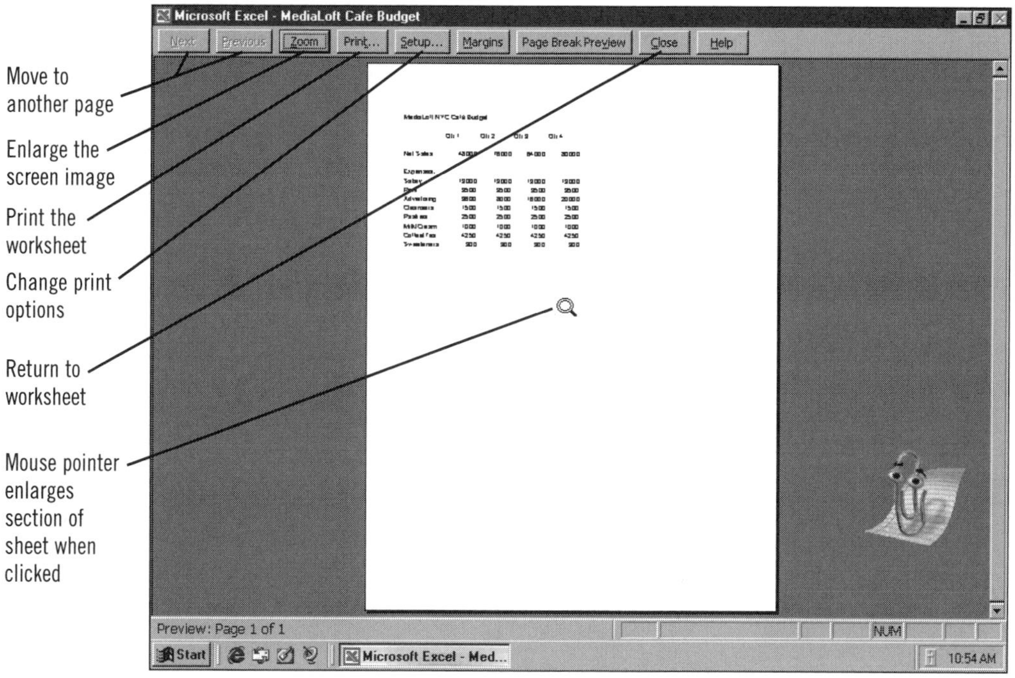

Move to another page

Enlarge the screen image

Print the worksheet

Change print options

Return to worksheet

Mouse pointer enlarges section of sheet when clicked

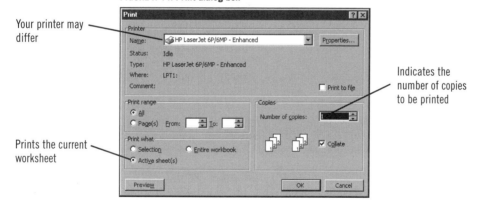

FIGURE A-14: Print dialog box

Your printer may differ

Indicates the number of copies to be printed

Prints the current worksheet

TABLE A-3: Worksheet printing tips

before you print	recommendation
Save your work	Make sure your work is saved to a disk
Check the printer	Make sure that the printer is turned on and is online, that it has paper, and that there are no error messages or warning signals
Preview the worksheet	Check the formatted image for page breaks, page setup (vertical or horizontal), and overall appearance of the worksheet
Check the printer selection	Use the Printer setup command in the Print dialog box to verify that the correct printer is selected
Check the Print what options	Verify that you are printing either the active sheet, the entire workbook, or just a selected range

Getting Help

Excel features an extensive **Help system** that gives you immediate access to definitions, explanations, and useful tips. The animated Office Assistant provides help in two ways. You can type a keyword to search on, or access a question and answer format to research your help topic. The Office Assistant provides **ScreenTips** (indicated by a light bulb) on the current action you are performing. You can click the light bulb to access further information in the form of a dialog box that you can resize and refer to as you work. In addition, you can press [F1] at any time to get immediate help. **Scenario** ▶ Jim wants to find out more about ranges so he can work more efficiently with them. He knows he can find more information using the animated Office Assistant.

QuickTip

If it's displayed, you can also click the Office Assistant to access Help.

1. **Click the Microsoft Excel Help button** 🔲 **on the Standard toolbar**
   An Office Assistant dialog box opens. You can get information by typing a word to search on in the query box, or by typing a question. If the text within the query box is already selected, any typed text will automatically replace what is highlighted. The Office Assistant provides help based on text typed in the query box.

2. **Type Define a range**
   See Figure A-16.

3. **Click Search**
   The Office Assistant searches for relevant topics from the help files in Excel and then displays the results.

QuickTip

Clicking the Print button in the Microsoft Excel Help window prints the information.

4. **Click See More** if necessary, click **Name cells in a workbook**, then click **Name a cell or a range of cells** in the Microsoft Excel Help window
   A Help window containing information about ranges opens. See Figure A-17.

5. **Read the text, then click the Close button on the Help window title bar**
   The Help window closes and you return to your worksheet.

6. **Right-click the Office Assistant, then click Hide**
   The Office Assistant is no longer visible on the worksheet.

Changing the Office Assistant

The default Office Assistant character is Clippit, but there are others from which you can choose. To change the appearance of the Office Assistant, right-click the Office Assistant, then click Choose Assistant. Click the Gallery tab, click the Back and Next buttons until you find an Assistant you want to use, then click OK. (You may need to insert your Microsoft Office 2000 CD to perform this task.) Each Office Assistant makes its own unique sounds and can be animated by right-clicking its window and clicking Animate! Figure A-15 shows the Office Assistant dialog box.

FIGURE A-15: Office Assistant dialog box

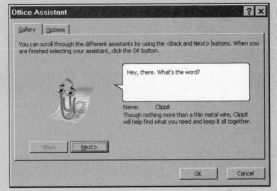

FIGURE A-16: Office Assistant

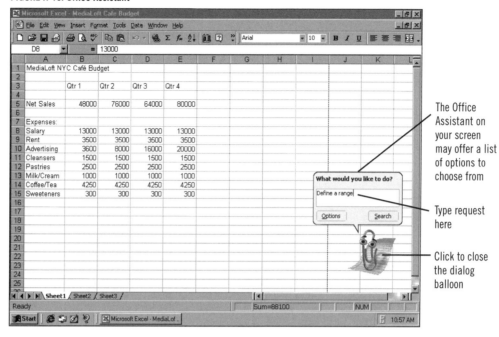

The Office Assistant on your screen may offer a list of options to choose from

Type request here

Click to close the dialog balloon

FIGURE A-17: Help window

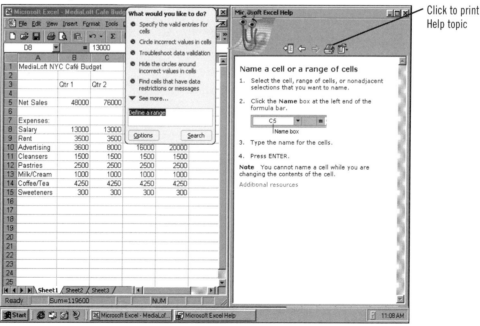

Click to print Help topic

Excel 2000

Closing a Workbook and Exiting Excel

When you have finished working you need to save the file and close it. When you have completed all your work in Excel you need to exit the program. You can exit Excel by clicking Exit on the File menu. **Scenario** Since Jim has completed his work on the MediaLoft Café budget, he is finished using Excel for the day. He closes the workbook and then exits Excel.

QuickTip

You could also click the workbook Close button instead of clicking the File menu.

1. Click **File** on the menu bar

The File menu opens. See Figure A-18.

2. Click **Close**

Excel closes the workbook and asks if you want to save your changes; if you have made any changes be sure to save them.

Trouble?

To exit Excel and close several files at once, click Exit on the File menu. Excel will prompt you to save changes to each open workbook before exiting.

3. Click **File** on the menu bar, then click **Exit**

You could also click the program Close button to exit the program. Excel closes and you return to the desktop. Memory is now freed up for other computing tasks.

FIGURE A-18: Closing a workbook using the File menu

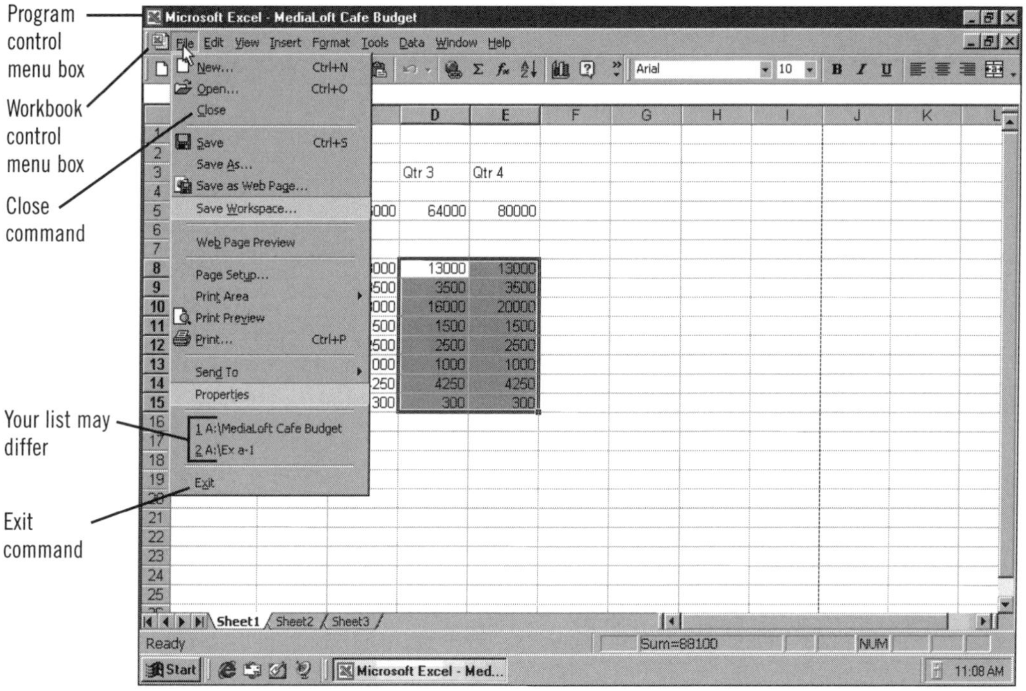

Program control menu box

Workbook control menu box

Close command

Your list may differ

Exit command

Excel 2000

Practice

► Concepts Review

Label the elements of the Excel worksheet window shown in Figure A-19.

FIGURE A-19

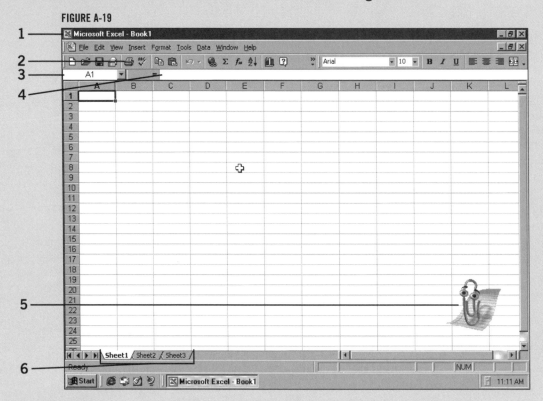

Match each term with the statement that describes it.

7. Cell pointer
8. Button
9. Worksheet window
10. Name box
11. Cell
12. Workbook

a. Collection of worksheets
b. The intersection of a column and row
c. Graphic symbol that depicts a task or function
d. Area that contains a grid of columns and rows
e. Rectangle indicating the active cell
f. Displays the active cell address

Select the best answer from the list of choices.

13. An electronic spreadsheet can perform all of the following tasks, *except*
   a. Recalculate updated information.
   b. Calculate data accurately.
   c. Plan worksheet objectives.
   d. Display information visually.

14. Each of the following is true about labels, *except*
   a. They can include numerical information.
   b. They are not used in calculations.
   c. They are right-aligned by default.
   d. They are left-aligned by default.

15. Each of the following is true about values, *except*
   a. They can include formulas.
   b. They are right-aligned by default.
   c. They are used in calculations.
   d. They can include labels.

16. What symbol is typed before a number to make the number a label?
   a. ;
   b. !
   c. '
   d. "

17. You can get Excel Help any of the following ways, *except*
   a. Minimizing the program window.
   b. Pressing [F1].
   c. Clicking 🔃.
   d. Clicking Help on the menu bar.

18. Each key(s) can be used to confirm cell entries, *except*
   a. [Shift][Enter].
   b. [Tab].
   c. [Esc].
   d. [Enter].

19. Which button is used to preview a worksheet?
   a. 🖨
   b. 🔍
   c. 💾
   d. 📋

Excel 2000

20. Which feature is used to enlarge a Print Preview view?

   a. Zoom

   b. Enlarge

   c. Amplify

   d. Magnify

21. Each of the following is true about the Office Assistant, *except*

   a. It can complete certain tasks for you.

   b. It provides help using a question and answer format.

   c. You can change the appearance of the Office Assistant.

   d. It provides tips based on your work habits.

► Skills Review

1. Start Excel 2000.

   a. Point to Programs in the Start menu.

   b. Click the Microsoft Excel program icon.

2. View the Excel window.

   a. Identify as many elements in the Excel worksheet window as you can without referring to the unit material.

3. Open and save a workbook.

   a. Open the workbook EX A-2 from your Project Disk by clicking the Open button.

   b. Save the workbook as "Totally Together Fashions" by clicking File on the menu bar, then clicking Save As.

4. Enter labels and values.

   a. Enter the labels shown in Figure A-20, the Totally Together Fashions worksheet.

   b. Enter values shown in Figure A-20.

   c. Type the label "New Data" in cell A2, then clear the cell contents in A2 using the Edit menu.

   d. Type your name in cell A10.

   e. Save the workbook by clicking the Save button.

FIGURE A-20

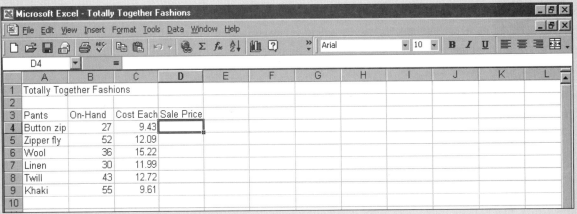

5. Preview and print a worksheet.

   a. Click the Print Preview button.

   b. Use the Zoom button to see more of your worksheet.

   c. Print one copy of the worksheet.

6. Get Help.

   a. Click the Office Assistant button if the Assistant is not displayed.

   b. Ask the Office Assistant for information about changing the Excel Office Assistant.

   c. Print information offered by the Office Assistant using the Print topic command on the Options menu.

   d. Close the Help window.

7. Close a workbook and exit Excel.

   a. Click File on the menu bar, then click Close.

   b. If asked if you want to save the worksheet, click No.

   c. If necessary, close any other worksheets you might have opened.

   d. Click File on the menu bar, then click Exit.

▶ Visual Workshop

Create a worksheet similar to Figure A-21 using the skills you learned in this unit. Save the workbook as "Carrie's Camera and Darkroom" on your Project Disk. Type your name in cell A11, then preview and print the worksheet.

FIGURE A-21

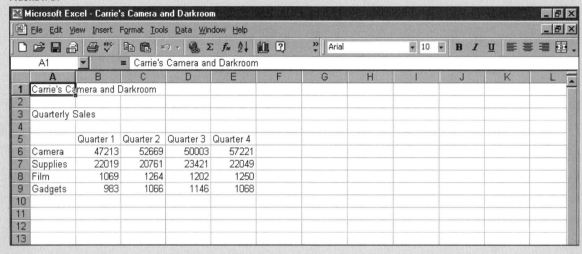

Building
and Editing Worksheets

Objectives

- ► **Plan and design a worksheet**
- `MOUS` ► **Edit cell entries and work with ranges**
- `MOUS` ► **Enter formulas**
- `MOUS` ► **Introduce Excel functions**
- `MOUS` ► **Copy and move cell entries**
- `MOUS` ► **Understand relative and absolute cell references**
- `MOUS` ► **Copy formulas with relative cell references**
- `MOUS` ► **Copy formulas with absolute cell references**
- `MOUS` ► **Name and move a sheet**

Using your understanding of the basics of Excel, you can now plan and build your own worksheets. When you build a worksheet, you enter text, values, and formulas into worksheet cells. Once you create a worksheet, you can save it in a workbook file and then print it. **Scenario** Jim Fernandez has received a request from the Marketing department for a forecast of this summer's author events and an estimate of the average number of author appearances. Marketing hopes that the number of appearances will increase 20% over last year's figures. Jim needs to create a worksheet that summarizes appearances for last year and forecasts the summer appearances for this year.

Planning and Designing a Worksheet

Before you start entering data into a worksheet, you need to know the purpose and approximate layout of the worksheet. You should also familiarize yourself with the mouse pointers you will encounter; refer to Table B-1. Scenario MediaLoft encourages authors to come to stores and sign their books. These author events are great for sales. Jim wants to forecast MediaLoft's 2001 summer author appearances. The goal, already identified by the Marketing department, is to increase the year 2000 signings by 20%. Using the planning guidelines below, work with Jim as he plans this worksheet.

In planning and designing a worksheet it is important to:

Determine the purpose of the worksheet and give it a meaningful title

Jim needs to forecast summer appearances for 2001. Jim titles the worksheet "Summer 2001 MediaLoft Author Events Forecast."

Determine your worksheet's desired results, or "output"

Jim needs to begin scheduling author events and will use these forecasts to determine staffing and budget needs if the number of author events increases by 20%. He also wants to calculate the average number of author events since the Marketing department uses this information for corporate promotions.

Collect all the information, or "input", that will produce the results you want

Jim gathers together the number of author events that occurred at four stores during the 2000 summer season, which runs from June through August.

Determine the calculations, or formulas, necessary to achieve the desired results

First, Jim needs to total the number of events at each of the selected stores during each month of the summer of 2000. Then he needs to add these totals together to determine the grand total of summer appearances. Because he needs to determine the goal for the 2001 season, the 2000 monthly totals and grand total are multiplied by 1.2 to calculate the projected 20% increase for the 2001 summer season. He'll use the Paste Function to select the Average function, which will determine the average number of appearances for the Marketing department.

Sketch on paper how you want the worksheet to look; identify where to place the labels and values

Jim decides to put store locations in rows and the months in columns. He enters the data in his sketch and indicates where the monthly totals and the grand total should go. Below the totals, he writes out the formula for determining a 20% increase in appearances for 2000. He also includes a label for the location of the average number of events calculations. Jim's sketch of his worksheet is shown in Figure B-1.

Create the worksheet

Jim enters the labels first to establish the structure of the worksheet. He then enters the values—the data about the events—into his worksheet. Finally, he enters the formulas necessary to calculate totals, averages, and forecasts. These values and formulas will be used to calculate the necessary output. The worksheet Jim creates is shown in Figure B-2.

FIGURE B-1: Worksheet sketch showing labels, values, and calculations

Summer 2001 MediaLoft Author Events Forecast

	June	July	August	Total	Average
Boston	15	10	23		
New York	14	10	12		
Seattle	12	13	6		
San Diego	10	24	15		
Total	June Total	July Total	August Total	Grand Total	
20% rise	Total X 1.2				

FIGURE B-2: Jim's forecasting worksheet

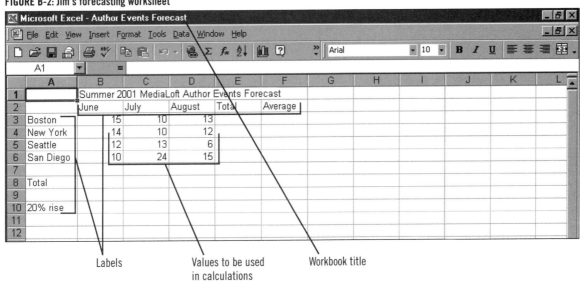

Labels — Values to be used in calculations — Workbook title

TABLE B-1: Commonly used pointers

name	pointer	use to
Normal	⊹	Select a cell or range; indicates Ready mode
Copy	⊳⁺	Create a duplicate of the selected cell(s)
Fill handle	＋	Create an alphanumeric series in a range
I-beam	I	Edit contents of formula bar
Move	⊳	Change the location of the selected cell(s)

Unit B
Excel 2000

Editing Cell Entries and Working with Ranges

You can change the contents of any cell at any time. To edit the contents of a cell, you first select the cell you want to edit. Then you have three options: you can click the formula bar, double-click the selected cell, or press [F2]. This puts Excel into Edit mode. To make sure you are in Edit mode, look at the **mode indicator** on the far left side of the status bar. Scenario After planning and creating his worksheet, Jim notices that he entered the wrong value for the August Seattle events, and that Houston should be entered instead of San Diego. He fixes the event figures, replaces the San Diego label, and corrects the value for July's Houston events.

Steps

1. Start Excel, click **Tools** on the menu bar, click **Customize**, click the **Options tab** in the Customize dialog box, click **Reset my usage data** to restore the default settings, click **Yes,** then click **Close**

2. Open the workbook **EX B-1** from your Project Disk, then save it as **Author Events Forecast**

3. Click cell **D5**
   This cell contains August Seattle events, which you want to change to reflect the correct numbers for the year 2000.

4. Click to **the right of 6** in the formula bar
   Excel goes into Edit mode, and the mode indicator on the status bar displays "Edit." A blinking vertical line called the **insertion point** appears in the formula bar, and if you move the mouse pointer to the formula bar, the pointer changes to I, which is used for editing. See Figure B-3.

5. Press **[Backspace]**, type **11**, then click the **Enter button** ✓ on the formula bar
   The value in cell D5 is changed or edited from 6 to 11. Additional modifications can also be made using the [F2] key.

6. Click cell **A6**, then press **[F2]**
   Excel is in Edit mode again, and the insertion point is in the cell.

QuickTip

The Redo command reverses the action of the Undo command. Click the Redo button ⤳ on the Standard toolbar if you change your mind after an undo.

7. Press **[Backspace]** nine times, type **Houston,** then press **[Enter]**
   The label changes to Houston. If you make a mistake, you can either click the Cancel button ✕ on the formula bar *before* accepting the cell entry, or click the Undo button ↺ on the Standard toolbar if you notice the mistake *after* you have accepted the cell entry. The Undo button allows you to reverse up to 16 previous actions, one at a time.

8. Double-click cell **C6**
   Double-clicking a cell also puts Excel into Edit mode with the insertion point in the cell.

9. Press **[Delete]** twice, then type **14**
   The number of book signings for July in Houston has been corrected. See Figure B-4.

10. Click ✓ to confirm the entry, then click the **Save button** 🖫 on the Standard toolbar

FIGURE B-3: Worksheet in Edit mode

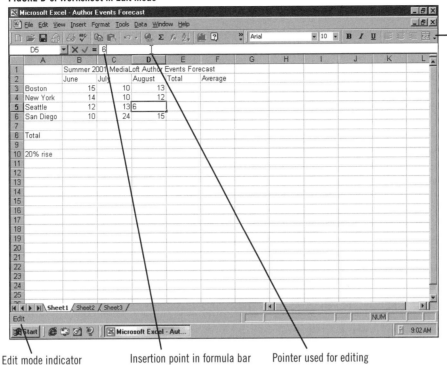

Your toolbars
may not
match the
toolbars in
the figures

Edit mode indicator   Insertion point in formula bar   Pointer used for editing

FIGURE B-4: Edited worksheet

Name box ——

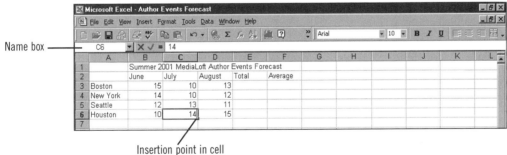

Insertion point in cell

Using range names in a workbook

Any group of cells (two or more) is called a **range**. To select a range, click the first cell and drag to the last cell you want to include in the range. The range address is defined by noting the first and last cells in the range separated by a colon, for example A8:B16. Once you select a range, the easiest way to give it a name is by clicking the name box and typing in a name. Range names—meaningful English names—are usually easier to remember than cell addresses. You can use a range

name in a formula (for example, Income-Expenses) or to move around the workbook more quickly. Simply click the name box list arrow, then click the name of the range you want to go to. The cell pointer moves immediately to select that range. To clear the name from a range, click Insert on the menu bar, point to Name, then click Define. Select the range name you want to delete from the Define Name dialog box, click Delete, then click OK.

Entering Formulas

You use **formulas** to perform numeric calculations such as adding, multiplying, and averaging. Formulas in an Excel worksheet usually start with the formula prefix—the equal sign (=)—and contain cell addresses and range names. Arithmetic formulas use one or more **arithmetic operators** to perform calculations; see Table B-2. Using a cell address or range name in a formula is called **cell referencing**. If you change a value in a cell, any formula containing that cell reference will be automatically recalculated using the new value. In formulas using more than one arithmetic operator, Excel uses the order of precedence rules to determine which operation to perform first. Scenario▶ Jim needs to total the values for the monthly author events for June, July, and August, and forecast what the 20% increase in appearances will be. He performs these calculations using formulas.

Steps

1. **Click cell B8**

   This is the cell where you want to enter the calculation that totals the June events.

2. **Type = (the equal sign)**

   Placing an equal sign at the beginning of an entry tells Excel that a formula is about to be entered, rather than a label or a value. "Enter" appears on the status bar. The total number of June events is equal to the sum of the values in cells B3, B4, B5, and B6.

Trouble?

If the formula instead of the result appears in the cell after you click ✓, make sure you began the formula with = (the equal sign).

3. **Type b3+b4+b5+b6, then click the Enter button ✓ on the formula bar**

   Notice that the result of 51 appears in cell B8, and the formula appears in the formula bar. Also, Excel is not case-sensitive: it doesn't matter if you type upper or lower-case characters when you enter cell addresses. See Figure B-5.

4. **Click cell C8, type =c3+c4+c5+c6, press [Tab]; in cell D8, type =d3+d4+d5+d6, then press [Enter]**

   The total appearances for July, 47, and for August, 51, appear in cells C8 and D8 respectively.

5. **Click cell B10, type =B8*1.2, then click ✓**

   To calculate the 20% increase, you multiply the total by 1.2. The formula in cell B10 multiplies the total events for June, cell B8, by 1.2. The result of 61.2 appears in cell B10 and is the projected value for an increase of 20% over the 51 June events. Now you need to calculate the 20% increase for July and August. You can use the **pointing method**, by which you specify cell references in a formula by selecting the desired cell with your mouse instead of typing its cell reference into the formula. Pointing is a preferred method because it eliminates typing errors.

QuickTip

Press [Esc] to turn off a moving border.

6. **Click cell C10, type =, then click cell C8**

   When you click cell C8, a moving border surrounds the cell. This **moving border**—as well as the mode indicator—indicates the cell that is copied in this operation. Moving borders can display around a single cell or a range of cells.

7. **Type *1.2, then press [Tab]**

   The calculated value 56.4 appears in cell C10.

8. **In cell D10, type =, click cell D8, type *1.2, then click ✓**

   Compare your results with Figure B-6.

9. **Click the Save button 🖫 on the Standard toolbar**

FIGURE B-5: Worksheet showing formula and result

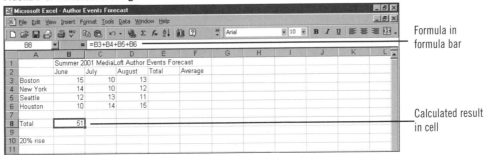

Formula in formula bar

Calculated result in cell

FIGURE B-6: Calculated results for 20% increase

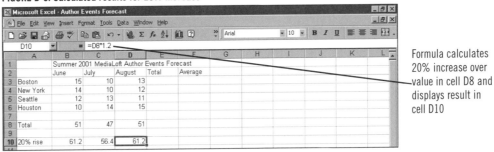

Formula calculates 20% increase over value in cell D8 and displays result in cell D10

TABLE B-2: Excel arithmetic operators

operator	purpose	example
+	Addition	=A5+A7
−	Subtraction or negation	=A5-10
*	Multiplication	=A5*A7
/	Division	=A5/A7
%	Percent	=35%
^ (caret)	Exponent	=6^2 (same as 6*6)

CLUES TO USE

Order of precedence in Excel formulas

A formula can include several mathematical operations. When you work with formulas that have more than one operator, the **order of precedence** is very important. If a formula contains two or more operators, such as 4 + .55/4000 * 25, the computer performs the calculations in a particular sequence based on these rules: Operations inside parentheses are calculated before any other operations. Exponents are calculated next, then any multiplication and division—from left to right. Finally, addition and subtraction is calculated from left to right. In the example 4 + .55/4000 * 25, Excel performs the arithmetic operations by first dividing 4000 into .55, then multiplying the result by 25, then adding 4. You can change the order of calculations by using parentheses. For example, in the formula (4+.55)/4000 * 25, Excel would first add 4 and .55, then divide that amount by 4000, then finally multiply by 25.

Introducing Excel Functions

Excel 2000

Functions are predefined worksheet formulas that enable you to do complex calculations easily. Like formulas, functions always begin with the formula prefix = (the equal sign). You can enter functions manually, or you can use the Paste Function to select the function you need from a list. **Scenario** Jim uses the SUM function to calculate the grand totals in his worksheet and the AVERAGE function to calculate the average number of author events per store.

1. **Click cell E3**
   This is the cell where you want to display the total of all author events in Boston for June, July, and August. You use **AutoSum** to create the totals. By default, AutoSum sets up the SUM function to add the values in the cells above the cell pointer. If there are one or fewer values in the cells above the cell pointer, AutoSum adds the values in the cells to the left of the cell pointer—in this case, the values in cells B3, C3, and D3.

Trouble?

If you don't see Σ on your toolbar, click the More Buttons button » on the Standard toolbar.

2. **Click the AutoSum button Σ on the Standard toolbar, then click the Enter button ✓ on the formula bar**
   The formula =SUM(B3:D3) appears in the formula bar. The result, 38, appears in cell E3. The information inside the parentheses is the **argument**, or the information to be used in calculating a result of the function. An argument can be a value, a range of cells, text, or another function.

3. **Click cell E4, click Σ , then click ✓**
   The values for the Boston and New York events are now totaled.

4. **Click cell E5, then click Σ**
   By default, AutoSum sets up a function to add the two values in the cells above the active cell, as you can see by the formula in the formula bar. You can override the current selection by manually selecting the correct range for this argument.

5. **Click cell B5, drag to cell D5 to select the range B5:D5, then click ✓**
   As you drag, the argument in the SUM function changes to reflect the selected range, and a ScreenTip appears telling you the size of the range by row and column.

6. **Click cell E6, type =SUM(, point to cell B6, drag to cell D6, press [Enter], click cell E8, type =SUM(, point to cell B8, drag to cell D8, press [Enter], click cell E10, type =SUM(, point to cell B10, drag to cell D10, then click ✓ to confirm the entry**
   See Figure B-7 to verify your results. Now the Paste Function can be used to select the function needed to calculate the average number of author events.

Trouble?

If the Office Assistant opens, click No, don't provide help now.

7. **Click cell F3, then click the Paste Function button fx on the Standard toolbar**
   The Paste Function dialog box opens. See Table B-3 for frequently used functions. The function needed to calculate averages—named AVERAGE—is included in the Most Recently Used function category.

QuickTip

Modify a function's range by clicking the Collapse dialog box button, defining the range with your mouse, then clicking the Expand dialog box button to return to the Paste Function window.

8. **Click AVERAGE in the Function name list box, click OK, the AVERAGE dialog box opens; type B3:D3 in the Number 1 text box, as shown in Figure B-8, then click OK**

9. **Click cell F4, click fx , verify that AVERAGE is selected, click OK, type B4:D4, click OK, click cell F5, click fx , click AVERAGE, click OK, type B5:D5, click OK, click cell F6, click fx , click AVERAGE, click OK, type B6:D6, then click OK**
   The result in Boston (cell F3) is 12.6667; the result in New York (cell F4) is 12; the result in Seattle (cell F5) is 12; and the result in Houston (cell F6) is 13, giving you the averages for all four stores.

FIGURE B-7: Worksheet with SUM functions entered

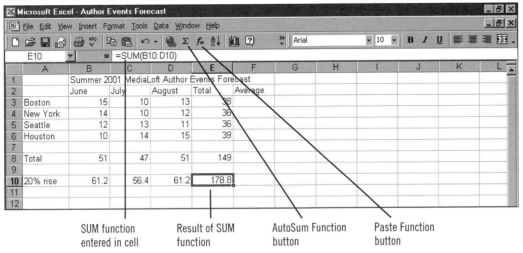

SUM function
entered in cell

Result of SUM
function

AutoSum Function
button

Paste Function
button

FIGURE B-8: Using the Paste Function to create a formula

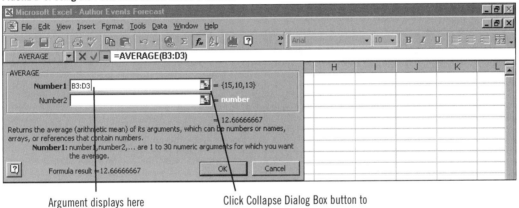

Argument displays here

Click Collapse Dialog Box button to
define an argument using your mouse

TABLE B-3: Frequently used functions

function	description
SUM(*argument*)	Calculates the sum of the arguments
AVERAGE(*argument*)	Calculates the average of the arguments
MAX(*argument*)	Displays the largest value among the arguments
MIN(*argument*)	Displays the smallest value among the arguments
COUNT(*argument*)	Calculates the number of values in the arguments

Using the MIN and MAX functions

Other commonly used functions include MIN and MAX. You use the MIN function to calculate the minimum or smallest value in a selected range; the MAX function calculates the maximum or largest value in a selected range. The MAX function is included in the Most Frequently Used function category in the Paste Function dialog box, while the MIN function can be found in the Statistical category. Like AVERAGE, MIN and MAX are preceded by an equal sign and the argument includes a range.

Excel 2000

Copying and Moving Cell Entries

Using the Cut, Copy, and Paste buttons or the Excel drag-and-drop feature, you can copy or move information from one cell or range in your worksheet to another. You can also cut, copy, and paste data from one worksheet to another to make corrections, and add information using the Office Clipboard, which can store up to 12 items. Scenario▶ Jim needs to include the 2001 forecast for Spring and Fall author events in his Author Events Forecast workbook. He's already entered the spring report in Sheet2 and will finish entering the labels and data for the fall report. Jim copies information from the spring report to the fall report.

Steps 123 4

1. Click Sheet 2 of the Author Events Forecast workbook

To work more efficiently, existing labels can be copied from one range to another and from one sheet to another. You see that the store names have to be corrected in cells A6:A7.

QuickTip

The Cut button ✂ removes the selected information from the worksheet and places it on the Office Clipboard.

2. Click Sheet 1, select the range A5:A6, then click the Copy button 🗈 on the Standard toolbar

The selected range (A5:A6) is copied to the **Office Clipboard**, a temporary storage file that holds the selected information you copy or cut. A moving border surrounds the selected range until you press [Esc] or copy additional information to the Clipboard. To copy the most recent item copied to the Clipboard to a new location, you click a new cell and then use the Paste command.

Trouble?

If the Clipboard toolbar does not open, click View on the menu bar, point to toolbars, then click Clipboard.

3. Click Sheet 2, select the range A6:A7, click the Paste button 🗈 on the Standard toolbar, select the range A4:A9, then click 🗈

The Clipboard toolbar opens when you copy a selection to the already occupied Clipboard. You can use the Clipboard toolbar to copy, cut, store, and paste up to 12 items.

QuickTip

To use the pop-up menu, right-click, click Copy, click the target cell, right-click, then click Paste to paste the last item copied to the Clipboard.

4. Click cell A13, place the pointer on the last 🗈 on the Clipboard toolbar, the contents of range A4:A9 display in a ScreenTip, click 🗈 to paste the contents in cell A13, then close the Clipboard toolbar

The item is copied into the range A13:A18. When pasting an item from the Clipboard into the worksheet, you only need to specify the top left cell of the range where you want the selection to go. The moving border remains active. Now you can use the drag-and-drop technique to copy the Total label, which does not copy the contents to the Clipboard.

5. Click cell E3, position the pointer on any edge of the cell until the pointer changes to ⬧, then press and hold down [Ctrl]

The pointer changes to the copy pointer ⬧. When you copy cells, the original data remains in the original cell. When you move cells, the original data does *not* remain in the original cell.

6. While still pressing [Ctrl], press and hold the left mouse button, drag the cell contents to cell E12, release the mouse button, then release [Ctrl]

As you drag, an outline of the cell moves with the pointer, as shown in Figure B-9, and a ScreenTip appears tracking the current position of the item as you move it. When you release the mouse button, the Total label appears in cell E12. You now decide to move the worksheet title over to the left. To use drag and drop to move data to a new cell, do not press [Ctrl].

Trouble?

When you drag and drop into occupied cells, Excel asks if you want to replace the existing cells. Click OK to replace the contents with the cell you are moving.

7. Click cell C1, position the pointer on the edge of the cell until it changes to ⬧, then drag the cell contents to A1

Once the labels are copied, you can easily enter the fall events data into the range B13:D16.

8. Using the information shown in Figure B-10, enter the author events data for the fall into the range B13:D16

Compare your worksheet to Figure B-10.

FIGURE B-9: Using drag and drop to copy information

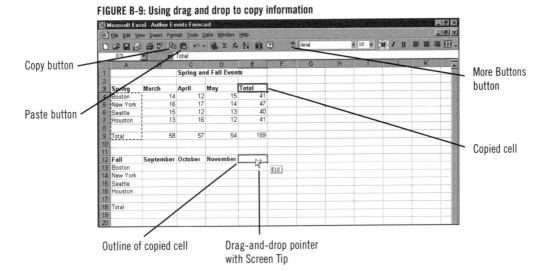

Copy button

Paste button

More Buttons button

Copied cell

Outline of copied cell

Drag-and-drop pointer with Screen Tip

FIGURE B-10: Worksheet with Fall author event data entered

Sum of selected range displays in status bar

Using the Office Clipboard

The Office Clipboard lets you copy and paste multiple items such as text, images, tables, or Excel ranges within or between the Microsoft Office applications. The Office Clipboard can hold up to 12 items copied or cut from any Office program. The Clipboard toolbar, shown in Figure B-11, displays the items stored on the Office Clipboard. You choose whether to delete the first item from the Clipboard when you copy the thirteenth item. The collected items remain in the Office Clipboard and are available to you until you close all open Office applications.

FIGURE B-11: The Office Clipboard

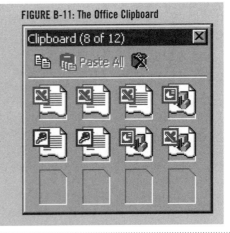

Excel 2000

Understanding Relative and Absolute Cell References

Like a label or value, an existing formula can be copied to a new location. This enables you to work efficiently by copying a working formula to multiple locations. When copied, a cell reference within a formula is automatically copied *relative* to its new location. This is called a **relative reference**. You can, however, choose to copy a cell reference with an absolute reference or a mixed reference. An **absolute reference** always cites a specific cell when the formula is copied. [Scenario ▶] Jim often copies existing worksheet formulas and makes use of many types of cell references.

Use relative references when cell relationships remain unchanged

When Excel copies a formula, all the cell references change to reflect the new location automatically. Each copied formula is identical to the original, except that the column or row is adjusted for its new location. The outlined cells in Figure B-12 contain formulas that contain relative references. For example, the formula in cell E5 is =SUM(B5:D5). When copied to cell E6, the resulting formula is =SUM(B6:D6). The original formula was copied from row 5 to row 6 within the same column, so the cell referenced in the copied formula increased by one row.

Use an absolute cell reference when one relationship changes

In most cases, you will use relative cell references—the default. Sometimes, however, this is not what is needed. In some cases, you'll want to reference a specific cell, even when copying a formula. You create absolute references by placing a $ (dollar sign) before both the column letter and row number for a cell's address using the [F4] function key (on the keyboard). Figure B-13 displays the formulas used in Figure B-11. Notice that each formula in range B15:D18 contains both a relative and absolute reference. By using an absolute reference when referring to cell $B$12 in a formula, Excel keeps that cell reference (representing the potential increase) constant when copying that formula.

Using a mixed reference

When copying formulas, the alternative to changing a cell reference relative to its new location and referring to a specific cell location as an absolute reference, is a mixed reference. A **mixed reference** contains both a relative and absolute reference. When copied, the mixed reference C$14 changes the column relative to its new location but prevents the row from changing. In the mixed reference $C14, the column would not change but the row would be updated relative to its location. Like the absolute reference, a mixed reference can be created using the [F4] function key. With each press of the [F4] key, you cycle through all the possible combinations of relative, absolute, and mixed references ($C$14, C$14, $C14, C14).

FIGURE B-12: Location of relative references

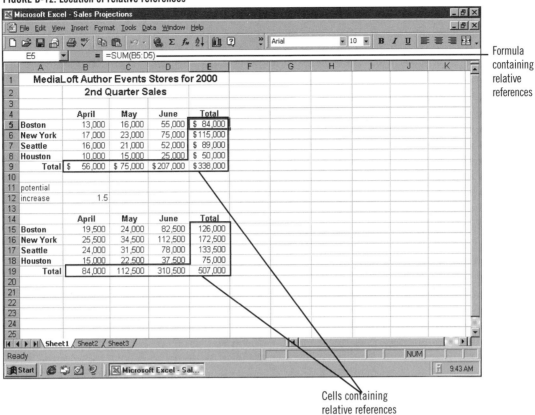

Formula containing relative references

Cells containing relative references

FIGURE B-13: Absolute and relative reference formulas

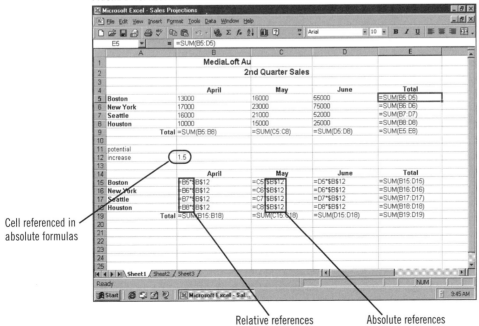

Cell referenced in absolute formulas

Relative references

Absolute references

Copying Formulas with Relative Cell References

Copying and moving formulas allows you to reuse formulas you've already created. Copying formulas, rather than retyping them, is faster and helps to prevent typing errors. **Scenario** Jim wants to copy the formulas that total the appearances by region and by month from the spring to the fall. He can use Copy and Paste commands and the Fill Right method to copy this information.

1. Click cell **E4,** then click the **Copy button** 📋 on the Standard toolbar

   The formula for calculating the total number of spring Boston author events is copied to the Clipboard. Notice that the formula =SUM(B4:D4) displays in the formula bar.

QuickTip

Click Edit on the menu bar, then click Paste Special to specify components of the copied cell or range prior to pasting. You can selectively copy formulas, values, comments, validation, and formatting attributes, as well as transpose cells or paste the contents as a link.

2. Click cell **E13,** then click the **Paste button** 📋 on the Standard toolbar

   The formula from cell E4 is copied into cell E13, where the new result of 39 appears. Notice in the formula bar that the cell references have changed, so that the range B13:D13 appears in the formula. This formula contains **relative cell references** which tell Excel to copy the formula to a new cell, but to substitute new cell references so that the relationship of the cells to the formula in its new location remains unchanged. In this case, Excel adjusted the formula so cells D13, C13, and B13—the three cell references immediately to the left of E13—replaced cells D4, C4, and B4, the three cell references to the left of E4.

   Notice that the bottom right corner of the active cell contains a small square, called the **fill handle.** You can use the fill handle to copy labels, formulas, and values. You use the fill handle to copy the formula in cell E13 to cells E14, E15, and E16.

QuickTip

As you drag the fill handle, the contents of the last filled cell appear in the name box.

3. Position the pointer over the **fill handle** until it changes to **+**, press the **left mouse button**, then drag the fill handle to select the range **E13:E16**

   See Figure B-14.

4. Release the mouse button

   Once you release the mouse button, the fill handle copies the formula from the active cell (E13) and pastes it into each cell of the selected range. Again, because the formula uses relative cell references, cells E14 through E16 correctly display the totals for the fall author events.

Trouble?

If the Clipboard toolbar opens, click the Close button. If the Office Assistant appears, right-click it, then click Hide.

5. Click cell **B9,** click **Edit** on the menu bar, then click **Copy**

6. Click cell **B18,** click **Edit** on the menu bar, then click **Paste**

   See Figure B-15. The formula for calculating the September events appears in the formula bar. You can use the Fill Right command to copy the formula from cell B18 to cells C18, D18, and E18.

7. Select the range **B18:E18**

8. Click **Edit** on the menu bar, point to **Fill,** then click **Right**

   The rest of the totals are filled in correctly. Compare your worksheet to Figure B-16.

9. Click the **Save button** 💾 on the Standard toolbar

Filling cells with sequential text or values

Often, we fill cells with sequential text: months of the year, days of the week, years, and text plus a number (Quarter 1, Quarter 2, . . .). You can easily fill cells using sequences by dragging the fill handle. As you drag the fill handle, Excel automatically extends the existing sequence. (The contents of the last filled cell appears in the name box.) Use the Fill Series command on the Edit menu to examine all of the available fill series options.

FIGURE B-14: Selected range using the fill handle

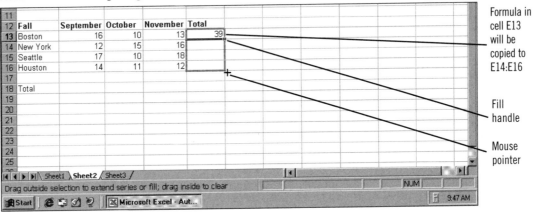

Formula in cell E13 will be copied to E14:E16

Fill handle

Mouse pointer

FIGURE B-15: Worksheet with copied formula

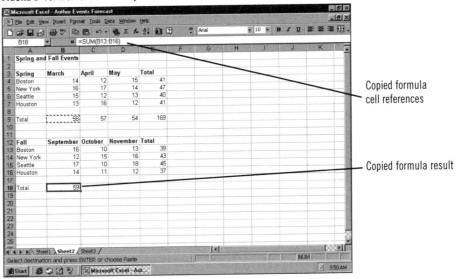

Copied formula cell references

Copied formula result

FIGURE B-16: Completed worksheet with all formulas copied

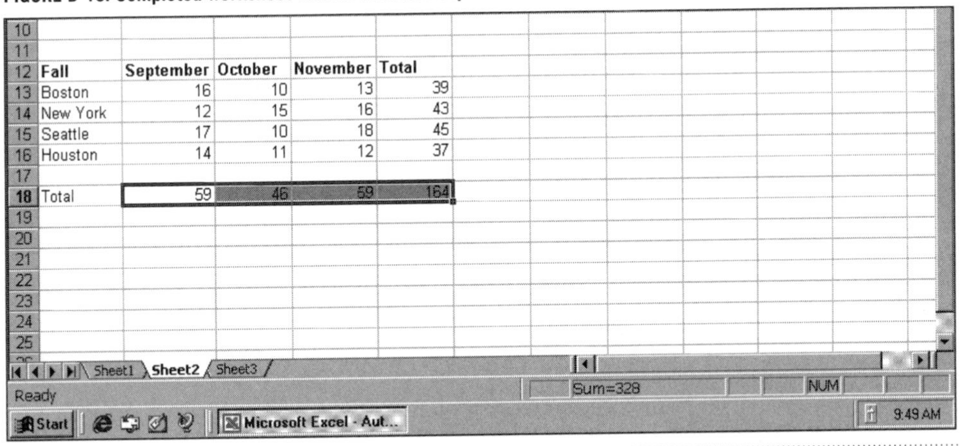

	Fall	September	October	November	Total
10					
11					
12	Fall	September	October	November	Total
13	Boston	16	10	13	39
14	New York	12	15	16	43
15	Seattle	17	10	18	45
16	Houston	14	11	12	37
17					
18	Total	59	46	59	164
19					
20					
21					
22					
23					
24					
25					

Copying Formulas with Absolute Cell References

When copying formulas, you might want a cell reference to always refer to a particular cell address. In such an instance, you would use an **absolute cell reference**. An absolute cell reference always refers to a specific cell address when the formula is copied. You identify an absolute reference by placing a dollar sign ($) before the row letter and column number of the address (for example $A$1). **Scenario** The staff in the Marketing department hopes the number of author events will increase by 20% over last year's figures. Jim decides to add a column that calculates a possible increase in the number of spring events in 2001. He wants to do a what-if analysis and recalculate the spreadsheet several times, changing the percentage that the number of appearances might increase each time.

1. Click cell **G1**, type **Change**, then press **[→]**

You can store the increase factor that will be used in the what-if analysis in cell H1.

2. Type **1.1**, then press **[Enter]**

The value in cell H1 represents a 10% increase in author events.

3. Click cell **G3**, type **What if?**, then press **[Enter]**

Now you create a formula that references a specific address: cell H1.

QuickTip

Before you copy or move a formula, check to see if you need to use an absolute cell reference.

4. In cell **G4**, type **=E4*H1**, then click the **Enter button** ☑ on the formula bar

The result of 45.1 appears in cell G4. This value represents the total spring events for Boston if there is a 10% increase. To determine the value for the remaining stores, you copy the formula in cell G4 to the range G5:G7.

5. Drag the fill handle to select the range **G4:G7**

The resulting values in the range G5:G7 are all zeros. When you copy the formula it adjusts so the formula in cell G5 is =E5*H2. Since there is no value in cell H2, the result is 0, an error. You need to use an absolute reference in the formula to keep the formula from adjusting. That way, cell H1 will always be referenced. You can change the relative cell reference to an absolute cell reference using [F4].

6. Click cell **G4**, press **[F2]** to change to Edit mode, then press **[F4]**

When you press [F2], the **range finder** outlines the equation's arguments in blue and green. When you press [F4], dollar signs appear, changing the H1 cell reference to an absolute reference. See Figure B-17.

7. Click the **Enter button** ☑ on the formula bar

The formula correctly contains an absolute cell reference and the value remains unchanged at 45.1. The fill handle can be used to copy the corrected formula in cell G4 to G5:G7.

8. Drag the fill handle to select the range **G4:G7**

The correct values for a 10% increase display in cells G4:G7. You complete the what-if analysis by changing the value in cell H1 from 1.1 to 1.25 to indicate a 25% increase in events.

9. Click cell **H1**, type **1.25**, then click ☑

The values in the range G4:G7 change to reflect the 25% increase. Compare your worksheet to Figure B-18. Since events only occur in whole numbers, the numbers' appearance can be changed later.

FIGURE B-17: Absolute cell reference in cell G4

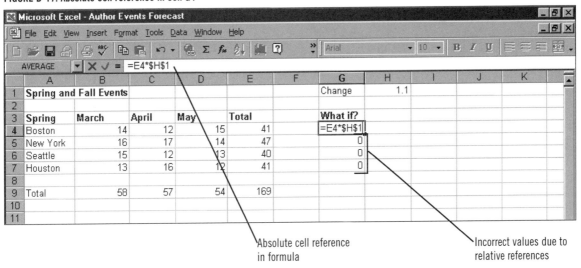

Absolute cell reference
in formula

Incorrect values due to
relative references

FIGURE B-18: Worksheet with what-if value

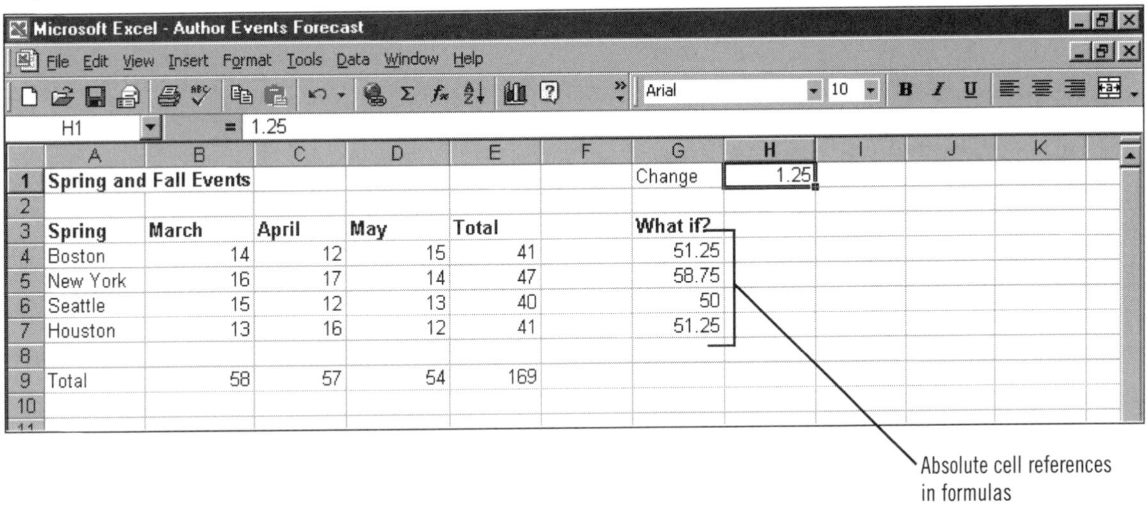

Absolute cell references
in formulas

Copying and moving using named ranges

You can give a range of cells an easy-to-remember meaningful name, such as "2001 Sales." If you move the named range, its name moves with it. Like any range, a named range can be referenced absolutely in a formula by using the $ symbol. To copy or move a named range, you can "go to" it quickly by clicking the name box list arrow and selecting its name.

Excel 2000

Naming and Moving a Sheet

Each workbook initially contains three worksheets named Sheet1, Sheet2, and Sheet3. When the workbook is opened, the first worksheet is the active sheet. To move from sheet to sheet, click the desired sheet tab located at the bottom of the worksheet window. Sheet tab scrolling buttons, located to the left of the sheet tabs, allow rapid movement among the sheets. To make it easier to identify the sheets in a workbook, you can rename each sheet and then organize them in a logical way. The name appears on the sheet tab. For instance, sheets within a single workbook could be named for individual salespeople to better track performance goals, and the sheets can be moved so they appear in alphabetical order. **Scenario** Jim wants to be able to easily identify the actual author events and the forecast sheets. He decides to name two sheets in his workbook, then changes their order.

1. Click the **Sheet1 tab**

   Sheet1 becomes active; this is the worksheet that contains the summer information you compiled for the Marketing department. Its tab moves to the front, and the tab for Sheet2 moves to the background.

2. Click the **Sheet2 tab**

   Sheet2, containing the spring and fall data, becomes active. Once you have confirmed which sheet is which, you can rename Sheet1 so it has a name that you can easily remember.

3. Double-click the **Sheet1 tab**

   The Sheet1 text becomes selected with the default sheet name ("Sheet1") selected. You could also click Format in the menu bar, point to Sheet, then click Rename to select the sheet name.

4. Type **Summer**, then press **[Enter]**

   See Figure B-19. The new name automatically replaces the default name in the tab. Worksheet names can have up to 31 characters, including spaces and punctuation.

   QuickTip

   To delete a worksheet, select the worksheet you want to delete, click Edit on the menu bar, then click Delete sheet. To insert a worksheet, click Insert on the menu bar, then click Worksheet.

5. Double-click the **Sheet2 tab**, then rename this sheet **Spring-Fall**

   Jim decides to rearrange the order of the sheets, so that Summer comes after Spring-Fall.

6. Click the **Summer sheet tab**, then drag it to the right of the **Spring-Fall sheet tab**

   As you drag, the pointer changes to ▣, the sheet relocation pointer. See Figure B-20. The first sheet in the workbook is now the Spring-Fall sheet. When there are multiple sheets in a workbook, the navigation buttons can be used to scroll through the sheet tabs. Click the leftmost navigation button to display the first sheet tab; click the rightmost navigation button to display the last sheet tab. The left and right buttons move one sheet in their respective directions.

7. Type your name in cell A12, click **File** on the menu bar, click **Print**, click the **Entire workbook option button**, then click the **Preview button**

   The Preview screen opens. Each worksheet is displayed on a separate page. You can preview the workbook sheets by clicking the Next and Previous buttons.

8. Click the **Print button** on the Preview toolbar

9. Save and close the workbook, then exit Excel

FIGURE B-19: Renamed sheet in workbook

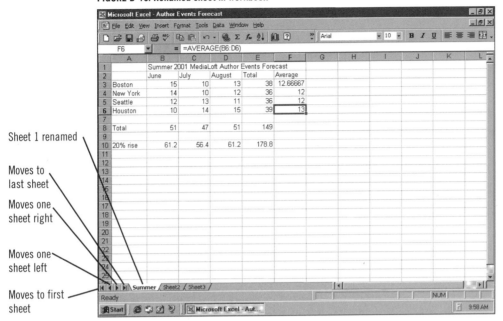

Sheet 1 renamed

Moves to
last sheet

Moves one
sheet right

Moves one
sheet left

Moves to first
sheet

FIGURE B-20: Moving Summer after Spring-Fall sheet

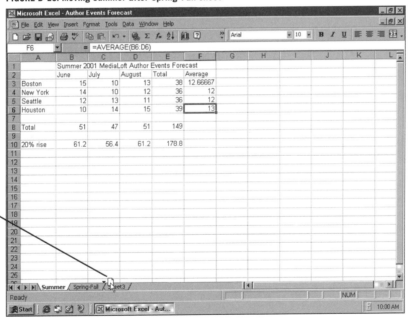

Sheet relocation
pointer

Moving and copying worksheets

There are times when you may want to move or copy sheets. To move sheets within the current workbook, drag the selected sheet tab along the row of sheet tabs to the new location. To copy, simply press CTRL as you drag the sheet tab and release the mouse button before you release CTRL. Although you have to be careful and carefully check the calculations when doing so, moving and copying worksheets to new workbooks is a relatively simple operation. You must have the workbook that you are copying to, as well as the workbook that you are copying from, open. Select the sheet to copy or move, click File on the menu bar, click Edit, then click Move or Copy sheet. Complete the information in the Move or Copy dialog box. Be sure to click the Create a Copy check box if you are copying rather than moving the worksheet.

CLUES TO USE

Practice

► Concepts Review

Label each element of the Excel worksheet window shown in Figure B-21.

FIGURE B-21

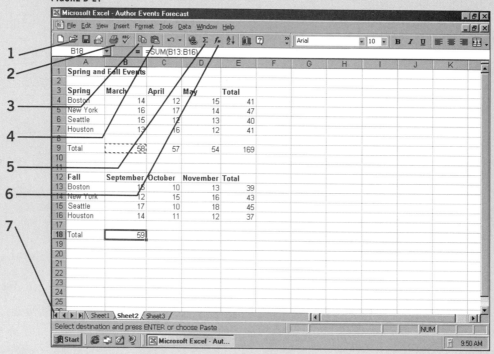

Match the term or button with the statement that describes it.

8. Range
9. Function
10. 🖺
11. 🖺
12. Formula

a. Used to copy cells
b. A cell entry that performs a calculation in an Excel worksheet
c. A specified group of cells, which can include the entire worksheet
d. A predefined formula that provides a shortcut for commonly used calculations
e. Used to paste cells

Select the best answer from the list of choices.

13. What type of cell reference changes when it is copied?
   a. Relative
   b. Circular
   c. Looping
   d. Absolute
14. What character is used to make a reference absolute?
   a. @
   b. ^
   c. $
   d. &

15. Which button is used to enter data in a cell?

   a. ☑   **c.** 🗐

   b. ☒   **d.** ↩

► Skills Review

1. Edit cell entries and work with ranges.

  a. Start Excel, open the workbook EX B-2 from your Project Disk and save it as "Office Furnishings."

  b. Change the quantity of Tables to 25.

  c. Change the price of each of the Desks to 250.

  d. Change the quantity of Easels to 17.

  e. Name the range B2:B5 "Quantity" and name the range C2:C5 "Price."

  f. Type your name in cell A20, then save and preview the worksheet.

2. Enter formulas.

  a. Click cell B6, then enter the formula B2+B3+B4+B5.

  b. Save your work, then preview the data in the Office Furnishings worksheet.

3. Introduce Excel functions.

  a. Type the label "Min Price" in cell A8.

  b. Click cell C8; enter the function MIN(C2:C5).

  c. Type the label "Max Price" in cell A9.

  d. Create a formula in cell C9 that determines the maximum price.

  e. Save your work, then preview the data.

4. Copy and move cell entries.

  a. Select the range A1:C6, then copy the range to cell A12.

  b. Use drag and drop to copy the range D1:E1 to cell D12.

  c. Save your work, then preview the worksheet.

5. Copy formulas with relative cell references.

  a. Click cell D2, then create a formula that multiplies B2 and C2.

  b. Copy the formula in D2 into cells D3:D5.

  c. Copy the formula in D2 into cells D13:D16.

  d. Save and preview the worksheet.

6. Copy formulas with absolute cell references.

  a. Click cell G2 and type the value 1.375.

  b. Click cell E2, then create a formula containing an absolute reference that multiplies D2 and G2.

  c. Use the Office Clipboard to copy the formula in E2 into cells E3:E5.

  d. Use the Office Clipboard to copy the formula in E2 into cells E13:E16.

  e. Change the amount in cell G2 to 2.873.

  f. Save the worksheet.

7. Name and move a sheet.

  a. Name the Sheet1 tab "Furniture."

  b. Move the Furniture sheet so it comes after Sheet3.

  c. Name the Sheet2 tab "Supplies."

  d. Move the Supplies sheet after the Furniture sheet.

  e. Save, preview, print and close the workbook, then exit Excel.

Visual Workshop

Create a worksheet similar to Figure B-22 using the skills you learned in this unit. Save the workbook as "Annual Budget" on your Project Disk. Type your name in cell A13, then preview and print the worksheet. (Your toolbars may look different from those shown in the figure.)

FIGURE B-22

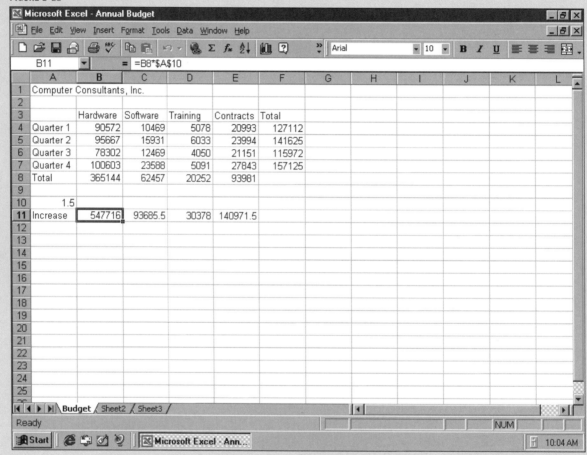

Formatting
a Worksheet

Objectives

MOUS ► **Format values**

MOUS ► **Use fonts and font sizes**

MOUS ► **Change attributes and alignment of labels**

MOUS ► **Adjust column widths**

MOUS ► **Insert and delete rows and columns**

MOUS ► **Apply colors, patterns, and borders**

MOUS ► **Use conditional formatting**

MOUS ► **Check spelling**

You use Excel's formatting features for a variety of reasons: to make a worksheet more attractive, to make it easier to read, or to emphasize key data. You do this by using colors and different fonts for the cell contents, adjusting column widths, and inserting and deleting columns and rows. Scenario ► The marketing managers at MediaLoft have asked Jim Fernandez to create a workbook that tracks advertising expenses for all MediaLoft stores. Jim has prepared a worksheet for the New York City store containing this information, which can be adapted later for the other stores. Now he uses formatting techniques to make the worksheet easier to read and to call attention to important data.

Formatting Values

Formatting determines how labels and values appear in cells; it does not alter the data in any way. To format a cell, first select it, then apply the formatting. Cells and ranges can be formatted before or after data is entered. If you enter a value in a cell and the cell appears to display the data incorrectly, adjust the cell's format to display the value correctly. Scenario> The Marketing department has requested that Jim begin by tracking the New York City store's advertising expenses. Jim developed a worksheet that tracks advertising invoices. He entered all the information and now wants to format some of the labels and values. Because some of the changes might also affect column widths, Jim makes all his formatting changes before changing the column widths.

Steps123

1. Start Excel, click **Tools** on the menu bar, click **Customize**, click the **Options tab** in the Customize dialog box, click **Reset my usage data** to restore the default settings, click **Yes**, then click **Close**

2. Open the worksheet **EX C-1** from your Project Disk, then save it as **Ad Expenses**
   The store advertising worksheet appears in Figure C-1. Numeric data can be displayed in a variety of ways, such as having a leading dollar sign. When formatting, you select the range to be formatted up to the last entry in a column or row by selecting the first cell, pressing and holding [Shift], pressing [End], then pressing [→] for the row, or [↓] for the column.

   > **Trouble?**
   > Click the More Buttons button [»] to locate buttons that are not visible on your toolbars.

3. Select the range **E4:E32**, then click the **Currency Style button** [$] on the Formatting toolbar
   Excel adds dollar signs and two decimal places to the Cost ea. column data. Excel automatically resizes the column to display all the information supplied by the new formatting. Another option for formatting dollar values is to apply the comma format, which does not include the $ sign.

   > **QuickTip**
   > Select any range by clicking the top left cell, pressing and holding [Shift], then clicking the bottom right cell. [Shift] acts as a "connector" for contiguous cells.

4. Select the range **G4:I32**, then click the **Comma Style button** [,] on the Formatting toolbar
   The values in columns G, H, and I display the comma format. You can also format percentages using the Formatting toolbar.

5. Select the range **J4:J32**, click the **Percent Style button** [%] on the Formatting toolbar, then click the **Increase Decimal button** [.00] on the Formatting toolbar to show one decimal place
   The % of Total column is now formatted with a percent sign (%) and one decimal place. Dates can be reformatted to display ranges in a variety of ways.

6. Select the range **B4:B31**, click **Format** on the menu bar, then click **Cells**
   The Format Cells dialog box opens with the Number tab in front and the Date format already selected. See Figure C-2. There are many types of date formats from which to choose.

   > **QuickTip**
   > The first DD-MM-YY format displays a single-digit date (such as May 1, 2000) as 1-May-00. The second format would display the same date as 01-May-00.

7. Select the (first) format **14-Mar-98** in the Type list box, then click **OK**
   You decide you don't need the year to appear in the Inv Due column.

8. Select the range **C4:C31**, click **Format** on the menu bar, click **Cells**, click **14-Mar** in the Type list box, then click **OK**
   Compare your worksheet to Figure C-3.

9. Save your work

FIGURE C-1: Advertising expense worksheet

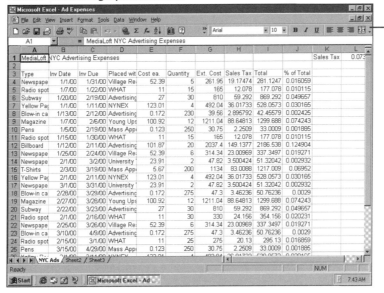

Your toolbars may not match the toolbars in the figures

FIGURE C-2: Format Cells dialog box

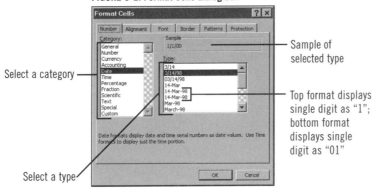

Select a category

Sample of selected type

Top format displays single digit as "1"; bottom format displays single digit as "01"

Select a type

FIGURE C-3: Worksheet with formatted values

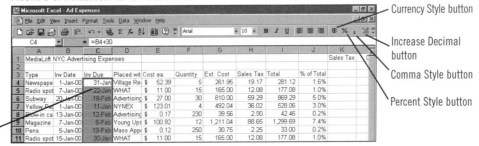

Currency Style button

Increase Decimal button

Comma Style button

Percent Style button

Modified date formats

Using the Format Painter

A cell's format can be "painted" into other cells using the Format Painter button 🖌 on the Standard toolbar. This is similar to using drag and drop to copy information, but instead of copying cell contents, you copy only the cell format. Select the cell containing the desired format, then click 🖌. The pointer changes to ⊕🖌. Use this pointer to select the cell or range you want to contain the painted format.

Using Fonts and Font Sizes

A **font** is the name given to a collection of characters (letters, numerals, symbols, and punctuation marks) with a specific design. The **font size** is the physical size of the text, measured in units called **points**. The default font in Excel is 10 point Arial. You can change the font, the size, or both of any entry or section in a worksheet by using the Format command on the menu bar or by using the Formatting toolbar. Table C-1 shows several fonts in different sizes. Scenario▶ Now that the data is formatted, Jim wants to change the font and size of the labels and the worksheet title so that they are better distinguished from the data.

1. Press **[Ctrl][Home]** to select cell A1

QuickTip

You can also open the Format Cells dialog box by right-clicking selected cells, then clicking Format Cells.

2. Click **Format** on the menu bar, click **Cells**, then click the **Font tab** in the Format Cells dialog box
   See Figure C-5.

3. Scroll down the **Font list** to see an alphabetical listing of the many fonts available on your computer, click **Times New Roman** in the Font list box, click **24** in the Size list box, then click **OK**
   The title font appears in 24 point Times New Roman, and the Formatting toolbar displays the new font and size information. Column headings can be enlarged to make them stand out. You can also change a font and increase the font size using the Formatting toolbar.

4. Select the range **A3:J3**, then click the **Font list arrow** on the Formatting toolbar
   Notice that the fonts on this font list actually look like the font they represent.

5. Click **Times New Roman** in the Font list, click the **Font Size list arrow**, then click **14** in the Font Size list
   Compare your worksheet to Figure C-6. Notice that some of the column headings are now too wide to display fully in the column. Excel does not automatically adjust column widths to accommodate formatting, you have to adjust column widths manually. You'll learn to do this in a later lesson.

6. Save your work

Using the Formatting toolbar to change fonts and font sizes

The font and font size of the active cell appear on the Formatting toolbar. Click the Font list arrow, as shown in Figure C-4, to see a list of available fonts. Notice that each font name is displayed in the selected font. If you want to change the font, first select the cell, click the Font list arrow, then click the font you want. You can change the size of selected text in the same way, by clicking the Font Size list arrow to display a list of available point sizes.

FIGURE C-4: Available fonts on the Formatting toolbar

Available fonts installed on your computer (yours may differ)   Font list arrow

FIGURE C-5: Font tab in the Format Cells dialog box

Currently selected font

Available fonts may differ on your computer

Effects options

Type a custom font size or select from the list

Font style options

Sample of selected font

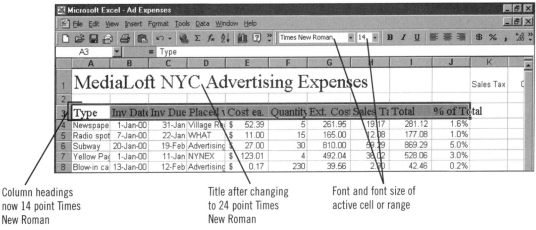

FIGURE C-6: Worksheet with formatted title and labels

Column headings now 14 point Times New Roman

Title after changing to 24 point Times New Roman

Font and font size of active cell or range

TABLE C-1: Types of fonts

font	12 point	24 point	font	12 point	24 point
Arial	Excel	Excel	Palatino	Excel	Excel
Comic Sans MS	Excel	Excel	Times	Excel	Excel

Changing Attributes and Alignment of Labels

Attributes are styling features such as bold, italics, and underlining that you can apply to affect the way text and numbers look in a worksheet. You can also change the **alignment** of labels and values in cells to be left, right, or center. Attributes and alignment can be applied from the Formatting toolbar, or from the Alignment tab of the Format Cells dialog box. See Table C-2 for a list and description of the available attribute and alignment buttons. `Scenario` Now that he has applied the appropriate fonts and font sizes to his worksheet labels, Jim wants to further enhance the worksheet's appearance by adding bold and underline formatting and centering some of the labels.

1. Press **[Ctrl][Home]** to move to cell A1, then click the **Bold button** 🅱 on the Formatting toolbar
   The title Advertising Expenses appears in bold.

2. Select the range **A3:J3**, then click the **Underline button** 🅤 on the Formatting toolbar
   Excel underlines the text in the column headings in the selected range.

QuickTip

Overuse of any attribute can be distracting and make a workbook less readable. Be consistent, adding emphasis the same way throughout.

3. Click cell **A3**, click the **Italics button** 🅘 on the Formatting toolbar, then click 🅱
   The word "Type" appears in boldface italic type. Notice that the Bold, Italics, and Underline buttons are indented. You can apply one or more attributes to text simultaneously.

4. Click 🅘
   Excel removes italics from cell A3 but the bold and underline formatting attributes remain.

QuickTip

Use formatting shortcuts on any selected range: [Ctrl][B] to bold, [Ctrl][I] to italicize, and [Ctrl][U] to underline.

5. Select the range **B3:J3**, then click 🅱
   Bold formatting is added to the rest of the labels in the column headings. You want to center the title over the data columns A through J.

6. Select the range **A1:J1**, then click the **Merge and Center button** 🔳 on the Formatting toolbar
   Merge creates one cell out of the 10 cells across the row, then Center centers the text in that newly created large cell. The title "MediaLoft NYC Advertising Expenses" is centered across ten columns. The alignment within individual cells can be changed using toolbar buttons.

QuickTip

To clear all formatting, click Edit on the menu bar, point to Clear, then click Formats.

7. Select the range **A3:J3**, then click the **Center button** 🔳 on the Formatting toolbar
   Compare your screen to Figure C-7. Although they may be difficult to read, notice that all the headings are centered within their cells.

8. Save your work

TABLE C-2: Attribute and Alignment buttons on the Formatting toolbar

button	description	button	description
🅱	Bolds text	▤	Aligns text on the left side of the cell
🅘	Italicizes text	▤	Centers text horizontally within the cell
🅤	Underlines text	▤	Aligns text on the right side of the cell
⊞	Adds lines or borders	🔳	Centers text across columns, and combines two or more selected adjacent cells into one cell

FIGURE C-7: Worksheet with formatting attributes applied

Title
centered
across
columns

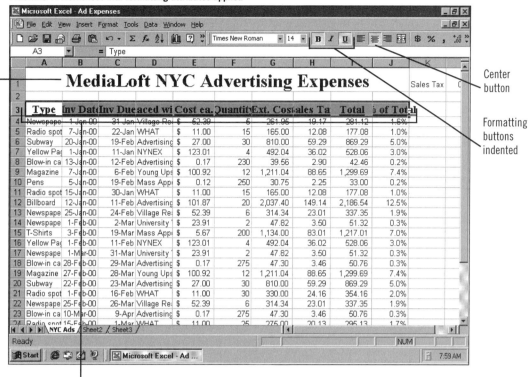

Center
button

Formatting
buttons
indented

Column headings
centered, bold, and
underlined

Using AutoFormat

Excel also has 17 predefined worksheet formats to make formatting easier and to give you the option of consistently styling your worksheets. AutoFormats are designed for worksheets with labels in the left column and top rows, and totals in the bottom row or right column. To use AutoFormatting, select the data to be formatted instantly—or place your mouse pointer anywhere within the range to be selected—click Format on the menu bar, click AutoFormat, then select a format from the sample boxes, as shown in Figure C-8.

FIGURE C-8: AutoFormat dialog box

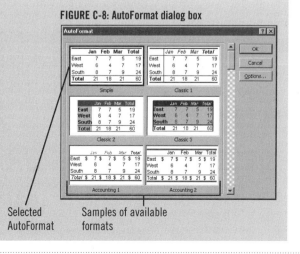

Selected
AutoFormat

Samples of available
formats

Excel 2000

Adjusting Column Widths

As your worksheet formatting continues, you might need to adjust the width of the columns to make your worksheet more usable. The default column width is 8.43 characters wide, a little less than one inch. With Excel, you can adjust the column width for one or more columns using the mouse or the Column command on the Format menu. Table C-3 describes the commands available on the Format Column menu. You can also adjust the height of rows to accommodate larger font sizes. Scenario▶ Jim notices that some of the labels in column A have been truncated and don't fit in the cells. He decides to adjust the widths of the columns so that the labels display fully.

Steps

1. **Position the pointer on the column line between columns A and B selector buttons**
   The pointer changes to ↔, as shown in Figure C-9. You position the pointer on the right edge of the column that you are adjusting. Then you can drag the column edge, resizing it using the mouse.

2. **Click and drag the ↔ pointer to the right until column A is wide enough to accommodate all of the text entries in column A**
   Yellow Pages is the widest entry. The **AutoFit** feature lets you use the mouse to resize a column so it automatically accommodates the widest entry in a cell.

3. **Position the pointer on the column line between columns B and C in the column selector until it changes to ↔, then double-click**
   The width of column B is automatically resized to fit the widest entry, in this case, the column label.

4. **Use AutoFit to resize columns C, D, and J**
   You can also use the Column Width command on the Format menu to adjust several columns to the same width. Columns can be adjusted by selecting any cell in the column.

5. **Select the range F5:I5**

6. **Click Format on the menu bar, point to Column, then click Width**
   The Column Width dialog box appears. Move the dialog box, if necessary, by dragging it by its title bar so you can see the contents of the worksheet. The column width measurement is based on the number of characters in the Normal font (in this case, Arial).

7. **Type 11 in the Column Width text box, then click OK**
   The column widths change to reflect the new settings. See Figure C-10. If "#######" displays after you adjust a column of values, the column is too narrow to display the contents. You need to increase column width until it is wide enough to display the values.

8. **Save your work**

> **QuickTip**
>
> To reset columns to the default width, select the columns, then use the Column Standard Width command on the Format menu. Click OK in the dialog box to accept the default width.

CLUES TO USE

Specifying row height

The Row Height command on the Format menu allows you to customize row height to improve readability. Row height is calculated in points, units of measure also used for fonts—one inch equals 72 points. The row height must exceed the size of the font you are using. Normally, you don't need to adjust row heights manually. If you format something in a row to be a larger point size, Excel will adjust the row to fit the largest point size in the row. You can also adjust row height by placing the ↔ pointer under the row selector button and dragging to the desired height.

FIGURE C-9: Preparing to change the column width

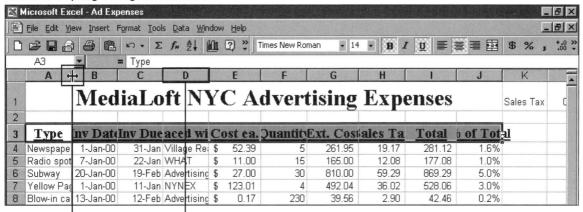

Resize pointer
between columns
A and B

Column D
selector button

FIGURE C-10: Worksheet with column widths adjusted

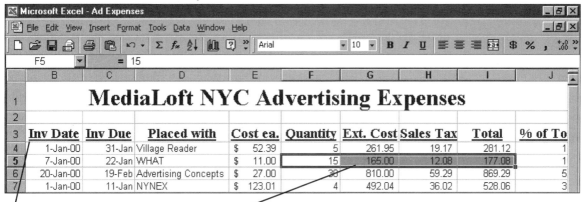

Columns widened
to display text

Columns widened to
same width

TABLE C-3: Format Column commands

command	description
Width	Sets the width to a specific number of characters
AutoFit Selection	Fits the widest entry
Hide	Hide(s) column(s)
Unhide	Unhide(s) column(s)
Standard Width	Resets to default widths

Excel 2000

Inserting and Deleting Rows and Columns

As you modify a worksheet, you might find it necessary to insert or delete rows and columns to keep your worksheet current. For example, you might need to insert rows to accommodate new inventory products or remove a column of yearly totals that are no longer current. Scenario Jim has already improved the appearance of his worksheet by formatting the labels and values in the worksheet. Now he decides to improve the overall appearance of the worksheet by inserting a row between the last row of data and the totals. Jim has located a row of inaccurate data that should be deleted, as well as a column that is not necessary.

1. Right-click cell **A32**, then click **Insert**
The Insert dialog box opens. See Figure C-11. You can choose to insert a column or a row, or you can shift the data in the cells in the active column right or in the active row down. An additional row between the last row of data and totals will visually separate the totals.

QuickTip

Inserting or deleting rows or columns that are specifically referenced in formulas can cause problems. Be sure to check formulas after inserting or deleting rows or columns.

2. Click the **Entire Row option button**, then click **OK**
A blank row is inserted between the totals and the Billboard data for March 2000. Excel inserts rows above the cell pointer and inserts columns to the left of the cell pointer. When you insert a new row, the contents of the worksheet shift down from the newly inserted row. Notice that the formula result in cell E33 has not changed. When you insert a new column, the contents of the worksheet shift to the right from the point of the new column. To insert a single row, you can also click the row selector immediately below where you want the new row, right-click, and then click Insert. To insert multiple rows, select the same number of rows as you want to insert. A row can easily be selected for deletion using its **row selector button**, the gray box containing the row number to the left of the worksheet.

3. Click the **row 27 selector button**
Hats from Mass Appeal Inc. will no longer be part of the advertising campaign. All of row 27 is selected, as shown in Figure C-12.

QuickTip

Use the Edit menu—or right-click the selected row and click Delete—to remove a selected row. Pressing [Delete] removes the contents of a selected row; the row itself remains.

4. Click **Edit** in the menu bar, then click **Delete**
Excel deletes row 27, and all rows below this shift up one row.

5. Click the **column J selector button**
The percentage information is calculated elsewhere and is no longer needed in this worksheet.

6. Click **Edit** in the menu bar, then click **Delete**
Excel deletes column J. The remaining columns to the right shift left one column. You are satisfied with the appearance of the worksheet and decide to save the changes.

7. Save your work

FIGURE C-11: Insert dialog box

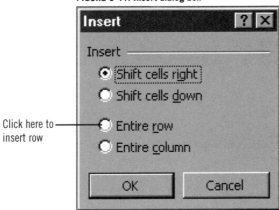

Click here to insert row

FIGURE C-12: Worksheet with row 27 selected

24	Radio spot	15-Feb-00	1-Mar	WHAT	$	11.00	25	275.00	20.13	295.13
25	Pens	15-Mar-00	29-Apr	Mass Appeal, Inc.	$	0.12	250	30.75	2.25	33.00
26	Yellow Pages	1-Mar-00	11-Mar	NYNEX	$	123.01	4	492.04	36.02	528.06
27	Hats	20-Mar-00	4-May	Mass Appeal, Inc.	$	7.20	250	1,800.00	131.76	1,931.76
28	Subway	20-Mar-00	19-Apr	Advertising Concepts	$	27.00	30	810.00	59.29	869.29
29	Newspaper	1-Apr-00	1-May	University Voice	$	23.91	2	47.82	3.50	51.32
30	Subway	10-Apr-00	10-May	Advertising Concepts	$	27.00	30	810.00	59.29	869.29
31	Billboard	28-Mar-00	27-Apr	Advertising Concepts	$	101.87	20	2,037.40	149.14	2,186.54
32										
33					$1,169.14		2034	16,311.75	1,194.02	17,505.77

NYC Ads / Sheet2 / Sheet3

Ready   Sum=77375.83035   NUM

Start   Microsoft Excel - Ad ...   8:04 AM

Row 27 selector button   Inserted row

CLUES TO USE

Using dummy columns and rows

When you add or delete a column or row within a range used in a formula, Excel automatically adjusts the formula to reflect the change. However, when you add a column or row at the end of a range used in a formula, you must modify the formula to reflect the additional column or row. To eliminate having to edit the formula, you can include a dummy column and dummy row which is a blank column or row included at the bottom of—but within—the range you use for that formula, as shown in Figure C-13. Then if you add another column or row to the end of the range, the formula will automatically be modified to include the new data.

FIGURE C-13: Formula with dummy row

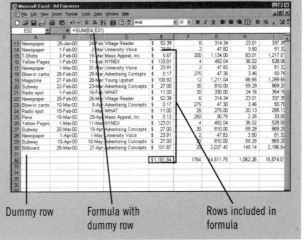

Dummy row   Formula with dummy row   Rows included in formula

Applying Colors, Patterns, and Borders

You can use colors, patterns, and borders to enhance the overall appearance of a worksheet and to improve its readability. You can add these enhancements using the Patterns tab in the Format Cells dialog box or by using the Borders and Color buttons on the Formatting toolbar. You can apply color or patterns to the background of a cell or range or to cell contents. And, you can apply borders to all the cells in a worksheet or only to selected cells. See Table C-4 for a list of border buttons and their functions. **Scenario** Jim decides to add a pattern, a border, and color to the title of the worksheet. This will give the worksheet a more professional appearance.

Steps

1. Press **[Ctrl][Home]** to select cell **A1**, then click the **Fill Color list arrow** 🖌▾ on the Formatting toolbar
   The color palette appears.

2. Click **Turquoise** (fourth row, fourth color from the right)
   Cell A1 has a turquoise background, as shown in Figure C-14. Notice that Cell A1 spans columns A-I because of the Merge and Center command used for the title.

   > **QuickTip**
   >
   > Use color sparingly. Excessive use can divert the reader's attention away from the data in the worksheet.

3. Click **Format** on the menu bar, then click **Cells**
   The Format Cells dialog box opens.

4. Click the **Patterns tab**, as shown in Figure C-15, if it is not already displayed
   When choosing a background pattern, consider that a high contrast between foreground and background increases the readability of the cell contents.

5. Click the **Pattern list arrow**, click the **Thin Diagonal Crosshatch Pattern** (third row, last pattern on the right), then click **OK**
   A border also enhances a cell's appearance. Unlike underlining, which is a text formatting tool, borders extend the width of the cell.

6. Click the **Borders list arrow** ▦▾ on the Formatting toolbar, then click the **Thick Bottom Border** (second row, second border from the left) on the Borders palette
   It can be difficult to view a border while the cell or range formatted with a border is selected.

7. Click cell **A3**
   The border is a nice enhancement. Font color can distinguish labels in a worksheet.

   > **QuickTip**
   >
   > The default color on the Fill Color and Font Color buttons changes to the last color you selected.

8. Select the range **A3:I3**, click the **Font Color list arrow** ▲▾ on the Formatting toolbar, then click **Blue** (second row from the top, third color from the right) on the palette
   The text changes color, as shown in Figure C-16.

9. Click the **Print Preview button** 🔍 on the Standard toolbar, preview the first page, click **Next** to preview the second page, click **Close** on the Print Preview toolbar, then save your work

Using color to organize a worksheet

You can use color to give a distinctive look to each part of a worksheet. For example, you might want to apply a light blue to all the rows containing one category of data and a light green to all the rows containing another category of data. Be consistent throughout a group of worksheets, and try to avoid colors that are too bright and distracting.

FIGURE C-14: Background color added to cell

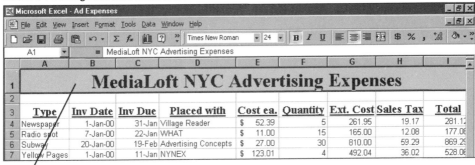

Cell A1 is affected by
fill color

FIGURE C-15: Patterns tab in the Format Cells dialog box

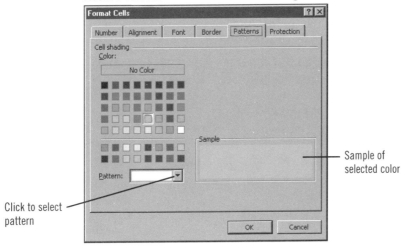

Click to select
pattern

Sample of
selected color

FIGURE C-16: Worksheet with colors, patterns, and border

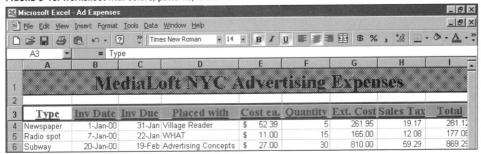

TABLE C-4: Border buttons

button	function	button	function	button	function
	Top Border		Inside Horizontal Border		Thick Bottom Border
	Bottom Border		Inside Vertical Border		Top and Bottom Border
	Left Border		Outside Border		Top and Double Bottom Border
	Right Border		No Border		Top and Thick Bottom Border
	Inside Border		Bottom Double Border		Thick Border

Using Conditional Formatting

Formatting attributes make worksheets look professional and help distinguish different data. These same attributes can be applied depending on specific outcomes in cells. Automatically applying formatting attributes based on cell values is called **conditional formatting**. If the data meets your criteria, Excel applies the formats you specify. You might, for example, want advertising costs above a certain number to display in red boldface and lower values to display in blue. Scenario▶ Jim wants the worksheet to include conditional formatting so that extended advertising costs greater than $175 display in red boldface. He creates the conditional format in the first cell in the extended cost column.

1. Click cell **G4**
   Use the scroll bars if necessary, to make column G visible.

2. Click **Format** on the menu bar, then click **Conditional Formatting**
   The Conditional Formatting dialog box opens, as shown in Figure C-17. Depending on the logical operator you've selected (such as "greater than" or "not equal to"), the Conditional Formatting dialog box displays different input fields. You can define up to three different conditions that let you determine outcome parameters, and then assign formatting attributes to each one. The condition is defined first. The default setting for the first condition is "Cell Value Is" "between."

Trouble?

If the Office Assistant appears, close it by clicking the No, Don't Provide Help Now button.

3. To change the current condition, click the **Operator list arrow**, then click **greater than or equal to**
   The first condition is that the cell value must be greater than or equal to some value. See Table C-5 for a list of options. You can use a constant, formula, cell reference, or date. That value is set in the third box.

4. Click the **Value text box**, then type **175**
   Once the value is assigned, the condition's formatting attributes are defined in the Format Cells dialog box.

5. Click **Format**, click the **Color list arrow**, click **Red** (third row, first column on the left), click **Bold** in the Font style list box, click **OK**, then click **OK** to close the Conditional Formatting dialog box
   The value, 261.95, in cell G4 is formatted in bold red numbers because it is greater than 175, meeting the condition to apply the format. The conditional format, like any other formatting, can be copied to other cells in a column.

6. With cell G4 selected, click the **Format Painter button** 🖊 on the Standard toolbar, then drag the Formatting pointer ⬇🖌 to select the range **G5:G30**
   Once the formatting is copied, you reposition the cell pointer to review the results.

7. Click cell **G4**
   Compare your results to Figure C-18. All cells with values greater than or equal to 175 in column G are displayed in bold red text.

8. Press **[Ctrl][Home]** to move to cell A1

9. Save your work

FIGURE C-17: Conditional Formatting dialog box

Click to select operator

Click to delete existing condition(s)

Click to add additional condition(s)

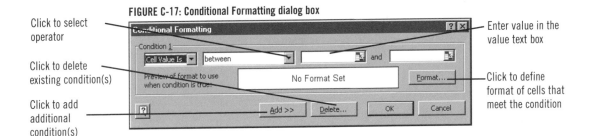

Enter value in the value text box

Click to define format of cells that meet the condition

FIGURE C-18: Worksheet with conditional formatting

Format Painter button

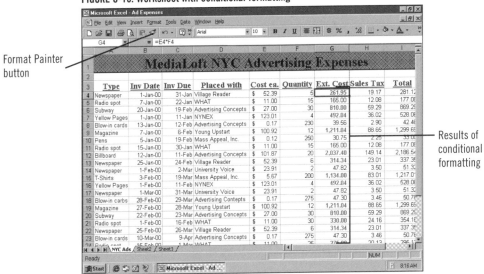

Results of conditional formatting

TABLE C-5: Conditional formatting options

option	mathematical equivalent	option	mathematical equivalent
Between	$X>Y<Z$	Greater than	$Z>Y$
Not between	$B \not> C \not< A$	Less than	$Y<Z$
Equal to	$A=B$	Greater than or equal to	$A>=B$
Not equal to	$A \neq B$	Less than or equal to	$Z<=Y$

CLUES TO USE

Deleting conditional formatting

Because it's likely that the conditions you define will change, any of the conditional formats defined can be deleted. Select the cell(s) containing conditional formatting, click Format on the menu bar, click Conditional Formatting, then click the Delete button. The Delete Conditional Format dialog box opens, as shown in Figure C-19. Click the check boxes for any of the conditions you want to delete, then click OK. The previously assigned formatting is deleted—leaving the cell's contents intact.

FIGURE C-19: Delete Conditional Format dialog box

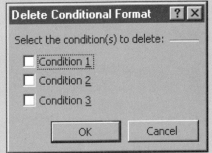

Excel 2000

Checking Spelling

You may think your worksheet is complete, but if you haven't checked for spelling errors, you risk undermining the professional value of your work. A single misspelled word can cast doubt on the validity of your numbers. The spell checker in Excel is also shared by Word, PowerPoint, and Access, so any words you've added to the dictionary using those programs are available in Excel. **Scenario** Jim has completed the formatting for his worksheet and is ready to check its spelling.

Steps 1 2 3 4

1. **Click the Spelling button 📖 on the Standard toolbar**

   The Spelling dialog box opens, as shown in Figure C-20, with MediaLoft selected as the first misspelled word in the worksheet. The spell checker starts from the active cell and compares words in the worksheet to those in its dictionary. Any word not found in the dictionary causes the spell checker to stop. At that point, you can decide to Ignore, Change, or Add the word to the active dictionary. For any word, (such as MediaLoft or "Inv", the abbreviation of invoice) you have the option to Ignore or Ignore All cases the spell checker cites as incorrect.

2. **Click Ignore All for MediaLoft**

   The spell checker found the word "cards" misspelled and offers "crabs" as one possible alternative. As words are found, you can choose to ignore them, fix the error, or select from a list of alternatives.

3. **Scroll through the Suggestions list, click cards, then click Change**

   The word "Concepts" is also misspelled and the spell checker suggests the correct spelling.

4. **Click Change**

   When no more incorrect words are found, Excel displays the message box shown in Figure C-21.

5. **Click OK**

6. **Press [Ctrl][Home]**

7. **Type your name in cell A2**

8. **Save your work, then preview and print the worksheet**

9. **Click File on the menu bar, then click Exit to close the workbook and exit Excel**

Modifying the spell checker

Each of us uses words specific to our profession or task. Because the dictionary supplied with Microsoft Office cannot possibly include all the words that each of us needs, it is possible to add words to the dictionary shared by all the components in the suite. To customize the Microsoft Office dictionary used by the spell checker, click Add when a word that you know to be correct (but was not in the dictionary) is found. From then on, that word will no longer be considered misspelled by the spell checker.

FIGURE C-20: Spelling dialog box

Misspelled word

Type replacement
word here or click a
suggestion

Click to ignore all
occurrences of
misspelled word

Click to add word to
dictionary

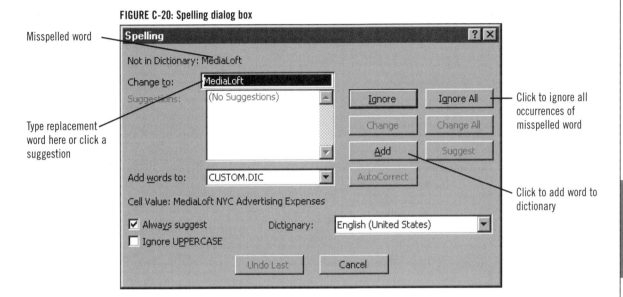

FIGURE C-21: Spelling completed alert box

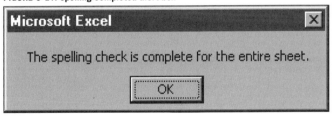

Practice

► Concepts Review

Label each element of the Excel worksheet window shown in Figure C-22.

FIGURE C-22

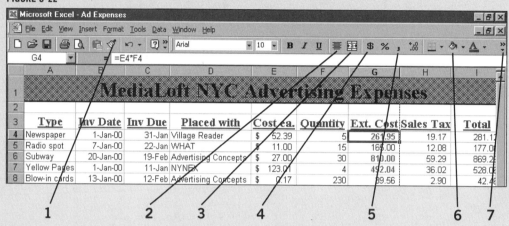

Match each command or button with the statement that describes it.

8. Format Cells	a. Changes the appearance of selected cells
9. Edit Delete	b. Erases the contents of a cell
10. Format Conditional Formatting	c. Checks the spelling in a worksheet
11.	d. Changes appearance of cell depending on result
12.	e. Pastes the contents of the Clipboard in the current cell
13.	f. Changes the format to Currency

Select the best answer from the list of choices.

14. Which button increases the number of decimal places in selected cells?
   a.
   b.
   c.
   d.

15. Each of the following operators can be used in conditional formatting, *except*
   a. Not between.
   b. Greater than.
   c. Similar to.
   d. Equal to.

16. How many conditional formats can be created in any cell?
   a. 4
   b. 2
   c. 3
   d. 1

17. Which button center-aligns the contents of a single cell?

a. ▤   c. ▤

b. ▤   d. ▦

18. Which of the following is an example of the comma format?

a. 5,555.55   c. 55.55%

b. 5555.55   d. $5,555.55

▶ Skills Review

1. Format values.

a. Start Excel and open a new workbook.

b. Enter the information from Table C-6 in your worksheet. Begin in cell A1, and do not leave any blank rows or columns.

c. Add the bold attribute to the equipment descriptions, as well as the Description and Totals labels.

d. Add the italics attribute to the Price and Sold labels.

e. Apply the Comma format to the Price and Sold data.

f. Insert formulas in the Totals column (multiply the price by the number sold).

g. Apply the Currency format to the Totals data.

h. Save this workbook as "Sports Equipment" on your Project Disk.

TABLE C-6

Best Sports Supreme, Inc.			
Quarterly Sales Sheet			
Description	Price	Sold	Totals
Ski boots	250	1104	
Rollerblades	175	1805	
Baseball bats	95	1098	
Footballs	35	1254	

2. Use fonts and font sizes.

a. Select the range of cells containing the column titles.

b. Change the font of the column titles to Times New Roman.

c. Increase the font size of the column titles to 14 point.

d. Resize the columns as necessary.

e. Select the range of values in the Price column.

f. Format the range using the Currency Style button.

g. Resize the columns, if necessary.

h. Save your changes.

3. Change attributes and alignment of labels.

a. Select the worksheet title Best Sports Supreme, Inc., then click the Bold button to apply boldface to the title.

b. Use the Merge and Center button to center the title over columns A through D.

c. Select the label Quarterly Sales Sheet, then click the Underline button to apply underlining to the label.

d. Select the range of cells containing the column titles, then click the Center button to center the column titles.

e. Save your changes, then preview and print the workbook.

4. Adjust column widths.

a. Use the AutoFit feature to resize the Price column.

b. Use the Format menu to resize the Description column to 16 and the Sold column to 9.

c. Save your changes.

5. Insert and delete rows and columns.

   a. Insert a new row between rows 4 and 5.

   b. Add Best Sports Supreme's newest product—a baseball jersey—in the newly inserted row. Enter "45" for the price and "360" for the number sold.

   c. Use the fill handle to copy the formula in cell D4 to cell D5.

   d. Add a new column between the Description and Price columns with the title "Location."

   e. Delete the "Location" column.

   f. Save your changes, then preview the workbook.

6. Apply colors, patterns, and borders.

   a. Add a border around the value data.

   b. Apply a lime background color to the Description column.

   c. Apply a green background to the column labels in cells B3:D3.

   d. Change the color of the font in the first row of the data to green.

   e. Add a pattern fill to the title in Row 1.

   f. Type your name in an empty cell, then save your work.

   g. Print the worksheet, then close the workbook.

7. Use conditional formatting.

   a. Open the file EX C-2 from your Project Disk and save it as "Quarterly Report."

   b. Create conditional formatting that changes values to blue if they are greater than 2500, and changes them to green if less than 700.

   c. Use the Bold button and Center button to format the column headings and row titles.

   d. Column A should be wide enough to accommodate the contents of cells A3:A9.

   e. AutoFit the remaining columns.

   f. Use Merge and Center in Row 1 to center the title over columns A:E.

   g. Format the title Reading Room, Inc. using 14 point Times New Roman text. Fill the cell with a color and pattern of your choice.

   h. Type your name in an empty cell, then apply a green background and make the text color yellow.

   i. Use the Edit menu to clear the cell formats of the cell with your name, then save your changes.

8. Check spelling.

   a. Check the spelling in the worksheet using the spell checker.

   b. Correct any spelling errors.

   c. Save your changes, then preview and print the workbook.

   d. Save, close the workbook, then exit Excel.

▶ Visual Workshop

Create the worksheet shown in Figure C-23, using skills you learned in this unit. Open the file EX C-5 on your Project Disk and save it as "Projected March Advertising Invoices." Create a conditional format in the Cost ea. column so that entries greater than 60 are displayed in red. (*Hint:* The only additional font used in this exercise is Times New Roman. It is 22 points in row 1, and 16 points in row 3.)

FIGURE C-23

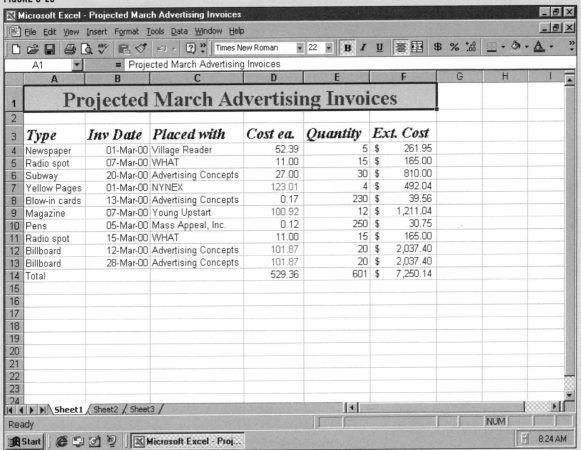

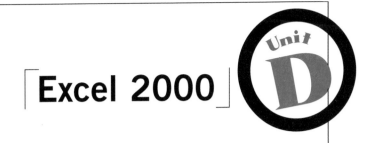

Working
with Charts

Objectives

► **Plan and design a chart**

MOUS ► **Create a chart**

MOUS ► **Move and resize a chart**

MOUS ► **Edit a chart**

MOUS ► **Format a chart**

MOUS ► **Enhance a chart**

MOUS ► **Annotate and draw on a chart**

MOUS ► **Preview and print a chart**

Worksheets provide an effective way to organize information, but they are not always the best format for presenting data to others. Information in a selected range or worksheet can easily be converted to the visual format of a chart. Charts graphically communicate the relationships of data in a worksheet. In this unit, you will learn how to create a chart, how to edit a chart and change the chart type, how to add text annotations and arrows to a chart, and how to preview and print a chart. Scenario► For the annual meeting Jim Fernandez needs to create a chart showing the six-month sales history at MediaLoft for the stores in the eastern division. He wants to illustrate the trend of growth in this division.

Planning and Designing a Chart

Before creating a chart, you need to plan the information you want your chart to show and how you want it to look. Scenario In early June, the Marketing department launched a regional advertising campaign for the eastern division. The results of the campaign were increased sales during the fall months. Jim wants his chart for the annual meeting to illustrate the growth trend of sales in MediaLoft's eastern division stores and to highlight this dramatic sales increase.

Jim uses the worksheet shown in Figure D-1 and the following guidelines to plan the chart:

 Determine the purpose of the chart, and identify the data relationships you want to communicate visually

You want to create a chart that shows sales throughout MediaLoft's eastern division from July through December. In particular, you want to highlight the increase in sales that occurred as a result of the advertising campaign.

 Determine the results you want to see, and decide which chart type is most appropriate to use

Different charts have different strengths and display data in various ways. How you want your data displayed—and how you want that data interpreted—can help you determine the best chart type to use. Table D-1 describes several different types of charts and when each one is best used. Because you want to compare data (sales in multiple locations) over a time period (the months July through December), you decide to use a column chart.

 Identify the worksheet data you want the chart to illustrate

You are using data from the worksheet titled "MediaLoft Eastern Division Stores" as shown in Figure D-1. This worksheet contains the sales data for the four stores in the eastern division from July through December.

 Sketch the chart, then use your sketch to decide where the chart elements should be placed

You sketch your chart as shown in Figure D-2. You put the months on the horizontal axis (the **x-axis**) and the monthly sales figures on the vertical axis (the **y-axis**). The **tick marks** on the y-axis create a scale of measure for each value. Each value in a cell you select for your chart is a **data point**. In any chart, a **data marker** visually represents each data point, which in this case is a column. A collection of related data points is a **data series**. In this chart, there are four data series (Boston, Chicago, Kansas City, and New York), so you include a **legend** to make it easy to identify them.

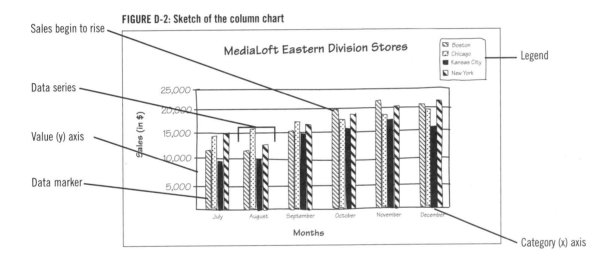

FIGURE D-2: Sketch of the column chart

Sales begin to rise

Data series

Value (y) axis

Data marker

Legend

Category (x) axis

MediaLoft Eastern Division Stores

Sales (in $)

25,000
20,000
15,000
10,000
5,000

July   August   September   October   November   December

Months

Boston
Chicago
Kansas City
New York

TABLE D-1: Commonly used chart types

type	button	description
Area		Shows how volume changes over time
Bar		Compares distinct objects over time using a horizontal format; sometimes referred to as a horizontal bar chart in other spreadsheet programs
Column		Compares distinct objects over time using a vertical format; the Excel default; sometimes referred to as a bar chart in other spreadsheet programs
Line		Compares trends over even time intervals; similar to an area chart
Pie		Compares sizes of pieces as part of a whole; can have slices pulled away from the pie, or "exploded"
XY (scatter)		Compares trends over uneven time or measurement intervals; used in scientific and engineering disciplines for trend spotting and extrapolation
Combination	none	Combines a column and line chart to compare data requiring different scales of measure

Excel 2000

Excel 2000

Creating a Chart

To create a chart in Excel, you first select the range containing the data you want to chart. Once you've selected a range, you can use the Excel Chart Wizard to lead you through the process of creating the chart. ▶Scenario▶ Using the worksheet containing the sales data for the eastern division, Jim creates a chart that shows the growth trend that occurred as a result of the advertising campaign.

Steps 1 2 3 4

QuickTip

To reset toolbars, click Tools on the menu bar, click Customize, click Reset my usage data, click Yes, then click Close.

1. **Start Excel, reset your toolbars to their default settings, open the workbook EX D-1 from your Project Disk, then save it as MediaLoft Sales-Eastern Division**
   You want the chart to include the monthly sales figures for each of the eastern division stores, as well as month and store labels. You don't include the Total columns because the monthly figures make up the totals and these figures would skew the chart.

Trouble?

Click the More Buttons button ▾ to locate buttons that are not visible on your toolbars.

2. **Select the range A5:G9, then click the Chart Wizard button 🔛 on the Standard toolbar**
   This range includes the cells that will be charted. The Chart Wizard opens. The Chart Wizard - Step 1 of 4 - Chart Type dialog box lets you choose the type of chart you want to create. See Figure D-3. You can see a preview of the chart by clicking and holding the Press and Hold to View Sample button.

3. **Click Next to accept Column, the default chart type**
   The Chart Wizard - Step 2 of 4 - Chart Source Data dialog box lets you choose the data being charted and whether the series are in rows or columns. You want to chart the effect of sales for each store over the time period. Currently, the rows are accurately selected as the data series, as specified by the Series in option button located under the Data range. Since you selected the data before clicking the Chart Wizard button, Excel converted the range to absolute values and the correct range =Sheet1!$A$5:$G$9 displays in the Data range text box.

4. **Click Next**
   The Chart Wizard - Step 3 of 4 - Chart Options dialog box shows a sample chart using the data you selected. Notice that the store locations (the rows in the selected range) are plotted according to the months (the columns in the selected range), and that the months were added as labels for each data series. Notice also that there is a legend showing each location and its corresponding color on the chart. Here, you can choose to keep the legend, add a chart title, gridlines, data labels, data table, and add axis titles.

5. **Click the Chart title text box, then type MediaLoft Sales - Eastern Division**
   After a moment, the title appears in the Sample Chart box. See Figure D-4.

6. **Click Next**
   In the Chart Wizard - Step 4 of 4 - Chart Location dialog box, you determine the placement of the chart in the workbook. You can display a chart as an object on the current sheet, on any other existing sheet, or on a newly created chart sheet. A **chart sheet** in a workbook contains only a chart that is linked to the worksheet data. Displaying the chart as an object in the sheet containing the data will help Jim emphasize his point at the annual meeting.

Trouble?

If you are using a small monitor, your chart may appear distorted. If so, you'll need to move it to a blank area of the worksheet and then enlarge it before continuing with the lessons in this unit. See your instructor or technical support person for assistance.

7. **Click Finish**
   The column chart appears and the Chart toolbar opens, either docked, as shown in Figure D-5, or floating. Your chart might be in a different location and look slightly different. You will adjust the chart's location and size in the next lesson. The **selection handles**, the small squares at the corners and sides of the chart's border, indicate that the chart is selected. Anytime a chart is selected, as it is now, a blue border surrounds the data range, a green border surrounds the row labels, and a purple border surrounds the column labels. If you want to delete a chart, select it, then press [Delete].

8. **Save your work**

FIGURE D-3: First Chart Wizard dialog box

Selected chart

Chart types

Chart sub-types for selected chart

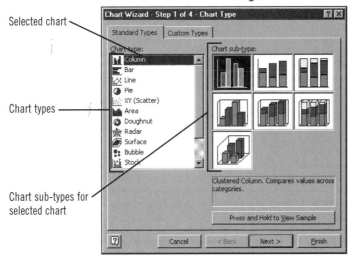

FIGURE D-4: Third Chart Wizard dialog box

Type the chart title here

Sample chart

Title added

Legend

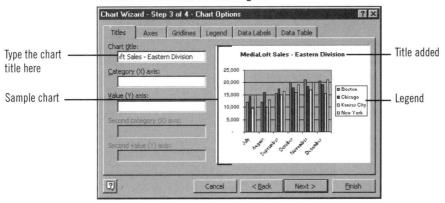

FIGURE D-5: Worksheet with column chart

Your toolbars may not match those in the figures

Column labels

Row labels

Data range

Month labels on x-axis

Title

Legend

Selection handles

Chart toolbar

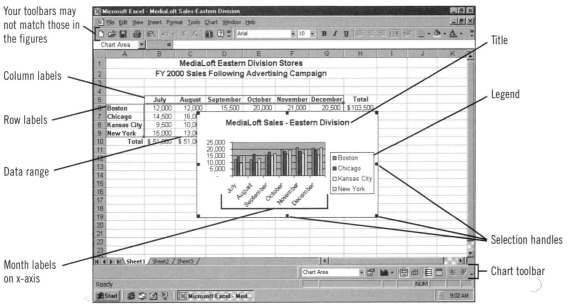

Moving and Resizing a Chart

Charts are graphics, or drawn **objects**, and are not in a specific cell or range address. You can move a chart anywhere on a worksheet without affecting formulas or data in the worksheet. Resize a chart to improve its appearance by dragging the selection handles. You can even put a chart on another sheet without worrying about cell formulas. Drawn objects such as charts contain other objects that you can move and resize. To move an object, select it, then drag it or cut and copy it to a new location. To resize an object, use the selection handles. When you select a chart object, the name of the selected object appears in the Chart Objects list box on the Chart toolbar, and in the name box. ▶Scenario▶ Jim wants to increase the size of the chart and position it below the worksheet data. He also wants to change the position of the legend.

QuickTip

When a chart is selected, the Chart menu appears on the menu bar.

1. Make sure the chart is still selected, then position the pointer over the chart
   The pointer shape ⌖ indicates that you can move the chart or use a selection handle to resize it. For a table of commonly used pointers, refer to Table D-2. On occasion, the Chart toolbar obscures your view. You can dock the toolbar to make it easier to see your work.

2. If the chart toolbar is floating, click the **Chart toolbar's title bar**, drag it to the **right edge of the status bar** until it docks, then release the mouse button
   The toolbar is docked on the bottom of the screen.

3. Place the ⌖ pointer on the chart, press and hold the left mouse button, using ✛ drag the upper left edge of the chart to the **top of row 13** and the left edge of the chart to the **left border of column A**, then release the mouse button
   A dotted outline of the chart perimeter appears as the chart is being moved. The chart is in the new location. Resizing a chart doesn't affect the data in the chart, only the way the chart looks on the sheet.

4. Position the pointer on the right-middle selection handle until it changes to ↔, then drag the right edge of the chart to the **right edge of column H**
   The chart is widened. See Figure D-6.

5. Position the pointer over the top middle selection handle until it changes to ↕, then drag it to the **top of row 12**

6. If the labels for the months do not fully display, position the pointer over the bottom middle selection handle until it changes to ↕, then drag down to display the months
   You can move the legend to improve the chart's appearance. You want to align the top of the legend with the top of the plot area.

7. Click the **legend** to select it, then drag the **legend** using the ⌖ to the **upper-right corner of the chart** until it is aligned with the plot area
   Selection handles appear around the legend when you click it; "Legend" appears in the Chart Objects list box on the Chart toolbar as well as in the name box, and a dotted outline of the legend perimeter appears as you drag. Changing the original Excel data modifies the legend text.

8. Click cell **A9**, type **NYC**, then click ☑
   See Figure D-7. The legend is repositioned and the legend entry for the New York City store is changed.

9. Save your work

FIGURE D-6: Worksheet with resized and repositioned chart

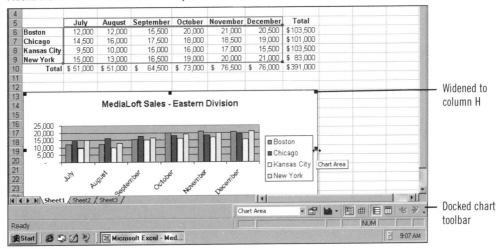

Widened to column H

Docked chart toolbar

FIGURE D-7: Worksheet with repositioned legend

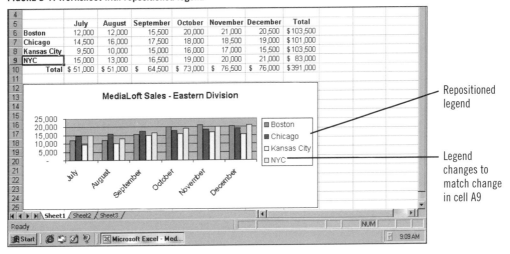

Repositioned legend

Legend changes to match change in cell A9

TABLE D-2: Commonly used pointers

name	pointer	use	name	pointer	use
Diagonal resizing	↖ or ↗	Change chart shape from corners	I-beam	I	Edit chart text
Draw	+	Create shapes	Move chart	✛	Change chart location
Horizontal resizing	↔	Change chart shape from left to right	Vertical resizing	↕	Changes chart shape from top to bottom

Identifying chart objects

There are many objects within a chart and Excel makes it easy to identify each of them. Placing your mouse pointer over a chart object causes a ScreenTip for that object to appear, whether the chart is selected or not. If a chart—or any object in it—is selected, the ScreenTips still appear. In addition, the name of the selected chart object appears in the name box and the Chart Object list box on the Chart toolbar.

Excel 2000

Editing a Chart

Once you've created a chart, it's easy to modify it. You can change data values in the worksheet, and the chart will automatically be updated to reflect the new data. You can also easily change chart types using the buttons on the Chart toolbar. Scenario▶ Jim looks over his worksheet and realizes he entered the wrong data for the Kansas City store in November and December. After he corrects this data, he wants to see how the same data looks using different chart types.

Trouble?

If you cannot see the chart and data together on your monitor, click View on the menu bar, click Zoom, then click 75%.

1. If necessary, scroll the worksheet so that you can see both the chart and row 8, containing the Kansas City sales figures, then place your mouse pointer over the data point to display **Series "Kansas City" Point "December" Value "15,500"**
   As you correct the values, the columns for November and December in the chart automatically change.

2. Click cell **F8**, type **18000** to correct the November sales figure, press [→], type **19500** in cell **G8**, then click ☑
   The Kansas City columns for November and December reflect the increased sales figures. See Figure D-9. The totals are also updated in column H and row 10.

3. Select the chart by clicking anywhere within the chart border, then click the **Chart Type list arrow** 📊▾ on the Chart toolbar
   The chart type buttons appear on the Chart Type palette. Table D-3 describes the chart types available.

4. Click the **Bar Chart button** 📊 on the palette
   The column chart changes to a bar chart. See Figure D-10. You look at the bar chart, take some notes, and then decide to convert it back to a column chart. You now want to see if the large increase in sales would be better presented with a three-dimensional column chart.

QuickTip

Experiment with different formats for your charts until you get just the right look.

5. Click the **Chart Type list arrow** 📊▾, then click the **3-D Column Chart button** 📊 on the palette
   A three-dimensional column chart appears. You notice that the three-dimensional column format is more crowded than the two-dimensional format but gives you a sense of volume.

6. Click the **Chart Type list arrow** 📊▾, then click the **Column Chart button** 📊 on the palette

7. Save your work

Rotating a chart

In a three-dimensional chart, columns or bars can sometimes be obscured by other data series within the same chart. You can rotate the chart until a better view is obtained. Double-click the chart, click the tip of one of its axes (select the Corners object), then drag the handles until a more pleasing view of the data series appears. See Figure D-8.

FIGURE D-8: 3-D chart rotated with improved view of data series

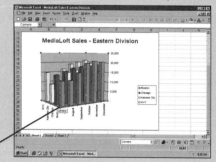

Click to rotate chart

FIGURE D-9: Worksheet with new data entered for Kansas City

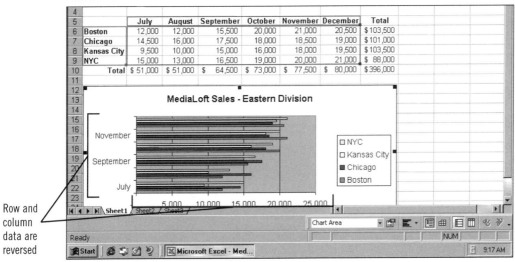

New data

Adjusted data points

FIGURE D-10: Bar chart

Row and column data are reversed

TABLE D-3: Commonly used chart type buttons

click	to display a	click	to display a	click	to display a	click	to display a
	area chart		pie chart		3-D area chart		3-D pie chart
	bar chart		(xy) scatter chart		3-D bar chart		3-D surface chart
	column chart		doughnut chart		3-D column chart		3-D cylinder chart
	line chart		radar chart		3-D line chart		3-D cone chart

Excel 2000

Formatting a Chart

After you've created a chart using the Chart Wizard, you can easily modify its appearance. Use the Chart toolbar and Chart menu to change the colors of data series and add or eliminate a legend and gridlines. **Gridlines** are the horizontal and vertical lines in the chart that enable the eye to follow the value on an axis. The button that selects the chart type changes to the last chart type selected. The corresponding Chart toolbar buttons are listed in Table D-4. Scenario> Jim wants to make some changes in the appearance of his chart. He wants to see if the chart looks better without gridlines, and he wants to change the color of a data series.

Steps

1. **Make sure the chart is still selected**
   Horizontal gridlines currently appear in the chart.

2. **Click Chart on the menu bar, click Chart Options, click the Gridlines tab in the Chart Options dialog box, then click the Major Gridlines checkbox for the Value (Y) axis to remove the check**
   The gridlines disappear from the sample chart in the dialog box, as shown in Figure D-11. Even though gridlines extend from the tick marks on an axis across the plot area, they are not always necessary to the chart's readability.

QuickTip

Minor gridlines show the values between the tick marks.

3. **Click the Major Gridlines checkbox for the Value (Y) axis, then click the Minor Gridlines checkbox for the Value (Y) axis**
   Both major and minor gridlines appear in the sample.

4. **Click the Minor Gridlines checkbox for the Value (Y) axis, then click OK**
   The minor gridlines disappear, leaving only the major gridlines on the Value axis. You can change the color of the columns to better distinguish the data series.

5. **With the chart selected, double-click any light blue column in the NYC data series**
   Handles appear on all the columns in the NYC data series, and the Format Data Series dialog box opens, as shown in Figure D-12.

QuickTip

Add values, labels, and percentages to your chart using the Data Labels tab in the Chart Options dialog box.

6. **Click the Patterns tab, if necessary, click the fuschia box (in the fourth row, first on the left), then click OK**
   All the columns for the series are fuschia, and the legend changes to match the new color. Compare your finished chart to Figure D-13.

7. **Save your work**

TABLE D-4: Chart enhancement buttons

button	use
	Displays formatting dialog box for the selected object on the chart
	Selects chart type (chart type on button changes to last chart type selected)
	Adds/Deletes legend
	Creates a data table within the chart
	Charts data by row
	Charts data by column
	Angles selected text downward
	Angles selected text upward

FIGURE D-11: Chart Options dialog box

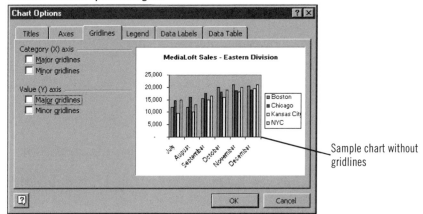

Sample chart without gridlines

FIGURE D-12: Format Data Series dialog box

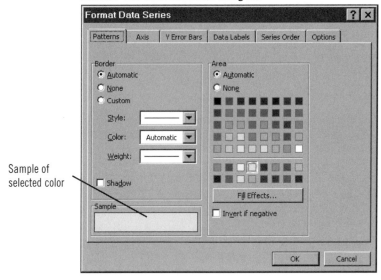

Sample of selected color

FIGURE D-13: Chart with formatted data series

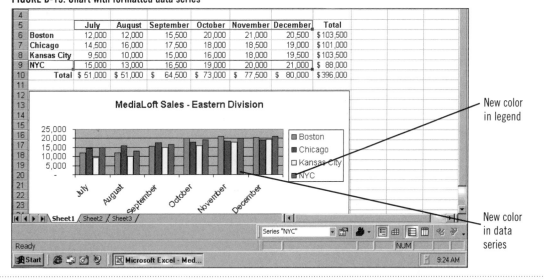

New color in legend

New color in data series

Enhancing a Chart

There are many ways to enhance a chart to make it easier to read and understand. You can create titles for the x-axis and y-axis, add graphics, or add background color. You can even format the text you use in a chart. **Scenario** Jim wants to improve the appearance of his chart by creating titles for the x-axis and y-axis. He also decides to add a drop shadow to the title.

Steps

1. **Make sure the chart is selected, click Chart on the menu bar, click Chart Options, click the Titles tab in the Chart Options dialog box, then type Months in the Category (X) axis text box**
   Descriptive text on the x-axis helps a user understand the chart. The word "Months" appears below the month labels in the sample chart, as shown in Figure D-14.

   QuickTip

   To edit the text, position the pointer over the selected text box until it changes to I, click, then edit the text.

2. **Click the Value (Y) axis text box, type Sales (in $), then click OK**
   A selected text box containing "Sales (in $)" appears rotated 90 degrees to the left of the y-axis. Once the Chart Options dialog box is closed, you can move the Value or Category axis titles to new positions by clicking on an edge of the object and dragging it.

3. **Press [Esc] to deselect the Value-axis title**
   Next you decide that a border with a drop shadow will enhance the chart title.

4. **Click the chart title MediaLoft Sales – Eastern Division to select it**
   You can create a drop shadow using the Format button on the Chart toolbar.

   QuickTip

   The Format button 🗐 opens a dialog box with the appropriate formatting options for the selected chart element. The ScreenTip for the button changes depending on the selected object.

5. **Click the Format Chart Title button 🗐 on the Chart toolbar to open the Format Chart Title dialog box, make sure the Patterns tab is selected, then click the Shadow checkbox**
   A border with a drop shadow surrounds the title. You can continue to format the title.

6. **Click the Font tab in the Format Chart Title dialog box, click Times New Roman in the Font list, click Bold Italic in the Font style list, click OK, then press [Esc] to deselect the chart title**
   A border with a drop shadow appears around the chart title, and the chart title text is reformatted.

7. **Click the Category Axis Title, click 🗐, click the Font tab, select Times New Roman in the Font list, then click OK**
   The Category Axis Title appears in the Times New Roman font.

8. **Click the Value Axis Title, click 🗐, click the Font tab, click Times New Roman in the Font list, click OK, then press [Esc] to deselect the title**
   The Value Axis Title appears in the Times New Roman font. Compare your chart to Figure D-15.

9. **Save your work**

Changing text font and alignment in charts

The font and the alignment of axis text can be modified to make it more readable or to better fit within the plot area. With a chart selected, double-click the axis text to be modified. The Format Axis dialog box appears. Click the Font or the Alignment tab, make the desired changes, then click OK.

FIGURE D-14: Sample chart with Category (X) axis text

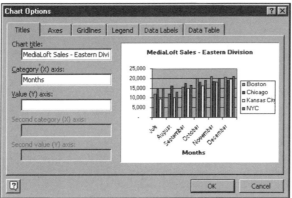

FIGURE D-15: Enhanced chart

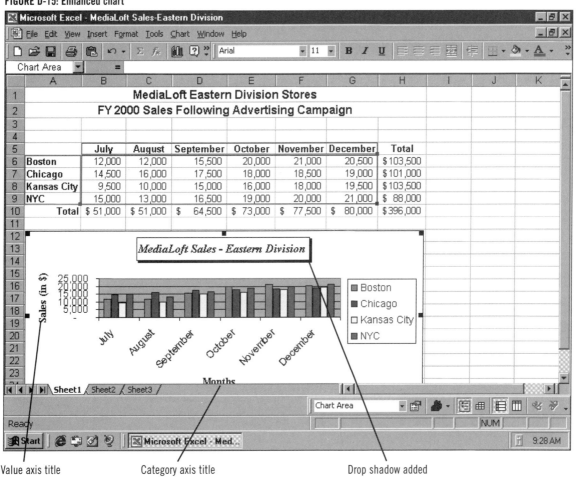

Value axis title   Category axis title   Drop shadow added

Annotating and Drawing on a Chart

You can add arrows and text annotations to point out critical information in your charts. Text annotations are labels that you add to a chart to further describe the data in it. You can draw lines and arrows that point to the exact locations you want to emphasize. **Scenario** Jim wants to add a text annotation and an arrow to highlight the October sales increase.

Steps

1. Make sure the chart is selected

To call attention to the Boston October sales increase, you can draw an arrow that points to the top of the Boston October data series with the annotation, "Due to ad campaign." With the chart selected, simply typing text in the formula bar creates annotation text.

2. Type **Due to ad campaign**, then click the **Enter button**

As you type, the text appears in the formula bar. After you confirm the entry, the text appears in a selected text box within the chart window.

3. Point to an edge of the text box so the pointer changes to

Trouble?

If the pointer changes to I or ↔, release the mouse button, click outside the text box area to deselect it, then select the text box and repeat Step 3.

4. Drag the text box **above the chart**, as shown in Figure D-16, then release the mouse button

You can add an arrow to point to a specific area or item in a chart using the Drawing toolbar.

5. Click the **Drawing button** on the Standard toolbar

The Drawing toolbar appears.

6. Click the **Arrow button** on the Drawing toolbar

The pointer changes to and the status bar displays "Click and drag to insert an AutoShape." When you draw an arrow, the point farthest from where you start will have the arrowhead.

QuickTip

You can insert text and an arrow in the data section of a worksheet by clicking the Text Box button on the Drawing toolbar, drawing a text box, typing the text, and then adding the arrow.

7. Position + under the 't' in the word "to" in the text box, press and hold the **left mouse button**, drag the line to the **Boston column in the October sales series**, then release the mouse button

An arrowhead appears, pointing to Boston October sales. The arrowhead is a selected object in the chart and can be resized, formatted, or deleted just like any other object. Compare your finished chart to Figure D-17.

8. Click to close the Drawing toolbar

9. Save your work

FIGURE D-16: Repositioning text annotation

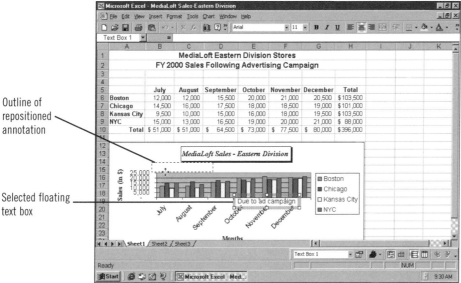

Outline of
repositioned
annotation

Selected floating
text box

FIGURE D-17: Completed chart with text annotation and arrow

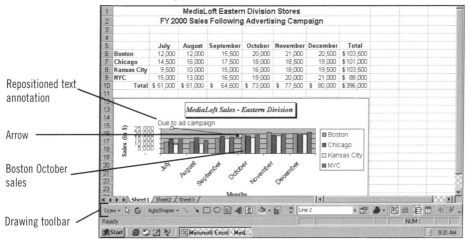

Repositioned text
annotation

Arrow

Boston October
sales

Drawing toolbar

Exploding a pie slice

Just as an arrow can call attention to a data
series, you can emphasize a pie slice by exploding it, or pulling it away from, the pie chart.
Once the pie chart is selected, click the pie to
select it, click the desired slice to select only the
slice, then drag the slice away from the pie, as
shown in Figure D-18. After you change the
chart type, you may need to adjust arrows
within the chart.

FIGURE D-18: Exploded pie slice

September sales
slice pulled from pie

Previewing and Printing a Chart

After you complete a chart to your satisfaction, you will need to print it. Previewing a chart gives you a chance to see what your chart looks like before you print it. You can print a chart by itself, or as part of the worksheet. ▸Scenario▸ Jim wants to print the chart for the annual meeting. He will print the worksheet and the chart together, so that the shareholders can see the actual sales numbers for the eastern division stores.

1. Press **[Esc]** twice to deselect the arrow and the chart, click cell **A35**, type your name, press **[Enter]**, then press **[Ctrl][Home]**

If you wanted to print only the chart without the data, you would leave the chart selected. Including your name on a worksheet ensures that you'll be able to identify your work when it is printed.

> **Trouble?**
>
> Click Margins on the Print Preview toolbar to display Margin lines in the Print Preview window.

2. Click the **Print Preview button** 🔍 on the Standard toolbar

The Print Preview window opens. You decide that the chart and data would make better use of the page if they were printed in **landscape** orientation—that is, with the text running the long way on the page. Altering the page setup changes the orientation of the page.

3. Click **Setup** on the Print Preview toolbar to open the Page Setup dialog box, then click the **Page tab**

4. Click the **Landscape option button** in the Orientation section as shown in Figure D-19, then click **OK**

Because each page has a left default margin of 0.75", the chart and data will print too far over to the left of the page. You can change this setting using the Margins tab.

5. Click **Setup**, click the **Margins tab**, click the **Center on page Horizontally checkbox**, then click **OK**

The data and chart are positioned horizontally on the page. See Figure D-20.

6. Click **Print** to display the Print dialog box, then click **OK**

The data and chart print and you are returned to the worksheet. If you want, you can choose to preview (and print) only the chart.

7. Select the **chart**, then click the **Print Preview button** 🔍

The chart appears in the Print Preview window. If you wanted to, you could print the chart by clicking the Print button on the Print Preview toolbar.

8. Click **Close** on the Print Preview toolbar

9. Save your work, then close the workbook and exit Excel

Using the Page Setup dialog box for a chart

When a chart is selected, a different Page Setup dialog box opens than when neither the chart nor data is selected. The Center on Page options are not always available. To accurately position a chart on the page, you could click the Margins button on the Print Preview toolbar. Margin lines appear on the screen and show you exactly how the margins display on the page. The exact placement appears in the status bar when you press and hold the mouse button on the margin line. You can drag the lines to the exact setting you want.

FIGURE D-19: Page tab of the Page Setup dialog box

Landscape option
button selected

FIGURE D-20: Chart and data ready to print

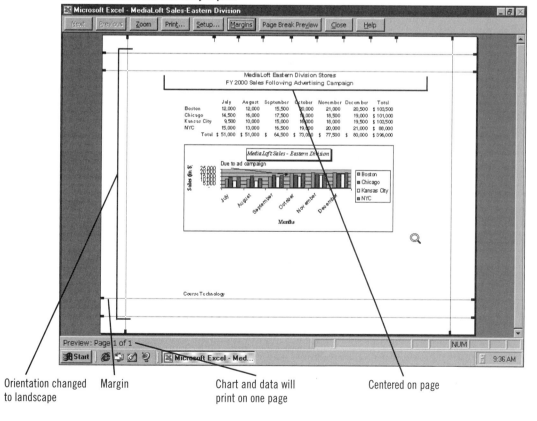

Orientation changed   Margin   Chart and data will   Centered on page
to landscape   print on one page

Practice

► Concepts Review

Label each element of the Excel chart shown in Figure D-21.

FIGURE D-21

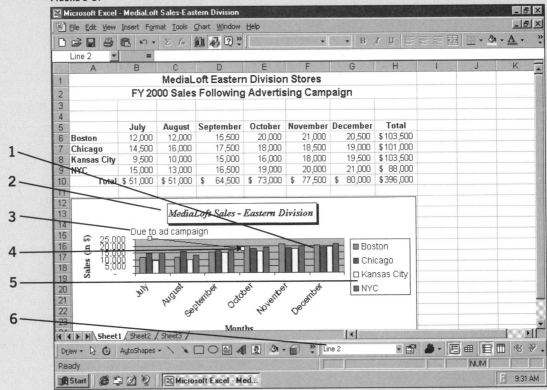

Match each chart type with the statement that describes it.

7. Column   a. Compares data over time—the Excel default

8. Area   b. Compares data as parts of a whole

9. Pie   c. Displays a column and line chart using different scales of measurement

10. Combination d. Compares trends over even time intervals

11. Line   e. Shows how volume changes over time

Select the best answer from the list of choices.

12. The object in a chart that identifies patterns used for each data series is a
   a. Range.
   b. Plot.
   c. Legend.
   d. Data point.

13. What is the term for a row or column on a chart?
   a. Data series
   b. Axis title
   c. Chart orientation
   d. Range address

14. The orientation of a page whose dimensions are 11" by 8½" is
   a. Landscape.
   b. Longways.
   c. Portrait.
   d. Sideways.

15. The Value axis is the
   a. Y-axis.
   b. Z-axis.
   c. D-axis.
   d. X-axis.

16. The Category axis is the
   a. Y-axis.
   b. Z-axis.
   c. D-axis.
   d. X-axis.

17. Which pointer is used to resize a chart object?
   a. +
   b. ↗
   c. ✥
   d. I

Skills Review

....

1. Create a chart.

a. Start Excel, open a new workbook, then save it as "Software Usage" to your Project Disk.

b. Enter the information from Table D-5 in your worksheet in range A1:F6. Resize columns and rows.

c. Save your work.

d. Select the range you want to chart.

e. Click the Chart Wizard button.

f. Complete the Chart Wizard dialog boxes and build a column chart on the same sheet as the data, having a different color bar for each department. Title the chart "Software Usage by Department."

g. Save your work.

TABLE D-5

	Excel	Word	PowerPoint	Access	Publisher
Accounting	22	15	2	2	1
Marketing	13	35	35	5	32
Engineering	23	5	3	1	0
Personnel	10	25	10	2	25
Production	6	5	22	0	22

2. Move and resize a chart.

a. Make sure the chart is still selected.

b. Move the chart beneath the data.

c. Drag the chart's selection handles so it is as wide as the screen.

d. Move the legend below the charted data. (*Hint:* Change the legend's position using the Legend button on the Chart toolbar.)

e. Save your work.

3. Edit a chart.

a. Change the value in cell B3 to "6." Notice the change in the chart.

b. Select the chart by clicking it.

c. Click the Chart Type list arrow on the Chart toolbar.

d. Click the 3-D Column Chart button.

e. Rotate the chart to move the data.

f. Change the chart back to a column chart.

g. Save your work.

4. Format a chart.

a. Make sure the chart is still selected.

b. Use the Chart Options dialog box to turn off the displayed gridlines.

c. Change the font used in the Category and Value labels to Times New Roman.

d. Turn the major gridlines back on.

e. Change the title's font to Times New Roman.

f. Save your work.

5. Enhance a chart.

   a. Make sure the chart is still selected, click Chart on the menu bar, click Chart Options, then click the Titles tab.

   b. Click the Category (X) axis text box, then type "Software" in the selected text box below the x-axis.

   c. Click the Value (Y) axis text box, type "Users" in the selected text box to the left of the y-axis, then click OK.

   d. Change the legend entry for "Production" to "Art."

   e. Add a drop shadow to the title.

   f. Save your work.

6. Annotate and draw on a chart.

   a. Select the chart.

   b. Create the text annotation "Need More Users."

   c. Drag the text annotation under the title.

   d. Click the Arrow button on the Drawing toolbar.

   e. Click below the text annotation, drag the arrow so it points to the area containing the Access columns, then release the mouse button.

   f. Save your work.

7. Preview and print a chart.

   a. Deselect the chart and type your name in cell A30.

   b. Preview the chart and data to see how it will look when printed.

   c. Change the paper orientation to landscape.

   d. Center the data and chart horizontally and vertically on the page.

   e. Click Print in the Print Preview window.

   f. Select the chart.

   g. Preview, then print only the chart.

   h. Save your work, close the workbook, then exit Excel.

Excel 2000

▶ Visual Workshop

Modify a worksheet using the skills you learned in this unit, using Figure D-22 for reference. Open the file EX D-5 from your Project Disk, and save it as "Quarterly Advertising Budget." Create the chart, then change the data to reflect Figure D-22. Type your name in cell A13, save, preview, and then print your results.

FIGURE D-22

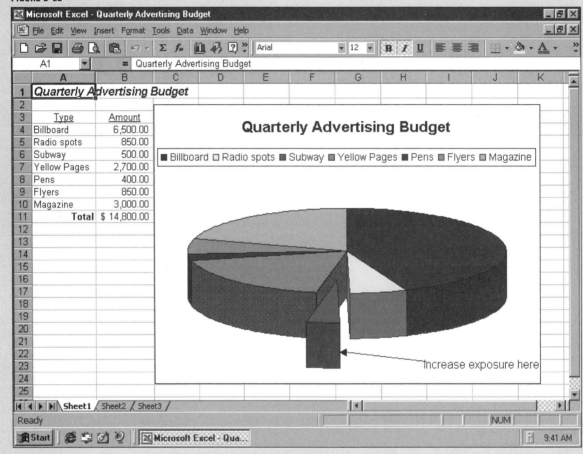

Excel 2000

Unit E

Working
with Formulas and Functions

Objectives

[MOUS] ▶ **Create a formula with several operators**

[MOUS] ▶ **Use names in a formula**

[MOUS] ▶ **Generate multiple totals with AutoSum**

[MOUS] ▶ **Use dates in calculations**

[MOUS] ▶ **Build a conditional formula with the IF function**

[MOUS] ▶ **Use statistical functions**

[MOUS] ▶ **Calculate payments with the PMT function**

[MOUS] ▶ **Display and print formula contents**

Without formulas, Excel would simply be an electronic grid with text and numbers. Used with formulas, Excel becomes a powerful data analysis software tool. As you learn how to analyze data using different types of formulas, including those that call for functions, you will discover more ways to use Excel. In this unit, you will gain a further understanding of Excel formulas and learn how to build several Excel functions. Scenario▶ Top management at MediaLoft has asked Jim Fernandez to analyze various company data. To do this, Jim creates several worksheets that require the use of formulas and functions. Because management is considering raising salaries for store managers, Jim's first task is to create a report that compares the payroll deductions and net pay for store managers before and after a proposed raise.

Excel 2000

Creating a Formula with Several Operators

You can create formulas that contain a combination of cell references (for example, Z100 and B2), operators (for example, * [multiplication] and − [subtraction]), and values (for example, 99 or 1.56). You also can create a single formula that performs several calculations. If you enter a formula with more than one operator, Excel performs the calculations in a particular sequence based on algebraic rules called **precedence**; that is, Excel performs the operation(s) within the parentheses first, then performs the other calculations. See Table E-1. **Scenario** Jim has been given the gross pay and payroll deductions for the first payroll period and needs to complete his analysis. He also has preformatted, with the Comma style, any cells that are to contain values. Jim begins by entering a formula for net pay that subtracts the payroll deductions from gross pay.

Steps 1 2 3 4

QuickTip

To return personalized toolbars and menus to their default state, click Tools on the menu bar, click Customize, click the Options tab in the Customize dialog box, click Reset my usage data to restore the default settings, click Yes, click Close, then close the Drawing toolbar if it is displayed.

1. Start Excel if necessary, open the workbook titled **EX E-1**, then save the workbook as **Pay Info for Store Mgrs**

The first part of the net pay formula will go in cell B11.

2. Click **Edit** on the menu bar, click **Go To**, then type **B11** in the Reference box and click **OK**

The Go To command is especially useful when you want to select a cell in a large worksheet.

3. Type **=B6-**

Remember that you can type cell references in either uppercase or lowercase letters. (Excel automatically converts lowercase cell reference letters to uppercase.) If you make a mistake while building a formula, press [Esc] and begin again. You type the equal sign (=) to tell Excel that a formula follows, B6 to reference the cell containing the gross pay, and the minus sign (−) to indicate that the next entry will be subtracted from cell B6.

Trouble?

If you receive a message box indicating "Parentheses do not match," make sure you have included both a left and a right parenthesis.

4. Type **(B7+B8+B9+B10)** then click the **Enter button** ☑ on the formula bar

The net pay for Payroll Period 1 appears in cell B11, as shown in Figure E-1. (*Note:* Your toolbars may differ from those in the figure.) Because Excel performs the operations within parentheses first, you can control the order of calculations on the worksheet. (In this case, Excel sums the values in cells B7 through B10 first.) After the operations within the parentheses are completed, Excel performs the operations outside the parentheses. (In this case, Excel subtracts the total of range B7:B10 from cell B6.)

5. Copy the formula in cell **B11** into cells **C11:F11**, then return to cell **A1**

The formula in cell B11 is copied to the range C11:F11 to complete row 11. See Figure E-2.

6. Save the workbook

Jim is pleased with the formulas that calculate net pay totals.

TABLE E-1: Example formulas using parentheses and several operators

formula	order of precedence	calculated result
=36+(1+3)	Add 1 to 3; then add the result to 36	40
=(10−20)/10−5	Subtract 20 from 10; divide that by 10; then subtract 5	−6
=(10*2)*(10+2)	Multiply 10 by 2; add 10 to 2; then multiply the results	240

FIGURE E-1: Worksheet showing formula and result

Result in cell B11

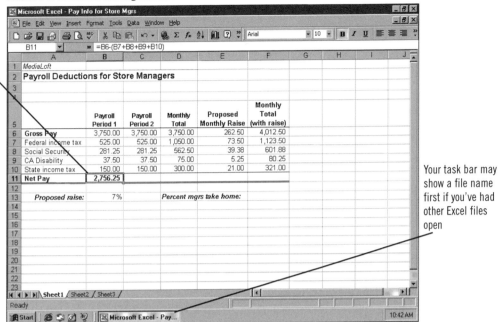

Your task bar may show a file name first if you've had other Excel files open

FIGURE E-2: Worksheet with copied formulas

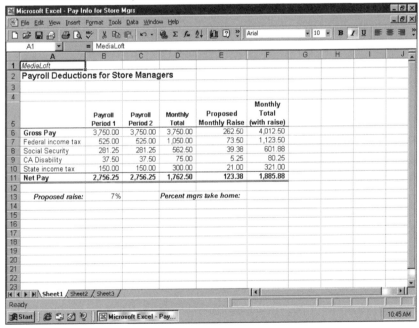

Excel 2000

Using Paste Special to paste formulas and values and to perform calculations

You can use the Paste Special command to quickly enter formulas and values or even to perform quick calculations. Click the cell(s) containing the formula or value you want to copy, click the Copy button on the Standard toolbar, then right-click the cell where you want the result to appear. In the pop-up menu, choose Paste Special, then choose the feature you want to paste and click OK.

Excel 2000

Using Names in a Formula

You can assign names to cells and ranges. Doing so reduces errors and makes a worksheet easier to follow. You also can use names in formulas. Using names in formulas facilitates formula building and provides a frame of reference for formula logic—the names make formulas easy to recognize and maintain. The formula Revenue − Cost, for example, is much easier to comprehend than the formula A2 − D3. You can produce a list of workbook names and their references at any time. Scenario Jim wants to include a formula that calculates the percentage of monthly gross pay the managers would actually take home (net pay) if a 7% raise is granted. He starts by naming the cells he'll use in the calculation.

Steps

1. **Click cell F6, click the name box on the formula bar to select the active cell reference, type Gross_with_Raise, then press [Enter]**
   The name assigned to cell F6, Gross_with_Raise, appears in the name box. Note that you must type underscores instead of spaces between words. Cell F6 is now named Gross_with_Raise to refer to the monthly gross pay amount that includes the 7% raise. The name box displays as much of the name as fits (Gross_with_...). The net pay cell needs a name.

QuickTip
To delete a name, click Insert on the menu bar, point to Name, then click Define. Select the name, click Delete, then click OK.

2. **Click cell F11, click the name box, type Net_with_Raise, then press [Enter]**
   The new formula will use names instead of cell references.

3. **Click cell F13, type =Net_with_Raise/Gross_with_Raise, then click the Enter button on the formula bar (make sure you begin the formula with an equal sign)**
   The formula bar now shows the new formula, and the result, 0.47, appears in the cell. If you add names to a worksheet after all the formulas have been entered, you must click Insert on the menu bar, point to Name, click Apply, click the name or names, then click OK. Cell F13 needs to be formatted in Percent style.

QuickTip
If you don't see ![%] on your toolbar, click the More Buttons button ![»] on the Formatting toolbar.

4. **Select cell F13, click Format on the menu bar, click Style, click the Style name list arrow, click Percent, then click OK**
   Notice that the result shown in cell F13, 47%, is rounded to the nearest whole percent as shown in Figure E-3. A **style** is a combination of formatting characteristics, such as bold, italic, and underlined. You can use the Style dialog box instead of the Formatting toolbar to apply styles. You can also use it to remove styles: select the cell that has a style and select Normal in the Style name list. To define your own style, select a cell, format it using the formatting toolbar (such as bold, italic, and 14 point), then open the Style dialog box and type a name for your style. Later, you can apply all those formatting characteristics simply by applying your new style from the dialog box.

5. **Enter your name into cell D1, return to cell A1, then save and print the worksheet**
   You can use the Label Ranges dialog box (Insert menu, Name submenu, Label command) to designate existing column or row headings as labels. Then instead of using cell references for the column or row in formulas, you can use the labels instead. (This feature is turned off by default. To turn it on, go to Tools/Options/Calculation tab/Accept labels in formulas.)

6. **Close the workbook**

FIGURE E-3: Worksheet formula that includes cell names

Formula with cell names

Name box

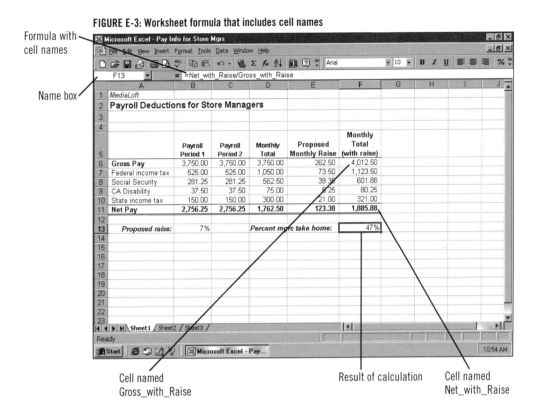

Cell named
Gross_with_Raise

Result of calculation

Cell named
Net_with_Raise

Producing a list of names

You might want to verify the names you have in a workbook and the cells they reference. To paste a list of names in a workbook, select a blank cell that has several blank cells beside and beneath it. Click Insert on the menu bar, point to Name, then click Paste. In the Paste Name dialog box, click Paste List. Excel produces a list that includes the sheet name and the cell or range the name identifies. See Figure E-4.

FIGURE E-4: Worksheet with pasted list of names

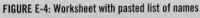
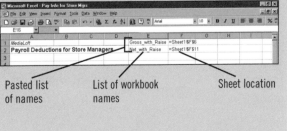

Pasted list of names

List of workbook names

Sheet location

Generating Multiple Totals with AutoSum

In most cases, the result of a function is a value derived from a calculation. Functions can also return results such as text, references, or other information about the worksheet. You enter a function, such as AVERAGE, directly into a cell; you can use the Edit Formula button; or you can insert it with the Paste Function. You can use cell references, ranges, names, and formulas as arguments between the parentheses. (Recall that arguments are the information used in calculating the results of a function.) As with other cell entries, you can cut, copy, and paste functions from one area of the worksheet to another and from one workbook to another. The most widely used Excel function, SUM, calculates worksheet totals and can be entered easily using the AutoSum button on the Standard toolbar. **Scenario** Maria Abbot, MediaLoft's general sales manager, has given Jim a worksheet summarizing store sales. He needs to complete the worksheet totals.

1. **Open the workbook titled EX E-2, type your name into cell D1, then save the workbook as MediaLoft Sales**
   You can use AutoSum to generate two sets of totals at the same time.

2. **Select range B5:E9, press and hold [Ctrl], then select range B11:E15**
   To select nonadjacent cells, you must press and hold [Ctrl] while selecting the additional cells. Compare your selections with Figure E-5. The totals will appear in the last line of each selection.

   Trouble?

   If you select the wrong combination of cells, simply click on a single cell and begin again.

3. **Click the AutoSum button [Σ] on the Standard toolbar**
   When the selected range you want to sum (B5:E9 and B11:E15, in this example) includes a blank cell with data values above it, AutoSum enters the total in the blank cell.

4. **Select range B5:F17, then click [Σ]**
   Whenever the selected range you want to sum includes a blank cell in the bottom row or right column, AutoSum enters the total in the blank cell. In this case, Excel ignores the data values and totals only the sums. Although Excel generates totals when you click the AutoSum button, it is a good idea to check the results.

5. **Click cell B17**
   The formula bar reads =SUM(B15,B9). See Figure E-6. When generating grand totals, Excel automatically references the cells containing SUM functions with a comma separator between cell references. Excel uses commas to separate multiple arguments in all functions, not just in SUM.

6. **Print the worksheet, then save and close the workbook**

FIGURE E-5: Selecting nonadjacent ranges using [Ctrl]

	A	B	C	D	E	F	G	H
1	MediaLoft			Jim Fernandez				
2	**1999 Sales Summary**							
3								
4	*MediaLoft East*	Qtr 1	Qtr 2	Qtr 3	Qtr 4	Total		
5	Boston	$ 147,000	$ 162,000	$ 157,000	$ 174,000			
6	Chicago	175,000	259,000	244,000	257,000			
7	Kansas City	162,000	207,000	215,000	225,000			
8	New York	183,000	230,000	225,000	247,000			
9	Total							
10	*MediaLoft West*							
11	Houston	$ 80,000	$ 117,000	$ 148,000	$ 182,000			
12	San Diego	63,000	96,000	152,000	186,000			
13	San Francisco	103,000	145,000	182,000	220,000			
14	Seattle	90,000	132,000	183,000	198,000			
15	Total							
16								
17	Grand Total							

Sum= $ 5,535,000

Start Microsoft Excel - Med...   11:09 AM

FIGURE E-6: Completed worksheet

B17   = =SUM(B15,B9)

Comma used to separate multiple arguments

	A	B	C	D	E	F	G	H
1	MediaLoft			Jim Fernandez				
2	**1999 Sales Summary**							
3								
4	*MediaLoft East*	Qtr 1	Qtr 2	Qtr 3	Qtr 4	Total		
5	Boston	$ 147,000	$ 162,000	$ 157,000	$ 174,000	$ 640,000		
6	Chicago	175,000	259,000	244,000	257,000	935,000		
7	Kansas City	152,000	207,000	215,000	225,000	799,000		
8	New York	183,000	230,000	225,000	247,000	885,000		
9	Total	$ 657,000	$ 858,000	$ 841,000	$ 903,000	$ 3,259,000		
10	*MediaLoft West*							
11	Houston	$ 80,000	$ 117,000	$ 148,000	$ 182,000	$ 527,000		
12	San Diego	63,000	95,000	152,000	186,000	$ 496,000		
13	San Francisco	103,000	145,000	182,000	220,000	$ 650,000		
14	Seattle	90,000	132,000	183,000	198,000	$ 603,000		
15	Total	$ 336,000	$ 489,000	$ 665,000	$ 786,000	$ 2,276,000		
16								
17	Grand Total	$ 993,000	$ 1,347,000	$ 1,506,000	$ 1,689,000	$ 5,535,000		

Start Microsoft Excel - Med...   11:19 AM

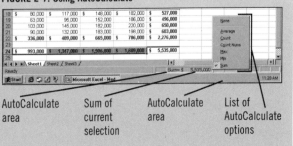

CLUES TO USE

Quick calculations with AutoCalculate

To check a total quickly without entering a formula, just select the range you want to sum, and the answer appears in the status bar next to SUM=. You also can perform other quick calculations, such as averaging or finding the minimum value in a selection. To do this, right-click the AutoCalculate area in the status bar and select from the list of options. The option you select remains in effect and in the status bar until you make another selection. See Figure E-7.

FIGURE E-7: Using AutoCalculate

18	$ 80,000	$ 117,000	$ 148,000	$ 182,000	$ 527,000	None
19	63,000	95,000	152,000	186,000	$ 496,000	Average
20	103,000	145,000	182,000	220,000	$ 650,000	Count
21	90,000	132,000	183,000	198,000	$ 603,000	Count Nums
22	336,000	489,000	665,000	786,000	$ 2,276,000	Max
23						Min
24	$ 993,000	$ 1,347,000	$ 1,506,000	$ 1,689,000	$ 5,535,000	Sum

Sum= $ 5,535,000   11:29 AM

AutoCalculate area | Sum of current selection | AutoCalculate area | List of AutoCalculate options

Excel 2000

Using Dates in Calculations

If you enter dates in a worksheet so that Excel recognizes them as dates, you can sort (arrange) the dates and perform date calculations. For example, you can calculate the number of days between your birth date and today, which is the number of days you have been alive. When you enter an Excel date format, Excel considers the entry a date function, converts the date to a serial date number, and stores that number in the cell. A date's converted serial date is the number of days to that date. Excel automatically assigns the serial date of "1" to January 1, 1900 and counts up from there; the serial date of January 1, 2000, for example, is 36,526. ►Scenario► Jim's next task is to complete the New York Accounts Payable worksheet. He remembers to enter the worksheet dates in a format that Excel recognizes so that he can use date calculation.

Steps 1 2 3 4

1. Open the workbook titled **EX E-3**, then save the workbook as **New York Payables** to the appropriate folder on your Project Disk
   The calculations will be based on the current date, 4/1/00.

2. Click cell **C4**, type **4/1/00**, then press **[Enter]**
   The date appears in cell C4 just as you typed it. You want to enter a formula that calculates the invoice due date, which is 30 days from the invoice date. The formula adds 30 days to the invoice date.

QuickTip
You also can perform time calculations in Excel. For example, you can enter an employee's starting time and ending time, then calculate how many hours and minutes he or she worked. You must enter time in a format that Excel recognizes; for example, 1:35 PM (h:mm AM/PM).

3. Click cell **E7**, type **=**, click cell **B7**, type **+30**, then click the **Enter button** ☑ on the formula bar
   Excel calculates the result by converting the 3/1/00 invoice date to a serial date number, adding 30 to it, then automatically formatting the result as a date. See Figure E-8. You can use the same formula to calculate the due dates of the other invoices.

4. Drag the fill handle to copy the formula in cell E7 into cells **E8:E13**
   Cell referencing causes the copied formula to contain the appropriate cell references. Now you are ready to enter the formula that calculates the age of each invoice. You do this by subtracting the invoice date from the current date. Because each invoice age formula must refer to the current date, you must make cell C4, the current date cell, an absolute reference in the formula.

QuickTip
If you perform date calculations and the intended numeric result displays as a date, format the cell(s) using a number format.

5. Click cell **F7**, type **=**, click cell **C4**, press **[F4]** to add the absolute reference symbols ($), type **−**, click **B7**, then click ☑
   The formula bar displays the formula $C$4−B7. The numerical result, 31, appears in cell F7 because there are 31 days between 3/1/00 and 4/1/00. You can use the same formula to calculate the age of the remaining invoices.

6. Drag the fill handle to copy the formula in F7 to the range **F8:F13**, then press **[Ctrl][Home]**
   The age of each invoice appears in column F, as shown in Figure E-9.

7. Save the worksheet

Using date functions

When you want Excel to perform a calculation using the current date, you can choose date and time options such as NOW, DATE, and TODAY. DATE inserts any date whose month, day, and year you specify as arguments in the formula palette: =DATE(2000,7,6) will produce July 6, 2000, NOW inserts the current date and time, while TODAY inserts today's date only (you don't have to enter arguments for NOW or TODAY).

FIGURE E-8: Worksheet with formula for invoice due date

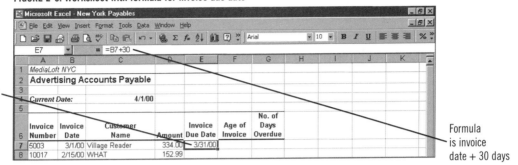

Formula result
automatically
calculated
as date

Formula
is invoice
date + 30 days

FIGURE E-9: Worksheet with copied formulas

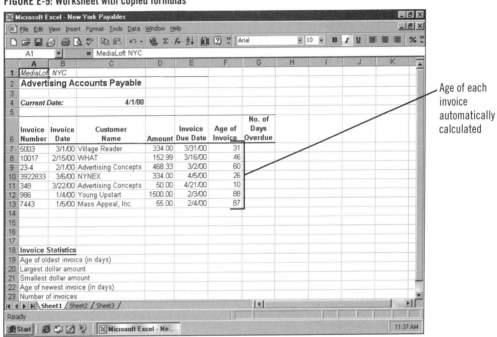

Age of each
invoice
automatically
calculated

Custom number and date formats

When you use numbers and dates in worksheets
or calculations, you can use built-in Excel formats
or create your own. The date you entered, 9/1/00,
uses the Excel format m/d/yy. You could change it
to the format d-mmm, or 1-Sep. The value $3,789
uses the number format $#,### where # represents
positive numbers. To apply number formats, click
Format on the menu bar, click Cells, then click the
Number tab. In the category list, click a category,
then specify the exact format in the list or scroll
box to the right. To create a custom format, click
Custom in the category list, then click a format
that resembles the one you want. In the Type box,
edit the symbols until they represent the format
you want, then click OK. See Figure E-10.

FIGURE E-10: Custom formats on the Number tab in the Format
Cells dialog box

Edit these
symbols to
customize this
format

Custom formats
category

Custom formats

Building a Conditional Formula with the IF Function

You can build a conditional formula using an IF function. A **conditional formula** is one that makes calculations based on stated conditions. For example, you can build a formula to calculate bonuses based on a person's performance rating. If a person is rated a 5 (the stated condition) on a scale of 1 to 5, with 5 being the highest rating, he or she receives 10% of his or her salary as a bonus; otherwise, there is no bonus. When the condition is a question that can be answered with a true or false response, Excel calls this stated condition a **logical test**. The IF function has three parts, separated by commas: a condition or logical test, an action to take if the logical test or condition is true, then an action to take if the logical test or condition is false. Another way of expressing this is: IF(test_cond,do_this,else_this). Translated into an Excel IF function, the formula to calculate bonuses would look something like this: IF(Rating=5,Salary*0.10,0). The translation would be: If the rating equals 5, multiply the salary by 0.10 (the decimal equivalent of 10%), then place the result in the selected cell. If the rating does not equal 5, place a 0 in the cell. When entering the logical test portion of an IF statement, you typically use some combination of the comparison operators listed in Table E-2. Scenario▶ Jim is almost finished with the worksheet. To complete it, he needs to use an IF function that calculates the number of days each invoice is overdue.

Steps 1 2 3 4

1. **Click cell G7**

   The cell pointer is now positioned where the result of the function will appear. You want the formula to calculate the number of days overdue as follows: If the age of the invoice is greater than 30, calculate the days overdue (Age of Invoice − 30), and place the result in cell G7; otherwise, place a 0 (zero) in the cell. The formula will include the IF function and cell references.

2. **Type =IF(F7>30, (be sure to type the comma)**

   You have entered the first part of the function, the logical test. Notice that you used the symbol for greater than (>). So far, the formula reads: If Age of Invoice is greater than 30 (in other words, if the invoice is overdue). The next part of the formula tells Excel the action to take if the invoice is over 30 days old.

3. **Type F7-30, (be sure to type the comma)**

   This part of the formula, between the first and second commas, is what you want Excel to do if the logical test is true (that is, if the age of the invoice is over 30). Continuing the translation of the formula, this part means: Take the Age of Invoice value and subtract 30. The last part of the formula tells Excel the action to take if the logical test is false (that is, if the age of the invoice is 30 days or less).

4. **Type 0, then click the Enter button ☑ on the formula bar (you do not have to type the closing parenthesis) to complete the formula**

   The formula is complete, and the result, 1 (the number of days overdue), appears in cell G7. See Figure E-11.

5. **Copy the formula in cell G7 into cells G8:G13 and return to cell A1**

   Compare your results with Figure E-12.

6. **Save the workbook**

FIGURE E-11: Worksheet with IF function

Action taken if test is true

Logical test

Commas separate parts of an IF function

Action taken if test is false

Result of function when test is true

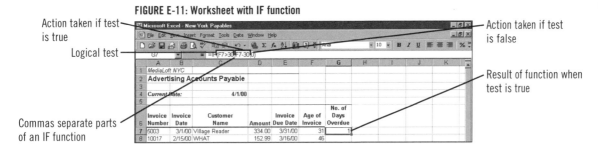

FIGURE E-12: Completed worksheet

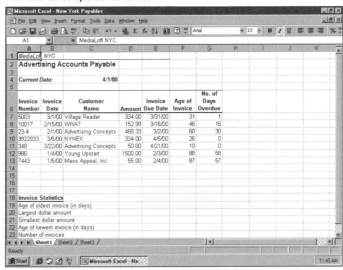

TABLE E-2: Comparison operators

operator	function
<	Less than
>	Greater than
=	Equal to
<=	Less than or equal to
>=	Greater than or equal to
<>	Not equal to

CLUES TO USE

Inserting and deleting selected cells

As you add formulas to your workbook, you may need to insert or delete cells, not entire rows or columns. When you do this, Excel automatically adjusts cell references to reflect their new locations. To insert cells, click Insert on the menu bar, then click Cells. The Insert dialog box opens, asking if you want to insert a cell and move the selected cell down or to the right of the new one. To delete one or more selected cells, click Edit on the menu bar, click Delete, and, in the Delete dialog box, indicate which way you want to move the adjacent cells. Be careful when using this option that you do not disturb row or column alignment that may be necessary to make sense of the worksheet.

Using Statistical Functions

Excel 2000

Excel offers several hundred worksheet functions. A small group of these functions calculates statistics such as averages, minimum values, and maximum values. See Table E-3 for a brief description of these commonly used functions. **Scenario** Jim wants to present detailed information about open accounts payable. To do this, he adds some statistical functions to the worksheet. He begins by using the MAX function to calculate the maximum value in a range.

Steps

Trouble?
If you have difficulty clicking cells or ranges when you build formulas, try scrolling to reposition the worksheet area until all participating cells are visible.

1. Click cell **D19**, type **=MAX(**, select range **G7:G13**, then press **[Enter]**

Excel automatically adds the right parenthesis after you press [Enter]. The age of the oldest invoice (or maximum value in range G7:G13) is 58 days, as shown in cell D19. Next, Jim builds a formula to calculate the largest dollar amount among the outstanding invoices.

2. In cell **D20**, type **=MAX(**, select range **D7:D13**, then press **[Enter]**

The largest outstanding invoice, for $1500.00, is shown in cell D20. The MIN function finds the smallest dollar amount and the age of the newest invoice.

Trouble?
If your results do not match those shown here, check your formulas and make sure you did not type a comma following each open parentheses. The formula in cell D20, for example, should be =MAX(D7:D13).

3. In cell **D21**, type **=MIN(**, select range **D7:D13**, then press **[Enter]**; in cell D22, type **=MIN(**, select range **F7:F13**, then press **[Enter]**

The smallest dollar amount owed is $50.00, as shown in cell D21, and the newest invoice is 10 days old. The COUNT function calculates the number of invoices by counting the number of entries in column A.

4. In cell **D23**, type **=**, then click the **Paste Function button** 🔧 on the Standard toolbar to open the Paste Function dialog box

QuickTip
If you don't see the desired function in the Function name list, scroll to display more function names.

5. Under Function category, click **Statistical**, then under Function name, click **COUNT**

After selecting the function name, notice that the description of the COUNT function reads, "Counts the number of cells that contain numbers…" Because the invoice numbers are formatted in General rather than in the Number format, they are considered text entries, not numerical entries, so the COUNT function will not work. There is another function, COUNTA, that counts the number of cells that are not empty and therefore can be used to count the number of invoice number entries.

6. Under Function name, click **COUNTA**, then click **OK**

Excel opens the Formula Palette and automatically references the range that is directly above the active cell as the first argument (in this case, range D19:D22, which is not the range you want to count). See Figure E-13. You need to select the correct range of invoice numbers. Because the desired invoice numbers are not visible, you need to collapse the dialog box so that you can select the correct range.

7. With the Value1 argument selected in the Formula Palette, click the Value1 **Collapse Dialog Box button** 📉, select range **A7:A13** in the worksheet, click the **Redisplay Dialog Box button** 📈, then click **OK**

Cell D23 confirms that there are seven invoices. Compare your worksheet with Figure E-14.

8. Type your name into cell D1, press **[Ctrl][Home]**, then save, print, and close the workbook

FIGURE E-13: Formula Palette showing COUNTA function

Edit Formula button
Click to pick a different function
Formula Palette

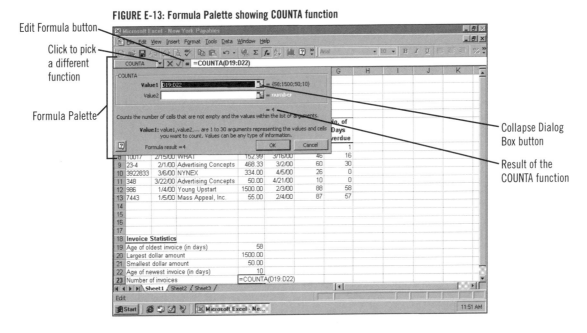

Collapse Dialog Box button
Result of the COUNTA function

FIGURE E-14: Worksheet with invoice statistics

TABLE E-3: Commonly used statistical functions

function	worksheet action
AVERAGE	Calculates an average value
COUNT	Counts the number of values
COUNTA	Counts the number of nonblank entries
MAX	Finds the largest value
MIN	Finds the smallest value
SUM	Calculates a total

Using the Formula Palette to enter and edit formulas

When you use the Paste Function to build a formula, the Formula Palette displays the name and description for the function and each of its arguments, the current result of the function, and the current result of the entire formula. You also can use the Formula Palette to edit functions in formulas. To open the Formula Palette from either a blank cell or one containing a formula, click the Edit Formula button ⊒ on the formula bar.

Calculating Payments with the PMT Function

PMT is a financial function that calculates the periodic payment amount for money borrowed. For example, if you want to borrow money to buy a car, the PMT function can calculate your monthly payment on the loan. Let's say you want to borrow $15,000 at 9% interest and pay the loan off in five years. The Excel PMT function can tell you that your monthly payment will be $311.38. The parts of the PMT function are: PMT(rate, nper, pv, fv, type). See Figure E-15 for an illustration of a PMT function that calculates the monthly payment in the car loan example. **Scenario** For several months, MediaLoft management has been discussing the expansion of the San Diego store. Jim has obtained quotes from three different lenders on borrowing $25,000 to begin the expansion. He obtained loan quotes from a commercial bank, a venture capitalist, and an investment banker. Now Jim can summarize the information using the Excel PMT function.

Steps

1. **Open the workbook titled EX E-4, then save the workbook as San Diego Financing**
   Jim has already entered all the lender data; you are ready to calculate the commercial loan monthly payment in cell E5.

QuickTip

It is important to be consistent about the units you use for *rate* and *nper*. If, for example, you express *nper* as the number of *monthly* payments, then you must express the interest rate as a *monthly* rate, not an annual rate.

2. **Click cell E5, type =PMT(C5/12,D5,B5) (make sure you type the commas); then click the Enter button ✓ on the formula bar**
   You must divide the annual interest by 12 because you are calculating monthly, not annual, payments. Note that the payment of ($543.56) in cell E5 is a negative amount. (It appears in red on a color monitor.) Excel displays the result of a PMT function as a negative value to reflect the negative cash flow the loan represents to the borrower. Because you want to show the monthly payment value as a positive number, you can convert the loan amount to a positive number by placing a minus sign in front of the cell reference.

3. **Edit cell E5 so it reads =PMT(C5/12,D5,−B5), then click ✓**
   A positive value of $543.56 now appears in cell E5. See Figure E-16. You can use the same formula to generate the monthly payments for the other loans.

4. **With cell E5 selected, drag the fill handle to select range E5:E7**
   A monthly payment of $818.47 for the venture capitalist loan appears in cell E6. A monthly payment of $1,176.84 for the investment banker loan appears in cell E7. The loans with shorter terms have much higher payments. You will not know the entire financial picture until you calculate the total payments and total interest for each lender.

5. **Click cell F5, type =E5*D5, then press [Tab]; in cell G5, type =F5−B5, then click ✓**

6. **Copy the formulas in cells F5:G5 into the range FG:G7, then return to cell A1**
   You can experiment with different interest rates, loan amounts, or terms for any one of the lenders; the PMT function generates a new set of values automatically. Compare your results with those in Figure E-17.

7. **Enter your name into cell D1, save the workbook, then print the worksheet**

FIGURE E-15: Example of PMT function for car loan

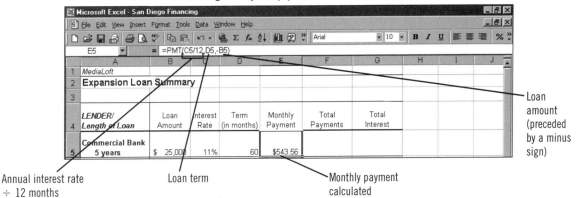

$$PMT(.09/12, 60, 15000) = \$311.38$$

| Interest rate per period | Number of payments | Present value of loan amount | Monthly payment calculated |

FIGURE E-16: PMT function calculating monthly loan payment

Microsoft Excel - San Diego Financing					
File Edit View Insert Format Tools Data Window Help					
E5		= =PMT(C5/12,D5,-B5)			

	A	B	C	D	E	F	G	H	I	J
1	MediaLoft									
2	Expansion Loan Summary									
3										
4	LENDER/ Length of Loan	Loan Amount	Interest Rate	Term (in months)	Monthly Payment	Total Payments	Total Interest			
5	Commercial Bank 5 years	$ 25,000	11%	60	$543.56					

Annual interest rate ÷ 12 months

Loan term

Monthly payment calculated

Loan amount (preceded by a minus sign)

FIGURE E-17: Completed worksheet

Microsoft Excel - San Diego Financing					
File Edit View Insert Format Tools Data Window Help					
A1		= MediaLoft			

	A	B	C	D	E	F	G	H	I	J
1	MediaLoft									
2	Expansion Loan Summary									
3										
4	LENDER/ Length of Loan	Loan Amount	Interest Rate	Term (in months)	Monthly Payment	Total Payments	Total Interest			
5	Commercial Bank 5 years	$ 25,000	11%	60	$543.56	$ 32,613.63	$ 7,613.63			
6	Venture Capitalist 3 years	$ 25,000	11%	36	$818.47	$ 29,464.85	$ 4,464.85			
7	Investment Banker 2 years	$ 25,000	12%	24	$1,176.84	$ 28,244.08	$ 3,244.08			

CLUES TO USE

Calculating future value with the FV function

You can use the FV (Future Value) function to determine the amount of money a given monthly investment will amount to, at a given interest rate after a given number of payment periods. The syntax is similar to that of the PMT function: FV(rate,nper,pmt,pv,type). For example, suppose you want to invest $1,000 every month for the next 12 months into an account that pays 12% a year, and you want to know how much you will have at the end of 12 months (that is, its future value). You would enter the function FV(.01,12,−1000), and Excel

would return the value $12,682.50 as the future value of your investment. As with the PMT function, the units for the rate and nper must be consistent. If you make monthly payments on a three-year loan at 6% annual interest, you would use the rate 6%/12 and 36 periods (12*3). The arguments pv and type are optional; pv is the present value, or the total amount the series of payments is worth now. If you omit it, Excel assumes the pv is 0. The Type argument indicates when the payments are made; 0 is the end of the period and 1 is the beginning of the period.

Displaying and Printing Formula Contents

Excel usually displays the result of formula calculations in the worksheet area and displays formula contents for the active cell in the formula bar. However, you can instruct Excel to display the formulas directly in the worksheet locations in which they were entered. You can document worksheet formulas by first displaying the formulas, then printing them. These formula printouts are valuable paper-based worksheet documentation. Because formulas are often longer than their corresponding values, landscape orientation is the best choice for printing formulas. **Scenario** Jim is ready to produce a formula printout to submit with the worksheet.

Steps 123 4

1. Click **Tools** on the menu bar, click **Options**, then click the **View tab**
   The View tab of the Options dialog box appears, as shown in Figure E-18.

2. Under Window options, click the **Formulas** check box to select it, then click **OK**
   The columns widen and retain their original formats.

3. Scroll horizontally to bring columns E through G into view
   Instead of formula results appearing in the cells, Excel shows the actual formulas. The column widths adjusted automatically to accommodate the formulas.

4. Click the **Print Preview button** 🔍 on the Standard toolbar
   The status bar reads Preview: Page 1 of 3, indicating that the worksheet will print on three pages. You want to print it on one page and include the row number and column letter headings.

QuickTip

All Page Setup options—such as Landscape orientation, Fit to scaling—apply to the active worksheet and are saved with the workbook.

5. Click the **Setup button** in the Print Preview window, then click the **Page tab**

6. Under Orientation, click the **Landscape option button**; then under Scaling, click the **Fit to option button**
   Selecting Landscape instructs Excel to print the worksheet sideways on the page. The Fit to option ensures that the document is printed on a single page.

7. Click the **Sheet tab**, under Print click the **Row and column headings check box** to select it, click **OK**, then position the **Zoom pointer** 🔍 over **column A** and click
   The worksheet formulas now appear on a single page, in landscape orientation, with row (number) and column (letter) headings. See Figure E-19.

8. Click **Print** in the Print Preview window, then click **OK**
   After you retrieve the printout, you want to return the worksheet to display formula results. You can do this easily by using a key combination.

9. Press **[Ctrl][`]** to redisplay formula results, save and close the workbook, then exit Excel
   [Ctrl][`] (grave accent mark) toggles between displaying formula results and displaying formula contents.

FIGURE E-18: View tab of the Options dialog box

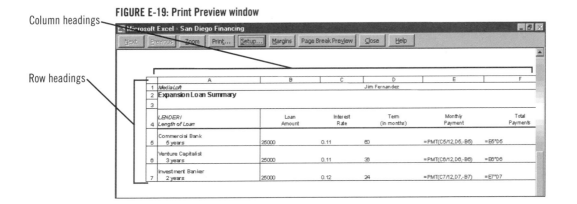

Click here to view formulas

FIGURE E-19: Print Preview window

Column headings

Row headings

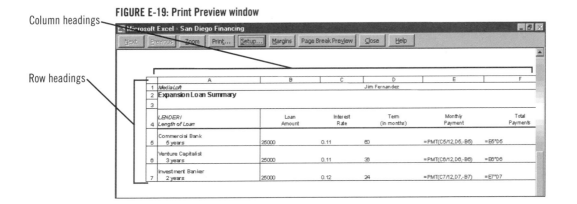

CLUES TO USE

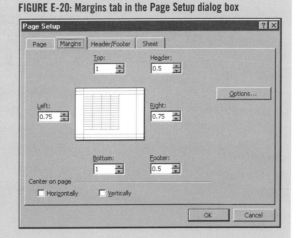

Setting margins and alignment when printing part of a worksheet

Sometimes you want to print one part of a worksheet. While you may have set margins for printing the whole worksheet, you can set custom margins to print the smaller section. Select the range you want to print, click File on the menu bar, click Print, under Print what click Selection, then click Preview. In the Print Preview window, click Setup, then click the Margins tab. See Figure E-20. Double-click the margin numbers and type new ones. Use the Center on page check boxes to center the range horizontally or vertically. If you plan to print the range again in the future, save the view after you print: Click View on the menu bar, click Custom Views, click Add, then type a view name and click OK.

FIGURE E-20: Margins tab in the Page Setup dialog box

Practice

▶ Concepts Review

Label each element of the Excel screen shown in Figure E-21.

FIGURE E-21

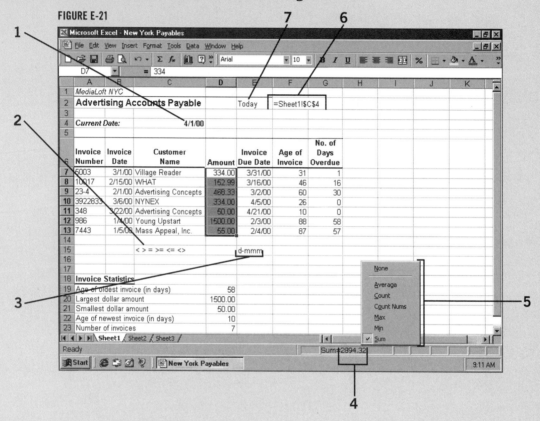

Match each term with the statement that best describes its function.

8. Parentheses
9. COUNTA
10. test_cond
11. COUNT
12. pv

a. Function used to count the number of nonblank entries
b. Function used to count the number of numerical entries
c. Part of the PMT function that represents the loan amount
d. Part of the IF function in which the conditions are stated
e. Symbols used in formulas to control formula calculation order

Select the best answer from the list of choices.

13. **To generate a positive payment value when using the PMT function, you must**
    a. Enter the interest rate divisor as a negative value.
    b. Enter the function arguments as negative values.
    c. Enter the amount being borrowed as a negative value.
    d. Enter the function arguments as positive values.

14. **When you enter the rate and nper arguments in a PMT function,**
    a. Use monthly units instead of annual units.
    b. Be consistent in the units used.
    c. Divide both values by 12.
    d. Multiply both units by 12.

15. **To express conditions such as less than or equal to, you can use a(n)**
    a. PMT function.
    b. Comparison operator.
    c. AutoCalculate formula.
    d. IF function.

16. **Which of the following statements is false?**
    a. m/d/yy is an Excel date format.
    b. You can create custom number and date formats in Excel.
    c. You can use only existing number and date formats in Excel.
    d. $#,### is an Excel number format.

▶ Skills Review

1. **Create a formula with several operators.**
    a. Open workbook EX E-5, enter your name into cell D1, and save the workbook as "Manager Bonuses".
    b. Select cell C15 using the Go To command.
    c. Enter the formula C13+(C14*7).
    d. Use the Paste Special command to paste the values in B4:B10 to G4:G10.

2. **Use names in a formula.**
    a. Name cell C13 "Dept_Bonus".
    b. Name cell C14 "Project_Bonus".
    c. In cell E4, enter the formula Dept_Bonus*D4+Project_Bonus.
    d. Copy the formula in cell E4 into the range E5:E10.
    e. Format range E4:E10 with the Comma Style button.
    f. In cell F4, enter a formula that sums C4 and E4.
    g. Copy the formula in cell F4 into the range F5:F10.
    h. Return to cell A1, then save your work.

3. **Generate multiple totals with AutoSum.**
    a. Select range E4:F11
    b. Enter the totals using AutoSum.
    c. Format range E11:F11 using the Currency Style button.
    d. Return to cell A1, save your work, then preview and print this worksheet.

4. Use dates in calculations.
   a. Make the Merit Pay sheet active.
   b. In cell D6, enter the formula B6+183.
   c. Copy the formula in cell D6 into the range D7:D14.
   d. Use the NOW function to insert the date and time in cell A3, widening the column as necessary.
   e. In cell E18, enter the text "Next Pay Date", and, in cell G18, use the Date function to enter the date 10/1/00.
   f. Save your work.

5. Build a conditional formula with the IF function.
   a. In cell F6, enter the formula IF(C6=5,E6*0.05,0).
   b. Copy the formula in cell F6 into the range F7:F14.
   c. Apply the comma format with no decimal places to F6:F14.
   d. Select the range A4:G4 and delete the cells using the Delete command on the Edit menu. Shift the remaining cells up.
   e. Repeat the procedure to delete the cells A15:G15.
   f. Use the Cells command on the Insert menu to insert a cell between Department Statistics and Average Salary, moving the remaining cells down.
   g. Check your formulas to make sure the cell references have been updated.
   h. Save your work.

6. Use statistical functions.
   a. In cell C18, enter a function to calculate the average salary in the range E5:E13 with no decimal places.
   b. In cell C19, enter a function to calculate the largest bonus in the range F5:F13.
   c. In cell C20, enter a function to calculate the lowest performance rating in the range C5:C13.
   d. In cell C21, enter a function to calculate the number of entries in range A5:A13.
   e. Enter your name in cell F3, then save, preview, and print this worksheet.

7. Calculate payments with the PMT function.
   a. Make the Loan sheet active.
   b. In cell B9, enter the formula PMT(B5/12,B6,−B4).
   c. In cell B10, enter the formula B9*B6.
   d. AutoFit column B, if necessary.
   e. In cell B11, enter the formula B10−B4.
   f. Enter your name in cell C1, then save and print the worksheet.

8. Display and print formula contents.
   a. Use the View tab in the Options dialog box to turn formulas on.
   b. Adjust the column widths as necessary.
   c. Save, preview, and print this worksheet in landscape orientation with the row and column headings.
   d. Close the workbook.

Visual Workshop

Create the worksheet shown in Figure E-22. (Hint: Enter the items in range C9:C11 as labels by typing an apostrophe before each formula.) Type your name in row 1, and save the workbook as "Car Payment Calculator" to the appropriate folder on your Project Disk. Preview, then print, the worksheet.

FIGURE E-22

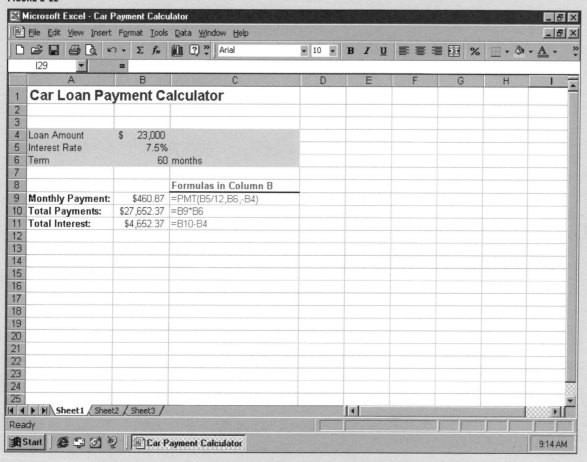

Managing

Workbooks and Preparing Them for the Web

Objectives

MOUS ▶ **Freeze columns and rows**

MOUS ▶ **Insert and delete worksheets**

MOUS ▶ **Consolidate data with 3-D references**

MOUS ▶ **Hide and protect worksheet areas**

▶ **Save custom views of a worksheet**

MOUS ▶ **Control page breaks and page numbering**

MOUS ▶ **Create a hyperlink between Excel files**

MOUS ▶ **Save an Excel file as an HTML document**

In this unit you will learn several Excel features to help you manage and print workbook data. You will also learn how to prepare workbooks for publication on the World Wide Web. Scenario MediaLoft's accounting department asks Jim Fernandez to design a timecard summary worksheet to track salary costs for hourly workers. He designs a worksheet using some employees from the MediaLoft Houston store. When the worksheet is complete, the accounting department will add the rest of the employees and place it on the MediaLoft intranet site for review by store managers. Jim will save the worksheet in HTML format for viewing on the site.

Excel 2000

Freezing Columns and Rows

As rows and columns fill up with data, you might need to scroll through the worksheet to add, delete, modify, and view information. Looking at information without row or column labels can be confusing. In Excel, you can temporarily freeze columns and rows, which enables you to view separate areas of your worksheets at the same time. **Panes** are the columns and rows that **freeze**, or remain in place, while you scroll through your worksheet. The freeze feature is especially useful when you're dealing with large worksheets. Sometimes, though, even freezing is not sufficient. In those cases, you can create as many as four areas, or panes, on the screen at one time and move freely within each of them. ▶Scenario▶ Jim needs to verify the total hours worked, hourly pay rate, and total pay for salespeople Paul Cristifano and Virginia Young. Because the worksheet is becoming more difficult to read as its size increases, Jim needs to freeze the column and row labels.

Steps 1 2 3 4

QuickTip

To return personalized toolbars and menus to their default state, click Tools on the menu bar, click Customize, click Reset my usage data on the Options tab, click Yes, then click Close.

1. Start Excel if necessary, open the workbook titled **EX F-1**, save it as **Timecard Summary**, scroll through the Monday worksheet to view the data and click cell **D6**

   You move to cell D6 because you want to freeze columns A, B, and C. By doing so, you will be able to see each employee's last name, first name, and timecard number on the screen when you scroll to the right. Because you want to scroll down the worksheet and still be able to read the column headings, you also freeze the labels in rows 1 through 5. Excel freezes the columns to the left and the rows above the cell pointer.

2. Click **Window** on the menu bar, then click **Freeze Panes**

   A thin line appears along the column border to the left of the active cell, and another line appears along the row above the active cell indicating that columns A through C and rows 1 through 5 are frozen.

QuickTip

To easily change worksheet data without manual scrolling, click Edit on the menu bar, click Replace, then enter text you want to find and text you want to replace it with. Use the Find Next, Replace, and Replace All buttons to find and replace occurrences of the found text with the replacement text.

3. Scroll to the right until columns **A** through **C** and **L** through **O** are visible

   Because columns A, B, and C are frozen, they remain on the screen; columns D through K are temporarily hidden from view. Notice that the information you are looking for in row 13 (last name, total hours, hourly pay rate, and total pay for Paul Cristifano) is readily available. You jot down Paul's data but still need to verify Virginia Young's information.

4. Scroll down until **row 26** is visible

   Notice that in addition to columns A through C, rows 1 through 5 remain on the screen as well. See Figure F-1. Jim jots down the information for Virginia Young. Even though a pane is frozen, you can click in the frozen area of the worksheet and edit the contents of the cells there, if necessary.

QuickTip

When you open an existing workbook, the cell pointer is in the cell it was in when you last saved the workbook. Press [Ctrl][Home] to return to cell A1 prior to saving and closing a workbook.

5. Press **[Ctrl][Home]**

   Because the panes are frozen, the cell pointer moves to cell D6, not A1.

6. Click **Window** on the menu bar, then click **Unfreeze Panes**

   The panes are unfrozen.

7. Return to cell A1, then save the workbook

FIGURE F-1: Scrolled worksheet with frozen rows and columns

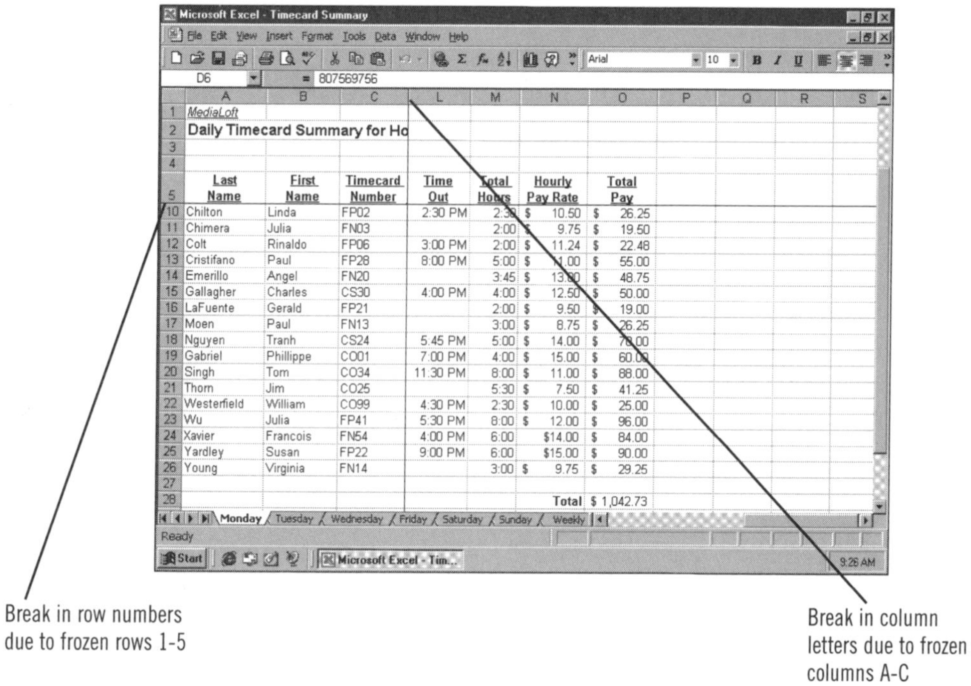

Break in row numbers due to frozen rows 1-5

Break in column letters due to frozen columns A-C

Splitting the worksheet into multiple panes

Excel provides a way to split the worksheet area into vertical and/or horizontal panes, so that you can click inside any one pane and scroll to locate desired information in that pane while the other panes remain in place. See Figure F-2. To split a worksheet area into multiple panes, drag the split box (the small box at the top of the vertical scroll bar or at the right end of the horizontal scroll bar) in the direction you want the split to appear. To remove the split, move the mouse over the split until the pointer changes to a double pointed arrow ✛, then double-click.

FIGURE F-2: Worksheet split into two horizontal panes

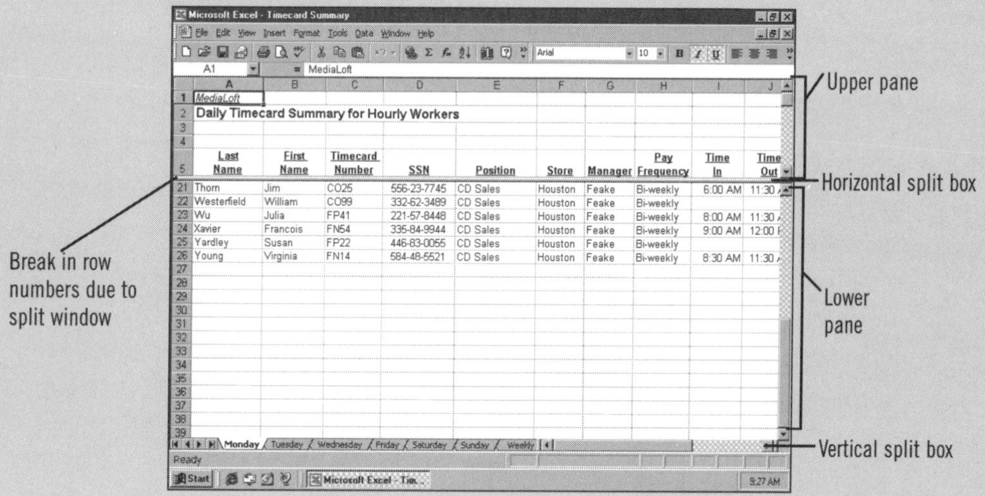

Upper pane

Horizontal split box

Lower pane

Vertical split box

Break in row numbers due to split window

Inserting and Deleting Worksheets

You can insert and delete worksheets in a workbook as needed. For example, because new workbooks open with only three sheets available (Sheet1, Sheet2, and Sheet3), you need to insert at least one more sheet if you want to have four quarterly worksheets in an annual financial budget workbook. You can do this by using commands on the menu bar or pop-up menu. ▸Scenario Jim was in a hurry when he added the sheet tabs to the Timecard Summary workbook. He needs to insert a sheet for Thursday and delete the sheet for Sunday because these Houston workers do not work on Sundays.

QuickTip

You also can copy the active worksheet by clicking Edit on the menu bar, then clicking Move or Copy Sheet. Choose the sheet the copy will precede, then select the Create a copy check box.

1. Click the **Friday sheet tab**, click **Insert** on the menu bar, then click **Worksheet**

Excel automatically inserts a new sheet tab labeled Sheet1 to the left of the Friday sheet.

2. Rename the Sheet1 tab **Thursday**

Now the tabs read Monday, Tuesday, Wednesday, Thursday, Friday, and Saturday. The tab for the Weekly Summary is not visible, but you still need to delete the Sunday worksheet.

3. Click the **Sunday sheet tab**, move the pointer over the **Sunday tab**, then click the **right mouse button**

A pop-up menu appears. See Figure F-3. The pop-up menu allows you to insert, delete, rename, move, or copy sheets, select all the sheets, or view any Visual Basic programming code in a workbook.

4. Click **Delete** on the pop-up menu

A message box warns that the selected sheet will be deleted permanently. You must acknowledge the message before proceeding.

5. Click **OK**

The Sunday sheet is deleted. Next, to check your work, you view a menu of worksheets in the workbook.

QuickTip

You can scroll several tabs at once by pressing [Shift] while clicking one of the middle tab scrolling buttons.

6. Move the mouse pointer over any tab scrolling button, then **right-click**

When you right-click a tab scrolling button, Excel automatically opens a menu of the worksheets in the active workbook. Compare your list with Figure F-4.

7. Click **Monday**, return to cell A1, then save the workbook

FIGURE F-3: Worksheet pop-up menu

Click to delete selected sheet

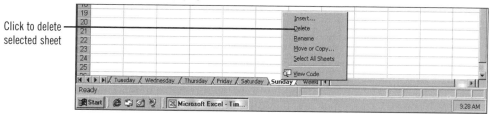

FIGURE F-4: Workbook with menu of worksheets

Active worksheet

Right-click any tab scrolling button to display menu of worksheets

Menu of worksheets

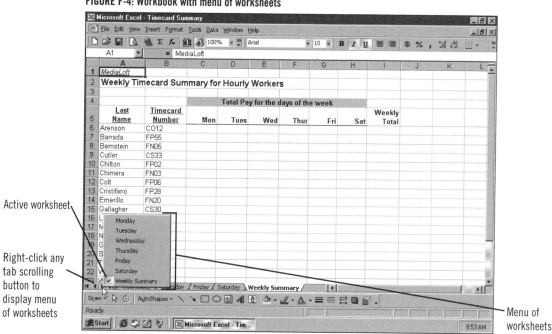

CLUES TO USE

Specifying headers and footers

As you prepare a workbook for others to view, it is helpful to give them as much data as possible about the worksheet—how many pages, who created it on what date, and the like. You can do this easily in a **header** or **footer**, information that prints at the top or bottom of each printed page. Headers and footers are visible on screen only in Print Preview. To add a header, for example, click View on the menu bar, click Header and Footer, click Custom Header, and you see a dialog box similar to that in Figure F-5. Both the header and the footer are divided into three sections, and you can enter information in any or all of them. Type information such as your name and click the icons to enter the page number 🔢, total pages 🔢, date 🔢, time 🕐, file name 🔢, or sheet name 🔲 to enter codes that represent these items. Click OK, view the preview on the Header and Footer tab, then click OK again.

FIGURE F-5: Header dialog box

Symbol for date

Click these icons to insert information into header sections

Symbol for page number

Excel 2000

Consolidating Data with 3-D References

When you want to summarize similar data that exists in different sheets or workbooks, you can combine and display it in one sheet. For example, you might have departmental sales figures on four different store sheets that you want to add together, or **consolidate**, on one summary sheet that shows total departmental sales for all stores. The best way to consolidate data is to use cell references to the various sheets on a consolidation, or summary, sheet. Because they reference other sheets that are usually behind the summary sheet, such references effectively create another dimension in the workbook and are called **3-D references**. You can reference data in other sheets and in other workbooks. Referencing cells is a better method than retyping calculated results because the data values on which calculated totals depend might change. If you reference the values instead, any changes to the original values are automatically reflected in the consolidation sheet. **Scenario** Although Jim does not have timecard data for the remaining days of the week, he wants to test the Weekly Summary sheet that will consolidate the timesheet data. He does this by creating a reference from the total pay data in the Monday sheet to the Weekly Summary sheet. First, he freezes panes to improve the view of the worksheets prior to initiating the reference between them.

Steps

1. On the Monday sheet, click cell **D6**, click **Window** on the menu bar, click **Freeze Panes**, then scroll horizontally to bring columns L through O into view

2. Right-click a **tab scrolling button**, then click **Weekly Summary**
   Because the Weekly Summary sheet (which is the consolidation sheet) will contain the reference, the cell pointer must reside there when you initiate the reference. To make a simple **reference** within the same sheet or between sheets, position the cell pointer in the cell to contain the reference, type = (equal sign), position the cell pointer in the cell to be referenced, and then enter the information.

   Trouble?

   If you have difficulty referencing cells between sheets, press [Esc] and begin again.

3. While in the Weekly Summary sheet, click cell **C6**, type **=**, activate the Monday sheet, click cell **O6**, then click the **Enter button** ☑ on the formula bar
   The formula bar reads =Monday!O6. See Figure F-6. *Monday* references the Monday sheet. The ! (exclamation point) is an **external reference indicator** meaning that the cell referenced is outside the active sheet; O6 is the actual cell reference in the external sheet. The result, $33.00, appears in cell C6 of the Weekly Summary sheet, showing the reference to the value displayed in cell O6 of the Monday sheet.

4. While in the Weekly Summary sheet, copy cell **C6** into cells **C7:C26**
   Excel copies the contents of cell C6 with its relative reference down the column. You can test a reference by changing one cell that it is based on and seeing if the reference changes.

5. Activate the Monday sheet, edit cell L6 to read **6:30 PM**, then activate the Weekly Summary sheet
   Cell C6 now shows $41.25. Changing Beryl Arenson's "time out" from 5:30 to 6:30 increased her pay from $33.00 to $41.25. This makes sense because Beryl's hours went from four to five, and her hourly salary is $8.25. The reference to Monday's total pay was automatically updated in the Weekly Summary sheet. See Figure F-7.

6. Preview, then print the Weekly Summary sheet
   To preview and print an entire workbook, click File on the menu bar, click Print, click to select the Entire Workbook option button, then click Preview. In the Preview window, you can page through the entire workbook. When you click Print, the entire workbook will print.

7. Activate the Monday sheet, then unfreeze the panes

8. Save the workbook

FIGURE F-6: Worksheet showing referenced cell

Sheet referenced

External reference indicator

Referenced value

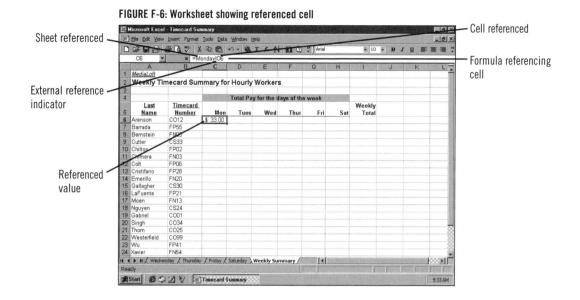

Cell referenced

Formula referencing cell

FIGURE F-7: Weekly Summary worksheet with updated reference

Updated value

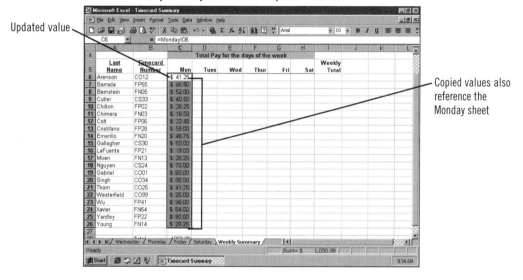

Copied values also reference the Monday sheet

CLUES TO USE

Consolidating data from different workbooks using linking

Just as you can reference data between cells in a worksheet and between sheets, you can reference data between workbooks dynamically so that changes made in referenced cells in one workbook are reflected in the consolidation sheet in the other workbook. This dynamic referencing is called **linking**. To link a single cell between workbooks, open both workbooks, select the cell to receive the linked data, press = (equal sign), select the cell in the other workbook containing the data to be linked, then press

[Enter]. Excel automatically inserts the name of the referenced workbook in the cell reference. To perform calculations, enter formulas on the consolidation sheet using cells in the supporting sheets. If you are linking more than one cell, you can copy the linked data to the Clipboard, select in the other workbook the upper-left cell to receive the link, click Edit on the menu bar, click Paste Special, then click Paste Link.

Excel 2000

Hiding and Protecting Worksheet Areas

Worksheets can contain sensitive information that you don't want others to view or alter. To protect such information, Excel gives you two basic options. You can **hide** the formulas in selected cells (or rows, columns, or entire sheets), and you can **lock** selected cells, in which case other people will be able to view the data (values, numbers, labels, formulas, etc.) in those cells but not to alter it in any way. See Table F-1 for a list of options you can use to protect a worksheet. You set the lock and hide options in the Format Cells dialog box. You lock and unlock cells by clicking the Locked check box in the Format Cells dialog box Protection tab, and hide and "unhide" cell formulas by clicking the Hidden check box. The lock and hide options will not function unless an Excel protection feature, which you access via the Tools menu, is also activated. A common worksheet protection strategy is to unlock cells in which data will be changed, sometimes referred to as the **data entry area**, and to lock cells in which the data should not be changed. Then, when you protect the worksheet, the unlocked areas can still be changed. Scenario Because Jim will assign someone to enter the sensitive timecard information into the worksheet, he plans to hide and lock selected areas of the worksheet.

Steps

1. Make sure the Monday sheet is active, select range **I6:L27**, click **Format** on the menu bar, click **Cells**, then click the **Protection tab**

   You include row 27, even though it does not contain data, in the event that new data is added to the row later. Notice that the Locked box in the Protection tab is already checked, as shown in Figure F-8. The Locked check box is selected by default, meaning that all the cells in a new workbook start out locked. (Note, however, that cell locking is not applied unless the protection feature is also activated. The protection feature is inactive by default.)

2. Click the **Locked check box** to deselect it, then click **OK**

   Excel stores time as a fraction of a 24-hour day. In the formula for total pay, hours must be multiplied by 24. This concept might be confusing to the data entry person, so you hide the formulas.

3. Select range **O6:O26**, click **Format** on the menu bar, click **Cells**, click the **Protection tab**, click the **Hidden check box** to select it, then click **OK**

   The screen data remains the same (unhidden and unlocked) until you set the protection in the next step.

QuickTip

To turn off worksheet protection, click Tools on the menu bar, point to Protection, then click Unprotect Sheet. If prompted for a password, type the password, then click OK. To remove passwords, open the workbook or worksheet using the password, then go to the window where you entered the password, highlight the password, and press [Delete]. Remember that passwords are case sensitive.

4. Click **Tools** on the menu bar, point to **Protection**, then click **Protect Sheet**

   The Protect Sheet dialog box opens. You choose not to use a password.

5. Click **OK**

   You are ready to test the new worksheet protection.

6. Click cell **O6**

   Notice that the formula bar is empty because of the hidden formula setting.

7. In cell O6, type **T** to confirm that locked cells cannot be changed, then click **OK**

   When you attempt to change a locked cell, a message box reminds you of the protected cell's read-only status. See Figure F-9.

8. Click cell **I6**, type **9**, and notice that Excel allows you to begin the entry, press **[Esc]** to cancel the entry, then save the workbook

   Because you unlocked the cells in columns I through L before you protected the worksheet, you can make changes to these cells. Jim is satisfied that the Time In and Time Out data can be changed as necessary.

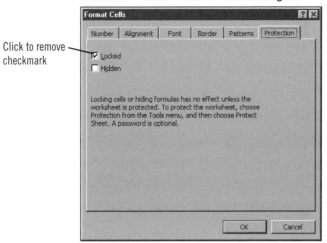

FIGURE F-8: Protection tab in Format Cells dialog box

Click to remove checkmark

FIGURE F-9: Reminder of protected cell's read-only status

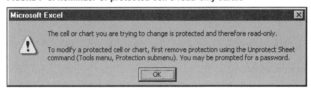

TABLE F-1: Options for hiding and protecting worksheet elements

task	menu commands
Hide/Unhide a column	Format, Column, Hide or Unhide
Hide/Unhide a formula	Format, Cells, Protection tab, select/deselect Hidden check box
Hide/Unhide a row	Format, Row, Hide or Unhide
Hide/Unhide a sheet	Format, Sheet, Hide or Unhide
Protect workbook	Tools, Protection, Protect Workbook, assign optional password
Protect worksheet	Tools, Protection, Protect Sheet, assign optional password
Unlock/Relock cells	Format, Cells, Protection tab, deselect/select Locked check box

Note: Some of the hide and protect options do not take effect until protection is enabled.

Changing workbook properties

You can also password-protect an entire workbook from being opened or modified by changing its file properties. Click File, click Save As, click Tools, then click General Options. Specify the password(s) for opening or modifying the workbook. You can also use this dialog box to offer users an option to open the workbook in read-only format. To make an entire workbook read-only so that users can open but not change it, click Start on the Taskbar, point to Programs, then click Windows Explorer. Locate and click the file name, click File on the menu bar, click Properties, click the General tab, then, under Attributes, select the Read-only check box.

Saving Custom Views of a Worksheet

A **view** is a set of display and/or print settings that you can name and save, then access at a later time. By using the Excel Custom Views feature, you can create several different views of a worksheet without having to create separate sheets. For example, if you often switch between portrait and landscape orientations when printing different parts of a worksheet, you can create two views with the appropriate print settings for each view. You set the display and/or print settings first, then name the view. **Scenario** Because Jim will generate several reports from his data, he saves the current print and display settings as a custom view. To better view the data to be printed, he decides to use the Zoom box to display the entire worksheet on one screen. The Zoom box has a default setting of 100% magnification and appears on the Standard toolbar.

Trouble?

If the Zoom box does not appear on your Standard toolbar, click the More Buttons button ⏩ to view it.

1. With the Monday sheet active, select range **A1:028**, click the **Zoom box list arrow** on the Standard toolbar, click **Selection**, then press **[Ctrl][Home]** to return to cell A1
   Excel automatically adjusts the display magnification so that the data selected fits on one screen. See Figure F-10. After selecting the **Zoom box**, you also can pick a magnification percentage from the list or type the desired percentage.

2. Click **View** on the menu bar, then click **Custom Views**
   The Custom Views dialog box opens. Any previously defined views for the active worksheet appear in the Views box. In this case, Jim had created a custom view named Generic containing default print and display settings. See Figure F-11.

QuickTip

To delete views from the active worksheet, select the view in the Views list box, then click Delete.

3. Click **Add**
   The Add View dialog box opens, as shown in Figure F-12. Here, you enter a name for the view and decide whether to include print settings and hidden rows, columns, and filter settings. You want to include the selected options.

4. In the Name box, type **Complete Daily Worksheet**, then click **OK**
   After creating a custom view of the worksheet, you return to the worksheet area. You are ready to test the two custom views. In case the views require a change to the worksheet, it's a good idea to turn off worksheet protection.

5. Click **Tools** on the menu bar, point to **Protection**, then click **Unprotect Sheet**

6. Click **View** on the menu bar, then click **Custom Views**
   The Custom Views dialog box opens, listing both the Complete Daily Worksheet and Generic views.

Trouble?

If you receive the message, "Some view settings could not be applied," repeat Step 5 to ensure worksheet protection is turned off.

7. Click **Generic** in the Views list box, click **Show**, preview the worksheet, then close the Preview
   The Generic custom view returns the worksheet to the Excel default print and display settings. Now you are ready to test the new custom view.

8. Click **View** on the menu bar, click **Custom Views**, click **Complete Daily Worksheet** in the Views list box, click **Show**
   The entire worksheet fits on the screen.

QuickTip

With Report Manager add-in on the View menu, you can group worksheets and their views to be printed in sequence as one large report. If Report Manager is not on your View menu, click Tools/Add-Ins to add it.

9. Return to the Generic view, then save your work
   Jim is satisfied with the custom view of the worksheet he created.

FIGURE F-10: Selected data fit to one screen

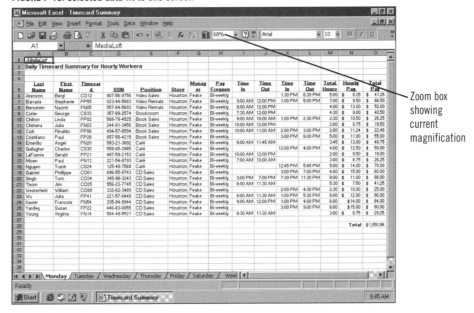

Zoom box showing current magnification

FIGURE F-11: Custom Views dialog box

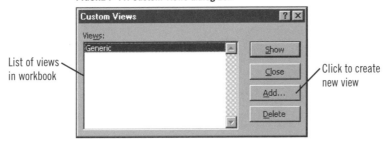

List of views in workbook

Click to create new view

FIGURE F-12: Add View dialog box

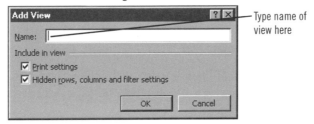

Type name of view here

Using a workspace

If you work with several workbooks at a time in a particular arrangement, you can create a **workspace** containing information about their location and window sizes. Then, instead of opening each workbook individually, you can just open the workspace, which will automatically display the workbooks in the sizes and locations saved in the workspace. To create a workspace, open the workbooks and locate and size them as you would like them to appear. Click File on the menu bar, click Save Workspace, then type a name for the workspace file. Then open the workspace file and open the workbooks in their saved locations and sizes. Remember, however, that the workspace file does not contain the workbooks themselves, so you still have to back up the original workbook files. To start the workspace automatically when you turn on your computer, place the workspace file only in your XLStart folder.

Controlling Page Breaks and Page Numbering

The vertical and horizontal dashed lines in worksheets indicate page breaks. Excel automatically inserts a page break when your worksheet data doesn't fit on one page. These page breaks are **dynamic**, which means they adjust automatically when you insert or delete rows and columns and when you change column widths or row heights. Everything to the left of the first vertical dashed line and above the first horizontal dashed line is printed on the first page. You can override the automatic breaks by choosing the Page Break command on the Insert menu. Table F-2 describes the different types of page breaks you can use. Scenario▶ Jim wants another report displaying no more than half the hourly workers on each page. To accomplish this, he must insert a manual page break.

1. Click cell **A16**, click **Insert** on the menu bar, then click **Page Break**
   A dashed line appears between rows 15 and 16, indicating a horizontal page break. See Figure F-13. After you set page breaks, it's a good idea to preview each page.

2. Preview the worksheet, then click **Zoom**
   Notice that the status bar reads "Page 1 of 4" and that the data for the employees up through Charles Gallagher appears on the first page. Jim decides to place the date in the footer.

   QuickTip

   To insert the page number in a header or footer section yourself, click 🔲 in the Header or Footer dialog box.

3. While in the Print Preview window, click **Setup**, click the **Header/Footer tab**, click **Custom Footer**, click the **Right section box**, click the **Date button** 🔳

4. Click the **Left section box**, type your name, then click **OK**
   Your name, the page number, and the date appear in the Footer preview area.

   QuickTip

   To remove a manual page break, select any cell directly below or to the right of the page break, click Insert on the menu bar, then click Remove Page Break.

5. In the Page Setup dialog box, click **OK**, and, still in Print Preview, check to make sure all the pages show your name and the page numbers, click **Print**, then click **OK**

6. Click **View** on the menu bar, click **Custom Views**, click **Add**, type **Half N Half**, then click **OK**
   Your new custom view has the page breaks and all current print settings.

7. Make sure cell H16 is selected, then click **Insert** on the menu bar and click **Remove Page Break**

8. Save the workbook

TABLE F-2: Page break options

type of page break	where to position cell pointer
Both horizontal and vertical page breaks	Select the cell below and to the right of the gridline where you want the breaks to occur
Only a horizontal page break	Select the cell in column A that is directly below the gridline where you want the page to break
Only a vertical page break	Select a cell in row 1 that is to the right of the gridline where you want the page to break

FIGURE F-13: Worksheet with horizontal page break

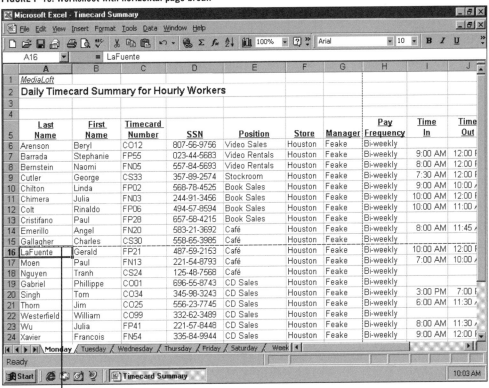

Dashed line indicates horizontal
break after row 15

Using Page Break Preview

By clicking View on the menu bar, then clicking Page Break Preview, or clicking Page Break Preview in the Print Preview window, you can view and change page breaks manually. (If you see a dialog box asking if you want help, just click OK to close it.) Simply drag the page break lines to the desired location. See Figure F-14. To exit Page Break Preview, click View on the menu bar, then click Normal.

FIGURE F-14: Page Break Preview window

Cell pointer in cell A16

Drag page break lines
to change page breaks

Creating a Hyperlink between Excel Files

As you manage the content and appearance of your workbooks, you may want the workbook user to have access to information in another workbook. It might be nonessential information or data that is too detailed to place in the workbook itself. In these cases, you can create a **hyperlink**, an object (a file name, a word, a phrase, or a graphic) in a worksheet that, when you click it, will jump to another worksheet, called the **target**. The target can be a document created in another software program or a site on the World Wide Web. For example, in a worksheet that lists customer invoices, at each customer's name, you might create a hyperlink to an Excel file containing payment terms for each customer. You can also use hyperlinks to navigate to other locations in a large worksheet. **Scenario** Jim wants managers who view the Timecard Summary worksheet to be able to view the pay categories for MediaLoft store employees. He creates a hyperlink at the Hourly Pay Rate column heading. Users will click the hyperlink to view the Pay Rate worksheet.

1. Display the Monday worksheet

2. Click **Edit**, click **Go To**, type **N5** (the cell containing **the text Hourly Pay Rate**), then click **OK**

3. Click the **Insert Hyperlink button** 📷 on the Standard toolbar, then click **Existing File or Web Page**, if necessary
   The Insert Hyperlink dialog box opens. See Figure F-15. The icons under Link to: on the left side of the dialog box let you specify the type of location you want the link to jump to: an existing file or Web page, a place in the same document, a new document, or an e-mail address. Since Jim wants users to display a document he has created, the first icon, Existing File or Web Page, is correct and is already selected.

4. Click **File** under Browse for, then in the Link to File dialog box, navigate to your Project Disk and double-click **Pay Rate Classifications**
   The Insert Hyperlink dialog box reappears with the file name you selected in the Type the file or Web page name text box. This document appears when users click this hyperlink. You can also specify the ScreenTip that users will see when they hold the pointer over the hyperlink.

5. Click **ScreenTip**, type **Click here to see MediaLoft pay rate classifications**, click **OK**, then click **OK** again
   Cell N5 now contains underlined blue text, indicating that it is a hyperlink. After you create a hyperlink, you should check it to make sure it jumps to the correct destination.

6. Move the pointer over the **Hourly Pay Rate text**, view the ScreenTip, then click once
   Notice that when you move the pointer over the text, the pointer changes to 🖑, indicating that it is a hyperlink, and the ScreenTip appears. After you click, the Pay Rate Classifications worksheet appears. See Figure F-16. The Web toolbar appears beneath the Standard and Formatting toolbars.

7. Click the **Back button** ⇐ on the Web toolbar, then save the workbook

Using hyperlinks to navigate large worksheets

Hyperlinks are useful in navigating large worksheets or workbooks. You can create a hyperlink from any cell to another cell in the same worksheet, a cell in another worksheet, or a defined name anywhere in the workbook. Under Link to in the Insert Hyperlink dialog box, click Place in This Document. Then type the cell reference and indicate the sheet, or select the named location in the scroll box.

FIGURE F-15: Insert Hyperlink dialog box

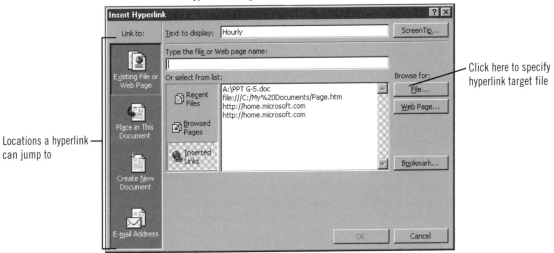

Locations a hyperlink can jump to

Click here to specify hyperlink target file

FIGURE F-16: Target document

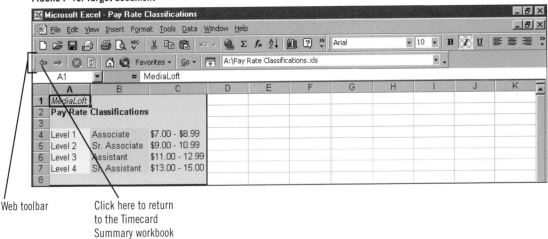

Web toolbar

Click here to return to the Timecard Summary workbook

Inserting a picture

As you prepare your workbooks for viewing by others on an intranet or on the Internet, you may want to enhance their appearance by adding pictures. You can easily add your own picture, such as a company logo or a scanned picture, or a picture from the Microsoft Clip Gallery. To insert a Clip Gallery picture on a worksheet, click Insert on the menu bar, point to Picture, then click Clip Art. Click a category, click the image you want to insert, then click the Insert Clip icon. Close the Insert Clip Art window. The picture is an **object** that you can move, resize, or delete. To move a picture, click and then drag it. To resize it, click it once to select it, then drag one of its corners. To delete it, click to select it, then press [Delete].

Excel 2000

Saving an Excel File as an HTML Document

One way to share Excel data is to publish, or **post**, it online over a network so that others can access it using their Web browsers. The network can be an **intranet**, which is an internal network site used by a particular group of people who work together, or the World Wide Web. The **World Wide Web** is a structure of documents, or pages, connected electronically over a large computer network called the **Internet**, which is made up of smaller networks and computers. If you save and post an entire workbook, users can click worksheet tabs to view each sheet. If you save a single worksheet, you can make the Web page interactive, meaning that users can enter, format, and calculate worksheet data. To post an Excel document to an intranet or the World Wide Web, you must first save it in **HTML (Hypertext Markup Language)**, which is the format that a Web browser can read. ▶Scenario Jim saves the entire Timecard Summary workbook in HTML format so it can be posted on the MediaLoft intranet for managers' use.

1. Click **File** on the menu bar, then click **Save as Web Page**
   The Save As dialog box opens. See Figure F-17. By default, the Entire Workbook option button is selected, which is what Jim wants. However, he wants the title bar of the Web page to be more descriptive than the file name.

2. Click **Change Title**
   The Set Page Title dialog box opens.

3. Type **MediaLoft Houston Timecard Summary**, then click OK
   The Page title area displays the new title. The Save as type list box indicates that the workbook will be saved as a Web page, which is in HTML format.

QuickTip

If you want, you can create a folder in the Save As dialog box. Click the Create new folder button 📄 and in the Save As dialog box, type the name of the new folder and click OK. The new folder automatically opens and appears in the Save in list. When you click Save, the HTML files will be saved in your new folder.

4. Change the file name to **Timecard Summary - Web**, then click the **Save in list arrow** and locate your Project Disk

5. Click **Save**
   A dialog box appears, indicating that the custom views you saved earlier will not be part of the HTML file.

6. Click **Yes**
   Excel saves the Web page version as an HTML file in the folder location you specified in the Save As dialog box, and in the same place creates a folder in which it places associated files, such as a file for each worksheet. To make the workbook available to others, you would post all these files on a network server. When the save process is complete, the original XLS file closes and the HTML file opens on your screen.

7. Click **File** on the menu bar, click **Web Page Preview**, then maximize the browser window
   The workbook opens in your default Web browser, which could be Internet Explorer or Netscape, showing you what it would look like if you opened it on an intranet or on the Internet. See Figure F-18. The Monday worksheet appears as it would if it were on a Web site or intranet, with tabs at the bottom of the screen for each daily sheet. If you wanted to use this document online, you would also need to save the target document (Pay Rate Classifications) in HTML format and post it to the Web site.

8. Click the **Weekly Summary tab**
   The Weekly Summary worksheet appears just as it would in Excel.

9. Close the Web browser window, then close the Timecard Summary - Web workbook and the Pay Rate Classifications workbook, then exit Excel

FIGURE F-17: Save As dialog box

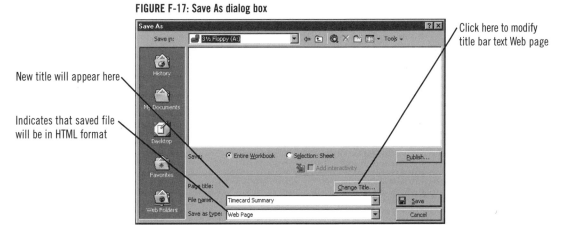

New title will appear here

Indicates that saved file will be in HTML format

Click here to modify title bar text Web page

FIGURE F-18: Workbook in Web page preview

Your browser may be Internet Explorer

Browser window

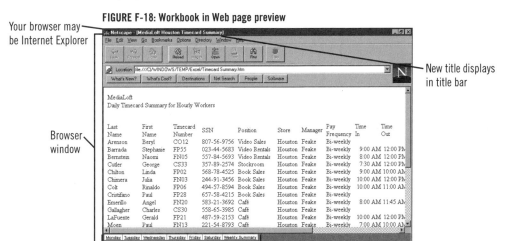

New title displays in title bar

Worksheet tabs allow users to view other sheets in browser

Send a workbook via e-mail

You can send an entire workbook or a worksheet to any e-mail recipient from within Excel. To send a workbook as an attachment to an e-mail message, click File, point to Send to, then click Mail Recipient (as attachment). Fill in the To and Cc information and click Send. See Figure F-19. (If Internet Explorer is not your default Web browser, you may need to respond to additional dialog boxes.) You can also route a workbook to one or more recipients on a routing list that you create. Click File, point to Send to, then click Routing Recipient. Click Create New Contact and enter contact information, then fill in the Routing slip. Depending on your e-mail program, you may have to follow a different procedure. See your instructor or lab resource person for help.

FIGURE F-19: E-mailing an Excel file as an attachment

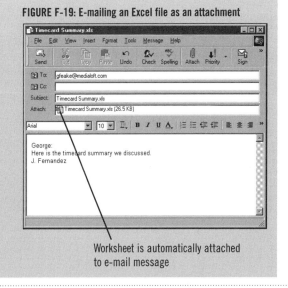

Worksheet is automatically attached to e-mail message

Practice

▶ Concepts Review

Label each element of the Excel screen shown in Figure F-20.

FIGURE F-20

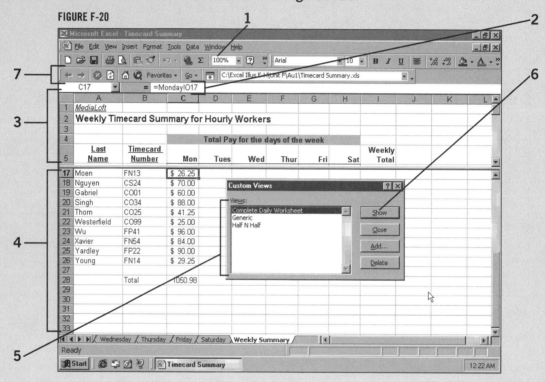

Match each of the terms with the statement that describes its function.

8.	**Dashed line**	a.	Inserts a code to print the sheet name in a header or footer
9.	**Hyperlink**	b.	Uses values from different workbooks
10.	**3-D reference**	c.	Indicates a page break
11.		d.	Inserts a code to print the total number of pages
12.		e.	An object you click to display a target

Select the best answer from the list of choices.

13. **You can save frequently used display and print settings by using the _____ feature.**
    a. Save command
    b. View menu
    c. Custom Views
    d. HTML

14. **You freeze areas of the worksheet to**
    a. Lock open windows in place.
    b. Lock column and row headings in place while you scroll through the worksheet.
    c. Freeze all data in place so that you can see it.
    d. Freeze data and unlock formulas.

15. **To protect a worksheet, you must first unlock those cells that _____, and then issue the Protect Sheet command.**
    a. are locked
    b. the user will be allowed to change
    c. have hidden formulas
    d. never change

▶ Skills Review

1. **Freeze columns and rows.**
   a. Open the workbook titled EX F-2, then save it as "Quarterly Household Budget".
   b. Freeze columns A and B and rows 1 through 3 for improved viewing. (*Hint:* Click cell C4 prior to issuing the Freeze Panes command.)
   c. Scroll until columns A and B and F through H are visible.
   d. Press [Ctrl][Home] to return to cell C4.
   e. Unfreeze the panes.

2. **Insert and delete worksheets.**
   a. With the 2001 sheet active, use the sheet pop-up menu to insert a new Sheet1 to its left.
   b. Delete Sheet1.
   c. Add a custom footer to the 2001 sheet with your name on the left side and the page number on the right side.
   d. Add a custom header with the worksheet name on the left side.
   e. Preview and print the worksheet.

3. **Consolidate data with 3-D references.**
   a. In cell C22, enter a reference to cell G7.
   b. In cell C23, enter a reference to cell G18.
   c. Activate the 2002 worksheet.
   d. In cell C4, enter a reference to cell C4 on the 2001 worksheet.
   e. In the 2002 worksheet, copy the contents of cell C4 into cells C5:C6.
   f. Preview the 2002 worksheet, view the Page Break Preview, and drag the page break so all the data fits on one page.
   g. Print the 2002 worksheet and save your work.

4. Hide and protect worksheet areas.

a. On the 2001 sheet, unlock the expense data in the range C10:F17.

b. Protect the sheet without using a password.

c. To make sure the other cells are locked, attempt to make an entry in cell D4.

d. Confirm the message box warning.

e. Change the first-quarter mortgage expense to $3,400.

f. Unprotect the worksheet.

g. Save the workbook.

5. Save custom views of a worksheet.

a. Set the zoom on the 2001 worksheet so all the data fits on your screen.

b. Make this a new view called "Entire 2001 Budget".

c. Use the Custom Views dialog box to return to Generic view.

d. Save the workbook.

6. Control page breaks and page numbering.

a. Insert a page break above cell A9.

b. Save the view as "Halves".

c. Preview and print the worksheet, then preview and print the entire workbook.

d. Save the workbook.

7. Create a hyperlink between Excel files.

a. On the 2001 worksheet, make cell A9 a hyperlink to the file Expense Details, with a ScreenTip that reads "Click here to see expense assumptions".

b. Test the link, then print the Expense Details worksheet.

c. Return to the Household Budget worksheet using the Web toolbar.

d. On the 2002 worksheet, enter the text "Based on 2001 budget" in cell A2.

e. Make the text in cell A2 a hyperlink to cell A1 in the 2001 worksheet. (*Hint:* Use the Place in this document button.)

f. Test the hyperlink.

g. Add any clip art picture to your worksheet, then move and resize it so it doesn't obscure any worksheet information.

8. Save an Excel file as an HTML document.

a. Save the entire budget workbook as a Web page with a title bar that reads "Our Budget" and the file named Quarterly Household Budget - Web.

b. Preview the Web page in your browser.

c. Test the worksheet tabs in the browser to make sure they work.

d. Return to Excel, then close the HTML document.

e. Close the Expense Details worksheet, then exit Excel.

► Visual Workshop

Create the worksheet shown in Figure F-21. Save the workbook as "Martinez Agency". Preview, then print, the worksheet. (*Hint:* Notice the hyperlink target on the sheet name at the bottom of the figure.)

FIGURE F-21

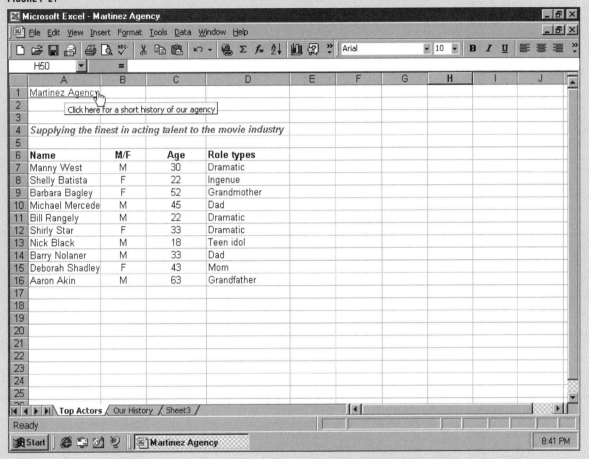

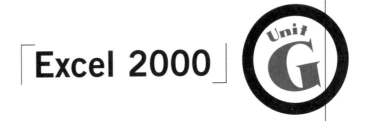

Automating
Worksheet Tasks

Objectives

► **Plan a macro**
[MOUS] ► **Record a macro**
[MOUS] ► **Run a macro**
[MOUS] ► **Edit a macro**
► **Use shortcut keys with macros**
► **Use the Personal Macro Workbook**
► **Add a macro as a menu item**
► **Create a toolbar for macros**

A **macro** is a set of instructions that performs tasks in the order you specify. You create macros to automate frequently performed Excel tasks that require a series of steps. For example, if you usually type your name and date in a worksheet footer, Excel can record the keystrokes in a macro that types the text and inserts the current date automatically. In this unit, you will plan and design a simple macro, then record and run it. Then you will edit the macro. You will also create a macro to run when you use shortcut keys, store a macro in the Personal Macro Workbook, add a macro option to the Tools menu, and create a new toolbar for macros. **Scenario** Jim is creating a macro for the accounting department. The macro will automatically insert text that will identify the worksheet as originating in the accounting department.

Planning a Macro

You create macros for tasks that you perform on a regular basis. For example, you can create a macro to enter and format text or to save and print a worksheet. To create a macro, you record the series of actions or write the instructions in a special format. Because the sequence of actions is important, you need to plan the macro carefully before you record it. You use commands on the Tools menu to record, run, and modify macros. Scenario Jim creates a macro for the accounting department that inserts the text "Accounting Department" in the upper-left corner of any worksheet. He plans the macro using the following guidelines:

Steps 1234

1. **Assign the macro a descriptive name, and write out the steps the macro will perform**
   This planning helps eliminate careless errors. Jim decides to name the macro "DeptStamp". He writes a description of the macro, as shown in Figure G-1. See Table G-1 for a list of macros Jim might create to automate other tasks.

2. **Decide how you will perform the actions you want to record**
   You can use the mouse, the keyboard, or a combination of the two. Jim decides to use both the mouse and keyboard.

3. **Practice the steps you want Excel to record and write them down**
   Jim wrote down the sequence of actions as he performed them, and he is now ready to record and test the macro.

4. **Decide where to locate the description of the macro and the macro itself**
   Macros can be stored in an unused area of the active workbook, in a new workbook, or in the Personal Macro Workbook. Jim stores the macro in a new workbook.

Macro to create stamp with the department name

Name: DeptStamp

Description: Adds a stamp to the top left of worksheet identifying it as an accounting department worksheet

Steps:
1. Position the cell pointer in cell A1
2. Type Accounting Department, then click the Enter button
3. Click Format on the menu bar, click Cells
4. Click Font tab, under Font style click Bold, under Underline click Single, and under Color click Red, then click OK

TABLE G-1: Possible macros and their descriptive names

description of macro	descriptive name
Enter a frequently used proper name, such as Jim Fernandez	JimFernandez
Enter a frequently used company name, such as MediaLoft	CompanyName
Print the active worksheet on a single page, in landscape orientation	FitToLand
Turn off the header and footer in the active worksheet	HeadFootOff
Show a frequently used custom view, such as a generic view of the worksheet, setting the print and display settings back to the Excel defaults	GenericView

CLUES TO USE

Macros and viruses

When you open an Excel Workbook that has macros, you will see a message asking you if you want to enable or disable macros. This is because macros can contain viruses, destructive software programs that can damage your computer files. If you know your workbook came from a trusted source, click Enable macros. If you are not sure of the workbook's source, click Disable macros. If you disable the macros in a workbook, you will not be able to use them in the workbook. For more information, see the Excel Help topic About Viruses and workbook macros.

Recording a Macro

The easiest way to create a macro is to record it using the Excel Macro Recorder. You simply turn the Macro Recorder on, enter the keystrokes, select the commands you want the macro to perform, then stop the recorder. As you record the macro, each action is translated into programming code that you can later view and modify. **Scenario** Jim wants to create a macro that enters a department stamp in cell A1 of the active worksheet. He creates this macro by recording his actions.

Steps

1. **Start Excel if necessary, click the New button** ▢ **on the Standard toolbar, then save the blank workbook as My Excel Macros**
   Now you are ready to start recording the macro.

2. **Click Tools on the menu bar, point to Macro, then click Record New Macro**
   The Record Macro dialog box opens. See Figure G-2. Notice the default name Macro1 is selected. You can either assign this name or type a new name. The first character of a macro name must be a letter; the remaining characters can be letters, numbers, or underscores; (spaces are not allowed in macro names; use underscores in place of spaces). This dialog box also allows you to assign a shortcut key for running the macro and to instruct Excel where to store the macro.

3. **Type DeptStamp in the Macro name box**

4. **If the Store macro in list arrow box does not read "This Workbook", click the list arrow and select This Workbook**

5. **If the Description text box does not contain your name, select the existing name, type your own name, then click OK**
   The dialog box closes. Excel displays the small Stop Recording toolbar containing the Stop Recording button ■, and the word "Recording" appears on the status bar. Take your time performing the steps below. Excel records every keystroke, menu option, and mouse action that you make.

6. **Press [Ctrl][Home]**
   The cell pointer moves to cell A1. When you begin an Excel session, macros record absolute cell references. By beginning the recording in cell A1, you ensure that the macro includes the instruction to select cell A1 as the first step.

7. **Type Accounting Department in cell A1, then click the Enter button** ✓ **on the formula bar**

8. **Click Format on the menu bar, then click Cells**

9. **Click the Font tab, in the Font style list box click Bold, click the Underline list arrow and click Single, then click the Color list arrow and click red (third row, first color on left)**
   See Figure G-3.

10. **Click OK, click the Stop Recording button** ■ **on the Stop Recording toolbar, click cell D1 to deselect cell A1, then save the workbook**
    Compare your results with Figure G-4.

FIGURE G-2: Record Macro dialog box

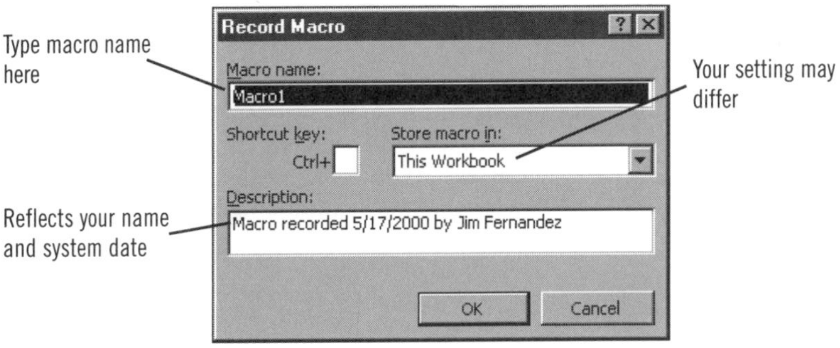

Type macro name here →

← Your setting may differ

Reflects your name and system date →

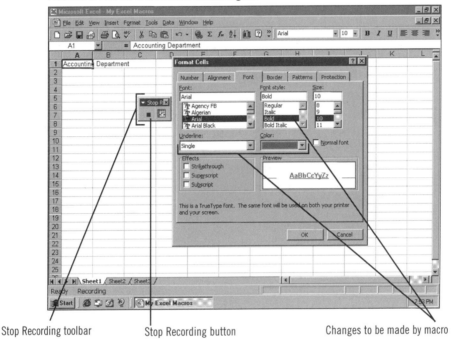

FIGURE G-3: Font tab of the Format Cells dialog box

Stop Recording toolbar   Stop Recording button   Changes to be made by macro

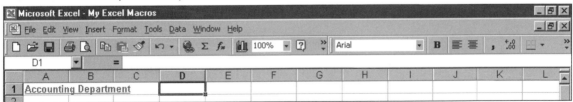

FIGURE G-4: Personalized department stamp

Using templates to create a workbook

You can create a workbook using an Excel **template**, a special-purpose workbook with formatting and formulas, such as an invoice or income statement. Click File on the menu bar, click New, click the Spreadsheet Solutions or Business planner templates tab, then double-click any template. Excel opens a workbook using that template design.

Running a Macro

Once you record a macro, you should test it to make sure that the actions performed are correct. To test a macro, you **run**, or execute, it. One way to run a macro is to select the macro in the Macros dialog box, then click Run. ▶Scenario Jim clears the contents of cell A1 and then tests the DeptStamp macro. After he runs the macro from the My Excel Macros workbook, he decides to test the macro once more from a newly opened workbook.

Steps

1. Click **cell A1**, click **Edit** on the menu bar, point to **Clear**, click **All**, then click any other cell to deselect cell A1

   When you delete only the contents of a cell, any formatting still remains in the cell. By using the Clear All option on the Edit menu, you can be sure that the cell is free of contents and formatting.

2. Click **Tools** on the menu bar, point to **Macro**, then click **Macros**

   The Macro dialog box, shown in Figure G-5, lists all the macros contained in the open workbooks.

3. Make sure **DeptStamp** is selected, click **Run**, then deselect cell A1

   Watch your screen as the macro quickly plays back the steps you recorded in the previous lesson. When the macro is finished, your screen should look like Figure G-6. As long as the workbook containing the macro remains open, you can run the macro from any open workbook.

4. Click the **New button** 🗋 on the Standard toolbar

   Because the new workbook automatically fills the screen, it is difficult to be sure that the My Excel Macros workbook is still open.

5. Click **Window** on the menu bar

   A list of open workbooks appears underneath the menu options. The active workbook name (in this case, Book2) appears with a check mark to its left. The My Excel Macros workbook appears on the menu, so you know it's open. See Figure G-7.

6. Deselect cell A1 if necessary, click **Tools** on the menu bar, point to **Macro**, click **Macros**, make sure **'My Excel Macros.xls'!DeptStamp** is selected, click **Run**, then deselect cell A1

   Cell A1 should look like Figure G-6. Notice that when multiple workbooks are open, the macro name includes the workbook name between single quotation marks, followed by an exclamation point, indicating that the macro is outside the active workbook. Since you use this workbook only to test the macro, you don't need to save it.

7. Close Book2 without saving changes

   The My Excel Macros workbook reappears.

FIGURE G-5: Macro dialog box

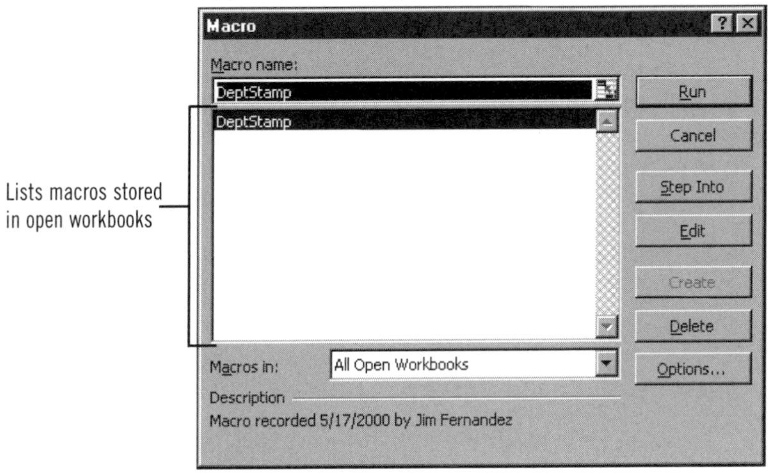

Lists macros stored in open workbooks

FIGURE G-6: Result of running DeptStamp macro

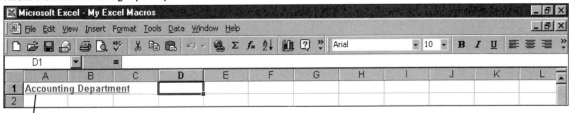

DeptStamp macro inserts formatted text in cell A1

FIGURE G-7: Window menu showing list of open workbooks

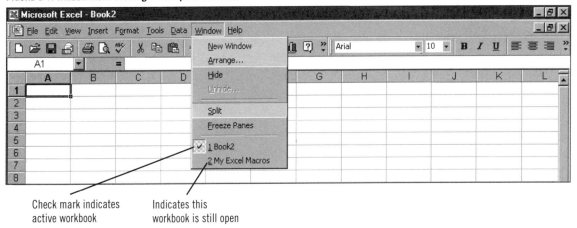

Check mark indicates active workbook

Indicates this workbook is still open

Editing a Macro

When you use the Macro Recorder to create a macro, the instructions are recorded automatically in Visual Basic for Applications programming language. Each macro is stored as a **module**, or program code container, attached to the workbook. Once you record a macro, you might need to change it. If you have a lot of changes to make, it might be best to re-record the macro. If you need to make only minor adjustments, you can edit the macro code, or program instructions, directly using the Visual Basic Editor. Scenario▶ Jim wants to modify his macro to change the point size of the department stamp to 12.

Steps 1234

QuickTip

Another way to start the Visual Basic Editor is to click Tools on the menu bar, point to Macro, then click Visual Basic Editor, or press [Alt][F11].

1. Make sure the My Excel Macros workbook is open, click **Tools** on the menu bar, point to **Macro**, click **Macros**, make sure **DeptStamp** is selected, then click **Edit**

The Visual Basic Editor starts showing the DeptStamp macro steps in a numbered module window (in this case, Module1).

2. Maximize the window titled **My Excel Macros.xls – [Module1 (Code)]**, then examine the steps in the macro

See Figure G-8. The name of the macro and the date it was recorded appear at the top of the module window. Notice that Excel translates your keystrokes and commands into words, known as macro code. For example, the line .FontStyle = "Bold" was generated when you clicked Bold in the Format Cells dialog box. When you make changes in a dialog box during macro recording, Excel automatically stores all the dialog box settings in the macro code. You also see lines of code that you didn't generate directly while recording the DeptStamp macro; for example, .Name = "Arial".

3. In the line .Size = 10, double-click **10** to select it, then type **12**

Because Module1 is attached to the workbook and not stored as a separate file, any changes to the module are saved automatically when the workbook is saved.

4. In the Visual Basic Editor, click **File** on the menu bar, click **Print**, then click **OK** to print the module

Review the printout of Module1.

5. Click **File** on the menu bar, then click **Close and Return to Microsoft Excel**

You want to rerun the DeptStamp macro to view the point size edit you made using the Visual Basic Editor.

6. Click cell **A1**, click **Edit** on the menu bar, point to **Clear**, click **All**, deselect cell A1, click **Tools** on the menu bar, point to **Macro**, click **Macros**, make sure **DeptStamp** is selected, click **Run**, then deselect cell A1

Compare your results with Figure G-9.

7. Save the workbook

FIGURE G-8: Visual Basic Editor showing Module1

Name of the macro

Project Explorer with open module selected

Properties window showing properties for selected objects

Macro programming code

Comments appear in green preceded by an apostrophe

Code window

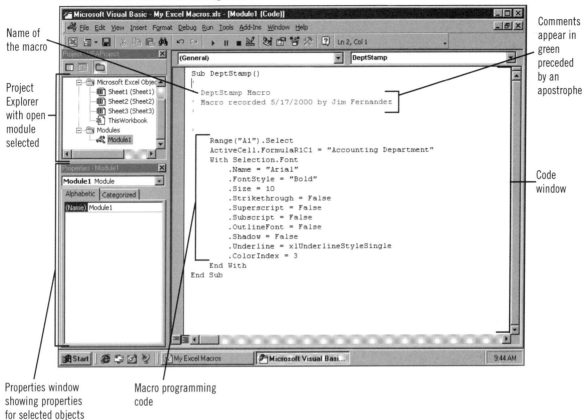

```
Sub DeptStamp()

' DeptStamp Macro
' Macro recorded 5/17/2000 by Jim Fernandez
'

    Range("A1").Select
    ActiveCell.FormulaR1C1 = "Accounting Department"
    With Selection.Font
        .Name = "Arial"
        .FontStyle = "Bold"
        .Size = 10
        .Strikethrough = False
        .Superscript = False
        .Subscript = False
        .OutlineFont = False
        .Shadow = False
        .Underline = xlUnderlineStyleSingle
        .ColorIndex = 3
    End With
End Sub
```

FIGURE G-9: Result of running edited DeptStamp macro

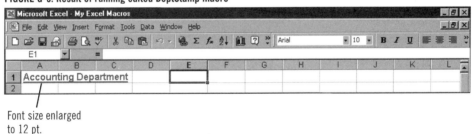

Font size enlarged to 12 pt.

Adding comments to code

With practice, you will be able to interpret the lines of code within your macro. Others who use your macro, however, might want to know the function of a particular line. You can explain the code by adding comments to the macro. Comments are explanatory text added to the lines of code. When you enter a comment, you must type an apostrophe (') before the comment

text. Otherwise, Excel thinks you have entered a command. On a color monitor, comments appear in green after you press [Enter]. See Figure G-8. You also can insert blank lines in the macro code to make the code more readable. To do this, type an apostrophe, then press [Enter].

Using Shortcut Keys with Macros

In addition to running a macro from the Macro dialog box, you can run a macro by assigning a shortcut key combination. Using shortcut keys to run macros reduces the number of keystrokes required to begin macro playback. You assign shortcut key combinations in the Record Macro dialog box. **Scenario** Jim also wants to create a macro called CompanyName to enter the company name into a worksheet. He assigns a shortcut key combination to run the macro.

Steps 1 2 3 4

1. **Click cell B2**
   You will record the macro in cell B2. You want to be able to enter the company name any-where in a worksheet. Therefore, you will not begin the macro with an instruction to posi-tion the cell pointer, as you did in the DeptStamp macro.

2. **Click Tools on the menu bar, point to Macro, then click Record New Macro**
   The Record Macro dialog box opens. Notice the option Shortcut key: Ctrl+ followed by a blank box. You can type a letter (A-Z) in the Shortcut key box to assign the key combina-tion of [Ctrl] plus that letter to run the macro. You use the key combination [Ctrl][Shift] plus a letter to avoid overriding any of the Excel's assigned [Ctrl][letter] shortcut keys, such as [Ctrl][C] for Copy.

3. **With the default macro name selected, type CompanyName, click the Shortcut key text box, press and hold [Shift], type C, then, if necessary, replace the name in the Description box with your name**
   Compare your screen with Figure G-10. You are ready to record the CompanyName macro.

4. **Click OK to close the dialog box**
   By default, Excel records absolute cell references in macros. Beginning the macro in cell B2 causes the macro code to begin with a statement to select cell B2. Because you want to be able to run this macro in any active cell, you need to instruct Excel to record relative cell ref-erences while recording the macro.

   QuickTip

   When you begin an Excel session, the Relative Reference button is toggled off, indicating that Excel is recording absolute cell ref-erences in macros. Once selected, and until it is tog-gled off again, the Relative Reference setting remains in effect during the current Excel session.

5. **Click the Relative Reference button 🔲 on the Stop Recording toolbar**
   The Relative Reference button is now indented to indicate that it is selected. See Figure G-11. This button is a toggle and retains the relative reference setting until you click it again to turn it off.

6. **Type MediaLoft in cell B2, click the Enter button ☑ on the formula bar, press [Ctrl][I] to italicize the text, click the Stop Recording button ■ on the Stop Recording toolbar, then deselect cell B2**
   MediaLoft appears in italics in cell B2. You are ready to run the macro in cell A5 using the shortcut key combination.

7. **Click cell A5, press and hold [Ctrl][Shift], type C, then deselect the cell**
   The result appears in cell A5. See Figure G-12. Because the macro played back in the selected cell (A5) instead of the cell where it was recorded (B2), Jim is convinced that the macro recorded relative cell references.

8. **Save the workbook**

FIGURE G-10: Record Macro dialog box with shortcut key assigned

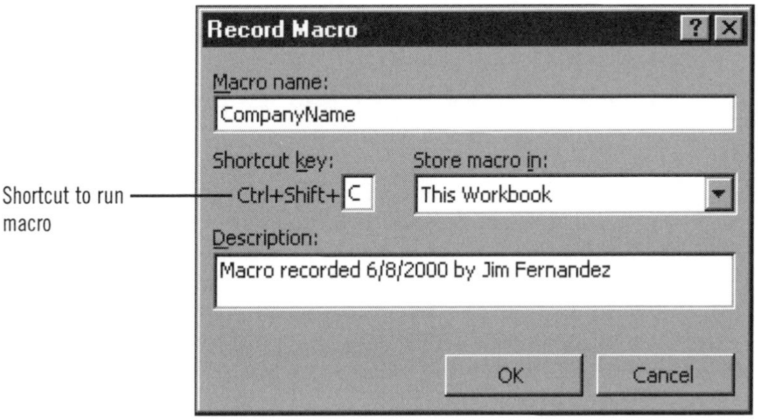

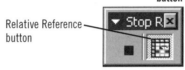

Shortcut to run macro ⟶

Record Macro

Macro name:
CompanyName

Shortcut key: Store macro in:
Ctrl+Shift+ C   This Workbook

Description:
Macro recorded 6/8/2000 by Jim Fernandez

OK   Cancel

FIGURE G-11: Stop Recording toolbar with Relative Reference button selected

Relative Reference button ⟶

FIGURE G-12: Result of running the CompanyName macro

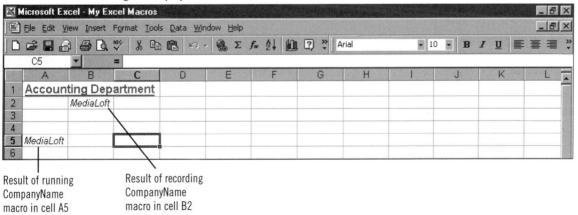

Result of running CompanyName macro in cell A5

Result of recording CompanyName macro in cell B2

Using the Personal Macro Workbook

You can store commonly used macros in a **Personal Macro Workbook**. The Personal Macro Workbook is always available, unless you specify otherwise, and gives you access to all the macros it contains, regardless of which workbooks are open. The Personal Macro Workbook file is created automatically the first time you choose to store a macro in it. Additional macros are added to the Personal Macro Workbook when you store them there. **Scenario** Jim often adds a footer to his worksheets identifying his department, the workbook name, the worksheet name, the page number, and the current date. He saves time by creating a macro that automatically inserts this footer. Because he wants this macro to be available whenever he uses Excel, Jim decides to store this macro in the Personal Macro Workbook.

1. From any cell in the active worksheet, click **Tools** on the menu bar, point to **Macro**, then click **Record New Macro**
   The Record Macro dialog box opens.

2. Type **FooterStamp** in the Macro name box, click the **Shortcut key box**, press and hold **[Shift]**, type **F**, then click the **Store macro in list arrow**
   You have named the macro FooterStamp and assigned it the shortcut combination [Ctrl][Shift][F]. Notice that This Workbook is selected by default, indicating that Excel automatically stores macros in the active workbook. See Figure G-13. You also can choose to store the macro in a new workbook or in the Personal Macro Workbook.

3. Click **Personal Macro Workbook**, replace the existing name in the Description text box with your own name, if necessary, then click **OK**
   The recorder is on, and you are ready to record the macro keystrokes. (If there is already a macro assigned to this shortcut, display the Personal Macro workbook and delete the FooterStamp macro. Then return to the My Excel Macro workbook and begin again from step 1.)

4. Click **File** on the menu bar, click **Page Setup**, click the **Header/Footer tab** (make sure to do this even if it is already active), click **Custom Footer**, in the Left section box, type **Accounting**, click the **Center section box**, click the **File Name button** 🖹, press **[Spacebar]**, type **/**, press **[Spacebar]**, click the **Tab Name button** 🖳 to insert the sheet name, click the **Right section box**, type your name followed by a comma, press **[Spacebar]**, click the **Date button** 🖾, click **OK** to return to the Header/Footer tab
   The footer stamp is set up, as shown in Figure G-14.

5. Click **OK** to return to the worksheet, then click the **Stop Recording button** ■ on the Stop Recording toolbar
   You want to ensure that the macro will set the footer stamp in any active worksheet.

6. Activate Sheet2, in cell A1 type **Testing the FooterStamp macro**, press **[Enter]**, press and hold **[Ctrl][Shift]**, then type **F**
   The FooterStamp macro plays back the sequence of commands.

7. Preview the worksheet to verify that the new footer was inserted

8. Print, then save the worksheet
   Jim is satisfied that the FooterStamp macro works in any active worksheet. Next, Jim adds the macro as a menu item on the Tools menu.

FIGURE G-13: Record Macro dialog box showing Store macro in options

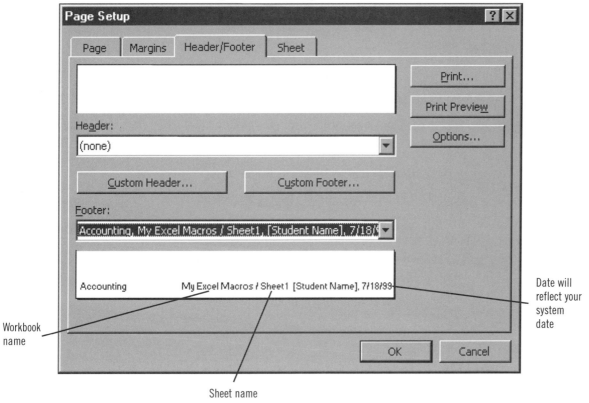

Click to store in new blank workbook

Click to store in active workbook

Click to store in Personal Macro Workbook

FIGURE G-14: Header/Footer tab showing custom footer settings

Workbook name

Date will reflect your system date

Sheet name

Working with the Personal Macro Workbook

Once created, the Personal Macro Workbook automatically opens each time you start Excel. By default, the Personal Macro Workbook is hidden as a precautionary measure so you don't accidentally add anything to it. When the Personal Macro Workbook is hidden, you can add macros to it but you cannot delete macros from it.

Excel 2000

Adding a Macro as a Menu Item

In addition to storing macros in the Personal Macro Workbook so that they are always available, you can add macros as items on the Excel Worksheet menu bar. The **Worksheet menu bar** is a special toolbar at the top of the Excel screen that you can customize. Scenario▶ To increase the availability of the FooterStamp macro, Jim decides to add it as an item on the Tools menu. First, he adds a custom menu item to the Tools menu, then he assigns the macro to that menu item.

Steps 1 2 3 4

QuickTip

If you want to add a command to a menu bar, first display the toolbar containing the menu to which you want to add the command.

1. Click **Tools** on the menu bar, click **Customize**, click the **Commands tab**, then under Categories, click **Macros**
   See Figure G-15.

2. Click **Custom Menu Item** under Commands, drag the selection to **Tools** on the menu bar (the menu opens), then point just under the last menu option, but do not release the mouse button
   Compare your screen to Figure G-16.

3. Release the mouse button
   Now, Custom Menu item is the last item on the Tools menu.

Trouble?

If you don't see PERSONAL.XLS!FooterStamp under Macro name, try repositioning the Assign Macro dialog box.

4. With the Tools menu still open, right-click **Custom Menu Item**, select the text in the Name box (&Custom Menu Item), type **Footer Stamp**, then click **Assign Macro**
   Unlike a macro name, the name of a custom menu item can have spaces between words, as do all standard menu items. The Assign Macro dialog box opens.

5. Click **PERSONAL.XLS!FooterStamp** under Macro name, click **OK**, then click **Close**

6. Click the **Sheet3 tab**, in cell A1 type **Testing macro menu item**, press [Enter], then click **Tools** on the menu bar
   The Tools menu appears with the new menu option at the bottom. See Figure G-17.

7. Click **Footer Stamp**, preview the worksheet to verify that the footer was inserted, then close the Print Preview window
   The Print Preview window appears with the footer stamp. Since others using your machine might be confused by the macro on the menu, it's a good idea to remove it.

8. Click **Tools** on the menu bar, click **Customize**, click the **Toolbars tab**, click **Worksheet Menu Bar** to select it, click **Reset**, click **OK** to confirm, click **Close**, then click **Tools** on the menu bar to make sure that the custom item has been deleted
   Because you did not make any changes to your workbook, you don't need to save it. Next, Jim creates a toolbar for macros and adds macros to it.

FIGURE G-15: Commands tab of the Customize dialog box

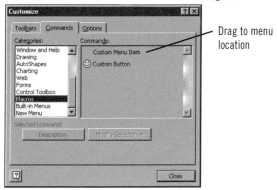

Drag to menu location

FIGURE G-16: Tools menu showing placement of Custom Menu Item

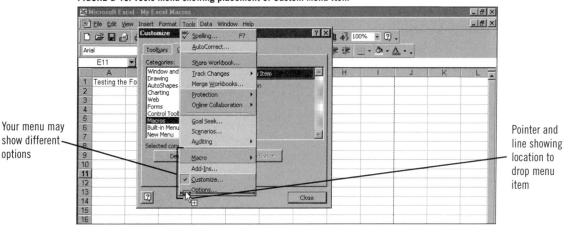

Your menu may show different options

Pointer and line showing location to drop menu item

FIGURE G-17: Tools menu with new Footer Stamp item

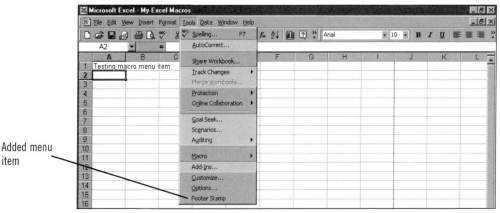

Added menu item

Creating a Toolbar for Macros

Toolbars contain buttons that allow you to access commonly used commands. You can create your own custom toolbars to organize commands so that you can find and use them quickly. Once you create a toolbar, you then add buttons to access Excel commands such as macros. Scenario▶ Jim has decided to create a custom toolbar called Macros that will contain buttons to run two of his macros.

Steps

QuickTip

Toolbars you create or customize are available to all workbooks on your PC. You also can ensure that a custom toolbar is available with a specific workbook by attaching the toolbar to the workbook using the Toolbar tab in the Customize dialog box.

1. **With Sheet3 active, click Tools on the menu bar, click Customize, click the Toolbars tab, if necessary, then click New**
   The New Toolbar dialog box opens, as shown in Figure G-18. Under Toolbar name, a default name of Custom1 is selected.

2. **Type Macros, then click OK**
   Excel adds the new toolbar named Macros to the bottom of the list and a small, empty toolbar named Macros opens. See Figure G-19. Notice that you cannot see the entire toolbar name. A toolbar starts small and automatically expands to fit the buttons you assign to it.

3. **Click the Commands tab in the Customize dialog box, click Macros under Categories, then drag the ☺ Custom Button over the new Macros toolbar and release the mouse button**
   The Macros toolbar now contains one button. You want the toolbar to contain two macros, so you need to add one more button.

4. **Drag the ☺ Custom Button over the Macros toolbar again**
   With the two buttons in place, you customize the buttons and assign macros to them.

5. **Right-click the left ☺ on the Macros toolbar, select &Custom Button in the Name box, type Department Stamp, click Assign Macro, click DeptStamp, then click OK**
   With the first toolbar button customized, you are ready to customize the second button.

6. **With the Customize dialog box open, right-click the right ☺ on the Macros toolbar, edit the name to read Company Name, click Change Button Image, click 🏃 (bottom row, third from the left), right-click 🏃, click Assign Macro, click CompanyName to select it, click OK, then close the Customize dialog box**
   The Macros toolbar appears with the two customized macro buttons.

7. **Move the mouse pointer over ☺ on the Macros toolbar to display the macro name (Department Stamp), then click to run the macro; click cell B2, move the mouse pointer over 🏃 on the Macros toolbar to display the macro name (Company Name), click 🏃, then deselect the cell**
   Compare your screen with Figure G-20. The DeptStamp macro automatically replaces the contents of cell A1.

8. **Click Tools on the menu bar, click Customize, click the Toolbars tab, if necessary, under Toolbars click Macros to select it, click Delete, click OK to confirm the deletion, then click Close**

Trouble?

If you are prompted to save the changes to the Personal Macro Workbook, click Yes.

9. **Save, then close the workbooks**

FIGURE G-18: New Toolbar dialog box

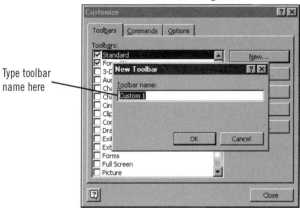

Type toolbar name here

FIGURE G-19: Customize dialog box with new Macros toolbar

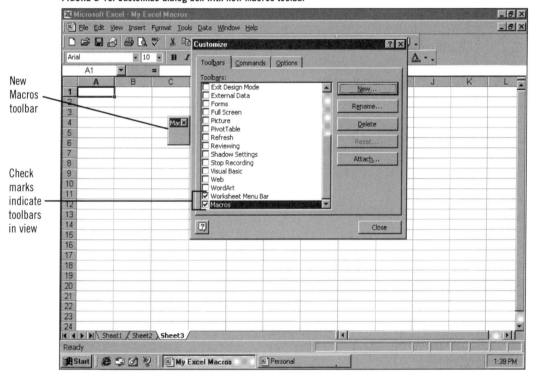

New Macros toolbar

Check marks indicate toolbars in view

FIGURE G-20: Worksheet showing Macros toolbar with two customized buttons

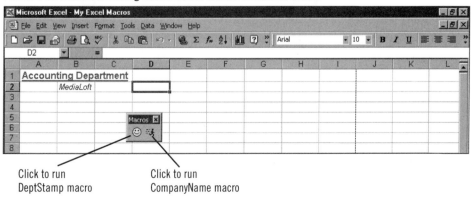

Click to run DeptStamp macro

Click to run CompanyName macro

Practice

► Concepts Review

Label each element of the Excel screen shown in Figure G-21.

FIGURE G-21

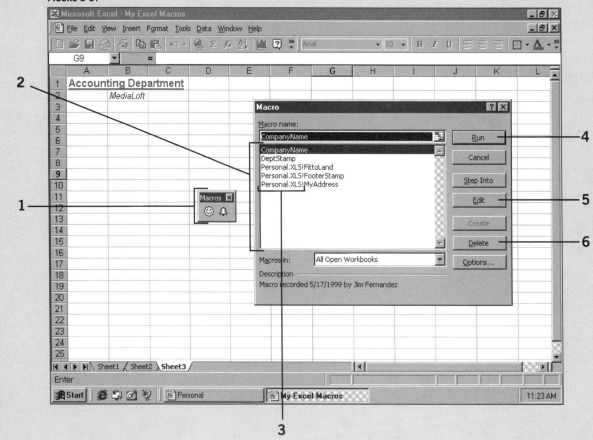

Select the best answer from the list of choices.

7. **Which of the following is the best candidate for a macro?**
   a. Nonsequential tasks
   b. Often-used sequences of commands or actions
   c. Seldom-used commands or tasks
   d. One-button or one-keystroke commands

8. **When you are recording a macro, you can execute commands by using**
   a. Only menu commands.
   b. Only the mouse.
   c. Any combination of the keyboard and the mouse.
   d. Only the keyboard.

9. **A macro is stored in**
   a. A Custom Menu Item.
   b. An unused area to the far right or well below the worksheet contents.
   c. A module attached to a workbook.
   d. The body of a worksheet used for data.

10. **Which of the following is *not* true about editing a macro?**
    a. You can make more than one editing change in a macro.
    b. A macro cannot be edited and must be recorded again.
    c. You can type changes directly in the existing macro code.
    d. You edit macros using the Visual Basic Editor.

11. **Why is it important to plan a macro?**
    a. Planning ensures that your macro will not contain errors.
    b. Planning helps prevent careless errors from being introduced into the macro.
    c. It is very difficult to correct errors you make in a macro.
    d. Macros won't be stored if they contain errors.

12. **Macros are recorded with relative references**
    a. Only if the Absolute Reference button is not selected.
    b. In all cases.
    c. Only if relative references are chosen while recording the macro.
    d. Only if the Relative Reference button is selected.

13. **You can run macros**
    a. Using all of the above.
    b. From shortcut key combinations.
    c. As items on menus.
    d. From the Macro dialog box.

Skills Review

1. Record a macro.

a. Create a new workbook, then save it as "Macros". You will record a macro titled "MyAddress" that enters and formats your name, address, and telephone number in a worksheet.

b. Store the macro in the current workbook.

c. Record the macro, entering your name in cell A1, your street address in cell A2, your city, state, and ZIP code in cell A3, and your telephone number in cell A4.

d. Format the information as 14-point Arial bold.

e. Add a border and make the text the color of your choice.

f. Save the workbook.

2. Run a macro.

a. Clear cell entries in the range affected by the macro.

b. Run the MyAddress macro in cell A1.

c. Clear the cell entries generated by running the MyAddress macro.

d. Save the workbook.

3. Edit a macro.

a. Open the MyAddress macro in the Visual Basic Editor.

b. Locate the line of code that defines the font size, then change the size to 18 point.

c. Edit the selected range to A1:E4, which increases it by three columns to accommodate the changed label size. (*Hint*: It is the second Range line in the macro.)

d. Add a comment line that describes this macro.

e. Save and print the module, then return to Excel.

f. Test the macro in Sheet1.

g. Save the workbook.

4. Use shortcut keys with macros.

a. You will record a macro in the current workbook called "MyName" that records your full name in cell G1.

b. Assign your macro the shortcut key combination [Ctrl][Shift][N] and store it in the current workbook.

c. After you record the macro, clear cell G1.

d. Use the shortcut key combination to run the MyName macro.

e. Save the workbook.

5. Use the Personal Macro Workbook.

a. You will record a new macro called "FitToLand" that sets print orientation to landscape, scaled to fit on a page.

b. Store the macro in the Personal Macro Workbook. If you are prompted to replace the existing FitToLand macro, click Yes.

c. After you record the macro, activate Sheet2, and enter some test data in row 1 that exceeds one page width.

d. In the Page Setup dialog box, return the orientation to portrait and adjust the capital A to 100 percent of normal size.

e. Run the macro.

f. Preview Sheet2 and verify that it's in landscape view and fits on one page.

6. Add a macro as a menu item.

a. On the Commands tab in the Customize dialog box, specify that you want to create a Custom Menu Item.

b. Place the Custom Menu Item at the bottom of the Tools menu.

c. Rename the Custom Menu Item "Fit to Landscape".

d. Assign the macro PERSONAL.XLS!FitToLand to the command.

e. Go to Sheet3 and change the orientation to portrait, then enter some test data in column A.

f. Run the Fit to Landscape macro from the Tools menu.

g. Preview the worksheet and verify that it is in landscape view.

h. Using the Tools, Customize menu options, select the Worksheet Menu bar, and reset.

i. Verify that the command has been removed from the Tools menu.

j. Save the workbook.

7. Create a toolbar for macros.

a. With the Macros workbook still open, you will create a new custom toolbar titled "My Info".

b. If necessary, drag the new toolbar onto the worksheet.

c. Display the Macros command category, then drag the Custom Button to the My Info toolbar.

d. Again, drag the Custom Button to the My Info toolbar.

e. Rename the first button "My Address", and assign the MyAddress macro to it.

f. Rename the second button "My Name", and assign the MyName macro to it.

g. Change the second button image to one of your choice.

h. On Sheet3, clear the existing cell data, then test both macro buttons on the My Info toolbar.

i. Use the Toolbars tab of the Customize dialog box to delete the toolbar named My Info.

j. Save and close the workbook, then exit Excel.

► Visual Workshop

Create the macro shown in Figure G-22. (*Hint:* Save a blank workbook as "File Utility Macros", then create a macro called SaveClose that saves a previously named workbook. Finally, include the line ActiveWorkbook. Close in the module, as shown in the figure.) Print the module. Test the macro. The line "Macro recorded...by..." will reflect your system date and name.

FIGURE G-22

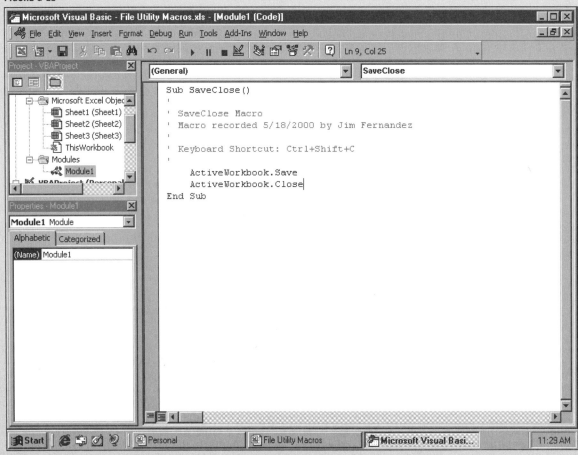

Using

Lists

Objectives

▶ **Plan a list**

▶ **Create a list**

MOUS ▶ **Add records with the data form**

MOUS ▶ **Find records**

MOUS ▶ **Delete records**

MOUS ▶ **Sort a list by one field**

MOUS ▶ **Sort a list by multiple fields**

MOUS ▶ **Print a list**

A **database** is an organized collection of related information. Examples of databases include a telephone book, a card catalog, and a roster of company employees. Excel refers to a database as a **list**. Using an Excel list, you can organize and manage worksheet information so that you can quickly find needed data for projects, reports, and charts. In this unit, you'll learn how to plan and create a list; add, change, find, and delete information in a list; and then sort and print a list.

Scenario▶ MediaLoft uses lists to analyze new customer information. Jim Fernandez needs to build and manage a list of new customers as part of the ongoing strategy to focus the company's advertising dollars.

Excel 2000

Planning a List

When planning a list, consider what information the list will contain and how you will work with the data now and in the future. Lists are organized into records. A **record** contains data about an object or person. Records, in turn, are divided into fields. **Fields** are columns in the list; each field describes a characteristic about the record, such as a customer's last name or street address. Each field has a **field name**, a column label that describes the field. See Table H-1 for additional planning guidelines. ▶Scenario Jim will compile a list of new customers. Before entering the data into an Excel worksheet, he plans his list using the following guidelines:

Identify the purpose of the list
Determine the kind of information the list should contain. Jim will use the list to identify areas of the country in which new customers live.

Plan the structure of the list
Determine the fields that make up a record. Jim has customer cards that contain information about each new customer. Figure H-1 shows a typical card. Each customer in the list will have a record. The fields in the record correspond to the information on the cards.

Write down the names of the fields
Field names can be up to 255 characters in length (the maximum column width), although shorter names are easier to see in the cells. Field names appear in the first row of a list. Jim writes down field names that describe each piece of information shown in Figure H-1.

Determine any special number formatting required in the list
Most lists contain both text and numbers. When planning a list, consider whether any fields require specific number formatting or prefixes. Jim notes that some ZIP codes begin with zero. Because Excel automatically drops a leading zero, Jim must type an apostrophe (') when he enters a ZIP code that begins with 0 (zero). The apostrophe tells Excel that the cell contains a label rather than a value. If a column contains both numbers and numbers that contain a text character, such as an apostrophe ('), you should format all the numbers as text. Otherwise, the numbers are sorted first, and the numbers that contain text characters are sorted after that; for example, 11542, 60614, 87105, '01810, '02115. To instruct Excel to sort the ZIP codes properly, Jim enters all ZIP codes with a leading apostrophe.

FIGURE H-1: Customer record and corresponding field names

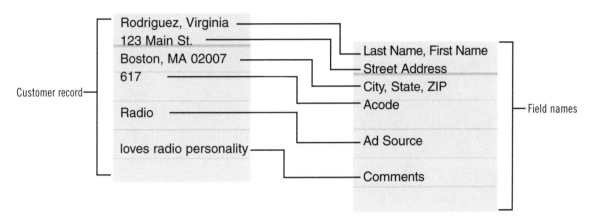

Excel 2000

TABLE H-1: Guidelines for planning a list

size and location guidelines	row and column content guidelines
Devote an entire worksheet to your list and list summary information because some list management features can be used on only one list at a time	Plan and design your list so that all rows have similar items in the same column
Leave at least one blank column and one blank row between your list and list summary data. Doing this helps Excel select your list when it performs list management tasks such as sorting	Do not insert extra spaces at the beginning of a cell because that can affect sorting and searching
Avoid placing critical data to the left or right of the list	Use the same format for all cells in a column

CLUES TO USE

Lists versus databases

If your list contains more records than can fit on one worksheet (that is, more than 65,536), you should consider using database software rather than spreadsheet software.

Excel 2000

Creating a List

Once you have planned the list structure, the sequence of fields, and any appropriate formatting, you need to create field names. Table H-2 provides guidelines for naming fields. **Scenario** Jim is ready to create the list using the field names he wrote down earlier.

Steps 1234

QuickTip

To return personalized toolbars and menus to their default state, click Tools on the menu bar, click Customize, click the Options tab in the Customize dialog box, click Reset my usage data to restore the default settings, click Yes, click Close, then close the Drawing toolbar if it is displayed.

1. Start Excel if necessary, open the workbook titled **EX H-1**, save it as **New Customer List**, rename Sheet1 as **Practice**, then if necessary maximize the Excel window
It is a good idea to devote an entire worksheet to your list.

2. Beginning in cell A1 and moving horizontally, type each field name in a separate cell, as shown in Figure H-2
Always put field names in the first row of the list. Don't worry if your field names are wider than the cells; you will fix this later.

Trouble?

If the Bold button or Borders button does not appear on your Formatting toolbar, click the More Buttons button to view it.

3. Select the field headings in range **A1:I1**, then click the **Bold button** B on the Formatting toolbar; with range A1:I1 still selected, click the **Borders list arrow**, then click the **thick bottom border** (second item from left in the second row)

4. Enter the information from Figure H-3 in the rows immediately below the field names, using a leading apostrophe (') for all ZIP codes; do not leave any blank rows
If you don't type an apostrophe, Excel deletes the leading zero (0) in the ZIP code. The data appears in columns organized by field name.

QuickTip

If the field name you plan to use is wider than the data in the column, you can turn on Wrap Text to stack the heading in the cell. Doing this allows you to use descriptive field names and still keep the columns from being unnecessarily wide. If you prefer a keyboard shortcut, you can press [Alt][Enter] to force a line break while entering field names.

5. Select the range **A1:I4**, click **Format** on the menu bar, point to **Column**, click **AutoFit Selection**, click anywhere in the worksheet to deselect the range, then save the workbook
Automatically resizing the column widths this way is faster than double-clicking the column divider lines between each pair of columns. Compare your screen with Figure H-4.

TABLE H-2: Guidelines for naming fields

guideline	explanation
Use labels to name fields	Numbers can be interpreted as parts of formulas
Do not use duplicate field names	Duplicate field names can cause information to be incorrectly entered and sorted
Format the field names to stand out from the list data	Use a font, alignment, format, pattern, border, or capitalization style for the column labels that are different from the format of your list data
Use descriptive names	Avoid names that might be confused with cell addresses, such as Q4

FIGURE H-2: Field names entered and formatted in row 1

Microsoft Excel - New Customer List
File Edit View Insert Format Tools Data Window Help
Arial
10
A1
= Last Name
Last Name
First Name
Street Address
City
State
Zip
ACode
Ad Source
Comments

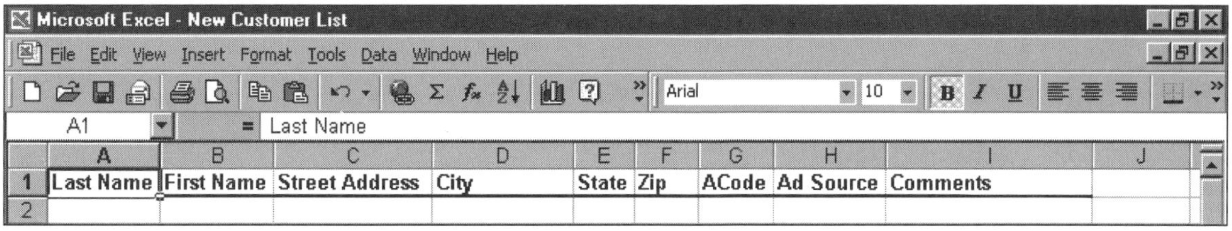

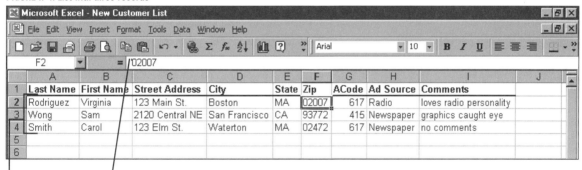

FIGURE H-3: Cards with customer information

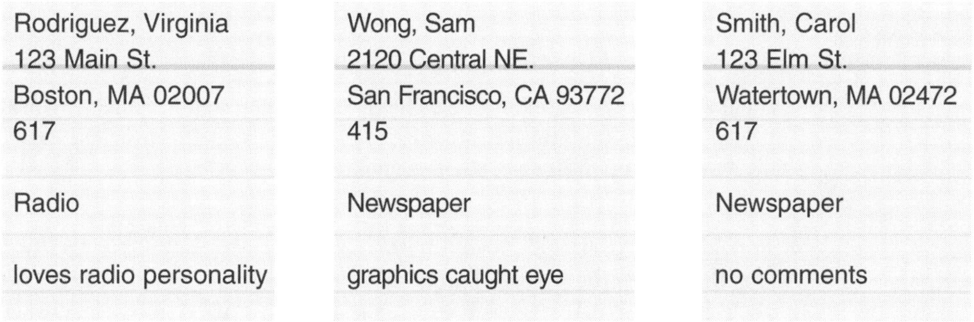

Rodriguez, Virginia
123 Main St.
Boston, MA 02007
617
Radio
loves radio personality
Wong, Sam
2120 Central NE.
San Francisco, CA 93772
415
Newspaper
graphics caught eye
Smith, Carol
123 Elm St.
Watertown, MA 02472
617
Newspaper
no comments

FIGURE H-4: List with three records

Microsoft Excel - New Customer List
File Edit View Insert Format Tools Data Window Help
Arial
10
F2
= '02007
Last Name | First Name | Street Address | City | State | Zip | ACode | Ad Source | Comments
Rodriguez | Virginia | 123 Main St. | Boston | MA | 02007 | 617 | Radio | loves radio personality
Wong | Sam | 2120 Central NE | San Francisco | CA | 93772 | 415 | Newspaper | graphics caught eye
Smith | Carol | 123 Elm St. | Waterton | MA | 02472 | 617 | Newspaper | no comments
New records
Leading apostrophe

CLUES TO USE

Maintaining the quality of information in a list

To protect the list information, make sure the data is entered in the correct field. Stress care and consistency to all those who enter the list data. Haphazardly entered data can yield invalid results later when it is manipulated.

Adding Records with the Data Form

You can add records to a list by typing data directly into the cells within the list range. Once the field names are created, you also can use the data form as a quick, easy method of data entry. A **data form** is a dialog box that displays one record at a time. By naming a list range in the name box, you can select the list at any time, and all new records you add to the list will be included in the list range. Scenario▶ Jim has entered all the customer records he had on his cards, but he receives the names of two more customers. He decides to use the Excel data form to add the new customer information.

Steps 1 2 3 4

1. **Make sure the New Customer List file is open, then rename Sheet2 Working List**
   Working List contains the nearly complete customer list. Before using the data form to enter the new data, you must define the list range.

2. **Select the range A1:I45, click the name box to select the reference to cell A1 there, type Database, then press [Enter]**
   The Database list range name appears in the name box. When you assign the name Database to the list, the commands on the Excel Data menu apply to the list named "Database".

3. **While the list is still selected, click Data on the menu bar, then click Form**
   A data form containing the first record appears, as shown in Figure H-5.

4. **Click New**
   A blank data form appears with the insertion point in the first field.

5. **Type Chavez in the Last Name box, then press [Tab] to move the insertion point to the next field**

6. **Enter the rest of the information for Jeffrey Chavez, as shown in Figure H-6**
   Press [Tab] to move the insertion point to the next field, or click in the next field's box to move the insertion point there.

7. **Click New to add Jeffrey Chavez's record and open another blank data form, enter the record for Cathy Relman as shown in Figure H-6, then click Close**
   The list records that you add with the data form are placed at the end of the list and are formatted in the same way as the previous records.

8. **Scroll down the worksheet to bring rows 46 and 47 into view, check both new records, return to cell A1, then save the workbook**

FIGURE H-5: Data form showing first record in the list

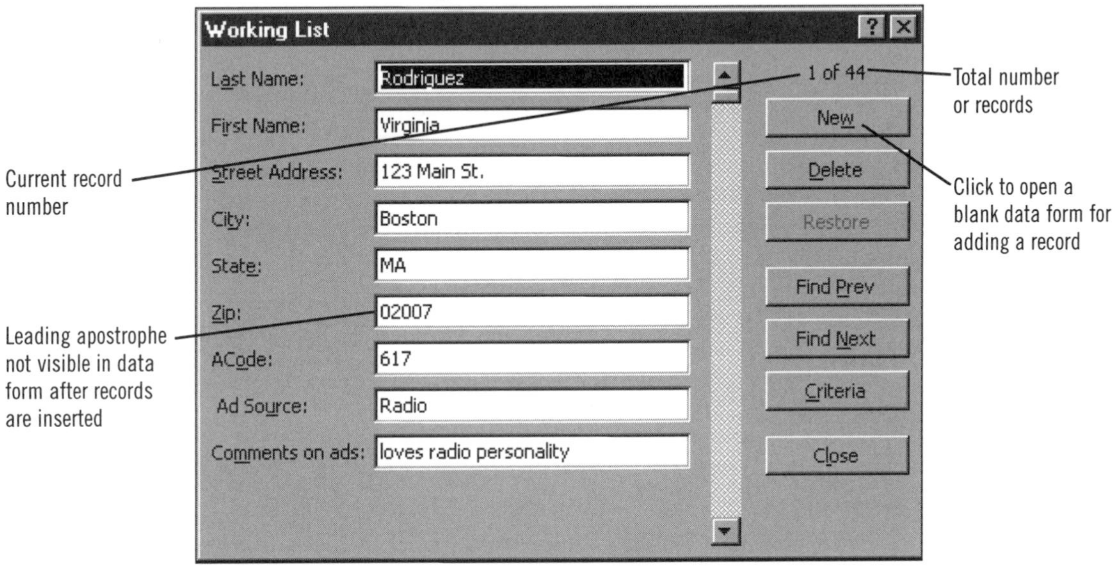

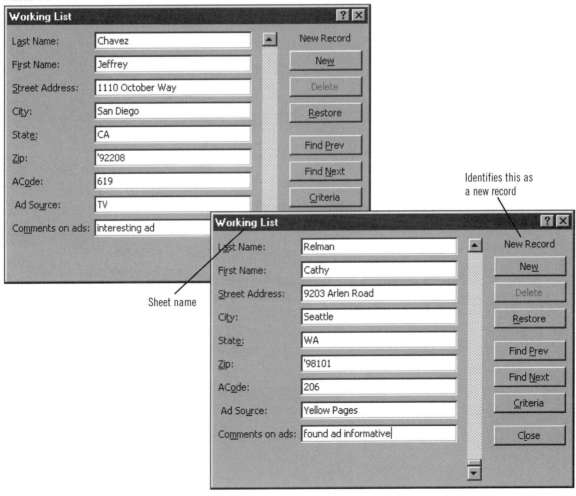

Current record number

Leading apostrophe not visible in data form after records are inserted

Total number or records

Click to open a blank data form for adding a record

FIGURE H-6: Two data forms with information for two new records

Sheet name

Identifies this as a new record

Finding Records

From time to time, you need to locate specific records in your list. You can use the Excel Find command on the Edit menu or the data form to search your list. Also, you can use the Replace command on the Edit menu to locate and replace existing entries or portions of entries with specified information. **Scenario** Jim wants to be more specific about the radio ad source, so he replaces "Radio" with "KWIN Radio." He also wants to know how many of the new customers originated from the company's TV ads. Jim begins by searching for those records with the ad source "TV".

Trouble?

If you receive the message "No list found", select any cell within the list, then repeat Step 1

1. **From any cell within the list, click Data on the menu bar, click Form, then click Criteria**

   The data form changes so that all fields are blank and "Criteria" appears in the upper-right corner. See Figure H-7. You want to search for records whose Ad Source field contains the label "TV".

2. **Press [Alt][U] to move to the Ad Source box, type TV, then click Find Next**

   Excel displays the first record for a customer who learned about the company through its TV ads. See Figure H-8.

QuickTip

You can also use comparison operators when performing a search using the data form. For example, you could specify >50,000 in a Salary field box to return those records in the Salary field with a value greater than $50,000.

3. **Click Find Next until there are no more matching records, then click Close**

   There are six customers whose ad source is TV. Next, Jim wants to make the radio ad source more specific.

4. **Return to cell A1, click Edit on the menu bar, then click Replace**

   The Replace dialog box opens with the insertion point located in the Find what box. See Figure H-9.

5. **Type Radio in the Find what box, then click the Replace with box**

   Jim wants to search for entries containing "Radio" and replace them with "KWIN Radio".

6. **Type KWIN Radio in the Replace with box**

   You are about to perform the search and replace option specified. Because you notice that there are other list entries containing the word "radio" with a lowercase "r" (in the Comments column), you need to make sure that only capitalized instances of the word are replaced.

7. **Click the Match case box to select it, then click Find Next**

   Excel moves the cell pointer to the first occurrence of "Radio".

8. **Click Replace All**

   The dialog box closes, and you complete the replacement and check to make sure all references to "Radio" in the Ad Source column now read "KWIN Radio". Note that in the Comments column, each instance of the word "radio" remains unchanged.

9. **Make sure there are no entries in the Ad Source column that read "Radio", then save the workbook**

FIGURE H-7: Criteria data form

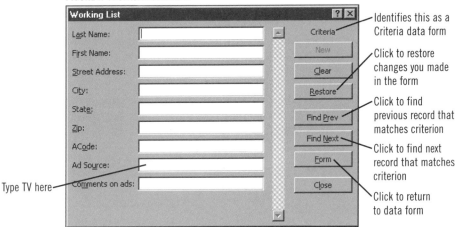

Identifies this as a
Criteria data form

Click to restore
changes you made
in the form

Click to find
previous record that
matches criterion

Click to find next
record that matches
criterion

Click to return
to data form

Type TV here

FIGURE H-8: Finding a record using the data form

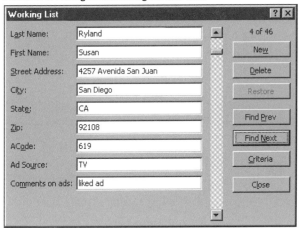

FIGURE H-9: Replace dialog box

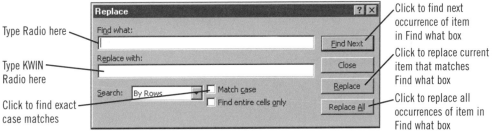

Type Radio here

Type KWIN
Radio here

Click to find exact
case matches

Click to find next
occurrence of item
in Find what box

Click to replace current
item that matches
Find what box

Click to replace all
occurrences of item in
Find what box

CLUES TO USE

Using wildcards to fine-tune your search

You can use special symbols called **wildcards** when defining search criteria in the data form or Replace dialog box. The question mark (?) wildcard stands for any single character. For example, if you do not know whether a customer's last name is Paulsen or Paulson, you can specify Pauls?n as the search criteria to locate

both options. The asterisk (*) wildcard stands for any group of characters. For example, if you specify Jan* as the search criteria in the First Name field, Excel locates all records with first names beginning with Jan (for instance, Jan, Janet, Janice, and so forth).

Excel 2000

Deleting Records

You need to keep your list up to date by removing obsolete records. One way to remove records is to use the Delete button on the data form. You can also delete all records that meet certain criteria—that is, records that have something in common. For example, you can specify a criterion for Excel to find the next record containing ZIP code 01879, then remove the record using the Delete button. If specifying one criterion does not meet your needs, you can set multiple criteria. **Scenario** After he notices two entries for Carolyn Smith, Jim wants to check the database for additional duplicate entries. He uses the data form to delete the duplicate record.

Steps 1234

1. Click **Data** on the menu bar, click **Form**, then click **Criteria**
The Criteria data form appears.

> **QuickTip**
> You can use the data form to edit records as well as to add, search for, and delete them. Just find the desired record and edit the data directly in the appropriate box.

2. Type **Smith** in the **Last Name box**, click the **First Name box**, type **Carolyn**, then click **Find Next**
Excel displays the first record for a customer whose name is Carolyn Smith. You decide to leave the initial entry for Carolyn Smith (record 5 of 46) and delete the second one, once you confirm it is a duplicate.

3. Click **Find Next**
The duplicate record for Carolyn Smith, number 40, appears as shown in Figure H-10. You are ready to delete the duplicate entry.

> **QuickTip**
> Clicking Restore on the data form will not restore deleted record(s).

4. Click **Delete**, then click **OK** to confirm the deletion
The duplicate record for Carolyn Smith is deleted, and all the other records move up one row. The data form now shows the record for Manuel Julio.

5. Click **Close** to return to the worksheet, scroll down until rows 41-46 are visible, then read the entry in row 41
Notice that the duplicate entry for Carolyn Smith is gone and that Manuel Julio moved up a row and is now in row 41. You also notice a record for K. C. Splint in row 43, which is a duplicate entry.

6. Return to cell A1, and read the record information for K. C. Splint in row 8
After confirming the duplicate entry, you decide to delete the row.

7. Click cell **A8**, click **Edit** on the menu bar, then click **Delete**
The Delete dialog box opens, as shown in Figure H-11.

> **QuickTip**
> You can also delete selected cells in a row. Highlight the cells to delete, choose Delete from the Edit menu, and, in the dialog box, indicate if the remaining cells should move up or to the left to replace the selection. Use this command with caution in lists, since with lists you usually delete an entire row.

8. Click the **Entire row option button**, then click **OK**
You have deleted the entire row. The duplicate record for K. C. Splint is deleted and the other records move up to fill in the gap.

9. Save the workbook
Recall that you can delete a range name by following these steps: click Insert on the menu bar, point to Name, click Define, highlight the range name, and click delete.

FIGURE H-10: Data form showing duplicate record for Carolyn Smith

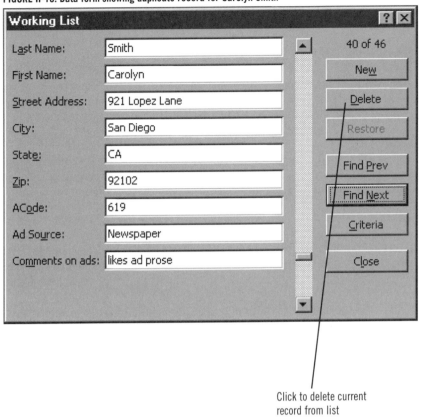

Click to delete current
record from list

FIGURE H-11: Delete dialog box

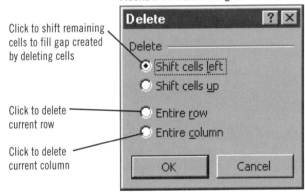

Click to shift remaining
cells to fill gap created
by deleting cells

Click to delete
current row

Click to delete
current column

CLUES TO USE

Advantage of deleting records from the worksheet

When you delete a record using the data form, you cannot undo your deletion. When you delete a record by deleting the row in which it resides inside the worksheet area, however, you can immediately restore the record by using the Undo command on the Edit menu, using the Undo button, or pressing [Ctrl][Z].

Sorting a List by One Field

Usually, you enter records in the order in which they are received, rather than in alphabetical or numerical order. When you add records to a list using the data form, the records are added to the end of the list. Using the Excel sorting feature, you can rearrange the order of the records. You can use the sort buttons on the Standard toolbar to sort records by one field, or you can use the Sort command on the Data menu to perform more complicated sorts. Alternatively, you can sort an entire list or any portion of a list, or you can arrange sorted information in ascending or descending order. In ascending order, the lowest value (the beginning of the alphabet, for instance, or the earliest date) appears at the top of the list. In a field containing labels and numbers, numbers come first. In descending order, the highest value (the end of the alphabet or the latest date) appears at the top of the list. In a field containing labels and numbers, labels come first. Table H-3 provides examples of ascending and descending sorts. ▸Scenario▸ Because Jim wants to be able to return the records to their original order following any sorts, he begins by creating a new field called Entry Order. Then he will perform several single field sorts on the list.

QuickTip

Before you sort records, it is a good idea to make a backup copy of your list or create a field that numbers the records so you can return them to their original order, if necessary.

Trouble?

If your sort does not perform as intended, press [Ctrl][Z] immediately to undo the sort and repeat the step.

▸ **1.** Enter the text and format in cell J1 shown in Figure H-12, then AutoFit column J

2. Type **1** in cell J2, press **[Enter]**, type **2** in cell J3, press **[Enter]**, select cells **J2:J3**, drag the fill handle to cell **J45**

With the Entry Order column complete, as shown in Figure H-12, you are ready to sort the list in ascending order by last name. You must position the cell pointer within the column you want to sort prior to issuing the sort command.

▸ **3.** Return to cell A1, then click the **Sort Ascending button** 🔼 on the Standard toolbar

Excel instantly rearranges the records in ascending order by last name, as shown in Figure H-13. You can easily sort the list in descending order by any field.

4. Click cell **G1**, then click the **Sort Descending button** 🔽 on the Standard toolbar

Excel sorts the list, placing those records with higher-digit area codes at the top. Jim wants to update the list range to include original entry order.

5. Select the range **A1:J45**, click the **name box**, type **Database**, then press **[Enter]**

You are now ready to return the list to original entry order.

6. Click cell **J1**, click the **Sort Ascending button** 🔼 on the Standard toolbar, then save the workbook

The list is back to its original order, and the workbook is saved.

TABLE H-3: Sort order options and examples

option	alphabetic	numeric	date	alphanumeric
Ascending	A, B, C	7, 8, 9	1/1, 2/1, 3/1	12A, 99B, DX8, QT7
Descending	C, B, A	9, 8, 7	3/1, 2/1, 1/1	QT7, DX8, 99B, 12A

FIGURE H-12: List with Entry Order field added

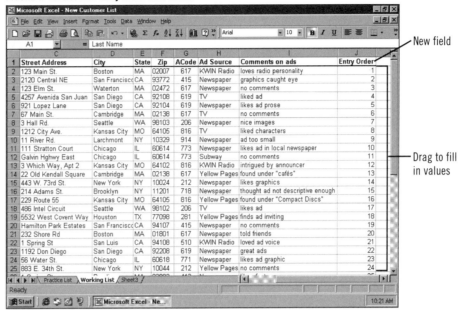

New field

Drag to fill in values

FIGURE H-13: List sorted alphabetically by Last Name

List sorted in ascending order by Last Name

Rotating and indenting to improve label appearance

The column label you added in cell J1 is considerably wider than the data in the column. In cases like this, you can adjust the format of any label or value: Select the cell, click Format on the menu bar, click Cells, and on the Alignment tab drag the red diamond under Orientation to 90 degrees. You can also add space to the left of any label or value by selecting the cell(s) and clicking the Increase Indent button on the Formatting toolbar.

Excel 2000

Sorting a List by Multiple Fields

You can sort lists by as many as three fields by specifying **sort keys**, the criteria on which the sort is based. To perform sorts on multiple fields, you must use the Sort dialog box, which you access through the Sort command on the Data menu. Scenario▶ Jim wants to sort the records alphabetically by state first, then within the state by ZIP code.

Steps 1234

1. Click the **name box list arrow**, then click **Database**
   The list is selected. To sort the list by more than one field, you will need to use the Sort command on the Data menu.

QuickTip

You can specify a capitalization sort by clicking Options in the Sort dialog box, then clicking the Case sensitive box. When you choose this option, lowercase entries precede uppercase entries.

2. Click **Data** on the menu bar, then click **Sort**
   The Sort dialog box opens, as shown in Figure H-14. You want to sort the list by state and then by ZIP code.

3. Click the **Sort by** list arrow, click **State**, then click the **Ascending option button** to select it, if necessary
   The list will be sorted alphabetically in ascending order (A-Z) by the State field. A second sort criterion will sort the entries within each state grouping.

4. Click the top **Then by list arrow**, click **Zip**, then click the **Descending option button**
   You also could sort by a third key by selecting a field in the bottom Then by list box.

5. Click **OK** to execute the sort, press **[Ctrl][Home]**, then scroll through the list to see the result of the sort
   The list is sorted alphabetically by state in ascending order, then within each state by ZIP code in descending order. Compare your results with Figure H-15.

6. Return to cell A1, then save the workbook

FIGURE H-14: Sort dialog box

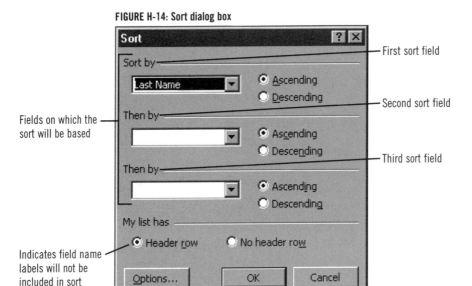

First sort field

Second sort field

Third sort field

Fields on which the sort will be based

Indicates field name labels will not be included in sort

FIGURE H-15: List sorted by multiple fields

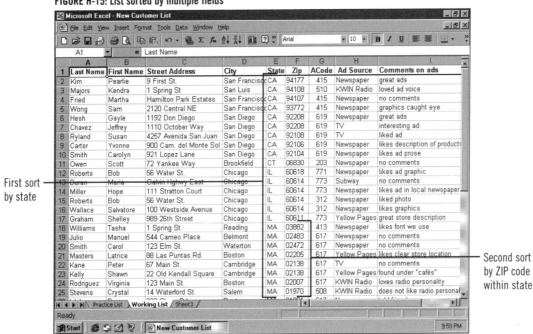

First sort by state

Second sort by ZIP code within state

CLUES TO USE

Specifying a custom sort order

You can identify a custom sort order for the field selected in the Sort by box. To do this, click Options in the Sort dialog box, click the First key sort order list arrow, then click the desired custom order.

Commonly used custom sort orders are days of the week (Mon, Tues, Wed, etc.) and months (Jan, Feb, Mar, etc.); alphabetic sorts do not sort these items properly.

Excel 2000

Printing a List

If a list is small enough to fit on one page, you can print it as you would any other Excel work-sheet. If you have more columns than can fit on a portrait-oriented page, try setting the page orientation to landscape. Because lists often have more rows than can fit on a page, you can define the first row of the list (containing the field names) as the **print title**, which prints at the top of every page. Most lists do not have any descriptive information above the field names on the worksheet. To augment the information contained in the field names, you can use headers and footers to add identifying text, such as the list title or report date. If you want to exclude any fields from your list report, you can hide the desired columns from view so that they do not print. Scenario▶ Jim has finished updating his list and is ready to print it. He begins by previewing the list.

Steps 1234

1. **Click the Print Preview button** 🔍 **on the Standard toolbar**
   Notice that the status bar reads Page 1 of 2. You want all the fields in the list to fit on a single page, but you'll need two pages to fit all the data. The landscape page orientation and the Fit to options will help you do this.

QuickTip

You can print multiple ranges at the same time by clicking the Print area box in the Sheet tab. Then drag to the select areas you wish to print.

2. **From the Print Preview window, click Setup, click the Page tab, click the Landscape option button** under Orientation, click the **Fit to option button** under Scaling, double-click the **tall box** and type **2**, click **OK**, then click **Next**
   The list still does not fit on a single page. Because the records on page 2 appear without column headings, you want to set up the first row of the list, containing the field names, as a repeating print title.

QuickTip

You can also use the sheet tab to specify whether you want gridlines, high or low print quality, and row and column headings.

3. **Click Close to exit the Print Preview window, click File on the menu bar, click Page Setup, click the Sheet tab, click the Rows to repeat at top box** under Print titles, click any cell in row 1, then click OK
   When you select row 1 as a print title, Excel automatically inserts an absolute reference to a beginning row to repeat at the top of each page—in this case, the print title to repeat beginning and ending with row 1. See Figure H-16.

4. **Click Print Preview, click Next to view the second page, then click Zoom**
   Setting up a print title to repeat row 1 causes the field names to appear at the top of each printed page. You can use the worksheet header to provide information about the list.

5. **Click Setup, click the Header/Footer tab, click Custom Header, click the Left section box** and type your name, then click the **Center section box** and type **MediaLoft—New Customer List**

6. **Select the header text in the Center section box, click the Font button** 🄰, change the font size to **14** and the style to **Bold**, click **OK**, click **OK** again to return to the Header/Footer tab, then click **OK** to preview the list
   Page 2 of the report appears as shown in Figure H-17.

QuickTip

To print a selected area instead of the entire work-sheet, select the area, click File, click Print, and, under Print what, click Selection.

7. **Click Print to print the worksheet, then save and close the workbook**
   To print more than one worksheet, select each sheet tab while holding down the [Shift] or [Ctrl] keys, then click the print button on the standard toolbar.

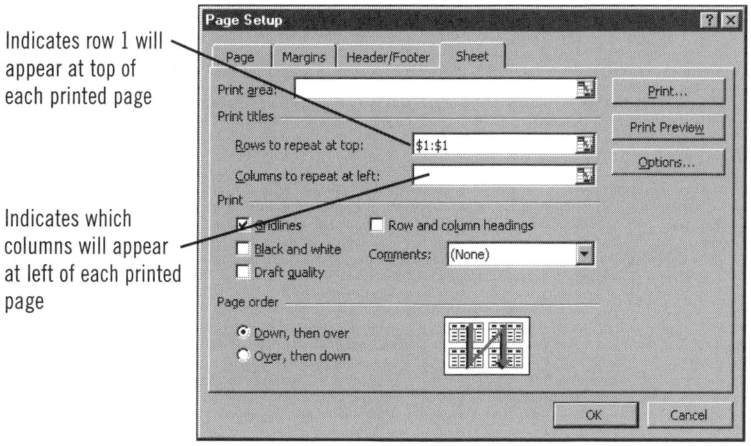

FIGURE H-16: Sheet tab of the Page Setup dialog box

Indicates row 1 will
appear at top of
each printed page

Indicates which
columns will appear
at left of each printed
page

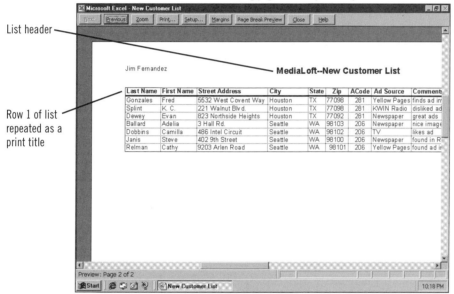

FIGURE H-17: Print Preview window showing page 2 of completed report

List header

Row 1 of list
repeated as a
print title

Setting a print area

There are times when you want to print only part
of a worksheet. You can do this in the Print dialog
box by choosing Selection under Print what. But if
you want to print a selected area repeatedly, it's
best to define a **print area**, which will print when
you click the Print button on the Standard toolbar. To set a print area, click View on the menu
bar, then click Page Break Preview. In the preview
window, select the area you want to print. Right-
click the area, then select Set Print Area. The print
area becomes outlined in a blue border. You can

drag the border to extend the print area (see
Figure H-18) or add nonadjacent cells to it by select-
ing them, right-clicking them, then selecting Add to
Print Area. To clear a print area, click File on the
menu bar, point to Print Area, then click Clear
Print Area.

FIGURE H-18: Defined print area

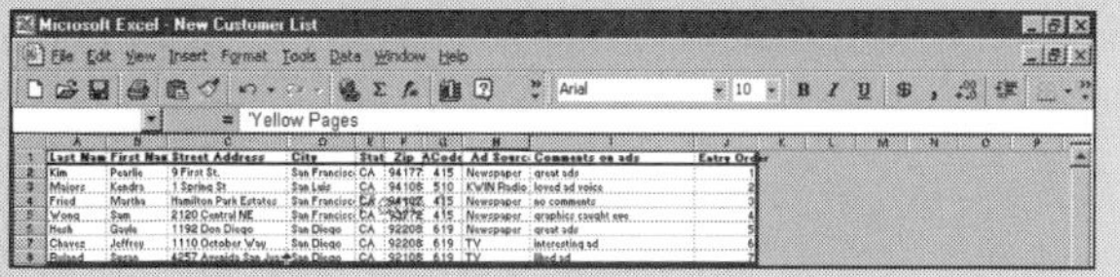

Practice

► Concepts Review

Label each of the elements of the Excel screen shown in Figure H-19.

FIGURE H-19

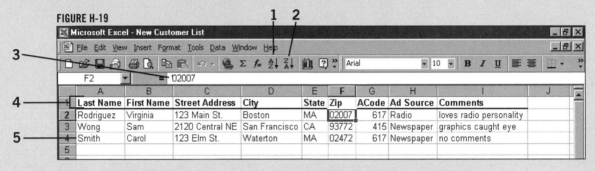

Match each term with the statement that best describes it.

6. List
7. Record
8. Database
9. Sort
10. Field name

a. Type of software used for lists containing more than 65,536 records
b. Organized collection of related information in Excel
c. Row in an Excel list
d. Arrange records in a particular sequence
e. Label positioned at the top of the column identifying data for that field

Select the best answer from the list of choices.

11. **Which of the following Excel sorting options do you use to sort a list of employee names in A-to-Z order?**
    a. Descending
    b. Absolute
    c. Alphabetic
    d. Ascending

12. **Which of the following series is in descending order?**
    a. 8, 6, 4, C, B, A
    b. C, B, A, 6, 5, 4
    c. 8, 7, 6, 5, 6, 7
    d. 4, 5, 6, A, B, C

13. **Once the _____ is defined, any new records added to the list using the data form are included in the _____.**
    a. list range, list range
    b. data form, data form
    c. worksheet, worksheet
    d. database, database

14. **When printing a list on multiple pages, you can define a print title containing repeating row(s) to**
    a. Exclude from the printout all rows under the first row.
    b. Include field names at the top of each printed page.
    c. Include the header in list reports.
    d. Include appropriate fields in the printout.

► Skills Review

1. **Create a list.**
   a. Create a new workbook, then save it as "MediaLoft New York Employee List".
   b. In cell A1, type the title "MediaLoft New York Employees".
   c. Enter the field names and records using the information in Table H-4.
   d. Apply bold formatting to the field names.
   e. Center the entries in the Years, Full/Part Time, and Training? fields.
   f. Adjust the column widths to make the data readable.
   g. Save, then print the list.

TABLE H-4

Last Name	First Name	Years	Position	Full/Part Time	Training?
Lustig	Sarah	3	Book Sales	F	Y
Marino	Donato	2	CD Sales	P	N
Khederian	Jay	4	Video Sales	F	Y
Finney	Carol	1	Stock	F	N
Rabinowicz	Miriam	2	Café Sales	P	Y

2. Add records with the data form.

  a. Select all the records in the list, including the field names, then define the range as "Database".

  b. Open the data form and add a new record for David Gitano, a one-year employee in Book Sales. David is full time and has not completed the training.

  c. Add a new record for George Worley, the café manager. George is full time, has worked there two years, and he has completed the training.

  d. Save the list.

3. Find and delete records.

  a. Find the record for Carol Finney.

  b. Delete the record.

  c. Save the list.

4. Sort a list by one field.

  a. Select the Database list range.

  b. Sort the list alphabetically in ascending order by last name.

  c. Save the list.

5. Sort a list by multiple fields.

  a. Select the Database list range.

  b. Sort the list alphabetically in ascending order, first by whether or not the employees have completed training and then by last name.

  c. Save the list.

6. Print a list.

  a. Add a header that reads "Employee Information" in the center and that includes your name on the right; format both header items in bold.

  b. Set the print area to include the range A1:F9.

  c. Delete the database range.

  d. Print the list, then save and close the workbook.

  e. Exit Excel.

Visual Workshop

Create the worksheet shown in Figure H-20. Save the workbook as "Famous Jazz Performers". Once you've entered the field names and records, sort the list by Contribution to Jazz and then by Last Name. Change the page setup so that the list is centered on the page horizontally and the header reads "Famous Jazz Performers". Preview and print the list, then save the workbook.

FIGURE H-20

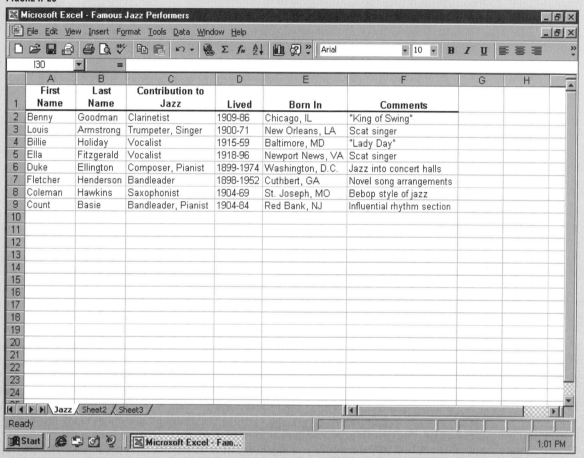

Analyzing

List Data

Objectives

- ▶ **Retrieve records with AutoFilter**
- ▶ **Create a custom filter**
- ▶ **Filter a list with Advanced Filter**
- ▶ **Extract list data**
- ▶ **Create subtotals using grouping and outlines**
- ▶ **Look up values in a list**
- ▶ **Summarize list data**
- ▶ **Use data validation for list entries**

There are many ways to **analyze**, or manipulate, list data with Excel. One way is to filter a list so that only the rows that meet certain criteria are retrieved. In this unit you will retrieve records using AutoFilter, create a custom filter, and filter a list using Excel's Advanced Filter feature. In addition, you will learn to insert automatic subtotals, use lookup functions to locate list entries, and apply database functions to summarize list data that meets specific criteria. You'll also learn how to restrict entries in a column using data validation. Scenario▶ Jim Fernandez recently conducted a survey for the MediaLoft Marketing department. He mailed questionnaires to a random selection of customers at all stores. After the questionnaires were returned, he entered all the data into Excel, where he will analyze the data and create reports.

Excel 2000

Retrieving Records with AutoFilter

The Excel AutoFilter feature searches for records that meet criteria the user specifies, and then lists those matching records. One way is to **filter** out, or hide, data that fails to meet certain criteria. You can filter specific values in a column, use the predefined Top 10 option to filter records based on upper or lower values in a column, or create a custom filter. For example, you can filter a customer list to retrieve names of only those customers residing in Canada. You also can filter records based on a specific field and request that Excel retrieve only those records having an entry (or no entry) in that field. Once you create a filtered list, you can print it or copy it to another part of the worksheet to manipulate it further. ▐Scenario▶ Jim is now ready to work on his survey information. He begins by retrieving data on only those customers who live in Chicago, Illinois.

Steps 123 4

QuickTip

To return personalized tool-bars and menus to their default state, click Tools on the menu bar, click Customize, click the Options tab in the Customize dialog box, click Reset my usage data to restore the default settings, click Yes, click Close, then close the Drawing toolbar if it is displayed.

1. Open the workbook titled **EX I-1**, then save it as **Survey Data**
The AutoFilter feature will enable you to retrieve the records for the report.

2. Click **Data** on the menu bar, point to **Filter**, then click **AutoFilter**
List arrows appear to the right of each field name.

3. Click the **City** list arrow
An AutoFilter list containing the different city options appears below the field name, as shown in Figure I-1. Because you want to retrieve data for only those customers who live in Chicago, "Chicago" will be your **search criterion**.

4. In the filter list, click **Chicago**
Only those records containing Chicago in the City field appear, as shown in Figure I-2. The status bar indicates the number of matching records (in this case, 5 of 35), the color of the row numbers changes for the matching records, and the color of the list arrow for the filtered field changes. Next, you want to retrieve information about those customers who purchased the most merchandise. To do so, you must clear the previous filter.

5. Click **Data** on the menu bar, point to **Filter**, then click **Show All**
All the records reappear.

Trouble?

If the column label in cell A1 covers the column headers, making it difficult to find the appropriate columns, select A2 before scrolling.

6. Scroll right until columns G through N are visible, click the **Purchases to Date** list arrow, then click **(Top 10 . . .)**
The Top 10 AutoFilter dialog box opens. The default is to select the ten records with the highest value. You need to display only the top 2.

7. With **10** selected in the middle box, type **2**, then click **OK**
The records are retrieved for the two customers who purchased the most merchandise, $3,200 and $2,530. See Figure I-3.

8. Click the **Purchases to Date** list arrow, click **(All)**, press **[Ctrl][Home]**, add your name to the right side of the footer, then print the list
You have cleared the filter and all the records reappear. Because you didn't make any changes to the list, there is no need to save the file.

FIGURE I-1: Worksheet showing AutoFilter options

City field

Click Chicago to filter by this city

Field list arrow

AutoFilter list for City field

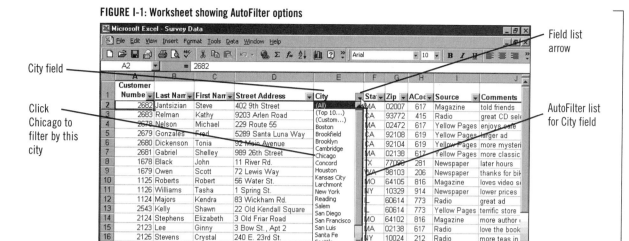

FIGURE I-2: List filtered with AutoFilter

Note break in record numbers

Search based on this field

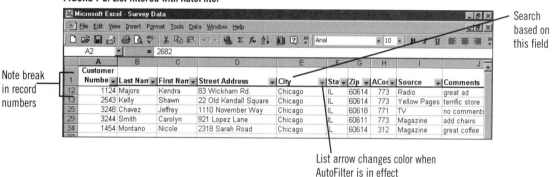

List arrow changes color when AutoFilter is in effect

FIGURE I-3: List filtered with Top 2 AutoFilter criteria

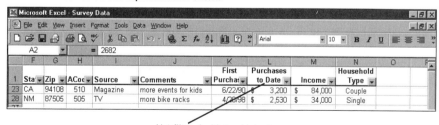

List filtered with two highest values in this field

Excel 2000

Creating a Custom Filter

So far, you have used the AutoFilter command to filter rows based on an entry in a single column. You can perform more complex filters using options in the Custom AutoFilter dialog box. For example, you can filter rows based on two entries in a single column or use comparison operators such as "greater than" or "less than" to display only those records with amounts greater than $50,000 in a particular column. ▸Scenario▸ Jim's next task is to locate those customers who live west of the Rocky Mountains, who live in a "single" household, and who heard about MediaLoft through a magazine advertisement.

Steps 1234

QuickTip

When specifying criteria in the Custom AutoFilter dialog box, use the ? wildcard to specify any single character and the * wildcard to specify any series of characters.

Trouble?

If no records are displayed in the worksheet, you may have forgotten to type the apostrophe before the number 81000. Repeat Steps 2 and 3, making sure you include the leading apostrophe.

1. Click the **Zip** list arrow, then click **(Custom . . .)**
The Custom AutoFilter dialog box opens. Because you know that all residents west of the Rockies have a ZIP code greater than 81000, you specify this criterion here. Because all the ZIP codes in the list were originally entered as labels with leading apostrophes, you need to include this apostrophe when entering the ZIP code value.

2. Click the **Zip** list arrow, click **is greater than**, press **[Tab]**, then type **'81000**
Your completed Custom AutoFilter dialog box should match Figure I-4.

3. Click **OK**
The dialog box closes, and only those records having a ZIP code greater than 81000 appear in the worksheet. Now, you'll narrow the list even further by displaying only those customers who live in a single household.

4. Scroll right until columns G through N are visible, click the **Household Type** list arrow, then click **Single**
The list of records retrieved has narrowed. Finally, you need to filter out all customers except those who heard about MediaLoft through a magazine advertisement.

5. Click the **Source** list arrow, then click **Magazine**
Your final filtered list now shows only customers in single households west of the Rocky Mountains who heard about MediaLoft through magazine ads. See Figure I-5.

6. Preview, then print the worksheet
The worksheet prints using the existing print settings—landscape orientation, scaled to fit on a single page.

7. Click **Data** on the menu bar, point to **Filter**, click **AutoFilter** to deselect it, then press **[Ctrl][Home]**
You have cleared the filter, and all the customer records appear.

FIGURE I-4: Custom AutoFilter dialog box

Value includes
leading apostrophe

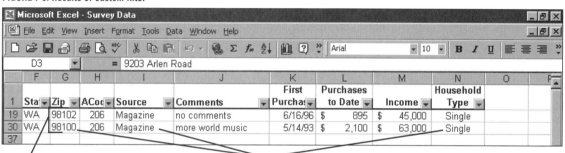

FIGURE I-5: Results of custom filter

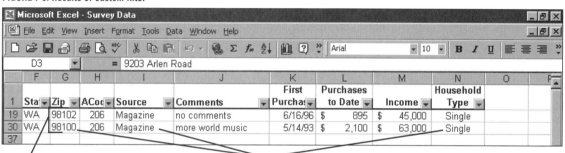

ZIP codes greater than 81000   Fields used in custom filter

And and Or logical conditions

You can narrow a search even further by using the
And or Or buttons in the Custom AutoFilter dialog box. For example, you can select records for
those customers with homes in California *and*
Texas as well as select records for customers with
homes in California *or* Texas. See Figure I-6. When
used in this way, "And" and "Or" are often referred
to as logical conditions. When you search for customers with homes in California *and* Texas, you
are specifying an And condition. When you search
for customers with homes in either California *or*
Texas, you are specifying an Or condition.

FIGURE I-6: Using the Custom AutoFilter dialog box

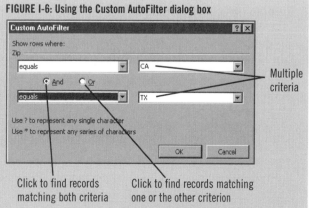

Multiple
criteria

Click to find records
matching both criteria

Click to find records matching
one or the other criterion

Filtering a List with Advanced Filter

The Advanced Filter command allows you to search for data that matches complicated criteria in more than one column, using And and Or conditions. To use advanced filtering, you must define a criteria range. A **criteria range** is a cell range containing one row of labels (usually a copy of the column labels) and at least one additional row underneath the row of labels that contains the criteria you want to match. Scenario Jim's next task is to identify customers who have been buying at MediaLoft since before May 1, 1999, and whose total purchases are less than or equal to $1,000. He will use the Advanced Filter command to retrieve this data. Jim begins by defining the criteria range.

1. Select **rows 1 through 6**, click **Insert** on the menu bar, then click **Rows**; click cell **A1**, type **Criteria Range**, click cell **A6**, type **List Range**, then click the **Enter button** [✓] on the formula bar

   See Figure I-7. Six blank rows are added above the list. Excel does not require the labels "Criteria Range" and "List Range," but they are useful because they help organize the worksheet. It will be helpful to see the column labels. (In the next step, if the column labels make it difficult for you to drag the pointer to cell N7, try clicking N7 first; then drag the pointer all the way left to cell A7.)

Trouble?

If the Copy button does not appear on your Standard tool-bar, click the More Buttons button [»] to view it.

2. Select range **A7:N7**, click the **Copy button** [📋] on the Standard toolbar, click cell **A2**, then press **[Enter]**

   Next, you need to specify that you want records for only those customers who have been customers since before May 1 and who have purchased no more than $1,000. In other words, you need records with a date before (less than) May 1, 1999 (<5/1/99) and a Purchases to Date amount that is less than or equal to $1,000 (<=1000).

3. Scroll right until columns H through N are visible, click cell **K3**, type **< 5/1/99**, click cell **L3**, type **<=1000**, then click [✓]

   This enters the criteria in the cells directly beneath the Criteria Range labels. See Figure I-8. Placing the criteria in the same row indicates that the records you are searching for must match both criteria; that is, it specifies an And condition.

4. Press **[Ctrl][Home]**, click **Data** on the menu bar, point to **Filter**, then click **Advanced Filter**

   The Advanced Filter dialog box opens, with the list range already entered. (Notice that the default setting under Action is to filter the list in its current location rather than copy it to another location. You will change this setting later.)

5. Click the **Criteria Range box**, select range **A2:N3** in the worksheet (move the dialog box if necessary), then click **OK**

   You have specified the criteria range. The filtered list contains 19 records that match both the criteria—their first purchase was before 5/1/99 and their purchases to date total less than $1,000. You'll filter this list even further in the next lesson.

FIGURE I-7: Using the Advanced Filter command

New rows —
New labels

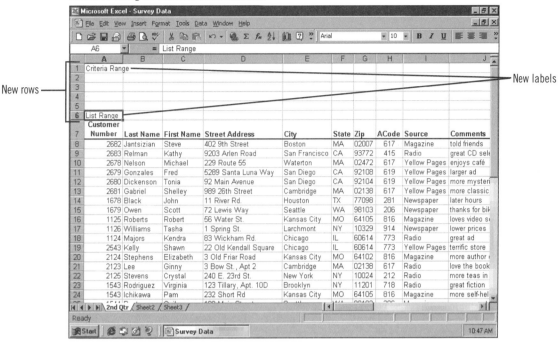

FIGURE I-8: Criteria in the same row

Subsequent filtered records will match these criteria

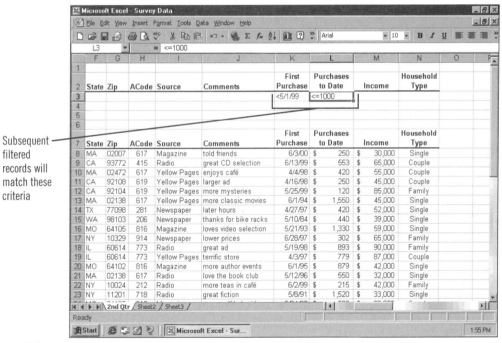

Understanding the criteria range

When you define the criteria range in the Advanced Filter dialog box, Excel automatically creates a name for this range in the worksheet (Criteria). The criteria range includes the field names and any criteria rows underneath the names.

Excel 2000

Extracting List Data

Whenever you take the time to specify a complicated set of search criteria, it's a good idea to extract the matching records. When you **extract** data, you place a copy of a filtered list in a range you specify in the Advanced Filter dialog box. That way, you won't accidentally clear the filter or lose track of the records you spent time compiling. **Scenario** Jim needs to filter the previous list one step further to reflect only those customers in the current filtered list who heard of MediaLoft through TV or a magazine ad. To complete this filter, he will specify an Or condition by entering two sets of criteria in two separate rows. He decides to save the matching records by extracting them to a different location in the worksheet.

Steps

1. **Click cell I3, type TV, then press [Enter]; in cell I4, type Magazine, click the Enter button ☑ on the formula bar, then copy the criteria in K3:L3 to K4:L4**
   See Figure I-9. This time, you'll indicate that you want to copy the filtered list to a range beginning in cell A50.

2. **Click Data on the menu bar, point to Filter, then click Advanced Filter; under Action, click the Copy to another location option button to select it, click the Copy to box, then type A50**
   The last time you filtered the list, the criteria range included only rows 2 and 3, and now you have criteria in row 4.

   > **Trouble?**
   >
   > Make sure the criteria range in the Advanced Filter dialog box includes the field names and the number of rows underneath the names that contain criteria. If you leave a blank row in the criteria range, Excel filters nothing and shows all records.

3. **In the Criteria Range box, edit the current formula to read $A$2:$N$4, click OK; then scroll down until row 50 is visible**
   You have changed the criteria range to include row 4. The matching records are copied to the range beginning in cell A50. The original list (starting in cell A7) contains the records filtered in the previous lesson. See Figure I-10.

4. **Select range A50:N61, click File on the menu bar, click Print, under Print what, click the Selection option button, click Preview, then click Print**
   The selected area prints.

5. **Press [Ctrl][Home], click Data on the menu bar, point to Filter, then click Show All**
   All the records in the range reappear. You return to the original list, which starts at its new location in cell A7.

6. **Save, then close the workbook**

FIGURE I-9: Criteria in separate rows

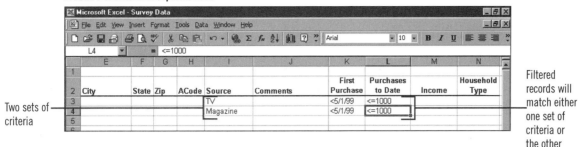

Two sets of criteria

Filtered records will match either one set of criteria or the other

FIGURE I-10: Extracted data records

Extracted records copied to the range starting at cell A50

	Street Address	City	State	Zip	ACode	Source	Comments	First Purchase	Purchases to Date	
50	Street Address	City	State	Zip	ACode	Source	Comments	First Purchase	Purchases to Date	
51	3 Old Friar Road	Kansas City	MO	64102	816	Magazine	more author events	6/1/95	$ 879	$
52	232 Short Rd	Kansas City	MO	64105	816	Magazine	more self-help videos	5/24/96	$ 530	$
53	100 Main Street	Seattle	WA	98102	206	Magazine	no comments	6/16/96	$ 895	$
54	123 Elm St.	Houston	TX	77098	281	Magazine	salespeople helpful	6/28/98	$ 320	$
55	1110 November Way	Chicago	IL	60618	771	TV	no comments	3/22/99	$ 250	$
56	42 Silver Street	Reading	MA	03882	413	TV	fun store	4/6/87	$ 420	$
57	921 Lopez Lane	Chicago	IL	60611	773	Magazine	add chairs	4/9/93	$ 480	$
58	900 Monument St.	Concord	MA	01742	508	Magazine	love the book club	6/15/97	$ 450	$
59	486 Intel Circuit	Houston	TX	77092	281	TV	very effective ad	5/26/96	$ 990	$
60	2318 Sarah Road	Chicago	IL	60614	312	Magazine	great coffee	4/29/97	$ 640	$
61	2120 Witch Way	Salem	MA	01970	508	Magazine	loves our staff	5/25/97	$ 820	$

Extracted records for customers with first purchase before 5/1/99 or purchases less than $1,000 and who heard about MediaLoft through TV or magazines

Understanding the criteria range and the copy-to location

When you define the criteria range and/or copy-to location in the Advanced Filter dialog box, Excel automatically creates names for these ranges in the worksheet (Criteria and Extract). The criteria range includes the field names and any criteria rows underneath them. The extract range includes just the field names above the extracted list. To extract a different list, simply select Extract as the copy-to location. Excel automatically deletes the old list in the extract area and generates a new list under the field names. Make sure the worksheet has enough blank rows underneath the field names for your data.

Excel 2000

Excel 2000

Creating Subtotals Using Grouping and Outlines

The Excel subtotals feature provides a quick, easy way to group and summarize data in a list. Usually, you create subtotals with the SUM function. You also can subtotal groups with functions such as COUNT, AVERAGE, MAX, and MIN. Your list must have field names and be sorted before you can issue the Subtotal command. **Scenario** Jim wants to create a list grouped by advertising source, with subtotals for purchases to date and household income. He starts by sorting the list in ascending order—first by advertising source, then by state, and, finally, by city.

1. Open the workbook titled **EX I-1**, then save it as **Survey Data 2**

2. Click the **Name Box** list arrow, click **Database**, click **Data** on the menu bar, then click **Sort**; click the **Sort by** list arrow, click **Source**, click the first **Then by** list arrow, click **State**, click the **Ascending option button** to set the Then by sort order; click the second **Then by** list arrow, click **City**, then click **OK**

   You have sorted the list in ascending order, first by advertising source, then by state, and, finally, by city.

Trouble?

You may receive the following message: "No list found. Select a single cell within your list and Microsoft Excel will select the list for you." If you do, this means that you did not select the list before issuing the Subtotals command. Click OK, then repeat Steps 2 and 3.

3. Press **[Ctrl][Home]**, click **Data** on the menu bar, then click **Subtotals**

   Before you use the Subtotals command, you must position the cell pointer within the list range (in this case, range A1:N36). The Subtotal dialog box opens. Here, you specify the items you want subtotaled, the function you want to apply to the values, and the fields you want to summarize.

4. Click the **At each change in** list arrow, click **Source**, click the **Use function** list arrow, click **Sum**; in the Add subtotal to list, click the **Purchases to Date** and **Income** check boxes to select them; if necessary, click the **Household Type** check box to deselect it; then, if necessary, click the **Replace current subtotals** and **Summary below data** check boxes to select them

   Your completed Subtotal dialog box should match Figure I-11.

5. Click **OK**, then scroll to and click cell **L41**

   The subtotaled list appears, showing the calculated subtotals and grand total in columns L and M. See Figure I-12. Notice that Excel displays an outline to the left of the worksheet showing the structure of the subtotaled lists.

6. Preview the worksheet, click **Setup** and place your name on the right side of the footer, then print the worksheet using the current settings

7. Press **[Ctrl][Home]**, click **Data** on the menu bar, click **Subtotals**, then click **Remove All**

   You have turned off the Subtotaling feature. The subtotals are removed, and the Outline feature is turned off automatically. Because you did not alter the worksheet data, there's no need to save the file.

FIGURE I-11: Completed Subtotal dialog box

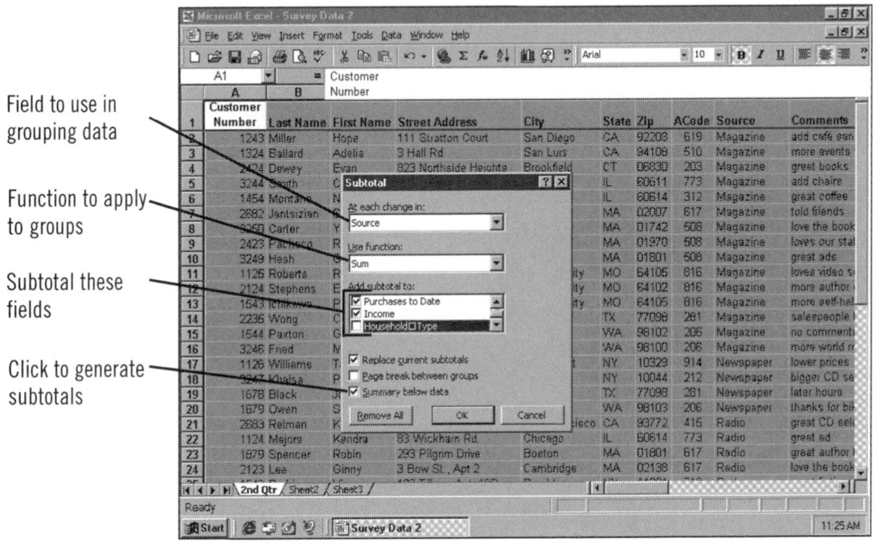

Field to use in grouping data

Function to apply to groups

Subtotal these fields

Click to generate subtotals

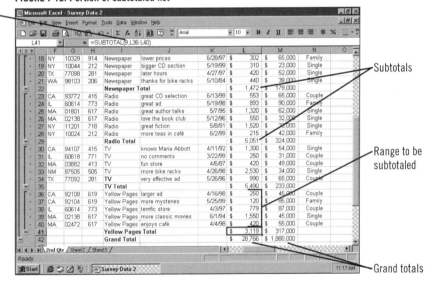

FIGURE I-12: Portion of subtotaled list

Number 9 indicates the SUM function

Subtotals

Range to be subtotaled

Grand totals

CLUES TO USE

Show or hide details in an Excel outline

Once subtotals have been generated, all detail records are displayed in an outline. See Figure I-13. You can then click the Hide Details button □ of your choice to hide that group of records, creating a summary report. You can also create a chart that shows the summary data. Any chart you create will be automatically updated as you show or hide data. You can also click the Show Details button ＋ for the group of data you want to display. To show a specific level of detail, click the row or column level button for the lowest level you want to display. For example, to display levels 1 through 3, click 3 .

FIGURE I-13: Subtotaled list with level 2 details hidden

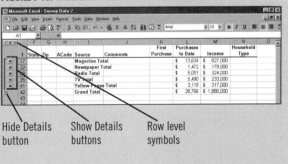

Hide Details button   Show Details buttons   Row level symbols

Unit I

Excel 2000

Looking Up Values in a List

The Excel VLOOKUP function helps you locate specific values in a list. The VLOOKUP searches vertically (V) down the leftmost column of a list and then reads across the row to find the value in the column you specify. The process of looking up a number in a phone book uses the same logic as the Excel VLOOKUP function: You locate a person's name and then read across the row to find the phone number you are looking for. **Scenario** At times, Jim wants to be able to find out what type of household a particular customer lives in simply by entering his or her specific customer number. To do this, he uses the VLOOKUP function. He begins by creating a special list, or table, containing the customer numbers he wants to look up. Then he copies names to a separate location.

Steps

QuickTip

Excel also has a Lookup Wizard to help you perform lookups. It is an Excel add-in (or extra) program. Open the Tools menu, point to Wizards, then click Lookup. If you don't see Wizards on the Tools menu, install the add-in from the Microsoft Office CD.

1. Click cell **C2**, click **Window** on the menu bar, then click **Freeze Panes**; scroll right until columns N through T and rows 1 through 15 are visible

2. Click cell **P1**, type **VLOOKUP Function**, click the **Enter button** ✓ on the formula bar; copy the contents of cell **A1** to cell **R1**, copy the contents of cell **N1** to cell **S1**, widen the columns as necessary to display the text, then click any blank cell
   See Figure I-14. Jim wants to know the household type for customer number 3247.

3. Click cell **R2**, type **3247**, then press **[→]**
   The VLOOKUP function in the Paste Function dialog box will let Jim find the household type for customer number 3247.

Trouble?

If the Office Assistant activates for this task, select the "No" option to indicate you don't want to learn more about this function at the present time. Continue with Step 5.

4. Make sure cell S2 is still selected, click the **Paste Function button** *fx* on the Standard toolbar, under Function category click **Lookup & Reference**, under Function name click **VLOOKUP**, then click **OK**
   The VLOOKUP dialog box opens. Because the value you want to find is in cell R2, that will be the Lookup_value. The list you want to search is the customer list, so its name ("Database") will be the Table_array.

5. Drag the **VLOOKUP dialog box** down so that at least rows 1 and 2 of the worksheet are visible; with the insertion point in the Lookup_value box, click cell **R2**, click the **Table_array box**, then type **DATABASE**
   The column you want to search (Household Type) is the fourteenth column from the left, so the Col_index_num will be 14. Because you want to find an exact match for the value in cell R2, the Range_lookup argument will be FALSE. (If you want to find only the closest match for a value, you enter TRUE in the Range_lookup box, as indicated in the bottom of the VLOOKUP dialog box.)

6. Click the **Col_index_num box**, type **14**, click the **Range_lookup box**, then type **FALSE**
   Your completed VLOOKUP dialog box should match Figure I-15.

Trouble?

If an exact match is not returned, make sure the Range_lookup is set to FALSE.

7. Click **OK**
   Excel searches down the leftmost column of the customer list until it finds a value matching the one in cell R2. Then it finds the household type for that record ("Single") and displays it in cell S2. Now, you'll use this function to determine the household type for one other customer.

8. Click cell **R2**, type **2125**, then click ✓
   The VLOOKUP function returns the value Family in cell S2.

9. Press **[Ctrl][Home]**, then save the workbook.

FIGURE I-14: Worksheet with headings for VLOOKUP

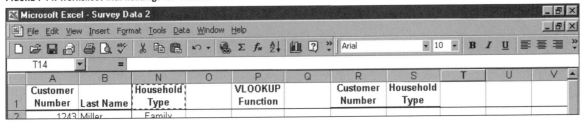

FIGURE I-15: Completed VLOOKUP dialog box

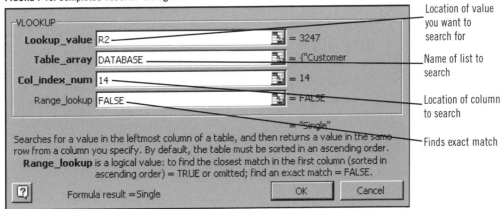

Using the HLOOKUP function

The VLOOKUP (Vertical Lookup) function is useful when your data is arranged vertically in columns. The HLOOKUP (Horizontal Lookup) function is useful when your data is arranged horizontally in rows. HLOOKUP searches horizontally across the topmost row of a list until the matching value is found, then looks down the number of rows you specify. The arguments for this function are identical to those for the VLOOKUP function, with one exception. Instead of a Col_index_number, HLOOKUP uses a Row_index_number, which indicates the location of the row you want to search. For example, if you want to search the fourth row from the top, the Row_index_number should be 4.

Summarizing List Data

Database functions allow you to summarize list data in a variety of ways. For example, you can use them to count, average, or total values in a field for only those records that meet specified criteria. When working with a sales activity list, for instance, you can use Excel to count the number of client contacts by sales representative or to total the amount sold to specific accounts by month. The format for database functions is explained in Figure I-16. **Scenario** Jim wants to summarize the information in his list in two ways. First, he wants to find the total purchases to date for each advertising source. He also wants to count the number of records for each advertising source. Jim begins by creating a criteria range that includes a copy of the column label for the column he wants to summarize, as well as the criterion itself.

1. **With the panes still frozen, scroll down until row 31 is the top row underneath the frozen headings, then enter and format the five labels shown in Figure I-17 in the range: I39:K41**

   The criteria range in I40:I41 tells Excel to summarize records with the entry "Yellow Pages" in the Source column. The functions will be in cells L39 and L41.

QuickTip

You can use a column label, such as "City", in place of a column number. Type the text exactly as it is entered in the list and enclose it in double quotation marks.

2. **Click cell L39, type =DSUM(DATABASE,12,I40:I41), then click the Enter button** 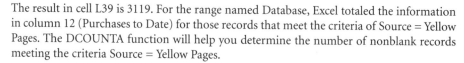 **on the formula bar**

   The result in cell L39 is 3119. For the range named Database, Excel totaled the information in column 12 (Purchases to Date) for those records that meet the criteria of Source = Yellow Pages. The DCOUNTA function will help you determine the number of nonblank records meeting the criteria Source = Yellow Pages.

Trouble?

If the result you receive is incorrect, make sure you entered the formula correctly, using the letter "I" in the criteria range address, and the number one (1) for the column number.

3. **Click cell L41, type =DCOUNTA(DATABASE,1,I40:I41), then click** ☑

   The result in cell L41 is 5, meaning that there are five customers who heard about MediaLoft through the Yellow Pages. This function uses the first field in the list, Customer Number, to check for nonblank cells within the criteria range Source = Yellow Pages. Jim also wants to see total purchases and a count for the magazine ads.

4. **Click cell I41, type Magazine, then click** ☑

   With total purchases of $13,634, it's clear that magazine advertising is the most effective way of attracting MediaLoft customers. Compare your results with Figure I-18.

5. **Press [Ctrl][Home], then save and close the workbook**

FIGURE I-16: Format of database function

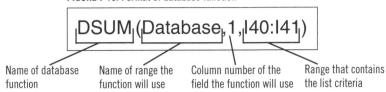

FIGURE I-17: Portion of worksheet showing summary area

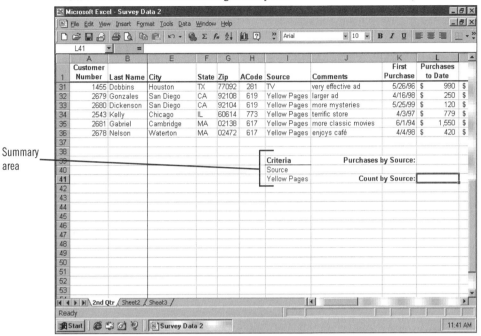

FIGURE I-18: Result generated by database function

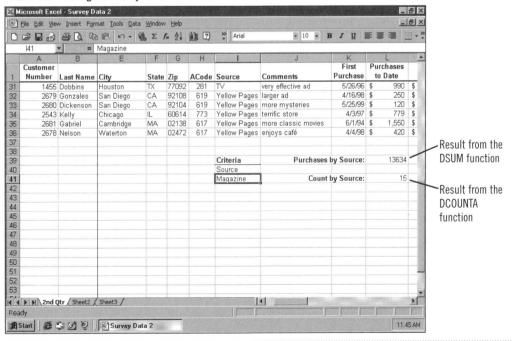

Using Data Validation for List Entries

The Excel Data Validation feature allows you to specify what data is valid for a range of cells. You can restrict data to whole numbers, decimal numbers, or text, or you can set limits on entries. You can also specify a list of acceptable entries. Once you've specified what data is considered valid, Excel prevents users from entering any other data (considered invalid) except your specified choices. **Scenario** Jim wants to make sure that information in the Household Type column is entered consistently in the future. He decides to restrict the entries in that column to three options: Couple, Single, and Family. First, he selects the column he wants to restrict.

Steps

1. Open the workbook titled **EX I-1**, then save it as **Survey Data 3**

2. Scroll right until column N is displayed, then click the **Column N** column header
   The entire column is selected.

QuickTip

To restrict entries to decimal or whole numbers, dates, or times, select the appropriate option in the Allow list. To specify a long list of valid entries, type the list in a column elsewhere in the worksheet, then type the address of the list in the Source box.

3. Click **Data** on the menu bar, click **Validation**, click the **Settings tab** if necessary, click the **Allow** list arrow, then click **List**
   Selecting the List option enables you to type a list of specific options.

4. Click the **Source** box, then type **Couple, Single, Family**
   You have entered the list of acceptable entries, separated by commas. See Figure I-19. Jim wants the data entry person to be able to select a valid entry from a drop-down list.

5. Click the **In-cell Drop-down check box** to select it if necessary, then click **OK**
   The dialog box closes, and you return to the worksheet. The new data restrictions will apply only to new entries in the Household Type column.

6. Click cell **N37**, then click the **list arrow** to display the list of valid entries
   See Figure I-20. You could click an item in the list to have it entered in the cell, but Jim first wants to know what happens if you enter an invalid entry.

7. Click the **list arrow** to close the list, type **Individual**, then press **[Enter]**
   A warning dialog box appears to prevent you from entering the invalid data. See Figure I-21.

8. Click **Cancel**, click the **list arrow**, then click **Single**
   The cell accepts the valid entry. The data restriction ensures that new records will contain only one of the three correct entries in the Household Type column. The customer list is finished and ready for future data entry.

9. Save and close the workbook

FIGURE I-19: Creating data restrictions

Restricts entries to a
list of valid options

List of valid options

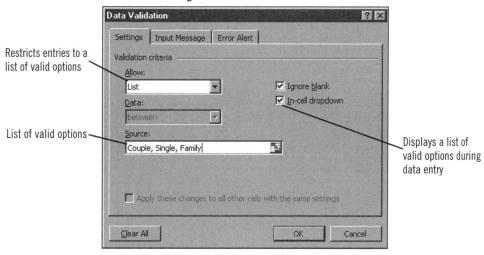

Displays a list of
valid options during
data entry

FIGURE I-20: Entering data in restricted cells

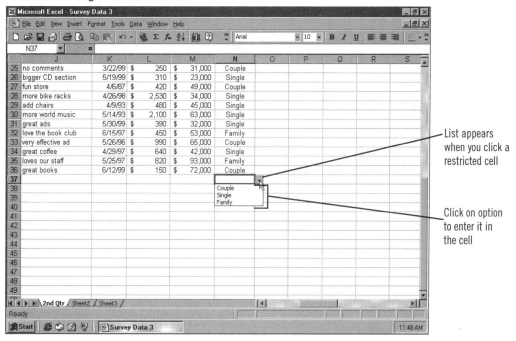

List appears
when you click a
restricted cell

Click on option
to enter it in
the cell

FIGURE I-21: Validation message

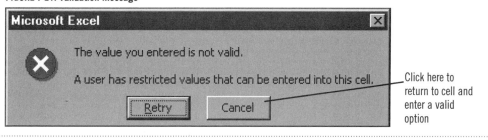

Click here to
return to cell and
enter a valid
option

Practice

► Concepts Review

Explain the function of each element of the Excel screen labeled in Figure I-22.

FIGURE I-22

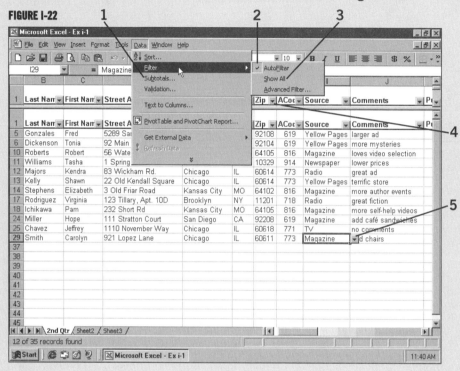

Match each term with the statement that describes it.

6. **HLOOKUP**
7. **Extracted list**
8. **Data validation**
9. **Criteria range**
10. **List range**

a. Range used to specify a database in database functions
b. Range in which search conditions are set
c. Restricts list entries to specified options
d. Cell range when advanced filter results are copied to another location
e. Function to use when data is arranged horizontally in rows

Select the best answer from the list of choices.

11. **You might perform an AutoFilter and search for nonblank entries in order to**
    a. Identify missing data.
    b. Sum records with data in a particular field.
    c. Find records with data in a particular field.
    d. b and c.

12. **What does it mean when you select the Or option when creating a custom filter?**
  a. Custom filter requires a criteria range.
  b. Either criterion can be true to find a match.
  c. Both criteria must be true to find a match.
  d. Neither criterion has to be 100% true.

13. **What must a list have before automatic subtotals can be inserted?**
  a. Formatted cells
  b. Grand totals
  c. Column or field headings
  d. Enough records to show multiple subtotals

▶ Skills Review

1. **Retrieve records with AutoFilter.**
  a. Open the workbook titled EX I-2, then save it as "Compensation Summary".
  b. Use AutoFilter to list records for employees in the Accounting department.
  c. Redisplay all employees, then use AutoFilter to show the three employees with the highest annual salary.
  d. Redisplay all the records.

2. **Create a custom filter.**
  a. Create a custom filter showing employees hired prior to 1/1/90 or after 1/1/94.
  b. Preview, then print the list in A1:J11.
  c. Redisplay all records.
  d. Turn off AutoFilter.

3. **Filter and extract a list with Advanced Filter.**
  a. You will retrieve a list of employees who were hired prior to 1/1/90 and earn more than $60,000 a year. Define a criteria range by copying the field names in range A1:J1 to cell A14.
  b. In cell D15, enter the criterion < 1/1/90, then in cell G15 enter >60000.
  c. Return to cell A1.
  d. Open the Advanced Filter dialog box.
  e. Indicate that you want to copy to another location, enter the criteria range A14:J15, then indicate that you want to copy to cell A18.
  f. If necessary, scroll so that rows 18 through 20 are visible to confirm that the retrieved list meets the criteria.
  g. Change the page setup to landscape orientation, then select and print only the extracted list in range A18:J20.
  h. Use the Edit menu to clear data and formats from the range A14:J20.

4. **Creating subtotals using grouping and outlines.**
  a. Move to cell A1. Sort the list in ascending order by department, then in descending order by monthly salary.
  b. Group and create subtotals by department, using the SUM function; select Monthly Salary in the Add Subtotal to list box, deselect Annual Comp., then click OK.
  c. AutoFit column E.
  d. Use the outline to display only the subtotals, preview, then print only the subtotaled list in landscape orientation fitting the data to one page.
  e. Remove the subtotals.

5. Look up values in a list.

   a. You will locate annual compensation information by entering a social security number. Scroll so that columns I through Q are visible.

   b. In cell N2, enter 556-53-7589.

   c. In cell O2, enter the following function: =VLOOKUP(N2,A2:J11,10,FALSE), then view the results.

   d. Enter another social security number, 356-93-2123, in cell N2 and view the annual compensation for that employee.

   e. Save your worksheet.

6. Summarize list data.

   a. You'll enter a database function to average the annual salaries by department, using the Marketing department as the initial criterion.

   b. Define the criteria area: In cell C14, enter "Criteria"; in cell C15, enter "Dept." (make sure you type the period); then in cell C16, enter "Marketing".

   c. In cell E14, enter "Average Annual Salary by Department:".

   d. In cell H14, enter the following database function: =DAVERAGE(Database,7,C15:C16).

   e. Test the function further by entering the text "Accounting" in cell C16. When the criterion is entered, cell H14 should display 58650 as the result.

   f. Save the workbook, then close it.

7. Use data validation for list entries.

   a. Open the workbook titled EX I-2 again, then save it as "Compensation Summary 2".

   b. Select column E.

   c. For the validation criteria, specify that you want to allow a list of valid options.

   d. Enter a list of valid options that restricts the entries to "Accounting", "Information Systems", and "Marketing". Remember to use a comma between each item in the list.

   e. Indicate that you want the options to appear in an in-cell dropdown list, then close the dialog box.

   f. Go to cell E12, then select "Accounting" in the dropdown list.

   g. Select column F.

   h. Indicate that you want to restrict the data entered to be only whole numbers.

   i. In the minimum box, enter 1000. In the Maximum box, enter 20000. Close the dialog box.

   j. Click cell F12, enter 25000, then press [Enter].

   k. Click Cancel, then enter 19000.50.

   l. Click Cancel, then enter 19000.

   m. Save, then close the workbook and exit Excel.

► Visual Workshop

Create the worksheet shown in Figure I-23. Save the workbook as "Commission Lookup" on your Project disk. (*Hint:* The formula in cell D5 accesses the commission from the table. Calculate the commission by multiplying the Amount of Sale by the Commission Rate. If an exact amount for the Amount of Sale does not exist, the next highest or lowest dollar value is used.) Add your name to the worksheet footer, then preview and print the worksheet.

FIGURE I-23

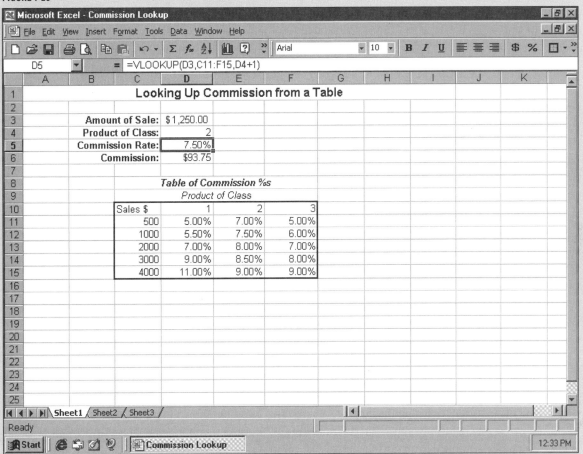

Enhancing
Charts and Worksheets

Objectives

► **Select a custom chart type**
► **Customize a data series**
► **Format a chart axis**
► **Add a data table to a chart**
► **Rotate a chart**
► **Enhance a chart with WordArt**
► **Rotate text**
► **Map data**

There are many ways to revise a chart or a worksheet to present its data with greater impact. In this unit, you enhance both charts and worksheets by selecting a custom chart type, customizing a data series, formatting axes, adding a data table, and rotating a chart. You also add special text effects and rotate text. Finally, you increase the impact of geographical data by plotting it on a map. Keep in mind that your goal in enhancing charts or worksheets is to communicate your data more clearly. Avoid excessive customization, which can be visually distracting. Scenario▶ MediaLoft's director of café operations, Jeff Shimada, has asked Jim Fernandez to produce two charts showing the sales of café pastry products in the first two quarters. He encourages Jim to enhance the charts and the worksheet data to improve their appearance and make the data more accessible. Finally, he asks Jim to create a map illustrating pastry sales by state.

Excel 2000

Selecting a Custom Chart Type

The Excel Chart Wizard offers a choice between standard and custom chart types. A **standard chart type** is a commonly used column, bar, pie, or area chart with several variations. For each standard chart type, you can choose from several subtypes, such as clustered column or stacked column. You can use the Wizard to add display options, and can later modify the formatting of any chart element. Excel supplies 20 built-in **custom chart types**, with special formatting already applied. You can also define your own custom chart type by modifying any of the existing Excel chart types. For example, you could define a company chart type that has the same title and then distribute it to other users in your office. Scenario ▶ Jim's first task is to create a chart showing the amount of each pastry type sold for the first quarter. To save time, he decides to use an Excel built-in custom chart.

Steps 1 2 3 4

QuickTip

To return personalized toolbars and menus to their default state, click Tools on the menu bar, click Customize, click the Options tab in the Customize dialog box, click Reset my usage data to restore the default settings, click Yes, click Close, then close the Drawing toolbar if it is displayed.

1. Open the workbook titled **EX J-1**, then save it as **Pastry Sales**
   The first step is to select the data you want to appear in the chart. In this case, you want the row labels in cells A6:A10 and the data for January and February in cells B5:C10.

2. Select the range **A5:C10**

3. Click the **Chart Wizard button** 📊 on the Standard toolbar, click the **Custom Types tab** in the Step 1 Chart Wizard dialog box, then under Select from, click the **Built-in option button** to select it if necessary
   See Figure J-1. When the built-in option button in the Custom Types tab is selected, all of the Excel custom chart types are displayed in the Chart type box, and a sample of the default chart appears in the Sample box. Once you make a selection in the Chart type box, the default chart disappears and a preview of the selected chart type appears in the Sample box. If the Chart Wizard button does not appear on your Standard toolbar, click the More Buttons button ⏩ to view it.

4. Click **Columns with Depth** in the Chart type box
   A preview of the chart appears in the Sample box. Notice that this custom chart type, with its 3-D bars and white background, has a more elegant appearance than the default chart shown in Figure J-1. Unlike the previous default chart, this chart doesn't have gridlines.

5. Click **Next**

6. Make sure = 'TotalSales'!A$5:$C$10 appears as the data range in the Data range box in the Step 2 Chart Wizard dialog box, then click **Next**

Trouble?

If the Chart toolbar does not open, right-click any toolbar and click Chart.

7. In the Step 3 Chart Wizard dialog box, click **Next**; if necessary, click the **As object in option button** in the Step 4 Chart Wizard dialog box to select it; then click **Finish**
   The completed chart appears, covering part of the worksheet data, along with the Chart toolbar. The Chart toolbar can appear anywhere within the worksheet window. As you complete the following steps, you may need to drag the toolbar to a new location.

Trouble?

Remember to drag the Chart toolbar out of the way if it blocks your view of the chart.

8. Scroll down the worksheet until **rows 13** through **28** are visible, click the **chart border** and drag the chart left and down until its upper-left corner is in cell **A13**, drag the **middle right sizing handle** right to the border between **column H** and **column I**, then check that its bottom border is between **rows 25** and **26**
   The new chart fills the range A13:H25, as shown in Figure J-2.

9. Save the workbook

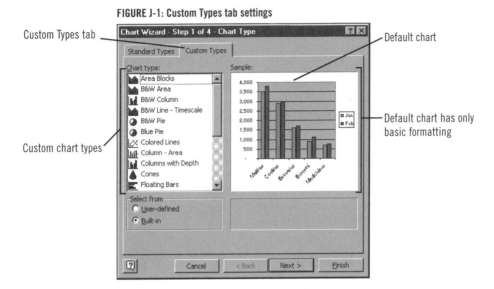

FIGURE J-1: Custom Types tab settings

Custom Types tab

Custom chart types

Default chart

Default chart has only basic formatting

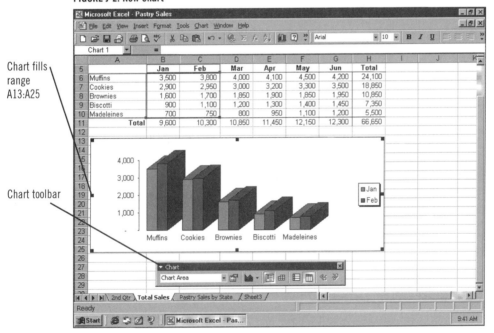

FIGURE J-2: New chart

Chart fills range A13:A25

Chart toolbar

Creating a custom chart type

You can create your own custom chart type by starting with a standard chart and then adding elements (such as a legend, color, or gridlines) that suit your needs. After you've finished creating the chart, click it to activate the Chart menu on the menu bar, click Chart, click Chart type, click the Custom Types tab,

then click User-defined. Click Add, then type a name for your chart type in the Name box. To use your custom chart type when creating additional charts, open the Chart Wizard dialog box, then click the User-defined button in the Custom Types tab.

Customizing a Data Series

A **data series** is the information, usually numbers or values, that Excel plots on a chart. You can customize the data series in a chart easily by altering the spreadsheet range that contains the chart data *or* by entering descriptive text, called a **data label**, that appears above a data marker in a chart. As with other Excel elements, you can change the borders, patterns, or colors of a data series. Scenario ► Jim notices that he omitted the data for March when he created his first-quarter sales chart. He needs to add this information to make the chart accurately reflect the entire first-quarter sales. Also, he wants to customize the updated chart by adding data labels to one of the data series to make it more specific. Then he'll change the color of another data series so its respective column figures will stand out more. He starts by adding the March data.

1. If necessary, click the **chart** to select it, scroll up until **row 5** is the top row in the worksheet area, select the range **D5:D10**, position the pointer over the lower border of cell D10 until it changes to ⌖, then drag the selected range anywhere within the chart area

   The chart now includes data for the entire first quarter: January, February, and March. Next, you will add data labels to the March data series.

QuickTip

If you have difficulty identifying the Chart Objects list arrow, rest your pointer on the first list arrow to the left on the Chart toolbar until the name "Chart Objects" appears.

2. Click the **Chart Objects list arrow** in the Chart toolbar, then click **Series "Mar"**

   See Figure J-3. Selection handles appear on each of the columns representing the data for March. Now that the data series is selected, you can format it by adding labels.

QuickTip

The ToolTip name for the Format Data Series button 🖳 changes, depending on what is selected. In this book it is called the Format Object button.

3. Click the **Format Object button** 🖳 on the Chart toolbar, then click the **Data Labels tab** in the Format Data Series dialog box

   The Data Labels tab opens. You want the value to appear on top of each selected data marker.

4. Under Data labels, click the **Show value option button** to select it, then click **OK**

   The data labels appear on the data markers, as shown in Figure J-4. The February data series could stand out more.

5. Click the **Chart Objects list arrow** on the Chart toolbar, click **Series "Feb"**, click 🖳, then click the **Patterns tab** in the Format Data Series dialog box

   The Patterns tab opens. See Figure J-5. The maroon color in the Sample box matches the current color displayed in the chart for the February data series. You decide that the series would show up better in a brighter shade of red.

QuickTip

You also can click outside the chart to deselect it.

6. Under Area, click the **red box** (third row, first color from the left), click **OK**, press **[Esc]** to deselect the data series, press **[Esc]** again to deselect the entire chart, then save the workbook

   The February data series now appears in a brighter shade of red.

Columns represent
data for March

FIGURE J-3: Selected data series

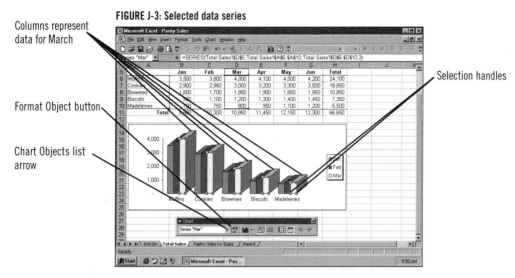

Selection handles

Format Object button

Chart Objects list
arrow

FIGURE J-4: Chart with data labels

Data labels

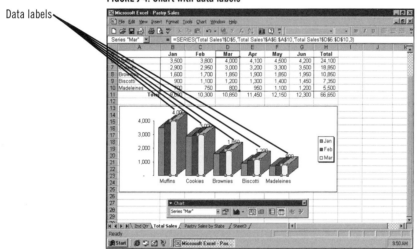

FIGURE J-5: Patterns tab settings

Bright red
color choice

Current color
of February
data series

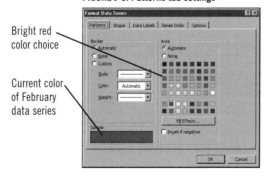

CLUES TO USE

Removing, inserting, and formatting legends

To insert or remove a legend, click the Legend button on the Chart toolbar to toggle the legend on or off. To format legend text, click Legend in the Chart

Objects list box of the Chart toolbar. Then click the Format Object button on the Chart toolbar and choose the options you want in the Font tab.

Formatting a Chart Axis

Excel automatically plots and formats all chart data and places chart axes within the chart's **plot area**. Data values in two-dimensional charts are plotted on the value (y) axis and categories are plotted on the category (x) axis. Excel creates a scale for the value (y) axis that is based on the highest and lowest values in the data series. Then Excel determines the intervals in which the values occur along the scale. In three-dimensional charts, like the one in Figure J-6, Excel generates three axes, where x remains the category axis but z becomes the value axis and y becomes the measure for the third dimension on the chart, depth. In 3-D charts, the value (z) axis usually contains the scale. For a list of the axes Excel uses to plot data, see Table J-1. You can override the Excel default formats for chart axes at any time by using the Format Axis dialog box. Scenario▶ Because the highest column is so close to the top of the chart, Jim wants to increase the maximum number on the value axis, which in this case is the y-axis, and change its number format. To begin, he selects the object he wants to format.

1. Click the **chart**, click the **Chart Objects list arrow** on the Chart toolbar, then click **Value Axis**
   The vertical axis becomes selected.

2. Click the **Format Object button** 🖼 on the Chart toolbar, then click the **Scale tab**
   The Scale tab of the Format Axis dialog box opens. The check marks under Auto indicate the default scale settings. You can override any of these settings by entering a new value.

3. In the Maximum box select **4000**, type **5000**, then click **OK**
   The chart adjusts so that 5000 appears as the maximum value on the value axis. Next, you want the minimum value to appear as a zero (0) and not as a hyphen (-).

4. With the Value Axis still selected, click 🖼 on the Chart toolbar, then click the **Number tab**
   The Number tab of the Format Axis dialog box opens. Currently, a custom format is selected under Category, which instructs Excel to use a hyphen instead of 0 as the lowest value.

5. Under Category click **General**, click **OK**, press **[Esc]** twice, then save the workbook
   The chart now shows 0 as the minimum value, as shown in Figure J-7.

FIGURE J-6: Chart elements in a 3-D chart

Tick marks

Plot area

Maximum value

Value (z) axis
with scale

Category (x)
axis

Minimum value

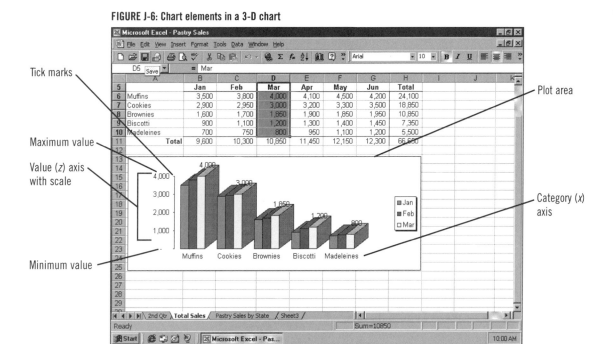

FIGURE J-7: Chart with formatted axis

New maximum
value

New minimum
value

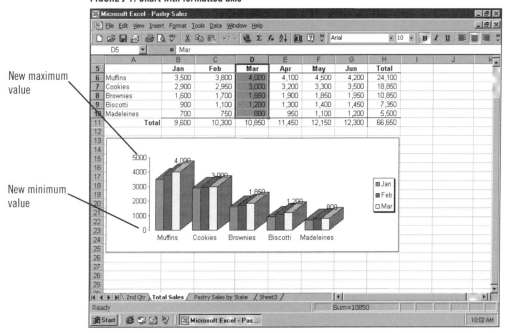

TABLE J-1: Axes used by Excel for chart formatting

axes in a two-dimensional chart	axes in a three-dimensional chart
Category (x) axis (horizontal)	Category (x) axis (horizontal)
Value (y) axis (vertical)	Series (y) axis (depth)
	Value (z) axis (vertical)

Adding a Data Table to a Chart

Excel 2000

A **data table**, attached to the bottom of a chart, is a grid containing the chart data. Data tables are useful because they highlight the data used to generate a chart, which might otherwise be difficult to find. Data tables can be displayed in line, area, column, and bar charts, and print automatically along with a chart. It's good practice to add data tables to charts stored separately from worksheet data. **Scenario** Jim wants to emphasize the first-quarter data used to generate his chart. He decides to add a data table.

1. **Click the chart to select it, click Chart on the menu bar, click Chart Options, then click the Data Table tab**
   The Data Table tab in the Chart Options dialog box opens, as shown in Figure J-8. The preview window displays the selected chart.

QuickTip

You also do this when creating a chart in the Step 3 Chart Wizard dialog box.

2. **Click the Show data table check box to select it**
   The chart in the preview window changes to show what the chart will look like with a data table added to the bottom. See Figure J-9. The data table crowds the chart labels, making them hard to read. (Your chart may look slightly different.) You'll fix this problem after you close the Chart Options dialog box.

QuickTip

To hide a data table, open the Data Table tab in the Chart Options dialog box, then clear the Show data table check box.

3. **Click OK, then, if necessary, scroll down to display the chart**
   The chart and the newly added data table look too crowded inside the current chart area. If you were to drag the chart borders to enlarge the chart, you wouldn't be able to see the entire chart displayed on the screen. It's more convenient to move the chart to its own sheet.

4. **If necessary, click the chart to select it, click Chart on the menu bar, click Location, click the As new sheet option button under Place chart, click OK**
   The chart is now located on a new sheet, where it is fully displayed in the worksheet window. See Figure J-10.

5. **Put your name in the sheet footer, save the workbook, then print the chart sheet**

FIGURE J-8: Data Table tab settings

Click to add a data table

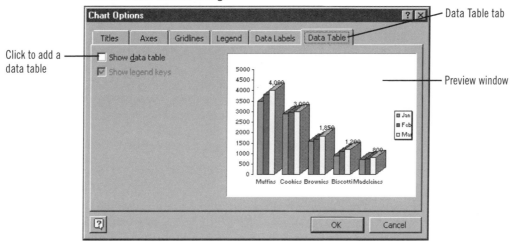

Data Table tab

Preview window

FIGURE J-9: Show Data Table box selected

Chart labels are hard to read

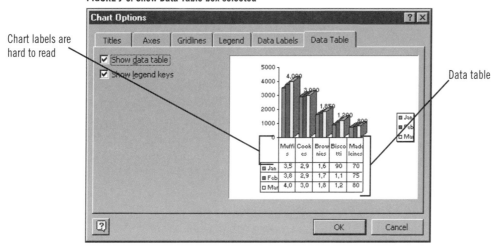

Data table

FIGURE J-10: Chart moved to chart sheet

Entire chart visible in window

Data table

New sheet tab

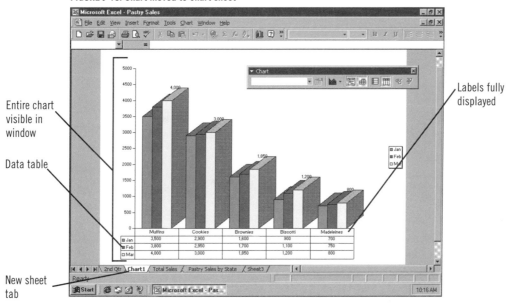

Labels fully displayed

Excel 2000

Rotating a Chart

Three-dimensional (3-D) charts do not always display data in the most effective way. In many cases, data in these charts can be obscured by one or more of the chart's data markers. By rotating and/or elevating the axes, you can improve the visibility of the chart's data. With Excel, you can adjust the rotation and elevation of a 3-D chart by dragging it with the mouse or using the 3-D View command on the Chart menu. **Scenario** Jim's workbook already contains a 3-D chart illustrating the sales data for the second quarter. He will display that chart, then rotate it so that the June columns are easier to see.

Steps

1. Click the **2nd Qtr sheet tab**, click the **Chart Objects list arrow** on the Chart toolbar, then click **Corners**
   Selection handles appear on the corners of the chart, as shown in Figure J-11.

2. Click the **lower-right corner handle** of the chart, press and hold the left mouse button, then drag the chart left approximately 2" until it looks like the object shown in Figure J-12, then release the mouse button
   The June columns are still not clearly visible. When using the dragging method to rotate a three-dimensional chart, you might need to make several attempts before you're satisfied with the view. It's usually more efficient to use the 3-D View option on the Chart menu.

   Trouble?
   Don't worry if your 3-D View dialog box settings are different from the ones shown in Figure J-13.

3. Click **Chart** on the menu bar, click **3-D View**, then drag the **3-D View dialog box** to the upper-right corner of the screen
   See Figure J-13. The preview box in the 3-D View dialog box allows you to preview changes to the chart's orientation in the worksheet.

4. Click **Default**
   The chart returns to its original position. Next, Jim decreases the chart's elevation, the height from which the chart is viewed.

   Trouble?
   If you have difficulty locating the Decrease Elevation button, refer to Figure J-13.

5. To the left of the preview box, click the **Decrease Elevation button**
   Notice how the preview image of the chart changes when you change the elevation.

6. Click **Apply**
   As the number in the Elevation box decreases, the viewpoint shifts downward. Note that the chart gains some vertical tick marks. Next, you'll change the rotation and **perspective**, or depth, of the chart.

7. In the Rotation box, select the current value, then type **55**; in the Perspective box, select the current value, type **0**, then click **Apply**
   The chart is reformatted. You notice, however, that the columns appear crowded. To correct this problem, you change the height as a percent of the chart base.

8. In the Height box, select the current value, type **70**, click **Apply**, then click **OK**
   The 3-D View dialog box closes. The chart columns now appear less crowded, making the chart easier to read.

9. Save your work

FIGURE J-11: Chart corners selected

Selection handles

Lower-right corner handle

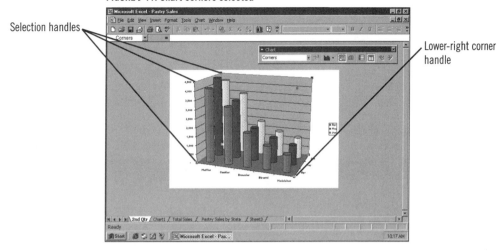

FIGURE J-12: Chart rotation in progress

Chart rotation pointer

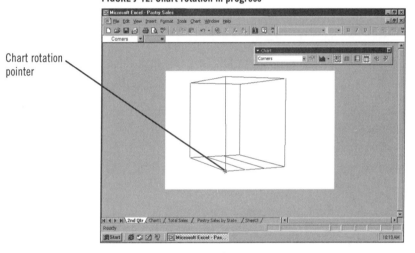

FIGURE J-13: Screen with chart and 3-D View dialog box

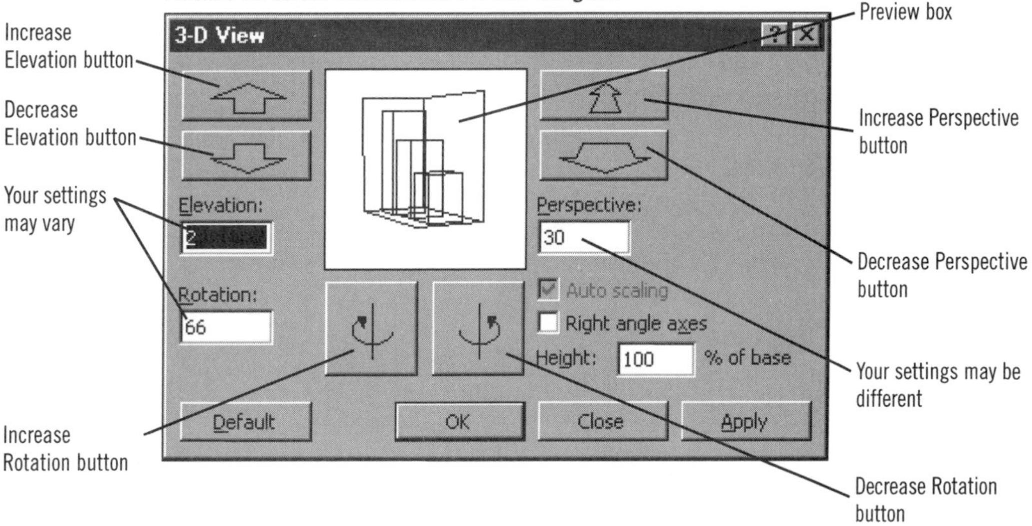

Increase Elevation button

Decrease Elevation button

Your settings may vary

Increase Rotation button

Preview box

Increase Perspective button

Decrease Perspective button

Your settings may be different

Decrease Rotation button

3-D View

Elevation:
2

Rotation:
66

Perspective:
30

Auto scaling

Right angle axes

Height: 100 % of base

Default   OK   Close   Apply

Enhancing a Chart with WordArt

You can enhance your chart or worksheet by adding specially formatted text using the WordArt tool on the Drawing toolbar. Once you've added a piece of WordArt to your workbook, you can edit or format it using the tools on the WordArt toolbar. Text formatted as WordArt is considered a drawing object rather than text. This means that WordArt objects cannot be treated as if they were labels entered in a cell; that is, you cannot sort, spell check, or use their cell references in formulas. Scenario Jim decides to add a WordArt title to the second-quarter chart. He begins by displaying the Drawing toolbar.

Steps

1. Click the **Drawing button** on the Standard toolbar
   The Drawing toolbar appears at the bottom of the Excel window. The WordArt text will be your chart title.

2. Click the **Insert WordArt button** on the Drawing toolbar
   The WordArt Gallery dialog box opens. This is where you select the style for your text.

3. In the second row, click the **second style from the left**, as shown in Figure J-14; then click **OK**
   The Edit WordArt Text dialog box opens, as shown in Figure J-15. This is where you enter the text you want to format as WordArt. You also can adjust the point size or font of the text or select bold or italic styles.

   QuickTip

   To delete a piece of WordArt, click it to make sure it is selected, then press [Delete].

4. Type **2nd Quarter Sales**, click the **Bold button** B, if necessary select **Times New Roman** in the Font list box and **36** in the Size list box, then click **OK**
   The Edit WordArt Text dialog box closes, and the chart reappears with the new title in the middle of the chart.

5. Place the pointer over 2nd Quarter Sales (the WordArt title) until the pointer changes to ⬚, then drag **2nd Quarter Sales** up until it appears in the upper-right corner of the chart
   The title is repositioned as shown in Figure J-16. Next, you decide to edit the WordArt to change "2nd" to the word "Second."

6. Click **Edit Text** on the WordArt toolbar, double-click **2nd** in the Edit WordArt Text box, type **Second**, then click **OK**
   The Edit WordArt Text dialog box closes, and the edited title appears over the chart.

   QuickTip

   To change the style of a piece of WordArt, click the WordArt Gallery button on the WordArt toolbar and select a new style.

7. Press **[Esc]** to deselect the WordArt, click, put your name in the chart sheet footer, save the workbook, then print the sheet

FIGURE J-14: Selecting a WordArt style

New style to apply to text

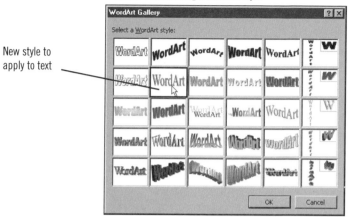

FIGURE J-15: Entering the WordArt text

Default font for this style

Replace with your text

Default point size for this style

Italic button

Bold button

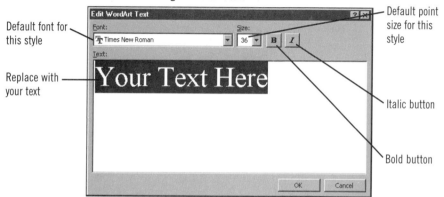

FIGURE J-16: Positioning the WordArt

New title location

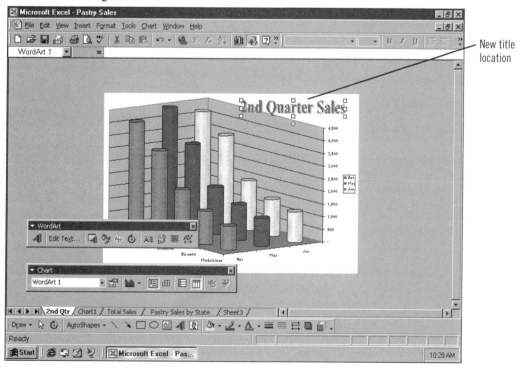

Rotating Text

By rotating text within a worksheet cell, you can draw attention to column labels or titles without turning the text into a drawing object (as in WordArt). Unlike WordArt, rotated text retains its usefulness as a worksheet entry, which means you can still sort it, spell check it, and use its cell reference in formulas. **Scenario** Now that he's finished enhancing the two charts in his workbook, Jim wants to improve the worksheet's appearance. He decides to rotate the column labels in cells B5 through G5.

Steps

1. Click the **Total Sales sheet tab**, make sure row 5 is the top row in the worksheet area, then select cells **B5:G5**

2. Click **Format** on the menu bar, click **Cells**, then click the **Alignment tab**
   The Alignment tab of the Format Cells dialog box opens. See Figure J-17. The settings under Orientation enable you to change the rotation of cell entries. Clicking the Vertical Text box on the left (the narrow one) allows you to display text vertically in the cell. To rotate the text to another angle, drag the rotation indicator in the Right Text box to the angle you want, or type the degree of angle you want in the Degrees box. You'll use the Degrees box to rotate the text entries.

3. Double-click the **Degrees box**, type **45**, then click **OK**
   The Format Cells dialog box closes.

4. If necessary, scroll up until row 1 is the top row in the worksheet area, then click cell **A1**
   The column labels for January through June now appear at a 45-degree angle in their cells, as shown in Figure J-18. The worksheet is now finished.

5. Put your name in the sheet footer, then save and print the worksheet

FIGURE J-17: Alignment tab settings

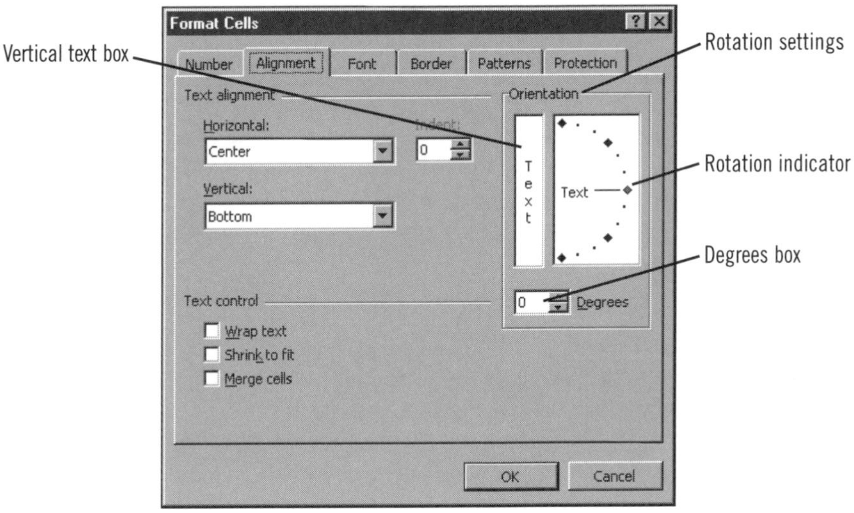

Vertical text box

Rotation settings

Rotation indicator

Degrees box

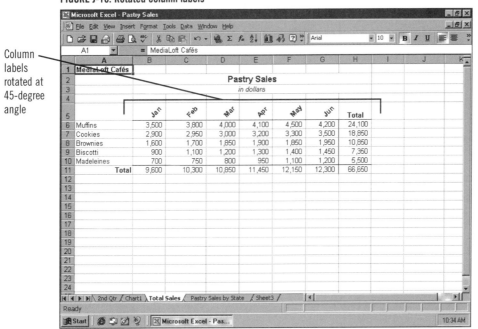

FIGURE J-18: Rotated column labels

Column labels rotated at 45-degree angle

Rotating chart labels

You can easily rotate the category labels on a chart by using the buttons on the Chart toolbar. First, you select the Category Axis in the Chart Objects list box.

Then you click either the Angle Text Downward button or the Angle Text Upward button on the Chart toolbar.

Excel 2000

Mapping Data

A **data map** shows geographic features and their associated data. To create a simple data map, arrange your worksheet data in two columns—with the first containing geographic data, such as the names of countries or states, and the second column containing the related data. Scenario ▶ Jim has compiled detailed sales figures for pastry by state. Now, he wants to create a map that clearly illustrates which states have the highest sales. He begins by selecting the data he wants to map.

Steps 1 2 3 4

1. Click the **Pastry Sales by State sheet tab**, then select the range **A4:B11**

   The first column of data contains the state names and the second contains the sales figures for each state. The column labels in row 4 (which you also selected) will be used in the legend title.

Trouble?

If you don't see the Map button, click Tools on the menu bar, click Command, and click Insert. Then under Commands, scroll to the Map icon and drag it to the Standard toolbar.

2. Click the **Map button** 🌐 on the Standard toolbar, drag the **crosshair pointer** from the middle of cell C4 to the lower-right corner of cell H23, then release the mouse button

   The map range is outlined on the worksheet, and the Multiple Maps Available dialog box opens on top.

3. Click **United States (AK & HI Inset) if necessary**, then click **OK**

   The map and the Microsoft Map Control dialog boxes appear.

4. Drag the **Microsoft Map Control dialog box** to the lower-left corner of the screen, then scroll up until most of the map is visible on your screen

   See Figure J-19. Excel automatically divides the sales data into intervals and assigns a different shade of gray to each interval, as the map legend indicates. The rectangular border indicates that the map is in Edit mode.

QuickTip

Click the Map Refresh button 🔄 to incorporate any changes to the data range into an existing map.

5. Double-click the **United States (AK & HI Inset) map title**, select the **default text** in the Edit Text Object dialog box, type **MediaLoft Pastry Sales**, then click **OK**

   The new title replaces the default map title. Next, to highlight the sales data more dramatically, you'll change the way values are represented using the Microsoft Map Control dialog box, shown in Figure J-20. You adjust the way data is represented on the map by dragging format buttons into the Format box. You want to change the format from shading to dots of varying density.

6. Click the **Dot Density button** in the Microsoft Map Control dialog box 🗺, then drag it over the top of the Value Shading button in the Format box

   When you release the mouse button, the map display changes from shading to dots, with one dot equal to $6,000 in pastry sales.

7. Click **Map** on the Menu bar, click **Features**, under Fill Color click the **Custom option button**, click the **Custom list arrow**, click the **turquoise square**, then click **OK**

   The map's background color changes to turquoise, as shown in Figure J-21. The legend could be more descriptive.

8. Double-click the **map legend**; click the **Legend Options tab** in the Format Properties dialog box if necessary; select the **default text** in the Title box, type **1st and 2nd Quarter**, then click **OK**

Trouble?

If your map doesn't print, your printer may not have enough memory. Try using another printer.

9. Press **[Esc]** three times to deselect the map, put your name in the sheet footer, save the workbook, print the worksheet, and exit Excel

FIGURE J-19: Newly created map

Section border

Microsoft Map Control dialog box

Default map title

Highest sales

Second highest sales

Map legend

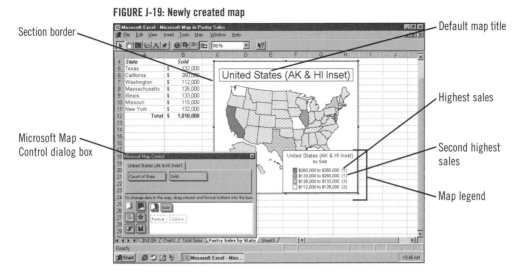

FIGURE J-20: Microsoft Map Control dialog box

Value Shading button

Dot Density button

Format buttons

Columns in data range

Format box

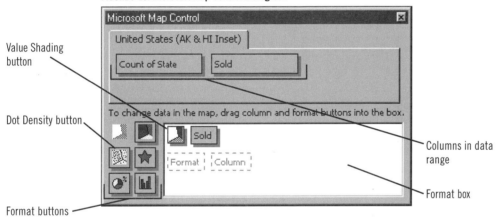

FIGURE J-21: Values formatted as dots

Dots

Dot Density button replaces Value Shading button

Turquoise backround

Updated legend

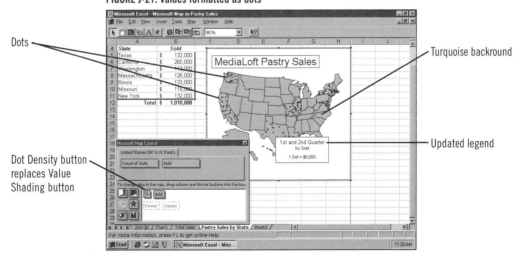

Practice

▶ Concepts Review

Label each element of the Excel screen shown in Figure J-22.

FIGURE J-22

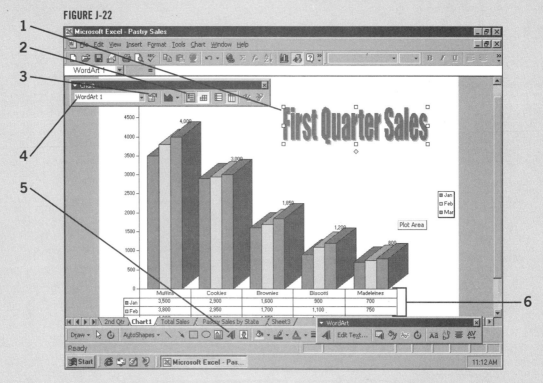

Match each button with the statement that describes it.

7. **a.** Opens the WordArt dialog boxes
8. **b.** Use to format the selected chart object
9. **c.** Use to create a data map
10. **d.** Use to change the style of a piece of WordArt
11. **e.** Use to display the Drawing toolbar

Select the best answer from the list of choices.

12. A chart's scale
   a. Cannot be modified.
   b. Displays values on the value (y) axis or the value (z) axis.
   c. Always appears on the value (y) axis.
   d. Appears on the category (x) axis.

13. What is the most efficient method of rotating a 3-D chart?
   a. Delete the chart, and start over with a new one.
   b. Adjust settings in the 3-D View dialog box.
   c. Select the chart corners, then drag a corner.
   d. Click Edit on the menu bar, then click Default.

14. How can you change the way data is represented on a map?
   a. Drag format buttons in the Microsoft Data Control dialog box.
   b. Click the Map Refresh button.
   c. Click Map, then click Data Representation.
   d. None of the above.

15. Which statement best describes the difference between two- and three-dimensional column charts?
   a. Two-dimensional charts have a value scale on the x-axis, and three-dimensional charts have a value scale on the z-axis.
   b. Two-dimensional charts show the data in three dimensions.
   c. Three-dimensional charts show the data in four dimensions.
   d. Two-dimensional charts have category (x) and value (y) axes; three-dimensional charts have category (x), series (y), and value (z) axes.

16. What is a data table?
   a. The data used to create a chart displayed in a grid.
   b. Worksheet data arranged geographically.
   c. A customized data series.
   d. A three-dimensional arrangement of data on the y-axis.

17. A custom chart type
   a. Is supplied only by Excel.
   b. Cannot be saved.
   c. Can be supplied by Excel or the user.
   d. All of the above.

18. To rotate text in a worksheet cell,
   a. Format the text as WordArt, then drag the WordArt.
   b. Click the Rotate button on the Standard toolbar.
   c. Select the text, then drag to rotate it the desired number of degrees.
   d. Adjust settings on the Alignment tab of the Format cells dialog box.

► Skills Review

1. **Select a custom chart type.**
   a. Open the workbook titled EX J-2, then save it as "MediaLoft Coffee Sales".
   b. On the 1st Quarter sheet, select the range A4:B7.
   c. Open the Chart Wizard, and on the Custom Types tab in the Chart Wizard dialog box, make sure the Built-in option button is selected.
   d. Select Blue Pie in the Chart type box.
   e. Go to the Step 2 Chart Wizard dialog box.
   f. Make sure the data range is correct, then go to the Step 3 Chart Wizard dialog box, read the contents, then go to the Step 4 Chart Wizard dialog box.
   g. Make sure the As Object In button is selected, then finish the Wizard.
   h. Drag the chart to a better location in the worksheet.
   i. Put your name in the sheet footer, then save, preview, and print the worksheet data and chart.

2. **Customize a data series.**
   a. On the 2nd Quarter sheet, move the June data in D4:D7 into the chart area.
   b. Select the April data series and display its data labels.
   c. Use the Format Data Series dialog box to change the color of the May data series to the green color of your choice.
   d. Save the workbook.

3. **Format a chart axis.**
   a. Select the value axis.
   b. Set its maximum to 10000 and its minimum to 0.
   c. On the Number tab in the Format Axis dialog box under Category, use the Currency format to add a dollar sign and two decimal places to the values, then close the dialog box.
   d. Save the workbook.

4. **Add a data table to a chart.**
   a. Show the data table.
   b. Use the Location command on the Chart menu to move the chart to its own sheet.
   c. Display the 3rd Quarter sheet tab.
   d. Use the Data Table tab in the Chart Options dialog box to hide the data table.
   e. Remove the chart legend.
   f. Save the workbook.

5. **Rotate a chart.**
   a. On the Chart1 sheet, use the Chart Objects list arrow to select the chart corners.
   b. Drag a chart corner to rotate the chart.
   c. Return the chart to its default rotation using the 3-D View command on the Chart menu.
   d. Change the rotation to 315.
   e. Change the elevation to 13.
   f. Deselect the chart corners.
   g. Save the workbook.

6. **Enhance a chart with WordArt.**
   a. Display the Drawing toolbar.
   b. Open WordArt and select the second style from the right in the second row.
   c. In the Edit WordArt Text dialog box, enter the text "Second Quarter Sales" and format it in italic.
   d. Position the new title above the chart.
   e. Make sure the WordArt is still selected, then use the WordArt Gallery button on the WordArt toolbar to select a new style for the title.
   f. Save the workbook.
   g. Close the Drawing toolbar.

7. **Rotate text.**
   a. On the 1st Quarter sheet tab, select cells B4:D4.
   b. Change the alignment to 45 degrees.
   c. On the 2nd Quarter sheet tab, select the range B4:D4.
   d. Use the rotation indicator on the Alignment tab in the Format Cells dialog box to change the rotation to 45 degrees.
   e. On the 3rd Quarter sheet tab, rotate the Category Axis labels downward.
   f. Save the workbook.

8. **Map worksheet data.**
   a. Make the Mail Order Contacts sheet active.
   b. Select the range A4:B16.
   c. Start Microsoft Map.
   d. Position the map in the range C4:H23, and use the United States (AK & HI Inset) map.
   e. Change the map title to "Western Region Contacts".
   f. Change the map's background color to bright pink.
   g. Change the data formatting to dot density.
   h. Change the legend title to "Mail Order".
   i. In cell B9, change the data for California to 25.
   j. Double-click the map to put it in Edit mode, then click the Map Refresh button on the Map toolbar to update the map.
   k. Put your name in the sheet footer, save the workbook, then select, preview, and print each sheet in the workbook.

▶ Visual Workshop

Create the worksheet and accompanying custom chart shown in Figure J-23. Save the workbook as "The Dutch Garden". Study the chart and worksheet carefully to make sure you start with the most appropriate chart type, and then make all the modifications shown. Put your name in the sheet footer, preview, and then print the worksheet and chart together in landscape orientation.

FIGURE J-23

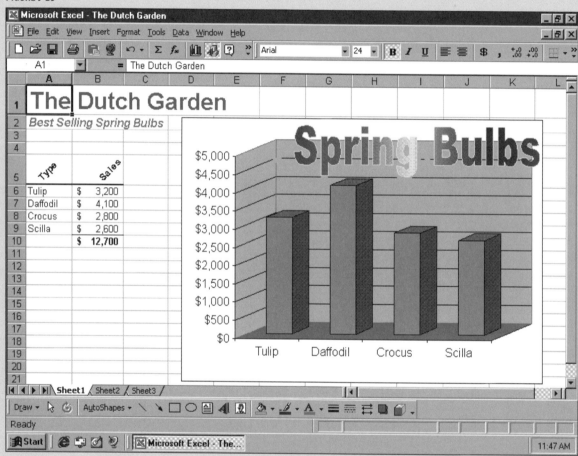

Using a
What-If Analysis

Objectives

► **Define a what-if analysis**
[MOUS] ► **Track a what-if analysis with Scenario Manager**
[MOUS] ► **Generate a scenario summary**
► **Project figures using a data table**
► **Create a two-input data table**
[MOUS] ► **Use Goal Seek**
[MOUS] ► **Set up a complex what-if analysis with Solver**
[MOUS] ► **Run Solver and generate an Answer Report**

Each time you use a worksheet to answer the question "what if?" you are performing a **what-if analysis**. For example, what would happen to a firm's overall expense budget if company travel expenses decreased by 30%? Using Excel, you can perform a what-if analysis in many ways. In this unit, you will learn to track what-if scenarios and generate summary reports using the Excel Scenario Manager. You will design and manipulate one-input and two-input data tables to project multiple outcomes. Also, you will use the Excel Goal Seek feature to solve a what-if analysis. Finally, you will use Solver to perform a complex what-if analysis involving multiple variables. **Scenario** The MediaLoft corporate office is considering the purchase of several pieces of capital equipment, as well as several vehicles.

Defining a What-If Analysis

By performing a what-if analysis in a worksheet, you can get immediate answers to questions such as "What happens if we sell 30% more of a certain product?" or "What happens if interest rates rise 2 points?" A worksheet used to produce a what-if analysis is often referred to as a **model** because it acts as the basis for multiple outcomes. To perform a what-if analysis in a worksheet, you change the value in one or more **input cells** (cells that contain data rather than formulas) and then observe the effects on dependent cells. A **dependent cell** is a cell—usually containing a formula—whose value changes depending on the values in the input cells. A dependent cell can be located either in the same worksheet as the changing value or in another worksheet. Scenario▶ Jim has created a worksheet model to perform an initial what-if analysis of equipment loan payments. See Figure K-1. Jim follows the guidelines below to perform a what-if analysis.

 Understand and state the purpose of the worksheet model
The worksheet model is designed to calculate a fixed-rate, monthly equipment loan payment.

 Determine the data input value(s) that, if changed, affect the dependent cell results
The model contains three data input values (labeled Loan Amount, Annual Interest Rate, and Term in months), in cells B4, B5, and B6, respectively.

 Identify the dependent cell(s), usually containing formulas, that will contain adjusted results once different data values are entered
There are three dependent cell formulas (labeled Monthly Payment, Total Payments, and Total Interest). The results appear in cells B9, B10, and B11, respectively.

 Formulate questions you want the what-if analysis to answer
Jim wants to answer the following questions with his model: (1) What happens to the monthly payments if the interest rate is 10%? (2) What happens to the monthly payments if the loan term is 60 months (5 years) instead of 48 months (4 years)? (3) What happens to the monthly payments if a less-expensive car with a lower loan amount is purchased?

 Perform the what-if analysis and explore the exact relationships between the input values and the dependent cell formulas, which depend on the input values
Jim wants to see what effect a 10% interest rate has on the dependent cell formulas. Because the interest rate is located in cell B5, any formula that references cell B5 will be directly affected by a change in interest rate—in this case, the Monthly Payment formula in cell B9. Because the formula in cell B10 references cell B9 and the formula in cell B11 references cell B10, however, a change in the interest rate in cell B5 affects these other two formulas as well. Figure K-2 shows the result of the what-if analysis described in this example.

FIGURE K-1: Worksheet model for a what-if analysis

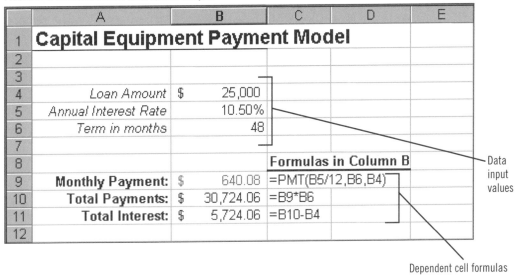

FIGURE K-2: What-if analysis with changed input value and dependent formula results

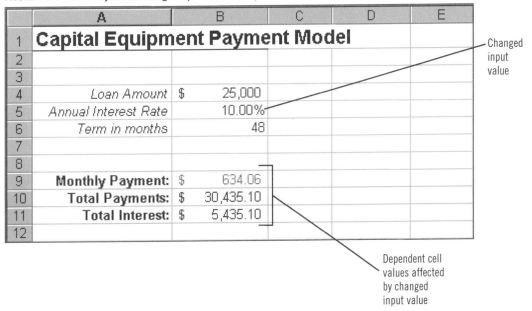

Excel 2000

Tracking a What-If Analysis with Scenario Manager

A **scenario** is a set of values you use to forecast worksheet results. The Excel Scenario Manager simplifies the process of what-if analysis by allowing you to name and save different scenarios with the worksheet. Scenarios are particularly useful when you work with uncertain or changing variables. If you plan to create a budget, for example, but are uncertain of your revenue, you can assign several different values to the revenue and then switch between the scenarios to perform a what-if analysis. Scenario ▶ Jim uses Scenario Manager to consider three equipment loan scenarios: (1) the original loan quote, (2) a longer-term loan, and (3) a reduced loan amount.

Steps

QuickTip

To return personalized tool-bars and menus to their default state, click Tools on the menu bar, click Customize, click the Options tab in the Customize dialog box, click Reset my usage data to restore the default settings, click Yes, click Close, then close the Drawing toolbar if it is displayed.

1. Open the workbook titled **EX K-1**, then save it as **Capital Equipment Payment Model**
   The first step in defining a scenario is choosing the cells that will vary in the different scenarios; these are known as **changing cells**.

2. Select range **B4:B6**, click **Tools** on the menu bar, then click **Scenarios**
   The Scenario Manager dialog box opens with the following message: "No Scenarios defined. Choose Add to add scenarios."

3. Click **Add** if necessary, drag the Add Scenario dialog box to the right until columns **A** and **B** are visible, then type **Original loan quote** in the Scenario name box
   The range in the Changing cells box reflects your initial selection, as shown in Figure K-3.

4. Click **OK** to confirm the Add Scenario settings
   The Scenario Values dialog box opens, as shown in Figure K-4. Notice that the existing values appear in the changing cell boxes. Because this first scenario reflects the original loan quote input values ($25,000 at 10.5% for 48 months), these values are correct.

5. Click **OK**
   The Scenario Manager dialog box reappears with the new scenario listed in the Scenarios box. Jim wants to examine a second scenario, this one with a loan term of 60 months.

6. Click **Add**; in the Scenario name box type **Longer term loan**, click **OK**; in the Scenario Values dialog box, select **48** in the third changing cell box, type **60**, then click **Add**
   Jim also wants to examine a scenario that uses $21,000 as the loan amount.

7. In the Scenario name box type **Reduced loan amount**, click **OK**; in the Scenario Values dialog box, change the **25000** in the first changing cell box to **21000**, then click **OK**
   The Scenario Manager dialog box reappears. See Figure K-5. All three scenarios are listed, with the most recent—Reduced loan amount—selected. Now that you have defined the three scenarios, you can apply them and see what effect they will have on the monthly payment.

8. Make sure Reduced loan amount is still selected, click **Show**, notice that the monthly payment in the worksheet changes from $640.08 to $537.67; click **Longer term loan**, click **Show**, notice that the monthly payment is now $537.35; click **Original loan quote**, click **Show** to return to the original values, then click **Close**

9. Save the workbook

CLUES TO USE

Merging scenarios

To bring scenarios from another workbook into the current workbook, click the Merge button in the Scenario Manager dialog box. The Merge Scenarios dialog box opens, letting you select scenarios from other workbooks.

FIGURE K-3: Add Scenario dialog box

Cell range to be changed

Your user name and date will be different

Scenario name

Click to confirm scenario settings

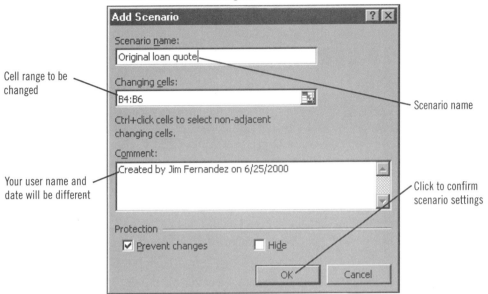

FIGURE K-4: Scenario Values dialog box

Changing cell boxes

Current cell values in B4, B5, B6

Click to return to Scenario Manager dialog box

Click to add current scenario and to return to Add Scenario dialog box

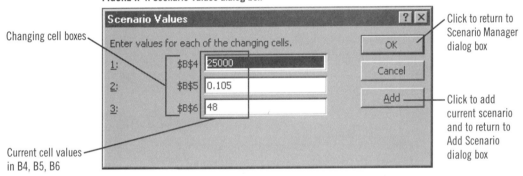

FIGURE K-5: Scenario Manager dialog box with three scenarios listed

Three scenarios

Click to show selected scenario

Click to delete selected scenario

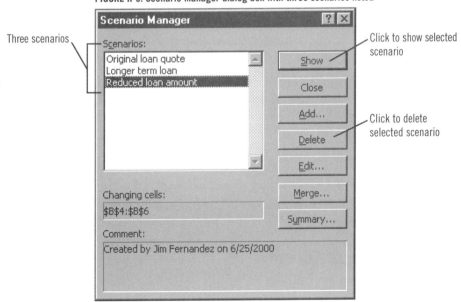

Excel 2000

Generating a Scenario Summary

Although it may be useful to switch between different scenarios when analyzing data, in most cases you will want to refer to a single report summarizing the results of the scenarios in a worksheet. A **scenario summary** is an Excel table that compiles data from the changing cells and corresponding result cells for each scenario. You can use a scenario summary to illustrate the best, worst, and most likely scenarios for a particular set of circumstances. **Scenario** Now that he's defined his scenarios, Jim needs to generate and print a scenario summary report. Naming the cells makes the summary easier to read because the names, not the cell references, are listed in the report. Jim begins by creating cell names in column B based on the labels in column A (the left column).

QuickTip

To delete a range, click Insert on the menu bar, click Define, click the range name, then click Delete.

1. Select range **A4:B11**, click **Insert** on the menu bar, point to **Name**, click **Create**, click the **Left column check box** to select it if necessary, then click **OK**
   Excel creates the names based on the cell contents.

2. Click cell **B4** to make sure Loan_Amount appears in the name box, then click the **name box list arrow**
   All six labels appear in the name box list, confirming that they were created. See Figure K-6. Now you are ready to generate the scenario summary report.

3. Press **[Esc]**, click **Tools** on the menu bar, click **Scenarios**, then click **Summary** in the Scenario Manager dialog box
   The Scenario Summary dialog box opens. Notice that Scenario summary is selected, indicating that it is the default report type.

4. Double-click the **Result cells box** to select it if necessary, then select range **B9:B11** in the worksheet
   The references in the Result cells box adjust to reflect those cells affected by the changing cells (that is, the references now refer to the result cells). See Figure K-7. With the report type and result cells specified, you are now ready to generate the report.

QuickTip

Scroll right to see all three scenarios included in the report. The scenario summary is not linked to the worksheet. If you change cells in the worksheet, you must generate a new scenario summary.

5. Click **OK**
   The summary of the worksheet's scenarios appears on a new sheet. The report appears in outline format so that you can hide or show report details. Because the Current Values column shows the same values as the Original loan quote column, Jim wants to delete column D.

6. Press **[Ctrl][Home]**, click the **Current Values column header** for column D, click the **right mouse button**, then click **Delete** in the pop-up menu
   The column containing the current values is deleted and the Original loan quote column data shifts left to fill column D. Next, Jim wants to delete the notes at the bottom of the report because they refer to the column that no longer exists. He also wants to make the report title more descriptive.

7. Select range **B13:B15**, press **[Delete]**, select cell **B2**, edit its contents to read **Scenario Summary for Equipment Loan**, then click cell **A1**
   The completed scenario summary is shown in Figure K-8.

8. Add your name to the report footer, save your work, then print the report in landscape orientation

FIGURE K-6: List box containing newly created names

Name box
list arrow

Names
match
labels in
column A

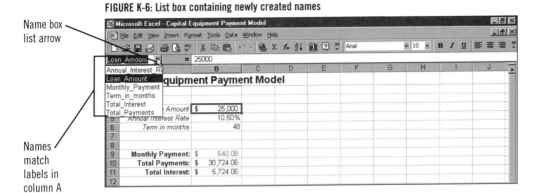

FIGURE K-7: Scenario Summary dialog box

Default report type

Cells to be recalculated when
a new scenario is applied

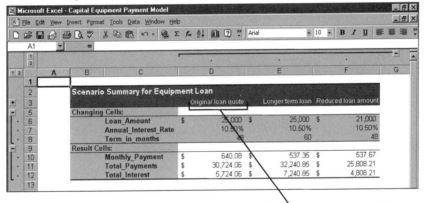

FIGURE K-8: Completed Scenario Summary report

Column D now contains original
loan quote

Using Report Manager

You can create customized, printed reports using the Excel Report Manager, an extra Excel program called an "add-in." A report can contain worksheets, views, or scenarios that you want to print repeatedly in a given order. To create a report, click View on the menu bar, click Report Manager, then click Add. In the Add Report dialog box, type a report name, select the sheets, views, or scenarios you want to include, then click Add. Repeat until you've added all the sections you need, click OK, select the report name, then click Print. The sections of the report print in the order in which you've listed them.

Excel 2000

Projecting Figures Using a Data Table

Another way to answer what-if questions in a worksheet is by using a data table. A **data table**, sometimes referred to as a **one-input data table**, is a range of cells that shows the resulting values when one input value is varied in a formula. For example, you could use a data table to calculate your monthly mortgage payment based on several different interest rates. Scenario Now that he's completed his analysis, Jim wants to find out how the monthly equipment payments would change as interest rates increase by increments of 0.25%. He estimates that the lowest interest rate would be about 9.75% and the highest 11.25%. To project these figures, Jim will generate a one-input data table. First, he creates a table structure, with the varying interest rates listed in the left column.

Steps 1 2 3 4

1. Click the **Single Loan sheet tab**, select cell **D4**, type **Interest**, select cell **D5**, type **9.75%**, select cell **D6**, type **10.00%**; select range **D5:D6**, drag the fill handle to select range **D7:D11**, then release the mouse button

   With the varying interest rates (that is, the input values) listed in column D, you need to enter a formula reference to cell B9. This tells Excel to use the formula in cell B9 to calculate multiple results in column E, based on the changing interest rates in column D.

2. Click cell **E4**, type **=B9**, then click the **Enter button** ☑ on the formula bar

   Notice that the value in cell B9, $640.08, now appears in cell E4, and the formula reference (=B9) appears in the formula bar. See Figure K-9. Because the value in cell E4 isn't a part of the data table (Excel uses it only to calculate the values in the table), Jim wants to hide the contents of cell E4 from view using a custom number format.

3. With cell E4 selected, click **Format** on the menu bar, click **Cells**, click the **Number tab** in the Format Cells dialog box if necessary; click **Custom** under Category, select the contents of the Type box, type **;;**, then click **OK**

   Because custom number formats usually specify the formats for positive and then negative numbers, with semicolons in between, the two semicolons actually specify no format, so the cell will remain blank. With the table structure in place, you can now generate monthly payment values for the varying interest rates.

Trouble?

If you receive the message "Selection not valid", repeat Step 4, taking care to select the entire range D4:E11.

4. Select range **D4:E11**, click **Data** on the menu bar, then click **Table**

   You have highlighted the range that makes up the table structure. The Table dialog box opens, as shown in Figure K-10. This is where you indicate in which worksheet cell you want the varying input values (the interest rates in column D) to be substituted. Because the monthly payments formula in cell B9 (which you just referenced in cell E4) uses the annual interest rate in cell B5, you'll enter a reference to cell B5. You'll place this reference in the Column input cell box, rather than the Row input cell box, because the varying input values are arranged in a column.

QuickTip

You cannot delete individual values in a data table; you must clear all values.

5. Click the **Column input cell box**, click cell **B5**, then click **OK**

   Excel generates monthly payments for each interest rate. The monthly payment values are displayed next to the interest rates in column E. The new data and the heading in cell D4 need formatting.

Trouble?

If the Bold button does not appear on your Formatting toolbar, click the More Buttons button ⁇ to view it.

6. Click cell **D4**, click the **Bold button** **B**, then click the **Align Right button** ▤ (both on the Formatting toolbar)

7. Select range **E5:E11**, click the **Currency Style button** 🖫 on the Formatting toolbar, deselect the range, add your name to the footer, then save and print the worksheet

   The completed data table appears as shown in Figure K-11. Notice that the monthly payment amount for a 10.50% interest rate is the same as the original loan quote in cell B9 and the reference to it in cell E4. You can use this information to cross-check the values Excel generates in data tables.

FIGURE K-9: One-input data table structure

Reference to formula in cell B9

Varying interest rates

Value displayed in cell B9

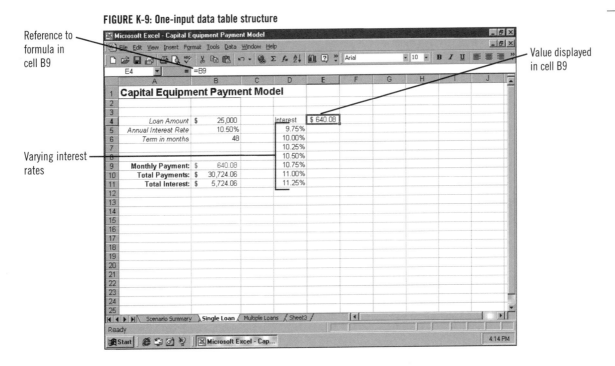

FIGURE K-10: Table dialog box

Enter reference to interest rate input cell here

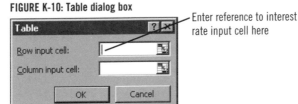

FIGURE K-11: Completed data table with resulting values

Formatted heading

Monthly payments

Completed data table

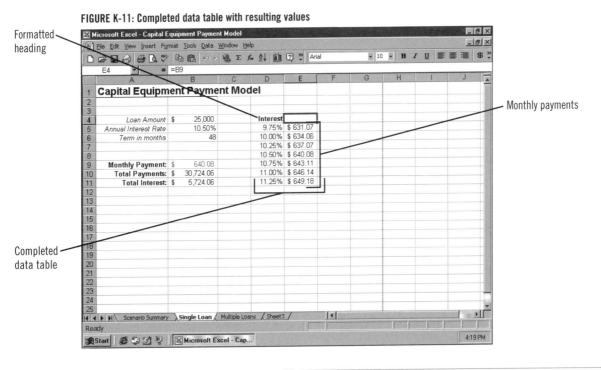

Excel 2000

Creating a Two-Input Data Table

A **two-input data table** shows the resulting values when two different input values are varied in a formula. You could, for example, use a two-input data table to calculate your monthly mortgage payment based on varying interest rates and varying loan terms. In a two-input data table, different values of one input cell appear across the top row of the table, while different values of the second input cell are listed down the left column of the table. ▶Scenario▶ Jim wants to use a two-input data table to see what happens if the various interest rates are applied across several different loan terms, such as 3, 4, and 5 years. He begins by changing the structure of the one-input data table to accommodate a two-input data table.

Steps 1234

1. Move the contents of cell **D4** to cell **C7**; click cell **C8**, type **Rates**, click the **Enter button** ☑ on the formula bar, then click the **Align Right button** ▤ and the **Bold button** ⓑ (both on the Formatting toolbar)

   The left table heading is in place. You don't need the old data table values, but you will need a heading for the values along the top row of the table.

2. Select range **E4:E11**, press **[Delete]**, click cell **F3**, type **Months**, click ☑, then click ⓑ

3. Click cell **E4**, type **36**, click ☑, click the **Comma Style button** ┘ on the Formatting toolbar, click the **Decrease decimal button** ⁺⁰₀ twice on the Formatting toolbar, press **[→]**, in cell F4 type **48**, press **[→]**, in cell G4 type **60**, then click ☑

   With both top row and left column values and headings in place, you are ready to reference the monthly payment formula in the upper-left cell of the table. Again, this is the formula Excel will use to calculate the values in the table. Because it is not part of the table (Excel uses it only to calculate the values in the table), it is best to hide the cell contents from view.

4. Click cell **D4**, type **=B9**, click ☑, click **Format** on the menu bar, click **Cells**, in the Format Cells dialog box click the **Number tab** if necessary, click **Custom**, select the contents of the Type box, type **;;**, then click **OK**

   The two-input data table structure is complete, as shown in Figure K-12. You are ready to enter the table values.

5. Select range **D4:G11**, click **Data** on the menu bar, then click **Table**

   The Table dialog box opens. The loan terms are arranged in a row, so you'll enter a reference to the loan term input cell (B6) in the Row input cell box. The interest rates are arranged in a column, so you'll enter a reference to the interest rate input cell (B5) in the Column input cell box.

6. With the insertion point positioned in the Row input cell box, click cell **B6** in the worksheet, click the **Column input cell box**, then click cell **B5**

   See Figure K-13. The row input cell (B6) references the loan term, and the column input cell (B5) references the interest rate. Now, you can generate the data table values.

7. Click **OK**, select range **F5:G11**, click the **Currency Style button** 💲 on the Formatting toolbar, then click cell **F8**

   The resulting values appear, as shown in Figure K-14. The value in cell F8 matches the original quote: a monthly payment of $640.08 for a 48-month loan term at a 10.50% interest rate.

8. Preview and print the worksheet, then save the workbook

Formula
reference

Table
headings

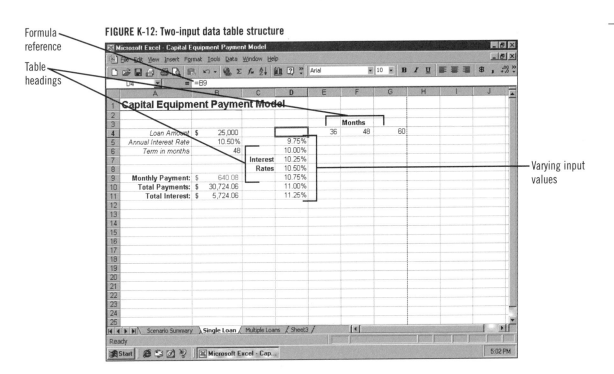

FIGURE K-12: Two-input data table structure

Varying input
values

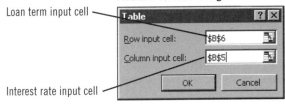

FIGURE K-13: Table dialog box

Loan term input cell

Interest rate input cell

Hidden reference
to cell B9

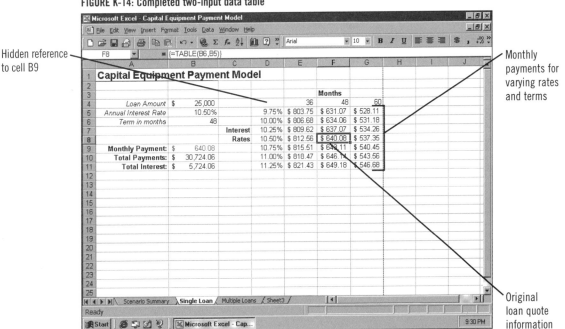

FIGURE K-14: Completed two-input data table

Monthly
payments for
varying rates
and terms

Original
loan quote
information

Excel 2000

Using Goal Seek

You can think of goal seeking as a what-if analysis in reverse. In goal seeking, you specify a solution and then find the input value that produces the answer you want. Backing into a solution in this way, sometimes referred to as **backsolving**, can save a significant amount of time. For example, you can use Goal Seek to determine how many units must be sold to reach a particular sales goal or to determine the expenses that must be cut to meet a budget. ▶Scenario▶ After reviewing his data table, Jim has a follow-up question: How much money could MediaLoft borrow if the company wanted to keep the total payment amount of all the equipment to $28,000? Jim uses Goal Seek to answer this question.

Steps

1. Click cell **B10**

The first step in using Goal Seek is to select a goal cell. A **goal cell** contains a formula in which you can substitute values to find a specific value, or goal. You use cell B10 as the goal cell because it contains the formula for total payments.

2. Click **Tools** on the menu bar, then click **Goal Seek**

The Goal Seek dialog box opens. Notice that the Set cell box contains a reference to cell B10, the Total Payments cell you selected in Step 1. You need to indicate that the figure in cell B10 should not exceed 28000.

3. Click the **To value box**, then type **28000**

The 28000 figure represents the desired solution that will be reached by substituting different values in the goal cell.

4. Click the **By changing cell box**, then click cell **B4**

You have specified that cell B4 will be changed to reach the 28000 solution. See Figure K-15. With the target value in the target cell specified, you can begin the Goal Seek.

> **QuickTip**
>
> Before you select another command, you can return the worksheet to its status prior to the Goal Seek by pressing [Ctrl][Z].

5. Click **OK, then move the dialog box as needed so that column B is visible**

The Goal Seek Status dialog box opens with the following message: "Goal Seeking with Cell B10 found a solution". Notice that by changing the Loan Amount figure in cell B4 from $25,000 to $22,783, Goal Seek achieves a Total Payments result of $28,000.

6. Click **OK**

Changing the loan amount value in cell B4 affects the entire worksheet. See Figure K-16.

7. Save, then print the workbook

FIGURE K-15: Completed Goal Seek dialog box

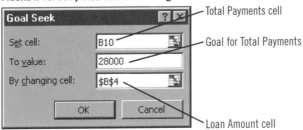

Total Payments cell

Goal for Total Payments

Loan Amount cell

FIGURE K-16: Worksheet with new values

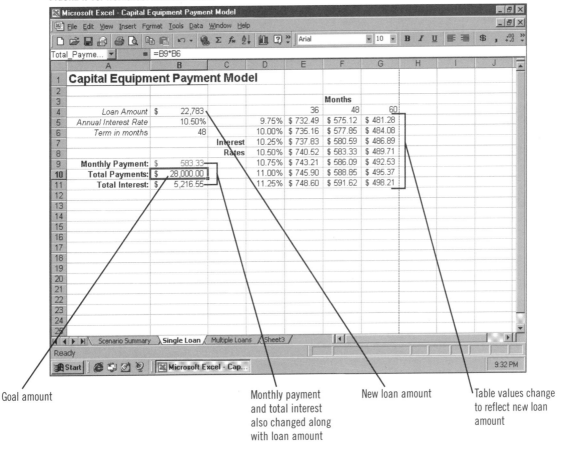

Goal amount

Monthly payment
and total interest
also changed along
with loan amount

New loan amount

Table values change
to reflect new loan
amount

Excel 2000

Setting Up a Complex What-If Analysis with Solver

The Excel Solver finds the most appropriate value for a formula by changing the input values in the worksheet. The cell containing the formula is called the **target cell**. Cells containing the values that change are called **changing cells**. Solver is helpful when you need to perform a complex what-if analysis involving multiple input values or when the input values must conform to specific constraints. Scenario▶ After seeing his analysis of interest rates and payments, Jim now addresses the vehicle purchase for the MediaLoft shuttle service. He decides that the best plan is to purchase a combination of vans, sedans, and compact cars that will accommodate a total of 44 passengers, the number of people Jim has estimated the company will need to transport to and from the stores for special events. In addition, the total monthly payments for the vehicles should not exceed $3,700. Jim uses Solver to find the best possible combination of vehicles.

Trouble?

If Solver is not an option on your Tools menu, you need to install the Solver add-in. See your instructor or technical support person for assistance.

Trouble?

If your Solver Parameters dialog box has entries in the By Changing Cells box or in the Subject to the Constraints box, click Reset All, then click OK, and continue with Step 3.

1. Click the **Multiple Loans sheet tab**

   See Figure K-17. This worksheet is designed to calculate total loans, payments, and passengers for a combination of vans, sedans, and compact cars. It assumes an annual interest rate of 10% and a loan term of 48 months. You will use Solver to change the purchase quantities in cells B7:D7 (the changing cells) to achieve your target of 44 passengers in cell B15 (the target cell). Your solution will include a constraint on cell C14, specifying that the total monthly payments must be less than or equal to $3,700.

2. Click **Tools**, then click **Solver**

   The Solver Parameters dialog box opens. This is where you indicate the target cell, the changing cells, and the constraints under which you want Solver to work. You begin by changing the value in the target cell.

3. With the Set Target Cell box selected in the Solver Parameters dialog box, click cell **B15** in the worksheet, click the **Value of option button**, double-click the **Value of box**, then type **44**

   $B$15 appears in the Set Target Cell box, and 44 appears in the Value of box.

4. Click the **By Changing Cells box**, then select cells **B7:D7** in the worksheet

   $B$7:$D$7 appears in the By Changing Cells box. You need to specify the constraints on the worksheet values, the values you don't want them to exceed.

5. Click **Add**

   The Add Constraint dialog box opens. This is where you specify the total monthly payment amount—in this case, no higher than $3,700.

6. Click the **Cell Reference box**, click cell **B14** in the worksheet, click the **list arrow** in the Add Constraint dialog box, select **<=**, click the **Constraint text box**, then type **3700**

   See Figure K-18. The Change Constraint dialog box specifies that cell B14 should contain a value that is less than or equal to 3700. Next, you need to specify that the purchase quantities should be as close as possible to integers. They should also be greater than or equal to zero.

7. Click **Add**, click the **Cell Reference box**, select range **B7:D7**, click the **list arrow** in the Add constraint dialog box, then select **int**

8. Make sure "integer" appears in the Constraint box, click **Add**, click the **Cell Reference box**, select cells **B7:D7** in the worksheet, in the Add Constraint dialog box select **>=**, click the **Constraint box**, type **0**, then click **OK**

   The Solver Parameters dialog box reappears, with the constraints listed as shown in Figure K-19. In the next lesson, you will run Solver and generate an answer report.

FIGURE K-17: Worksheet setup for complex what-if analysis

Interest rate

Loan term

Adjustable cells

Amount must be less than $3,700

Target cell

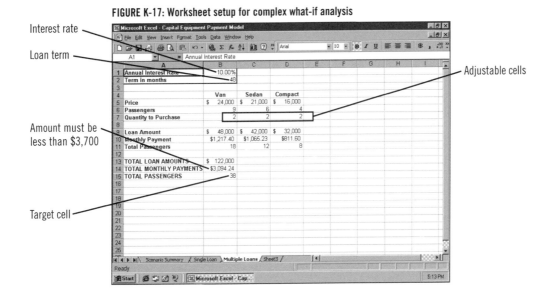

FIGURE K-18: Adding constraints

Constraints will affect this cell

Less than or equal to symbol

Highest possible monthly payment

Cell containing total monthly payments

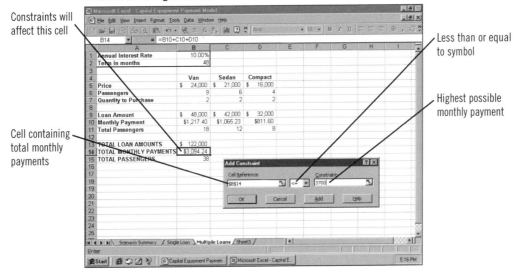

FIGURE K-19: Completed Solver Parameters dialog box

Target cell

Changing cells

Constraints on worksheet values

Target value

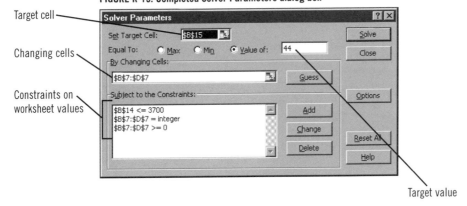

Excel 2000

Running Solver and Generating an Answer Report

After entering all the parameters in the Solver Parameters dialog box, you can run Solver to find an answer. In some cases, Solver may not be able to find a solution that meets all of your constraints; then you would need to enter new constraints and try again. Once Solver finds a solution, you can choose to create a special report explaining the solution. **Scenario** Jim has finished entering his parameters in the Solver Parameters dialog box. Now he's ready to run Solver and create an answer report.

Steps 1234

1. Make sure your Solver Parameter dialog box matches Figure K-19 in the previous lesson

2. Click **Solve**
   After a moment, the Solver Results dialog box opens, indicating that Solver has found a solution. See Figure K-20. The solution values appear in the worksheet, but you decide to move them to a special Answer Report and display the original values in the worksheet.

3. Click **Restore Original Values**, click **Answer** in the Reports list box, then click **OK**
   The Solver Results dialog box closes, and the original values are displayed in the worksheet. The Answer Report appears on a separate sheet.

4. Click the **Answer Report 1 sheet tab**
   The Answer Report displays the solution to the vehicle-purchase problem, as shown in Figure K-21. To accommodate 44 passengers and keep the monthly payments to less than $3,700, you need to purchase two vans, three sedans, and two compact cars. Notice that Solver's solution includes two long decimals that are so small as to be insignificant. You'll now format the worksheet cells to display only integers. Also, because the Original Value column doesn't contain any useful information, you'll delete it.

5. Press **[Ctrl]**, click cell **E8** and cell **E14**, click the **Decrease Decimal button** on the Standard toolbar until the cells display no decimal places

6. Right-click the **column D column header**, click **Delete** in the pop-up menu, press **[Ctrl][Home]**, then put your name in the worksheet footer, save the workbook, and print the worksheet
   You've successfully found the best combination of vehicles using Solver. The settings you specified in the Solver Parameters for the Multiple Loans worksheet are saved along with the workbook.

7. Close the workbook and exit Excel

FIGURE K-20: Solver Results dialog box

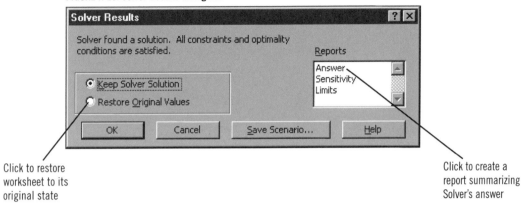

Click to restore
worksheet to its
original state

Click to create a
report summarizing
Solver's answer

FIGURE K-21: Answer Report

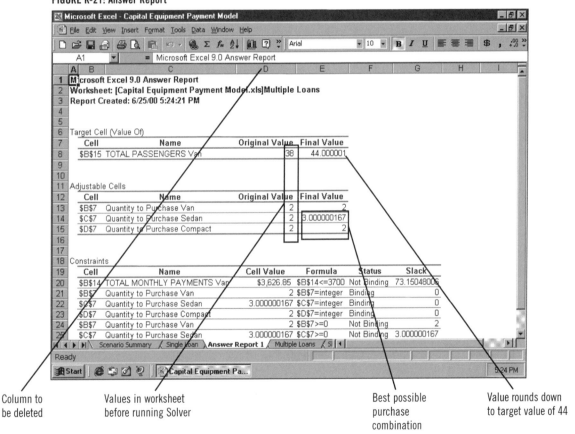

Column to
be deleted

Values in worksheet
before running Solver

Best possible
purchase
combination

Value rounds down
to target value of 44

Practice

► Concepts Review

Label each element of the Excel screen shown in Figure K-22.

FIGURE K-22

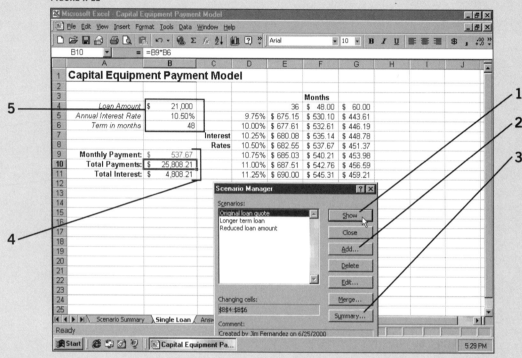

Match each term with the statement that describes it.

6. Two-input data table
7. Scenario summary
8. Goal Seek
9. One-input data table
10. Solver

a. Helps you backsolve what-if scenarios
b. Separate sheet with results from the worksheet's scenarios
c. Generates values resulting from a formula and input values variations across the top row and left column
d. Add-in that helps you solve complex what-if scenarios
e. Generates values resulting from a formula and input values variations across the top row or left column

Select the best answer from the list of choices.

11. **A scenario is**
    a. The same as a dependent cell.
    b. A set of values used to forecast worksheet results.
    c. The same as a changing cell.
    d. A worksheet model.

12. **What are changing cells?**
    a. Cells that change positions during a what-if analysis.
    b. Formulas that change, depending on their input cells.
    c. Input cells whose values can be changed in a scenario.
    d. Input cells that change, depending on their formulas.

13. **Dependent cells are usually**
    a. Formula cells that depend on the results of a scenario.
    b. Data cells that depend on their formulas.
    c. Input cells that depend on the results of a data table.
    d. Formula cells that depend on input from other cells.

14. **In Solver, the cell containing the formula is called the**
    a. Target cell.
    b. Input cell.
    c. Output cell.
    d. Changing cell.

▶ Skills Review

1. **Define a what-if analysis.**
   a. Open the workbook titled EX K-2, then save it as "Capital Equipment Repair Models" and make sure the Cappuccino Machine Repair sheet is active.
   b. State the purpose of the worksheet model.
   c. Locate the data input cells.
   d. Locate any dependent cells.
   e. Write three questions this what-if analysis model could answer.
2. **Track a what-if analysis with Scenario Manager.**
   a. Set up the most likely scenario with the current data input values. Select range B3:B5, then create a scenario called Most Likely.
   b. Add a scenario called Best Case using the same changing cells, but change the $B$3 value to 50, change the $B$4 value to 45, then change the $B$5 value to .75. Add the scenario to the list.
   c. Add a scenario called Worst Case. Change the $B$3 value to 75, change the $B$4 value to 70, then change the $B$5 value to 2.
   d. If necessary, drag the Scenario Manager dialog box to the right until columns A and B are visible.
   e. Show the Worst Case scenario results.
   f. Show the Best Case scenario results. Finally, display the Most Likely scenario results.
   g. Close the Scenario Manager dialog box.
   h. Save your work.

Excel 2000

3. **Generate a scenario summary.**
   a. Create names for the input value cells and the dependent cell in the range A3:B7 (based on the left column).
   b. Verify that the names were created.
   c. Create a Scenario Summary report in the result cell B7.
   d. Edit cell B2 to read "Scenario Summary for Cappuccino Machine Repair".
   e. Delete the Current Values column.
   f. Delete the notes beginning in cell B11.
   g. Return to cell A1, add your name to the sheet footer, then print the Scenario Summary report in landscape orientation and save your work.

4. **Project figures using a data table.**
   a. Click the Cappuccino Machine Repair sheet tab.
   b. Enter the label "Labor $" in cell D3.
   c. Adjust the formatting of the label so that it is boldfaced and right-aligned.
   d. In cell D4, enter 50; then in cell D5, enter 55.
   e. Select range D4:D5, then use the fill handle to extend the series to cell D9.
   f. Reference the job cost formula in the upper-right corner of the table structure: In cell E3, enter =B7.
   g. Format the contents of cell E3 as hidden, using the ;; Custom formatting type on the Number tab of the Format Cells dialog box.
   h. Generate the new job costs based on the varying labor costs: Select range D3:E9 and create a data table. In the Table dialog box, make cell B3 the Column Input Cell.
   i. Format range E3:E9 as currency.
   j. Add your name to the footer, save the workbook, then preview and print the worksheet.

5. **Create a two-input data table.**
   a. Move the contents of cell D3 to cell C6.
   b. Delete the contents of range E4:E9.
   c. Format cell E3 using the Currency Style button, then move the contents of cell E3 to cell D3.
   d. Format the contents of cell D3 as hidden, using the ;; Custom formatting type on the Number tab of the Format Cells dialog box.
   e. Enter "Hrs. per job" in cell F2, and format it so it is boldfaced.
   f. Enter "1" in cell E3, enter 1.5 in cell F3, then enter 2 in cell G3.
   g. Select range D3:G9 and make it a data table, making cell B5 the row input cell and cell B3 the column input cell.
   h. Format range F4:G9 as currency.
   i. Save the workbook, preview, then print the worksheet.

6. **Use Goal Seek.**
   a. Determine what the parts would have to cost so that the cost to complete the job is $125: Click cell B7, and open the Goal Seek dialog box.
   b. Enter 125 as the To value, and B4 as the By changing cell.
   c. Return to the worksheet and note the cost of the parts.
   d. Save the workbook.
   e. Determine what the labor would have to cost so that the cost to complete the job is $100. Note the result.
   f. Save the workbook.
   g. Determine what the number of hours would have to be for the cost to complete the job to equal $90. Note the result.
   h. On a blank area of the worksheet, enter the results you obtained when the job cost equaled $125, the labor costs when the job cost equaled $100, and the hours when the job cost equaled $90.
   i. Save the workbook, then preview and print the worksheet.

7. Perform a complex what-if analysis with Solver and generate an Answer Report.

   a. Click the Vehicle Repair sheet tab to make it active, then open the Solver dialog box.

   b. Make B16 the target cell, with a target value of 146.

   c. Use cells B6:D6 as the changing cells.

   d. Specify that cell B14 must be greater than or equal to 4000.

   e. Specify that cell B15 must be greater than or equal to 6000.

   f. Use Solver to find a solution.

   g. Generate an Answer Report and restore the original values to the worksheet.

   h. Edit the Answer Report to delete the original values column.

   i. Add your name to the footer, save the workbook, preview and print the Answer Report, then close the workbook.

▶ Visual Workshop

Create the worksheet shown in Figure K-23. Make sure to generate the table on the right as a data table. Save the workbook as "Color Laptop Loan Payment Model". Add your name to the footer, then preview and print the worksheet. Print the worksheet again with the formulas displayed.

FIGURE K-23

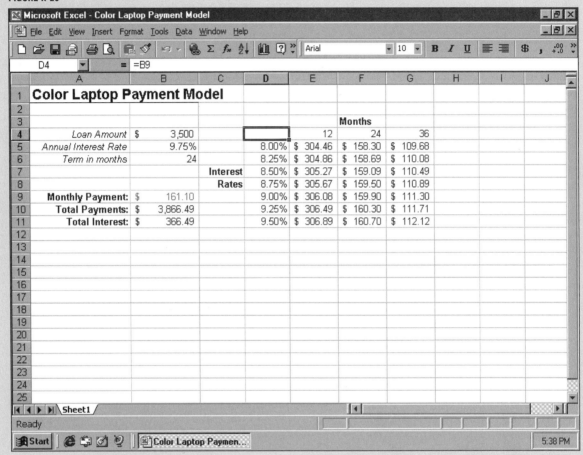

Summarizing
Data with PivotTables

Objectives

▶ **Plan and design a PivotTable report**
MOUS ▶ **Create a PivotTable report**
MOUS ▶ **Change the summary function of a PivotTable report**
MOUS ▶ **Analyze three-dimensional data**
▶ **Update a PivotTable report**
MOUS ▶ **Change the structure and format of a PivotTable report**
MOUS ▶ **Create a PivotChart report**
▶ **Use the GETPIVOTDATA function**

With the Excel PivotTable feature, you can summarize selected data in a worksheet, then list and display that data in a table format. The interactive quality of a PivotTable allows you to freely rearrange, or "pivot," parts of the table structure around the data and summarize any data values within the table. You also can designate a PivotTable page field that lets you view list items three-dimensionally, as if they were arranged in a stack of pages. There are two PivotTable features in Excel: PivotTable reports and PivotChart reports. In this unit, you will plan, design, create, update, and change the layout and format of a PivotTable report. You will also add a page field to a PivotTable report, then create a PivotChart report. Scenario▶ It's nearing the end of the fiscal year, and the Accounting department has asked Jim Fernandez to develop a departmental salary analysis for selected corporate and management positions. Jim uses a PivotTable report to do this.

Planning and Designing a PivotTable Report

Creating a PivotTable report (often called a PivotTable) involves only a few steps. Before you begin, however, you need to review the data and consider how a PivotTable can best summarize it. **Scenario** Jim plans and designs his PivotTable using the following guidelines:

Review the list information

Before you can effectively summarize list data in a PivotTable, you need to know what information each field contains and understand the list's scope. Jim is working with a list of corporate and managerial staff that he received from Karen Rosen, MediaLoft's human resource manager. This list is shown in Figure L-1.

Determine the purpose of the PivotTable, then write down the names of the fields you want to include

The purpose of Jim's PivotTable is to summarize corporate salary information by position across various departments. Jim will include the following fields in the PivotTable: department, position, and annual salary.

Determine which field contains the data you want summarized and which summary function will be used

Jim intends to summarize salary information by averaging the salary field for each department and position. He'll do this by using the Excel Average function.

Decide how you want to arrange the data

The layout of a PivotTable is crucial in delivering its intended message. Jim will define department as a column field, position as a row field, and annual salary as a data summary field. See Figure L-2.

Determine the location of the PivotTable

You can place a PivotTable in any worksheet of any workbook. Placing a PivotTable on a separate worksheet makes it easier to locate, however, and prevents you from accidentally overwriting parts of an existing sheet. Jim decides to create the PivotTable as a new worksheet in the current workbook.

FIGURE L-1: Management salary worksheet

	First Name	Last Name	Hire Date	Department	Position	Mgmt Level	Annual Salary	Perf Rating
2	Maria	Abbott	10/18/93	Corporate Manager	General Sales Manager	2	70,000	2
3	Tyler	Amodo	9/5/94	Corporate Staff	Division Manager	3	65,000	3
4	Michael	Cole	2/6/97	Management Staff	Accounting Staff	2	42,000	3
5	Katherine	DeNiro	4/29/99	Corporate Staff	Accounting Staff	3	55,000	2
6	David	Dumont	4/7/86	Section Manager	Director of Training	3	53,500	4
7	Catherine	Favreau	3/19/99	Corporate Manager	Director of Advertising	2	55,500	3
8	George	Feake	8/1/94	Store	Store Manager	3	46,000	3
9	Jim	Fernandez	1/2/96	Corporate Manager	Office Manager	2	58,000	5
10	Louis	Grazio	5/24/96	Management Staff	Payroll Manager	3	45,000	3
11	Lois	Greenwood	5/2/94	Store	Store Manager	3	42,000	4
12	Patrick	Ikutu	3/12/98	Corporate Staff	Division Manager	3	48,000	4
13	Robert	Jaworski	3/1/98	Corporate Staff	Accounting Staff	2	42,000	4
14	John	Kim	3/3/99	Section Manager	Dir. Of Shipping	3	57,500	1
15	Mike	MacDowell	2/8/99	Management Staff	Web Manager	3	55,000	2
16	Goran	Manchevski	4/5/95	Store	Store Manager	3	47,500	2
17	Michael	Martin	2/15/98	Store	Store Manager	3	48,000	3
18	Eileen	Murphy	2/10/94	Corporate Staff	Ad Copy Writer	4	45,000	3
19	Patricia	Fabel	6/21/96	Management Staff	Accounting Staff	3	48,000	3
20	Elizabeth	Reed	2/1/96	Corporate Manager	Vice President	1	85,000	5
21	Evelyn	Storey	1/10/92	Corporate Staff	Circulation Manager	3	55,000	4
22	Alice	Wegman	1/5/97	Corporate Manager	Marketing Manager	2	65,000	4

Manager List

Ready

Start | Microsoft Excel - Ex I-1 | 10:45 PM

FIGURE L-2: Example of a PivotTable report

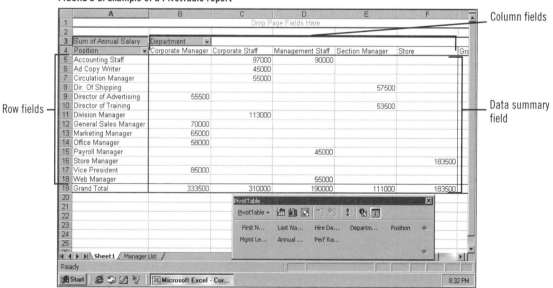

Column fields

Row fields

Data summary field

SUMMARIZING DATA WITH PIVOTTABLES EXCEL L-3

Creating a PivotTable Report

Excel 2000

Once you've planned and designed your PivotTable, you can create it. The PivotTable Wizard takes you through the process step-by-step. Scenario With the planning and design stage complete, Jim is ready to create a PivotTable that summarizes corporate salary information. After they add the remaining salary information, the Accounting and Human Resources departments will use this information to budget salaries for the coming year.

QuickTip

To return personalized toolbars and menus to their default state, click Tools on the menu bar, click Customize, click the Options tab in the Customize dialog box, click Reset my usage data to restore the default settings, click Yes, click Close, then close the Drawing toolbar if it is displayed.

1. **Open the workbook titled EX L-1, then save it as Corporate Salaries**

   This worksheet contains information about some of MediaLoft's corporate employees and managers, including hire date, department, position, management level, salary, and performance rating. Notice that the records are sorted alphabetically by last name.

2. **Click cell A1 if necessary, click Data on the menu bar, then click PivotTable and PivotChart report**

   The first PivotTable and PivotChart Wizard dialog box opens, as shown in Figure L-3. This is where you specify the type of data source you want to use for your PivotTable: an Excel list or database, an external data source (for example, a Microsoft Access file), or multiple consolidation ranges (another term for worksheet ranges). You also have the option of choosing a PivotTable or PivotChart report.

3. **Make sure the Microsoft Excel list or database option button is selected, make sure PivotTable is selected, then click Next**

   The second PivotTable and PivotChart Wizard dialog box opens. Because the cell pointer was located within the list before you opened the PivotTable Wizard, Excel automatically completes the Range box with the table range that includes the selected cell—in this case, $A$1:$H$22. You can either type a new range in the Range box or confirm that the PivotTable will be created from the existing range.

4. **Click Next**

   The third PivotTable Wizard dialog box opens. You use this dialog box to specify the location of the PivotTable.

Trouble?

If your PivotTable toolbar does not appear, click View on the menu bar, click Toolbars, then click PivotTable to select it. If the PivotTable toolbar blocks your view of the worksheet, drag it to the bottom of the worksheet window.

5. **Make sure New Worksheet is selected, then click Finish**

   A worksheet appears with an empty PivotTable, as shown in Figure L-4. The PivotTable toolbar also appears. It contains buttons that allow you to manipulate data as well as field names that you can drag into various "drop areas" of the PivotTable to analyze your data.

6. **Drag the Department field button from the PivotTable toolbar to the area marked Drop Column Fields here, then drag the Position field button to the Drop Row Fields Here area**

   This format will create a PivotTable with the departments as column headers and the management positions as row labels. To display the entire field name in a ToolTip in the PivotTable toolbar, place the pointer over the field button.

QuickTip

You can use more than one summary function in a PivotTable by simply dragging multiple field buttons to the data area.

7. **Drag the Annual Salary field button to the Drop Data Items Here area**

   Because SUM is the Excel default function for data fields containing numbers, Excel automatically calculates the sum of the salaries by department and by position. See Figure L-5. Notice that the position titles now appear as row labels in the left column, and the department names are listed across the columns as field names.

FIGURE L-3: First PivotTable Wizard dialog box

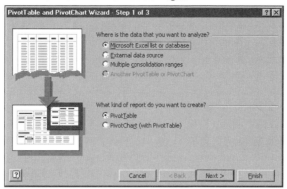

FIGURE L-4: New PivotTable ready to receive field data

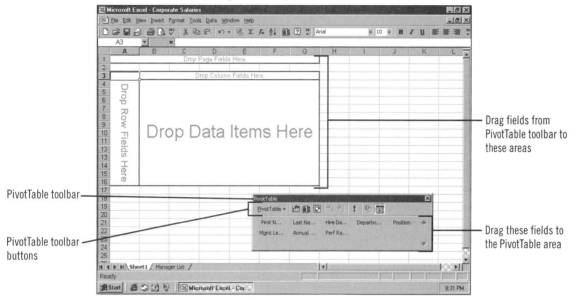

PivotTable toolbar

PivotTable toolbar
buttons

Drag fields from
PivotTable toolbar to
these areas

Drag these fields to
the PivotTable area

FIGURE L-5: New PivotTable with fields in place

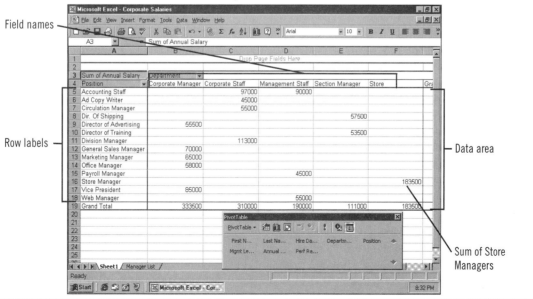

Field names

Row labels

Data area

Sum of Store
Managers

Changing the Summary Function of a PivotTable Report

A PivotTable's **summary function** controls what type of calculation is applied to the table data. Unless you specify otherwise, Excel applies the SUM function to numeric data and the COUNT function to data fields containing text. However, you can easily change the SUM function in the PivotTable Wizard dialog box to a different function, such as AVERAGE (which calculates the average of all values in the field), PRODUCT (which multiplies all the values in a field), or MAX (which finds the highest value in a field). **Scenario** Jim wants to calculate the average salary for the managers using the AVERAGE function.

Steps 1 2 3 4

1. Click any cell in the data area, then click the **Field Settings button** 📲 on the PivotTable toolbar

   The PivotTable Field dialog box opens. The functions listed in the Summarize by list box designate how the data will be calculated. Other buttons on the PivotTable toolbar are described in Table L-1.

2. In the Summarize by list box, click **Average**, then click **OK**

   The PivotTable Field dialog box closes. The data area of the PivotTable shows the average salary for each position by department. See Figure L-6. The numbers representing sums in the last column and row now represent averages of annual salary. After reviewing the data, you decide that it would be more useful to sum the salary information than to average it.

3. Click the **Field Settings button** 📲 on the PivotTable toolbar; in the Summarize by list box, click **Sum**, then click **OK**

   The PivotTable Field dialog box closes and Excel recalculates the PivotTable—this time, summing the salary data instead of averaging it.

4. Rename Sheet1 **PivotTable**, add your name to the worksheet footer, save the workbook, then preview and print the worksheet in landscape orientation

FIGURE L-6: PivotTable showing averages

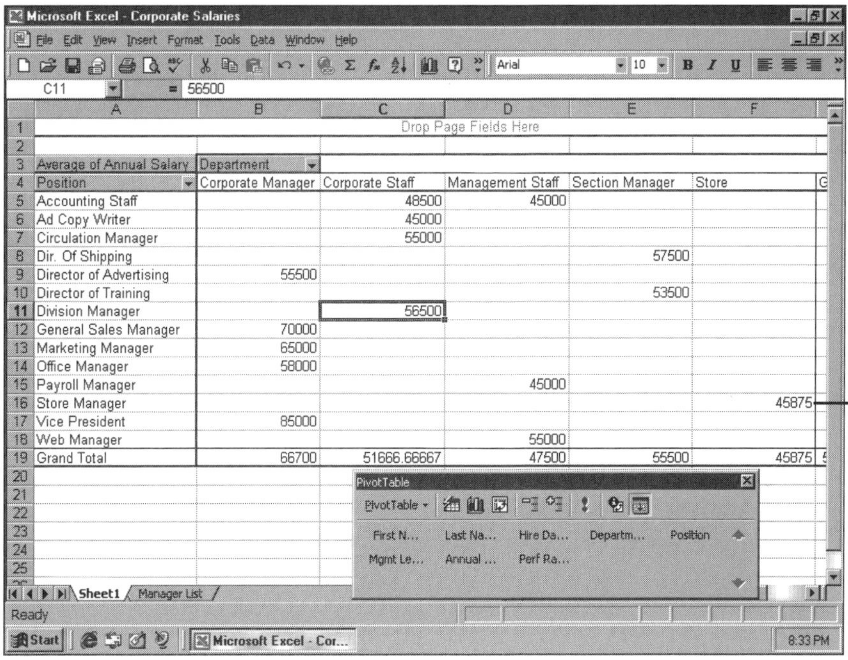

Average salary for Store Managers

TABLE L-1: PivotTable toolbar buttons

button	name	description
PivotTable ▾	**PivotTable Menu**	Displays menu of PivotTable commands
🔲	**Format Report**	Displays a list of PivotTable formats
🔲	**Chart Wizard**	Creates a PivotChart report
🔲	**PivotTable Wizard**	Starts PivotTable Wizard
🔲	**Hide Detail**	Hides detail in table groupings
🔲	**Show Detail**	Shows detail in table groupings
❗	**Refresh Data**	Updates list changes within the table
🔲	**Field Settings**	Displays a list of field settings
🔲	**Show/Hide Fields**	Displays/hides PivotTable fields on toolbar; in a chart, displays or hides outlines and labels

Analyzing Three-Dimensional Data

When row and column field positions are established in a PivotTable, you are working with two-dimensional data. You can convert a PivotTable to a three-dimensional data analysis tool by adding a **page field**. Page fields make the data appear as if it is stacked in pages, thus adding a third dimension to the analysis. When using a page field, you are in effect filtering data through that field. To add the page field, you simply drag it to the Drop Page Fields Here area. **Scenario** Jim wants to filter the PivotTable so that only one department's data is visible at one time. He uses the PivotTable Wizard to add the Department page field.

Steps

1. Drag the **Department field button** from the column area to the **Drop Page Fields Here** area

   The PivotTable is re-created with a page field showing data for each department. See Figure L-7. You can select and view the data for each department, page by page, by clicking the Department list arrow and selecting the page you want to view.

2. Click the **Department list arrow**

3. Click **Management Staff**, then click **OK**

   The PivotTable displays the salary data for the management staff only, as shown in Figure L-8.

4. Click the **Department list arrow**, click **Corporate Staff**, then click **OK**

   The salaries for the corporate staff appear.

5. Save the workbook, then print the worksheet

QuickTip

To display each page of the page field on a separate worksheet, click PivotTable on the PivotTable toolbar, then click Show Pages, then click OK.

FIGURE L-7: PivotTable with Department as page field

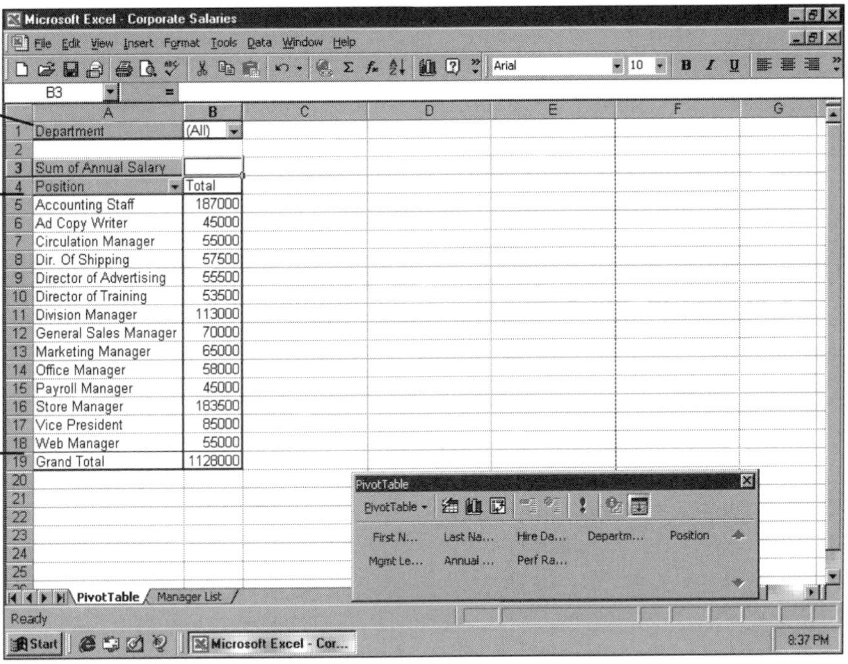

Department now in Page field area

Data now shows total salaries for each position in all departments

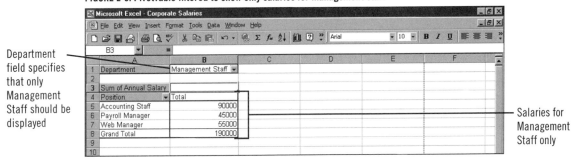

FIGURE L-8: PivotTable filtered to show only salaries for management staff

Department field specifies that only Management Staff should be displayed

Salaries for Management Staff only

Excel 2000

Updating a PivotTable Report

The data displayed in a PivotTable looks like typical worksheet data. Because the PivotTable data is linked to a source list, however, the values and results in the PivotTable are read-only values. That means you cannot move or modify part of a PivotTable by inserting or deleting rows, editing results, or moving cells. To change PivotTable data, you must edit the items directly in the list you used to create the table, called the **source list**, and then update, or **refresh**, the PivotTable to reflect the changes. Scenario⟩ Jim just learned that the training manager, Howard Freeberg, was never entered into the workbook. Jim needs to add information about this manager to the current list; he starts by inserting a row for Freeberg's information.

1. Click the **Manager List sheet tab**
By inserting the new row in the correct position alphabetically, you will not need to sort the list again. Also, by adding the new manager within the named range, Database, the new row data will be included automatically in the named range.

2. Right-click the **row 10 header**; then on the pop-up menu, click **Insert**
A blank row appears as the new row 10, and the data in the old row 10 moves down to row 11. You'll enter the data on Freeberg in the new row 10.

3. Enter the data for the new manager based on the following information

field name	new data item
First Name	Howard
Last Name	Freeberg
Hire Date	10/29/98
Department	Corporate Staff
Position	Training Manager
Mgmt Level	2
Annual Salary	59,000
Perf Rating	2

After you add data, you must refresh the PivotTable so that it reflects the additional data.

4. Click the **PivotTable sheet tab**, then make sure the Corporate Staff page is in view
Notice that the Corporate Staff list does not currently include a training manager and that the grand total is $310,000. Before you select the Refresh Data command to refresh the PivotTable, you need to make sure the cell pointer is located within the current table range.

5. Click anywhere within the table range (A3:B9), then click the **Refresh Data button** 🔼 on the PivotTable toolbar
A message dialog box opens with the message "The Refresh Data operation changed the PivotTable report" to confirm that the update was successful.

QuickTip

Clicking a row label in a PivotTable selects the entire row. Clicking a data cell selects only that cell.

6. Click **OK**
The PivotTable now includes the training manager in row 9, and the grand total has increased by the amount of his salary (59,000) to $369,000. See Figure L-9.

7. Save the workbook and print the worksheet

FIGURE L-9: Refreshed PivotTable

New record for
Training
Manager now
appears in
Corporate Staff
salaries

Total reflects
new record for
Training
Manager

	A	B	C	D	E	F	G
1	Department	Corporate Staff					
2							
3	Sum of Annual Salary						
4	Position	Total					
5	Accounting Staff	97000					
6	Ad Copy Writer	45000					
7	Circulation Manager	55000					
8	Division Manager	113000					
9	Training Manager	59000					
10	Grand Total	369000					
11							
12							
13							

Maintaining original table data

Once you select the Refresh Data command, you cannot undo the operation. If you want the PivotTable to display the original source data, you must change the source data list, then re-select the Refresh Data command. If you're concerned about the effect refreshing the PivotTable might have on your work, save a second (working) copy of the workbook so that your original data remains intact.

Changing the Structure and Format of a PivotTable Report

Although you cannot change the actual data in a PivotTable, you can alter its structure and format at any time. You might, for example, want to rename a PivotTable field button, add another column field, or switch the positions of existing fields. You can quickly change the way data is displayed in a PivotTable by dragging field buttons in the worksheet from a row position to a column position, or vice versa. Alternatively, you may want to enhance the appearance of a PivotTable by changing the way the text or values are formatted. It's a good idea to format a PivotTable using AutoFormat, because once you refresh a PivotTable any formatting that has not been applied to the cells through AutoFormat is removed. **Scenario** Jim wants to add the performance ratings to the PivotTable in order to supply the Accounting department with additional data needed for salary budgeting. Once the new field is added, Jim will format the PivotTable.

Steps

1. Make sure that the **PivotTable sheet** is active, that the Corporate Staff page is in view, and that the cell pointer is located anywhere inside the PivotTable (range A3:B10)

   When you move fields in a PivotTable, you can drag them as you did when you moved the Department field into the page area. Sometimes, however, you may want to drag fields while looking only at the PivotTable structure, without the data. You can do this by using the PivotTable Wizard Layout dialog box.

2. Click the **PivotTable Wizard button** 🔳 on the PivotTable toolbar

3. Click **Layout**, drag the **Perf Rating button** to the **COLUMN** area and compare your screen with Figure L-10

4. Click **OK**, then click **Finish**

   The PivotTable is re-created, and the new field is added. In addition to displaying the manager's position and annual salary on each department page, each manager's last performance rating on a scale from 1 to 5 appears as a column label. Now you are ready to format the PivotTable.

5. Click cell **B5**, click the **Field Settings button** 🔳 on the PivotTable toolbar, then in the PivotTable Field dialog box, click **Number**

6. Under Category in the Format Cells dialog box, click **Accounting**, edit the Decimal Places box to read **0**, click **OK**, then click **OK** again

   The PivotTable Field dialog box closes, and the annual salaries are formatted with commas and dollar signs.

7. Click cell **A3**; click the **Format Report button** 🔳 on the PivotTable toolbar bar; in the AutoFormat dialog box, scroll down and then click **Table 2**, click **OK**, then click outside the range to deselect it

   The PivotTable appears as shown in Figure L-11. The AutoFormat is applied to all pages of the PivotTable.

8. Click the **Department list arrow**, click **Management Staff**, then click **OK**

   The Management Staff page has the same formatting.

9. Save the workbook, then preview and print the active sheet

FIGURE L-10: Revised PivotTable structure

Performance Rating now in COLUMN area

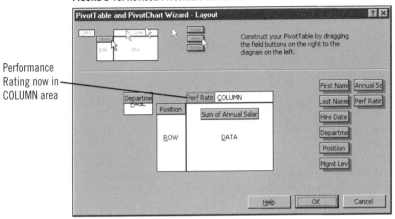

FIGURE L-11: Corporate Staff page with AutoFormat applied

AutoFormat has applied shading as well as blue headings and totals

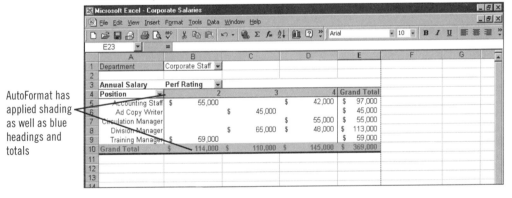

Excel 2000

Creating a PivotChart Report

A PivotChart report is a chart that you create from data or from a PivotTable report. Like a PivotTable report, a PivotChart report has fields that you can drag to explore new data relationships. Table L-2 describes how the elements in a PivotTable report correspond to the elements in a PivotChart report. When you create a PivotChart directly from data, Excel automatically creates a corresponding PivotTable report. When you change a PivotChart report by dragging fields, Excel updates the corresponding PivotTable report to show the new layout. You can create a PivotChart report from any PivotTable report to reflect that view of your data, but if you use an indented PivotTable report format, your chart will not have series fields; indented PivotTable report formats do not include column fields. **Scenario** Jim wants to chart the annual salary and performance rating information for the Corporate Manager department. He uses the PivotTable and PivotChart Wizard to create a column chart from the PivotTable data.

Steps

1. Click the **Manager List tab**, click anywhere in the data range, click **Data**, then click **PivotTable and PivotChart Report**
   The PivotTable and PivotChart Wizard opens.

2. Make sure Excel list or database is selected, then click to select **PivotChart (with PivotTable)** as shown in Figure L-12, click **Next**, then click **Next** again
   A message tells you that your existing PivotTable was created from the same source data and recommends using the same data to save memory.

3. Click **Yes**, click **Next**, then click **Finish**
   A new chart sheet opens, shown in Figure L-13. Jim wants to explore salary levels as they relate to performance ratings and management level.

4. Drag fields to PivotChart areas as follows:

Field	Area
Department	Page Fields
Management Level	Category Fields
Performance Rating	Series Fields
Annual Salary	Data

   The chart representing your data appears in the chart area.

Trouble?

If the Chart toolbar does not appear on your screen, open it: Click View on the menu bar, point to Toolbars, then click Chart.

5. Click **Sum of Annual Salary** on the PivotChart, click the **Field Settings button** 📇 on the PivotTable toolbar, click **Average** in the PivotTable Field dialog box, then click **OK**
   The PivotChart report is recalculated, as shown in Figure L-14.

6. Click the **Department list arrow**, click **Corporate Manager**, click **OK**, then drag the **Position field** from the PivotTable toolbar to the Series fields area (the legend).
   The positions and ratings appear in the legend. Jim now has more detail on which to base his discussions with Human Resources and upper management.

7. Save the workbook, place your name in the chart sheet footer, then preview and print the PivotChart report

FIGURE L-12: PivotTable and PivotChart Wizard

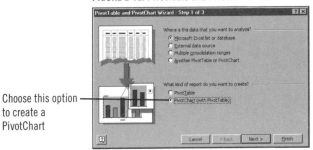

Choose this option to create a PivotChart

FIGURE L-13: New chart sheet, ready to receive fields

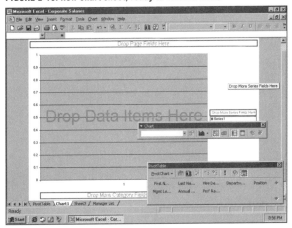

FIGURE L-14: PivotChart report recalculated to show averages

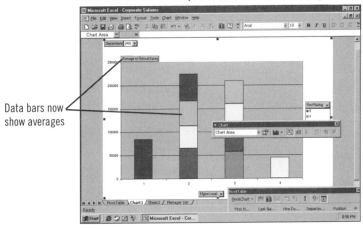

Data bars now show averages

TABLE L-2: PivotTable and PivotChart elements

PivotTable items	become	PivotChart items
row fields		category fields
column fields		series fields
page fields		page fields

Excel 2000

Using the GETPIVOTDATA Function

Because a PivotTable is rearranged so easily, you can't use an ordinary cell reference when you want to reference a PivotTable cell in another worksheet. If you change the way data is displayed in a PivotTable (for example, by displaying a different page), the data moves, rendering an ordinary cell reference incorrect. Instead, to retrieve summary data from a PivotTable, you need to use the Excel GETPIVOTDATA function. Its syntax is displayed in Figure L-15. ▶Scenario In creating next year's budget, the Accounting department is allocating money toward the payroll budget for the office manager. The department has asked Jim to include the current total salary for the office manager on the Manager List sheet. Jim uses the GETPIVOTDATA function to retrieve this information from the PivotTable.

1. Click the **PivotTable sheet tab**
   The Management Staff page is currently visible. You need the salary information for marketing managers in all departments.

2. Click the **Department list arrow**, click **(All)**, then click **OK**
   The PivotTable displays the salary data for all positions. Next, you will reference the total for marketing managers in the Manager List sheet.

   Trouble?
   If the Align Right button does not appear on your Formatting toolbar, click the More Buttons button 》 to view it.

3. Click the **Manager List sheet tab**, click cell **D25**, type **Office Manager Salary:**, click the **Enter button** ✓ on the formula bar, click the **Align Right button** on the Formatting toolbar, then click the **Bold button** on the Formatting toolbar
   The new label appears formatted in cell D25. Now, you'll enter a GETPIVOTDATA function in cell E25 that will retrieve the total salary for marketing managers from the PivotTable.

4. Click cell **E25**, click the **Paste Function button** 𝑓ₓ on the Standard toolbar; under Function category in the Paste Function dialog box, click **Lookup & Reference**; under Function name, click **GETPIVOTDATA**; then click **OK**
   The GETPIVOTDATA formula palette opens. The function's first argument, Pivot_table, can contain a reference to any cell within the PivotTable range. The second argument, Name, can contain the row or column label for the summary information you want (in this case, the column label Grand Total) enclosed in quotation marks.

5. With the pointer in the Pivot_table box, click the **PivotTable sheet tab**; click cell **F14** (or any other cell in the PivotTable range); in the formula palette, click the **Name box**; then type **"Office Manager"**
   Be sure to type the quotation marks. See Figure L-16.

6. Click **OK**, then click the **Currency Style button** $ on the Formatting toolbar
   The current total salary for Office Manager is $58,000, as shown in Figure L-17. This is the same value displayed in cell F14 of the PivotTable. The GETPIVOTDATA function will work correctly only when the salary for all departments is displayed in the PivotTable. You can verify this by displaying a different page in the PivotTable and viewing the effect on the Manager List worksheet.

7. Click the **PivotTable sheet tab**, click the **Department list arrow**, click **Corporate Manager**, click **OK**, then click the **Manager List sheet tab**
   The error message in cell E25 will disappear when you redisplay the (All) page.

8. Click the **PivotTable sheet tab**, click the **Department list arrow**, click **(All)**, click **OK**, then click the **Manager List sheet tab**
   Note that the correct value—$58,000.00—is once again displayed in cell E25.

9. Put your name in the footer, save the workbook, print the Manager List worksheet, then close the file and exit Excel

FIGURE L-15: Syntax of GETPIVOTDATA function

GETPIVOTDATA(pivot_table,name)

Reference to any page in the
PivotTable that shows the
data you want to retrieve.

The row or column label (enclosed in
quotation marks) describing the summary value you want to retrieve. For
example, "January 2000" for the grand
total for January 2000.

FIGURE L-16: Completed GETPIVOTDATA formula palette

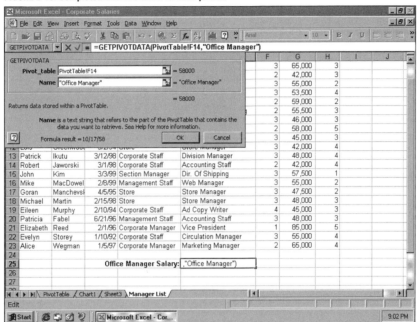

FIGURE L-17: Results of GETPIVOTDATA function

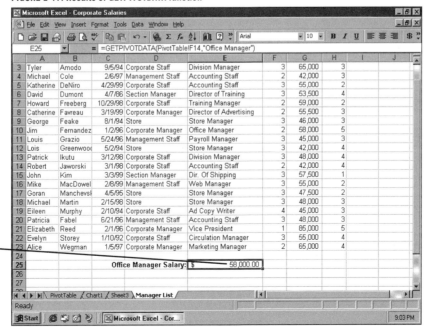

Results of
GETPIVOTDATA
function

Excel 2000

Practice

► Concepts Review

Label each element of the Excel screen shown in Figure L-18.

FIGURE L-18

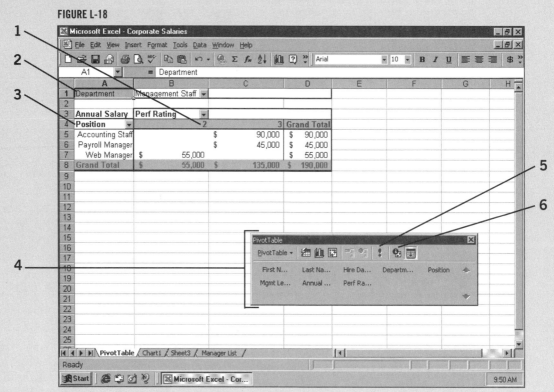

Match each term with the statement that describes it.

7. COLUMN area
8. GETPIVOTDATA function
9. DATA area
10. PivotTable page
11. Summary function

a. Displays summarized values
b. Displays fields as column labels
c. Shows data for one item at a time in a table
d. Determines how data will be calculated
e. Retrieves information from a PivotTable

Select the best answer from the list of choices.

12. **A PivotTable report is best described as an Excel feature that**
    a. Requires a source list.
    b. "Stacks" pages of data.
    c. Allows you to display, summarize, and analyze list data.
    d. Displays columns and rows of data.

13. **Which PivotTable report field allows you to average values?**
    a. Column field
    b. Data field
    c. Page field
    d. Row field

14. **To make changes to PivotTable data, you must**
    a. Drag a column header to the column area.
    b. Edit cells in the source list and then refresh the PivotTable.
    c. Edit cells in the PivotTable and then refresh the source list.
    d. Create a page field.

► Skills Review

1. **Plan and design a PivotTable.**
   a. Open the workbook titled EX L-2, then save it as "October CDs".
   b. You'll create a PivotTable to show the sum of sales across products and regions. Study the list, then write down the field names you think should be included in the PivotTable. Determine which fields you think should be column fields, row fields, and data fields, then sketch a draft PivotTable.

2. **Create a PivotTable report**
   a. Using the data on the Sales List, generate a PivotTable report on a new worksheet, and arrange the data fields as follows: (*Hint:* In the Row area, place the Store field to the left of the Sales Rep field.)

Field	Area
Store	Row
Sales Rep	Row
Product	Column
Sales $	Data

3. **Change the summary function of a PivotTable report.**
   a. Change the PivotTable summary function to Average, then change it back to Sum.
   b. Rename the new sheet "Oct. 99 PivotTable".
   c. Save your work.

4. Analyze three-dimensional data.

    a. Place the Region field in the page area.

    b. Display sales for only the East region.

    c. Add your name to the worksheet footer, then print the worksheet in landscape orientation.

    d. Save your work.

5. Update a PivotTable.

    a. On the PivotTable, note the Boston total for The Sunset Trio.

    b. Go to the Sales List sheet.

    c. Create a new blank row 8 and enter the following data:

Field name	New data item
Period	Oct-99
Product	The Sunset Trio
Region	East
Store	Boston
Sales $	4,900
Sales Rep	L. Smith

    d. Refresh the PivotTable so it reflects the new data item.

    e. Note the Boston total for The Sunset Trio and verify that it increased by $4,900.

    f. Add your name to the worksheet footer then print the PivotTable.

    g. Save your work.

6. Change the structure and format of a PivotTable.

    a. In the PivotTable, redisplay data for all regions and return the summary function to Sum of sales.

    b. Drag fields so that the following areas contain the following fields: (*Hint:* To remove fields from an area, drag them back over to the field area in the PivotTable toolbar.)

Field	Area
Product	Row
Sales Rep	Column
Store	Page

    c. Change the numbers to Currency format with 0 decimal places.

    d. Apply the Report 6 AutoFormat and print the PivotTable.

    e. Apply the Table 4 AutoFormat and print the PivotTable in landscape orientation, fitting the information on one page.

    f. Save your work.

7. **Create a PivotChart report.**
   a. Go to the Sales List sheet.
   b. Create a PivotChart report (with PivotTable), using the existing PivotTable data on a new worksheet.
   c. Place fields in the PivotChart report areas as follows:

Field	Area
Product	Series
Region	Category
Store	Category
Sales$	Data

   d. Change the Summary function to Average.
   e. Add your name to the chart sheet, then preview and print the chart.
   f. Save the workbook.

8. **Use the GETPIVOTDATA function.**
   a. In cell E27 of the Sales List, create a function to retrieve the grand total for S. Gupta from the October 99 PivotTable.
   b. Format the figure in E27 as currency with no decimal places.
   c. Save the workbook, then preview and print the worksheet.
   d. Close the workbook and exit Excel.

► Visual Workshop

Open the workbook titled EX L-7, then save it as "Corner Fruit Stand". Using the data in the workbook provided, create the PivotTable shown in Figure L-19. (*Hint:* There are two data summary fields.) Add your name to the worksheet footer, then preview and print the PivotTable. Save the worksheet, then close the workbook.

FIGURE L-19

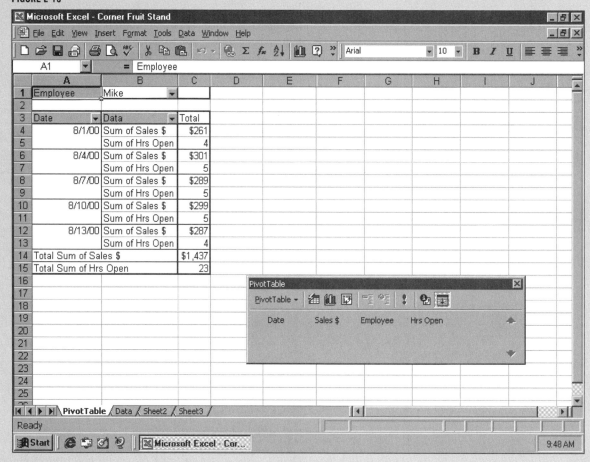

Excel 2000

Exchanging
Data with Other Programs

Objectives

► **Plan a data exchange**

_{MOUS} ► **Import a text file**

_{MOUS} ► **Import a database table**

_{MOUS} ► **Insert a graphic file in a worksheet**

_{MOUS} ► **Embed a worksheet**

_{MOUS} ► **Link a worksheet to another program**

_{MOUS} ► **Embed an Excel chart into a PowerPoint slide**

► **Convert a list to an Access table**

In a Windows environment, you can freely exchange data between Excel and most other Windows programs. In this unit, you will plan a data exchange with Excel. **Scenario►** MediaLoft's upper management has asked MediaLoft office manager Jim Fernandez to research the possible purchase of CafeCorp, a small company that operates cafés in large businesses, hospitals, and, more recently, drug stores. Jim is reviewing the broker's paper documents and electronic files and developing a presentation on the feasibility of acquiring this company. To complete this project, Jim will exchange data between Excel and other programs.

Planning a Data Exchange

Because the tools available in Windows and Windows-supported programs are so flexible, exchanging data between Excel and other programs is easy. The first step involves planning what you want to accomplish with each data exchange. **Scenario** Jim uses the following guidelines to plan data exchanges between Excel and other programs in order to complete the business analysis project.

1. Identify the data you want to exchange, its file type, and, if possible, the program used to create it

Whether the data you want to exchange is contained in a graphic file or a worksheet or consists only of text, it is important to identify the data's **source program**, the file type, and the program used to create it. Once the source program has been identified, you can determine options for exchanging that data with Excel. Jim has been asked to analyze a text file containing the CafeCorp product data. Although he does not know the source program, Jim knows that the file contains unformatted text. A file that consists of text but no formatting is sometimes referred to as an **ASCII file**. Because an ASCII file is a universally accepted text file format, Jim can easily import it into Excel.

2. Determine the program with which you want to exchange the specified data

You might want to insert a graphic object into an Excel worksheet or add a spreadsheet to a WordPad document. Data exchange rules vary from program to program. Besides knowing which program created the data to be exchanged, you must also identify which program will receive the data (that is, the **destination program**). Jim received a database table of CafeCorp's corporate customers created with the dBASE IV program. After determining that Excel can import dBASE IV tables, he plans to import that database file into Excel to perform his analysis.

3. Determine the goal of your data exchange

Although it is convenient to use the Clipboard to cut, copy, and paste data within and between programs, you cannot retain a connection with the source program or document using this method. However, there are two ways to transfer data within and between programs that allow you to retain some connection with the source document and/or the source program. These data-transfer options involve using a Windows technology known as object linking and embedding, or **OLE**. The data to be exchanged, called an **object**, may consist of text, a worksheet, or any other type of data. You use **embedding** to insert a copy of the original object in the destination document and, if necessary, to subsequently edit this data separately from the source document. This process is illustrated in Figure M-1. You use **linking** when you want the information you inserted to be updated automatically when the data in the source document changes. This process is illustrated in Figure M-2. Embedding and linking are discussed in more detail later in this unit. Jim has determined that he needs to use both object embedding and object linking for his analysis and presentation project.

4. Set up the data exchange

When you exchange data between two programs, it is best to start both programs prior to initiating the exchange. You might also want to tile the programs on the screen either horizontally or vertically so that you can see both while the data is exchanged. See Table M-1 for a list of file formats that Excel can import. Jim will work with Excel and WordPad when exchanging data for this project.

5. Execute the data exchange

The steps you use will vary, depending on the type of data exchanged. Jim is eager to attempt the data exchanges to complete his business analysis of CafeCorp.

FIGURE M-1: Embedded object

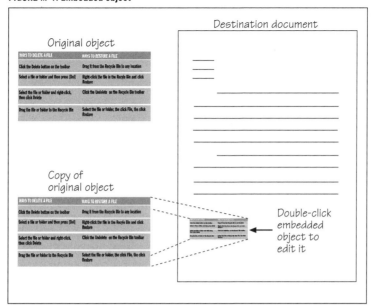

FIGURE M-2: Linked object

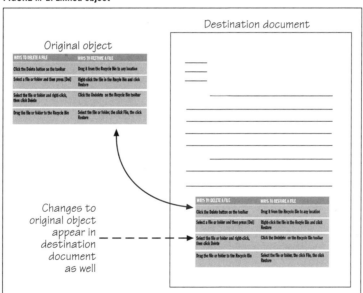

TABLE M-1: Importable file formats and extensions

file format	file extension(s)	file format	file extensions
dBASE II, III, IV	DBF	CSV (Comma Separated Values)	CSV
Excel 4.0	XLS, XLW, XLC, XLM	DIF (Data Interchange Format, i.e., VisiCalc)	DIF
Excel 5.0/7.0	XLS, XLT	Formatted Text (Space or column delimited)	TXT, PRN
Lotus 1-2-3	WKS, WK1, WK3, ALL, FMT, WK3, FM3, WK4	Text (Tab delimited)	TXT
Quattro/Quattro Pro	WQ1, WBI	SYLK (Symbolic Link: Multiplan, Microsoft Works)	SLK

Excel 2000

Importing a Text File

You can import data stored in other programs into Excel by simply opening the file, so long as Excel can read the file type. After importing the file, use the Save As command on the File menu to save the data in Excel format. Text files use a tab or space as the **delimiter**, or column separator, to separate columns of data. When you import a text file into Excel, the Text Import Wizard automatically opens and describes how text is separated in the imported file. **Scenario** Now that he's planned his data exchange, Jim wants to import a tab-delimited text file containing product cost and pricing data from CafeCorp.

1. In a blank workbook, click the **Open button** 🖼 on the Standard toolbar, click the **Look in list arrow**, then click the drive containing your Project Disk

   The Open dialog box shows only those files that match the file types listed in the Files of type box—usually Microsoft Excel files. In this case, however, you're importing a text file.

Trouble?

If the Preview window in the Text Import Wizard dialog box contains odd-looking characters, make sure you selected the correct original data type.

2. Click the **Files of type list arrow**, click **Text Files,** click **EX M-1** if necessary, then click **Open**

   The first Text Import Wizard dialog box opens. See Figure M-3. Notice that under Original data type, the Delimited option button is selected. In the Preview of file box, line 1 indicates that the file contains three columns of data: Item, Cost, and Price. No changes are necessary in this dialog box.

3. Click **Next**

   The second Text Import Wizard dialog box opens. Under Delimiters, the tab character is selected as the delimiter, and the Data preview box contains an image showing where the delimiters divide the data into columns.

4. Click **Next**

   The third Text Import Wizard dialog box opens with options for formatting the three columns of data. Notice that under Column data format, the General option button is selected. This is the best formatting option for text mixed with numbers.

5. Click **Finish**

   Excel imports the text file into the blank worksheet as three columns of data: Item, Cost, and Price.

6. Click **File** on the menu bar, click **Save As**, make sure the drive containing your Project Disk appears in the Save in box, click the **Save as type list arrow**, click **Microsoft Excel Workbook**, edit the File name box to read **CafeCorp - Product Info**, then click **Save**

   The file is saved as a workbook, and the new name appears in the title bar. The worksheet is automatically named after the imported file, EX M-1. The worksheet information would be easier to read if it were formatted and if it showed the profit for each item.

QuickTip

To format numbers with dollar signs, use the Currency or Accounting format on the Numbers tab of the Format Cells dialog box.

7. Double-click the border between the headers in **Columns A** and **B**, click cell **D1**, type **Profit**, click cell **D2**, type **=C2-B2**, click the **Enter button** ☑ on the Formula bar, copy the contents of cell D2 to range **D3:D18**, then center the column labels, apply bold formatting to them, and format the data in columns B, C, and D with two decimal places using the Number style

   The completed worksheet, which analyzes the text file imported into Excel, is shown in Figure M-4.

8. Add your name to the worksheet footer, preview and print the list in portrait orientation, then save and close the workbook

FIGURE M-3: First Text Import Wizard dialog box

Original data type
is delimited

Three column
headings

Preview of file box

Text appears in
three columns

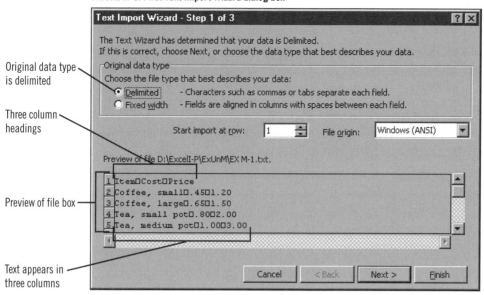

FIGURE M-4: Completed worksheet with imported text file

Columns from
text file

Added column
with new
profit data

Column A
widened to
longest entry

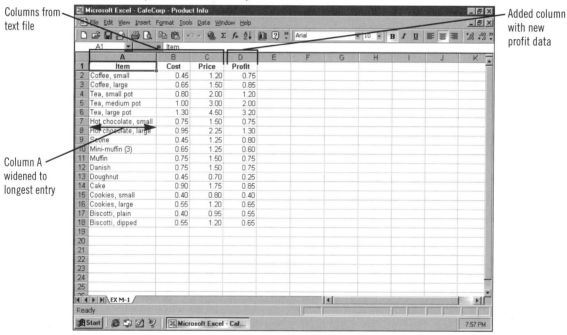

Other ways to import text files

Although the Text Import Wizard gives you the most flexibility, there are other ways to import text files. On the Windows desktop, drag your text file over the Excel program icon. Excel opens your text file. You can also click Insert on the menu bar, click Object, click Create from File, click the Browse button and locate the text file, click Insert, then click OK. The text file is inserted as an icon on your worksheet. Double-click the icon to open the text file in WordPad. You can then copy it into your worksheet.

Importing a Database Table

In addition to importing text files, you can also use Excel to import files from other programs or database tables. To import files that contain supported file formats, simply open the file, then you are ready to work with the data in Excel. **Scenario** Jim received a database table of CafeCorp's corporate customers, which was created with dBASE IV. He will import this table into Excel, then format, sort, and total the data.

1. Click the **Open button** on the Standard toolbar, make sure the drive containing your Project Disk appears in the Look in box, click the **Files of type list arrow**, scroll down and click **dBase Files**, click **EX M-2**, if necessary, then click **Open**
Excel opens the database table and names the sheet tab EX M-2. See Figure M-5. Before manipulating the data, you should save the table as an Excel workbook.

2. Click **File** on the menu bar; click **Save As**; make sure the drive containing your Project Disk appears in the Save in box; click the **Save as type list arrow**; scroll up, if necessary, and click **Microsoft Excel Workbook**; edit the File name box to read **CafeCorp - Corporate Customer Info**; click **Save**; then rename the sheet tab **Corporate Customer Info**
The truncated column labels in row 1 are not very readable; they would look better if the text wrapped to two lines.

3. Edit cell A1 to read **COMPANY NAME** (no underscore), click cell **F1**, type **1994**, press **[Alt][Enter]** to force a new line, type **ORDER**, press **Tab**, type **1995**, press **[Alt][Enter]**, type **ORDER**, then press **[Enter]**
Pressing [Alt][Enter] as you create cell entries forces the text to wrap to the next line. Columns F and G could be wider, and the column labels would look better if they were formatted.

4. Format the numbers in **columns F** and **G** using the Comma style with no decimal places, center and apply bold formatting to all the column labels, then widen the columns as necessary

5. Save the workbook, click cell **G2**, then click the **Sort Descending button** on the Standard toolbar
Columns F and G need totals.

6. Select range **F19:G19**, click the **AutoSum button** on the Standard toolbar, then format the range F19:G19 with the Comma style and no decimal places, add a border around it, then click cell A1
Your completed worksheet should match Figure M-6.

7. Add your name to the worksheet footer, preview and print the list in landscape orientation, fit the list to one page if necessary, then save the workbook

FIGURE M-5: Imported dBASE table

Excel substitutes underscores in place of spaces

Truncated column label

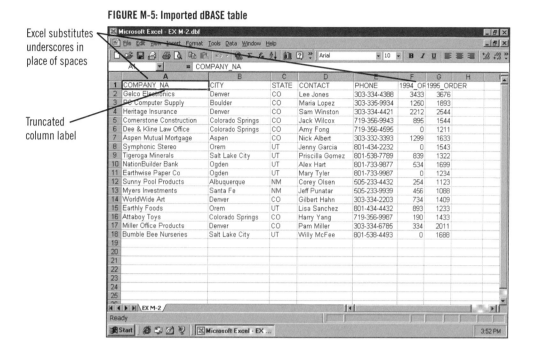

FIGURE M-6: Completed worksheet containing imported data

Adjusted and formatted column labels

Figures for 1995 arranged in descending order

New totals

Renamed sheet tab

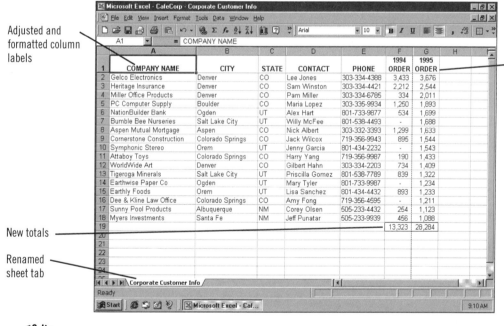

Exporting Excel data

Most of the file types that Excel can import (listed in Table M-1) are also the file types to which Excel can **export**, or deliver data. Excel can also export Text and CSV formats for Macintosh and OS/2. To export an Excel worksheet, use the Save As command on the File menu, click the Save as type list arrow, then select the desired format. Saving to a non-Excel format might result in the loss of formatting that is unique to Excel.

Excel 2000

Inserting a Graphic File in a Worksheet

A graphic object (such as a drawing, logo, or photograph) can greatly enhance a worksheet's visual impact. The Picture options on the Insert menu make it easy to insert graphics into an Excel worksheet. Once you've inserted a picture, you can edit it using the tools available on the Picture toolbar. **Scenario** Jim wants to insert a copy of the MediaLoft logo at the top of his corporate customer database table. He has a copy of the logo, previously created by the company's Marketing department, saved as a graphics file on a disk. He starts by creating a space for it.

QuickTip

You can insert shapes, clip art, scanned pictures, and special text effects into your worksheet. You can use a graphic as a hyperlink to another file or as a way to start a macro. Search the keyword "text graphics" in Excel help to find "About using graphics in Microsoft Excel."

1. Select **rows 1** through **5**, click **Insert** on the menu bar, then click **Rows**
   Five blank rows appear above the header row. To insert a picture, you start with the Insert menu.

2. Click cell **A1**, click **Insert** on the menu bar, then point to **Picture**
   The Picture menu opens. See Figure M-7. This menu offers several options for inserting graphics. You will insert a picture that you already have in a file.

3. Click **From File**; in the Insert Picture dialog box, make sure the drive containing your Project Disk appears in the Look in box; then click **EX M-3**, if necessary, to select it
   A preview of the selected graphic displays on the right side of the Insert Picture dialog box. See Figure M-8.

4. Click **Insert**
   Excel inserts the graphic and opens the Picture toolbar.

5. Drag the lower-right corner up and to the left so the logo fits within rows 1–5
   See Figure M-9. To improve the look of the graphic, you'll add a border.

QuickTip

You can also use the Line Style button on the Drawing toolbar to add a border for a selected object.

6. With the graphic still selected, click the **Line Style button** ▤ on the Picture toolbar and click the **1½ pt** line style, then press **[Esc]** to deselect the graphic and close the Picture toolbar
   The Drawing toolbar closes and the graphic is displayed with a border.

7. Preview and print the worksheet, save the workbook, then close the workbook and exit Excel

FIGURE M-7: Picture menu

Inserts a ready-made piece of art

Click to insert a graphic saved in a file

Inserts an electronic image captured with a scanner or digital camera

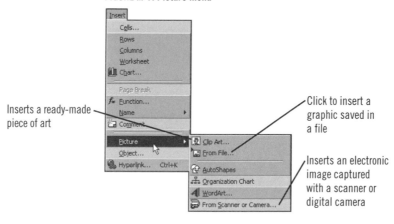

FIGURE M-8: Insert Picture dialog box

File to be inserted

Preview of selected graphic

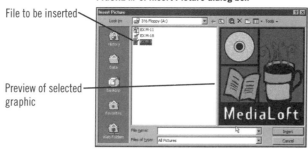

FIGURE M-9: Worksheet with inserted picture

Inserted graphic

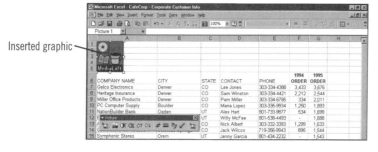

Importing data from HTML files

You can easily import information from HTML files and Web pages into Excel by using drag and drop or the Insert Object command. To use drag and drop, open Internet Explorer, then open the HTML file or Web page that contains the data you want to import. Resize the Explorer window so it covers only half of the screen, then open the Excel file to which you want to import the data and resize the Excel window so it covers the other half of the screen. In the Explorer window, highlight the table or information you want to import, then drag it over to the Excel window. When the pointer changes to a white arrow with a plus sign, release the mouse button. The table will appear in your Excel document, ready for analysis.

You can use this method to update worksheets you have published on the Web. You can also open an HTML file from your intranet or a Web site in Excel and modify it, which is known as HTML round tripping. To use the Object command on the Insert menu to embed an HTML file in an Excel worksheet, click Insert on the menu bar, click Object, click the Create from File tab, click Browse, then navigate to the HTML file you want to Import and click OK. The page appears as an icon in your Excel document. Double-click the icon to view the file. To retrieve data from a particular Web page on a regular basis, use a Web query, which you'll learn about in the next unit.

Embedding a Worksheet

Excel 2000

Microsoft Office programs work together to make it easy to copy an object (such as text, data, or a graphic) in a source program and then insert it into a document in a different program (the destination program). If you insert the object using a simple Paste command, however, you retain no connection to the source program. That's why it is often more useful to embed objects rather than simply paste them. **Embedding** allows you to edit an Excel workbook from within a different program using Excel commands and tools. You can embed a worksheet so the data is visible in the destination program or so it appears as an icon in the destination document. To access data embedded as an icon, you simply double-click the icon. ▷Scenario▷ Jim decides to update Maria on the project status. He uses a WordPad memo, which includes the projected sales revenue worksheet embedded as an icon. First, he starts the WordPad program and opens the memo.

1. Press **[Ctrl][Esc]** to open the Windows Start menu; point to **Programs**; point to **Accessories**; click **WordPad**; then, if necessary, maximize the WordPad window
   The WordPad program opens, with a blank document displayed in the WordPad window.

2. Click **File** on the WordPad menu bar, click **Open**, make sure the drive containing your Project Disk appears in the Look in box, click **EX M-4**, then click **Open**
   The memo opens.

3. Click **File** on the menu bar, click **Save As**, make sure the Save in box contains the drive containing your Project Disk, edit the File name box to read **CafeCorp - Sales Projection Memo**, then click **Save**
   You want to embed the worksheet below the last line of the document.

4. Press **[Ctrl][End]**, click **Insert** on the menu bar, then click **Object**
   After a moment, the Insert Object dialog box opens. You are embedding an existing file.

5. Click the **Create from File option button**

Trouble?

If the entire worksheet appears, not just the icon, you might not have checked the Display As Icon box.

6. Click **Browse**, make sure the drive containing your Project Disk appears in the Look in box, click **EX M-5**, click **Insert**; then in the Insert Object dialog box, select the **Display As Icon check box**
   The Insert Object dialog box now shows the file to be embedded. See Figure M-10. You are now ready to embed the object.

7. Click **OK**, then click outside the object to deselect it
   The memo now contains an embedded copy of the sales projection worksheet, displayed as an icon. See Figure M-11.

QuickTip

To edit an embedded object, double-click the object to open the source program, then make the desired changes. When you save and exit the source program, the embedded object reflects the changes.

8. Double-click the **Microsoft Excel Worksheet icon** 📊
   The Excel program starts and displays the embedded worksheet. See Figure M-12.

9. Click **File** on the Excel menu bar, click **Close & Return to CafeCorp - Sales Projection**, then save the memo

FIGURE M-10: Insert Object dialog box

Click to embed an existing worksheet

Your drive may differ

Click to display object as an icon

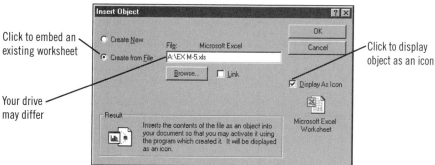

FIGURE M-11: Memo with embedded worksheet

Memo is in WordPad program

Icon representing embedded worksheet

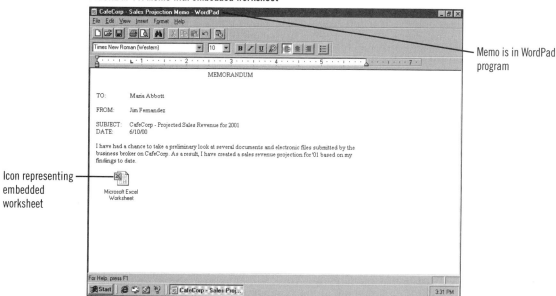

FIGURE M-12: Embedded worksheet opened in Excel

Excel program window

Description of embedded object

Your Excel window may be a different shape or size

Embedded worksheet

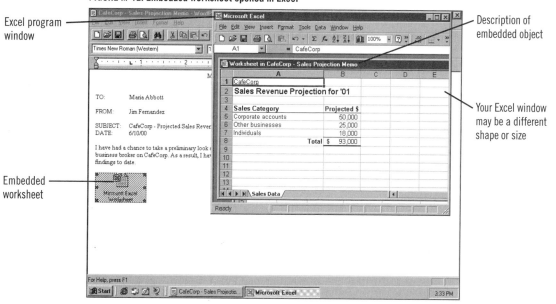

Excel 2000

Linking a Worksheet to Another Program

You use **linking** when you want to insert a worksheet into another program and retain a connection with the original document as well as the original program. When you link a worksheet to another program, the link contains a pointer to the source document so that, when you double-click it, the source document opens for editing. Once you link a worksheet to another program, any changes you make to the original worksheet document are reflected in the linked object. Scenario▶ Jim realizes he may be making some changes to the workbook he embedded in the memo to Maria. To ensure that these changes will be reflected in the memo, he decides to link a copy of the worksheet to the source document rather than simply embed it. First, he deletes the embedded worksheet icon; he then replaces it with a linked version of the same worksheet.

1. With the WordPad memo still displayed in your window, click the Microsoft Excel Worksheet icon 📄 to select it if necessary, then press **[Delete]**

   The embedded worksheet is removed. Now, you will link the same worksheet to the memo.

2. Make sure the insertion point is below the last line of the memo, click **Insert** on the WordPad menu bar, click **Object**, then click the **Create from File option button** in the Insert Object dialog box

3. Click **Browse**, make sure the drive containing your Project Disk appears in the Look in box, click **EX M-5**, click **Insert**, then select the **Link check box**

   With the file containing the worksheet object selected, you are ready to link the worksheet object to the memo.

4. Click **OK**; drag the worksheet's **lower-right selection handle** to the right margin to enlarge the window, then click outside the worksheet to deselect it

   The memo now displays a linked copy of the sales projection worksheet. See Figure M-13. In the future, any changes made to the source file (EX M-5) will also be made to the linked copy in the WordPad memo. In the next step, you'll verify this by making a change to the source file and viewing its effect on the WordPad memo.

   QuickTip

   When you open an Excel workbook containing a linked object, a dialog box will appear asking if you want to update the links.

5. Click the **Save button** 🖫 on the WordPad Standard toolbar, click **File** on the WordPad menu bar, then click **Exit**; start Excel if necessary, then open the file **EX M-5**

   The worksheet appears in the Excel window. You will test the link by changing the sales projection for other businesses to $20,000.

6. Click cell **B6**, type **20,000**, then press **[Enter]**

   Now you will open the WordPad memo to verify that the same change was made automatically to the linked copy of the worksheet.

   Trouble?

   If you can't read the worksheet clearly, select it, then drag the lower-right selection handle to enlarge it. Continue with Step 8.

7. Press **[Ctrl][Esc]** to open the Windows Start menu, point to **Programs**, point to **Accessories**, click **WordPad**; click **File** on the WordPad menu bar, then click **1 CafeCorp - Sales Projection Memo**

   After a message about updating the link appears briefly, the memo re-displays on your screen with the new amount automatically inserted. See Figure M-14.

8. Click **File** on the WordPad menu bar, click **Exit**, click **No** if you are asked if you want to save changes; click **File** on the Excel menu bar, click **Exit**, then click **No** to close the workbook without saving changes

FIGURE M-13: Memo with linked worksheet

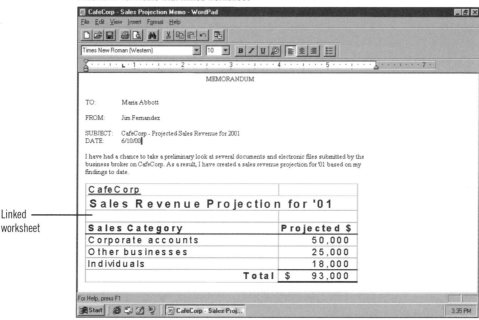

Linked worksheet

FIGURE M-14: Viewing updated WordPad memo

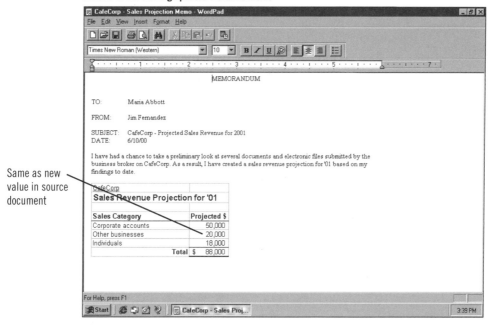

Same as new value in source document

Managing links

When you make changes to a source file, the link is updated automatically each time you open the destination document. You can manage linked objects further by choosing Links on the Edit menu. This opens the Links dialog box, which allows you to update a link or to change the source file of a link. You can also **break**, or delete, a link by selecting the linked object in the Links dialog box, then pressing [Delete].

Excel 2000

Embedding an Excel Chart into a PowerPoint Slide

Microsoft PowerPoint is a presentation graphics program that you can use to create slide show presentations. For example, you can create a slide show to present a sales plan to management or to inform potential clients about a new service. PowerPoint slides can include a mix of text, data, and graphics. Adding an Excel chart to a slide helps to illustrate complicated data, which gives your presentation more visual appeal. ▸Scenario▸ Based on his analysis thus far, upper management asks Jim to brief the Marketing department on the possible acquisition of CafeCorp. Jim will make his presentation using PowerPoint slides. He decides to add an Excel chart to one of the presentation slides illustrating the 2001 sales projection data. He begins by starting PowerPoint.

Trouble?

If you don't see Microsoft PowerPoint on your Programs menu, look for something with a similar name somewhere on the Programs menu or the Start menu. If you still can't find it, Microsoft PowerPoint may not be installed on your computer. See your instructor or technical support person for assistance. If the Office Assistant opens when you start PowerPoint, click close and continue with Step 2.

1. Press **[Ctrl][Esc]** to open the Windows Start menu, point to **Programs**, then click **Microsoft PowerPoint**

   The PowerPoint dialog box opens within the Microsoft PowerPoint window. This is where you indicate whether you want to create a new presentation or open a previously created one. You want to open a previously created presentation.

2. Click the **Open an existing presentation option button** if necessary; click **OK**; make sure the drive containing your Project Disk appears in the Look in box; click **EX M-6** if necessary; then click **Open**, then save the presentation as **Marketing Department Presentation**

   The presentation appears in Normal view and contains three panes, as shown in Figure M-15. Notice that the outline of the presentation in the outline pane on the left shows the title and text included on each slide. You will add an Excel chart to slide 2, "2001 Sales Projections". To add the chart, you first need to select the slide, then display it in Slide view.

3. Click the **slide 2 icon** ☐ in the outline pane

   The slide appears in the slide pane on the right.

QuickTip

The Insert Chart button on the Standard toolbar allows you to create a new chart using a limited spreadsheet program called Microsoft Graph. Experienced Excel users will find it easier to create a chart in Excel.

4. Click **Insert** on the PowerPoint menu bar, then click **Object**

   The Insert Object dialog box opens. You want to insert an object (the Excel chart) that has already been saved in a file.

5. Click the **Create from file option button**, click **Browse**, make sure the drive containing your Project Disk appears in the Look in box, click **EX M-7**, click **OK**; in the Insert Object dialog box click **OK** again, then press **[Esc]** to select the object

   After a moment, a pie chart illustrating the 2001 sales projections appears in the slide. The chart is difficult to read in Normal view, so you'll switch to Slide Show view to display the slide on the full screen.

QuickTip

The Excel worksheet you see in the PowerPoint slide is the one that was active when the workbook was last saved.

6. Click **View** on the PowerPoint menu bar, then click **Slide Show**

   After a pause, the first slide appears on the screen. You need to display slide 2, which contains your graphic.

7. Press **[Enter]**

   The finished sales projection slide appears, as shown in Figure M-16. The presentation for the Marketing department is complete.

8. Press **[Esc]**, click the **Save button** 🖫 on the PowerPoint Standard toolbar, click **File** on the menu bar, then click **Exit**

FIGURE M-15: Presentation in Normal view

Slide 2 icon

Slide 2 title

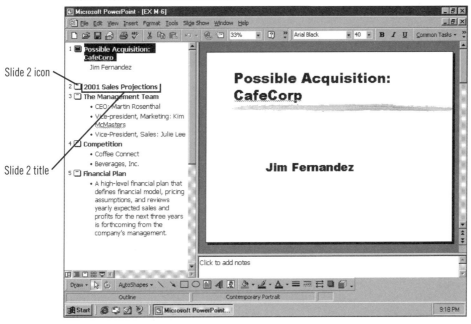

FIGURE M-16: Completed Sales Projections slide in Slide Show view

Excel chart inserted into slide

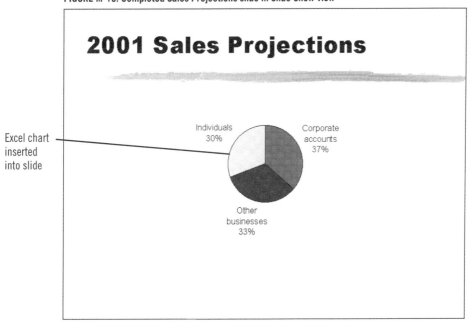

Excel 2000

Converting a List to an Access Table

An Excel data list can be easily converted for use in Microsoft Access, a sophisticated database program. You need to make sure, however, that the list's column labels don't contain spaces between words or any of the following special characters: a period (.), an exclamation point (!), an accent mark (`), or brackets ([ ]) so that Access can interpret the labels correctly. Once converted to Access format, a data list is called a **table**. **Scenario** Upper management has just received a workbook containing salary information for the managers at CafeCorp. One of the managers asks Jim to convert the list to a Microsoft Access table so that it can be added to MediaLoft's database of compensation information for all employees. Jim begins by opening the list in Excel.

Steps 1 2 3 4

1. Start Excel, open the workbook **EX M-8**, then save it as **CafeCorp Management**

Trouble?

If you don't see the Convert to MS Access command on the Excel Data menu, you need to install the Microsoft AccessLinks Add-in program. See your instructor or technical support person for assistance.

2. With cell A1 selected, click **Data** on the menu bar, then click **Convert to MS Access**; in the Convert to Microsoft Access dialog box, make sure the **New database option button** is selected, then click **OK**

   The Microsoft Access window opens, followed by the First Import Spreadsheet Wizard dialog box. See Figure M-17. In the next step, you'll indicate that you want to use the column headings in the Excel list as the field names in the Access database.

3. Select the **First Row Contains Column Headings check box** if necessary, then click **Next**

   In the next Import Spreadsheet Wizard dialog box, you specify whether you want to store the Excel data in a new or an existing table. In this case, you want to store it in a new table.

4. Make sure the **In a New Table option button** is selected, then click **Next**

   The next Import Spreadsheet Wizard dialog box opens. This is where you specify information about the fields (the Excel columns) you are converting. Notice that the column headings from the Excel list are used as the field names. You can also indicate which columns from the Excel list you do not want to import. In this case, you do not want to import the Annual Salary column.

5. Scroll right until the **Annual Salary column** is in view; click anywhere in the column to select it, then select the **Do not import field (Skip) check box** under Field Options

   Your completed Import Spreadsheet Wizard dialog box should match Figure M-18.

6. Click **Next**

   The next Import Spreadsheet Wizard dialog box opens. This is where you specify the table's primary key. A **primary key** is the field that contains unique information for each record (or row) of information. Specifying a primary key allows you to retrieve data more quickly in the future. In this case, you use the Social Security field as the primary key because the Social Security number for each person in the list is unique.

QuickTip

If Access chooses your primary key, it will select a field with unique data or create a new field that assigns a unique number.

7. Click the **Choose my own primary key option button**; make sure Social Security appears in the list box next to the selected option button; click **Next**; in the next Import Spreadsheet Wizard dialog box, click **Finish**; click **OK**; then click the **Maximize button** 🔲 on the Microsoft Access window

   The icon and name representing the new Access table are shown in the new database. See Figure M-19. Next, you'll open the table to make sure it was imported correctly.

8. Make sure **Compensation** is selected, then click **Open**

   The data from the Excel workbook is displayed in the new Access table. When you click the Save button on the Access toolbar, Access automatically saves the database to the same location as the original Excel workbook.

9. Click the **Save button** 🔲 on the Access toolbar, click **File** on the Access menu bar, then click **Exit**; in the Excel window, save the workbook, then exit Excel

FIGURE M-17: First Import Spreadsheet Wizard dialog box

Column labels will become field names

Preview of Access table

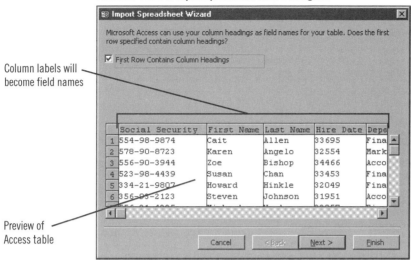

FIGURE M-18: Completed Input Spreadsheet Wizard dialog box

Click to select

Field names

Horizontal scroll bar

Annual Salary column

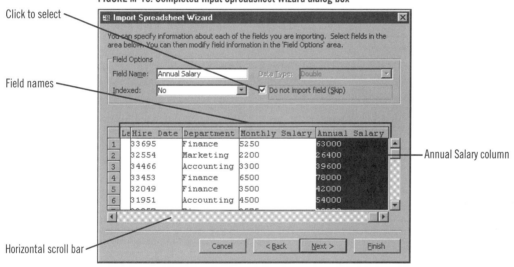

FIGURE M-19: Maximized Microsoft Access window

Database name taken from Excel workbook name

Icon indicates new table

New table name taken from sheet name in Excel workbook

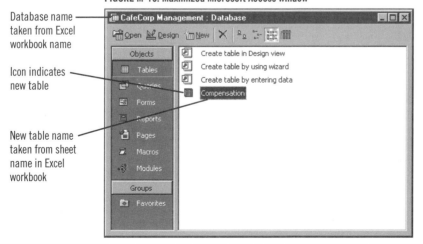

Practice

▶ Concepts Review

Label each element of the Excel screen shown in Figure M-20.

FIGURE M-20

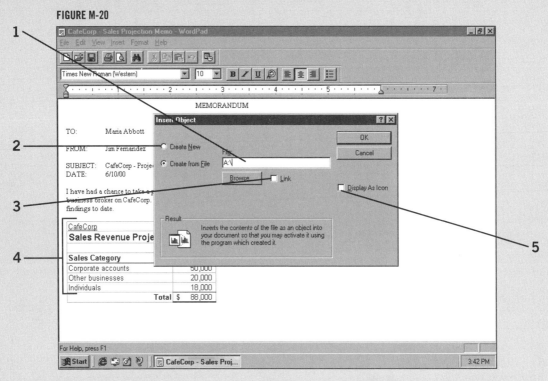

Match each term with the statement that describes it.

6. Source document
7. Linking
8. Destination document
9. Embedding
10. Presentation program
11. Table

a. An Excel list converted to Access format
b. Copies and retains a connection with the source program and source document
c. Document receiving the object to be embedded or linked
d. Used to create slide shows
e. Copies and retains a connection with the source program
f. File from which the object to be embedded or linked originates

Select the best answer from the list of choices.

12. **An ASCII file**
    a. Contains a PowerPoint presentation.
    b. Contains an unformatted worksheet.
    c. Contains text but no formatting.
    d. Contains formatting but no text.

13. **An object consists of**
    a. Database data only.
    b. Text, a worksheet, or any other type of data.
    c. A worksheet only.
    d. Text only.

14. **Which of the following is true about converting an Excel list to an Access table?**
    a. The column headings cannot be used as the table's field names.
    b. You must convert all the columns in the list to an Access table.
    c. The column labels cannot contain spaces.
    d. All of the above.

15. **To view a worksheet that has been embedded as an icon in a WordPad document, you need to**
    a. Double-click the worksheet icon.
    b. Drag the icon.
    c. Click File, then click Open.
    d. Click View, then click Worksheet.

16. **To diplay numbers with a dollar sign you can use the following format:**
    a. Number
    b. Currency
    c. Accounting
    d. a and b

▶ Skills Review

1. **Import a text file.**
    a. Start Excel, then open the tab-delimited text file EX M-9.
    b. Save the file as an Excel workbook with the name "Sunshine Temporary - Income Summary".
    c. Widen the columns so that all the data is visible.
    d. Center the column labels and apply bold formatting.
    e. Add your name to the worksheet footer, preview and print your work, then save and close the workbook and close Excel.
    f. At the Windows desktop, drag the text file EX M-9 over the Excel program icon. When the file opens, save it as an Excel file named "Sunshine Temporary - Income Summary 2", then close the file.
    g. Use the Object command on the Insert menu to insert the text file EX M-9 into a blank worksheet as an icon. Double-click the icon to open the file in Notepad, then copy the data into the worksheet below the icon.
    h. Save the file as "Sunshine Temporary - Income Summary 3", then close the file.

2. Import a database table.

    a. In Excel, open the dBase file EX M-10.

    b. Save the file as an Excel workbook with the name "Sunshine Temporary - Company Budget".

    c. Rename the sheet tab "Company Budget".

    d. Change the column labels so they read as follows: BUDGET CATEGORY, BUDGET ITEM, MONTH, and AMOUNT BUDGETED.

    e. Use AutoSum to calculate a total in cell D26, then add a top and bottom border to the cell.

    f. Format range D2:D26 using the Accounting style with no decimal places.

    g. Add bold formatting to the column labels, then wrap the text on two lines.

    h. Center the column labels and manually adjust the column widths as necessary.

    i. Save your work.

3. Embed a graphic file in a worksheet.

    a. Add four rows above row 1 to create space for the graphic file.

    b. Insert the picture file EX M-11 in the space.

    c. Make the graphic smaller so it doesn't cover up any column headings.

    d. Open the Drawing toolbar, if necessary.

    e. Use the Line style button to add a 1-point border around the graphic.

    f. Adjust the size and position as necessary, using [Ctrl] with the arrow keys to move it in small increments.

    g. Press [Esc] to deselect the graphic, then close the Drawing toolbar, if necessary.

    h. Add your name to the worksheet footer, preview and print the worksheet, then save your work.

4. Embed a worksheet in another program.

    a. In cell A33, type "For details on Green Hills salaries, click this icon:".

    b. In cell D33, embed the worksheet object EX M-12 and display it as an icon.

    c. Double-click the icon to verify that the worksheet opens, then close it.

    d. Preview, then print the Sunshine Temporary - Company Budget worksheet.

    e. Save your work.

5. Link a worksheet.

    a. Delete the embedded object icon.

    b. Link the spreadsheet object EX M-12 to cell D33, displaying the worksheet, not an icon.

    c. Save, then close the Sunshine Temporary - Company Budget worksheet.

    d. Open the EX M-12 workbook, change the Manager salary to 5,000, correct the first and last name order of employees Smith and Hargrove, then open the Sunshine Temporary - Company Budget worksheet; click Yes when you are asked if you want to update links, then verify that the manager salary has changed to 5,000 and that the name order is correct in the linked workbook.

    e. Preview, then print the worksheet with the linked object on one page.

    f. Close both workbooks without saving changes, then exit Excel.

6. Paste an Excel chart into a PowerPoint slide.

    a. Open the Microsoft PowerPoint program.

    b. Open the PowerPoint presentation file EX M-13.

    c. Save the presentation as "Monthly Budget Meeting".

    d. Display Slide 2, January Expenditures.

    e. Embed the Excel file EX M-14, then drag the chart until it is centered in the blank area of the slide.

f. View the slide with the chart in Slide Show view.

g. Press [Esc] to return to Normal view, save the file, and exit PowerPoint.

7. **Converting an Excel list to an Access database.**

   a. Start Excel, open the workbook EX M-15, then save it as Budget List.

   b. Convert the worksheet into a new Access database table, using the first row as column headings. Do not import the month column, and let Access add the primary key.

   c. Open the January Budget table in the Budget List in Access and drag the column borders as necessary to fully display the field names.

   d. Save the database file and exit Access.

   e. In the Excel window, add your name to the worksheet footer, print the worksheet (along with the conversion notice), then save the workbook and exit Excel.

► Visual Workshop

Create the worksheet shown in Figure M-21. Insert the graphic file EX M-18, resizing it as necessary. (*Hint*: Drag the resize handles as necessary to enlarge the art to the proper size.) Save the workbook as "Atlantic Price List". Preview, add your name to the worksheet footer, then print the worksheet.

FIGURE M-21

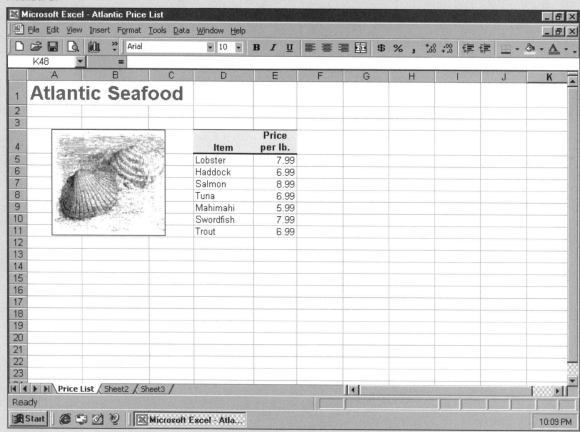

Unit
N

Sharing

Excel Files and Incorporating Web Information

Objectives

▶ Share Excel Files
▶ Set up a shared workbook
▶ Track changes in a shared workbook
▶ Apply and remove passwords
▶ Create an interactive worksheet for an intranet or the Web
▶ Create an interactive PivotTable for an intranet or the Web
▶ Create hyperlinks between Excel files and the Web
▶ Run queries to retrieve data on the Web

With the recent growth of networks, company intranets, and the World Wide Web, people are increasingly sharing electronic spreadsheet files with others for review, revision, and feedback. They are also incorporating information from intranets and the World Wide Web into their worksheets. Scenario▶ Jim Fernandez has some MediaLoft corporate information he wants to share with corporate office employees and store managers. He also wants to track information on MediaLoft's competitors.

Sharing Excel Files

Microsoft Excel provides many different ways to share spreadsheets electronically with people in your office, company, or anywhere on the World Wide Web. Users can not only retrieve and review your workbooks and worksheets, but they can modify them electronically and return their revisions to you for incorporation with others' changes. When you share workbooks, you also have to consider how you will protect information that you don't want everyone to see. You can post workbooks, worksheets, or other parts of workbooks for users to interact with on a company intranet or on the World Wide Web. You can also use Excel workbooks to run queries to retrieve data from the Web. ▶Scenario▶ Jim considers the best way to share his Excel workbooks with corporate employees and store managers. He also thinks about how to get Web data for use in his workbooks. He considers the following issues:

Details

 Allowing others to use a workbook

When you pass on Excel files to others, you could just have them write their comments on a printed copy. But it's easier to set up your workbook so that several users can simultaneously open the workbook from a network server and modify it. Then you can view each user's name and the date the change was made. Jim wants to get feedback on selected store sales and customer information from MediaLoft corporate staff and store managers.

 Controlling access to workbooks on a server

When you set up a workbook on a network server, you may want to control who can open and make changes to it. You can do this easily with Excel passwords. Jim assigns a password to his workbook and gives it to the corporate staff and store managers, so only they will be able to open it and make changes.

 Distributing workbooks to others

There are several ways of making workbook information available to others. You can send it to recipients simultaneously as an e-mail attachment or as the body of an e-mail message; you can **route** it, or send it sequentially to each user, who then forwards it on to the next user using a **routing slip**, or list of recipients. You can also save the file in HTML format and post it on a company intranet server or on the Web, where people can view it with their Web browsers. Jim decides to make an Excel workbook available to others by putting it on a central company server.

 Publishing a worksheet for use on an intranet or the World Wide Web

When you save a workbook in HTML format, you can save the entire workbook or just part of it— a worksheet, a chart, a filtered list, a cell range, or a print area. When you save only part of a workbook, you can specify that you want to make that particular part, or object, **interactive**, meaning that users can make changes to it when they view it in their browsers. They do not have to have the Excel program on their machines. See Figure N-1. The changes remain in effect until users close their browsers. Jim decides to publish part of a worksheet about MediaLoft café pastry sales.

 Interactive PivotTables

You can save a PivotTable in HTML format so people can only view it, but the data is much more useful if people can interact with it from their browsers, just as they would in Excel. To make an Excel PivotTable interactive, you need to save it as a PivotTable list. Jim wants corporate staff to explore some sales data using their browsers just as he would with Excel.

 Creating hyperlinks to the Web

You can make Web information available to users by creating hyperlinks to any site on the Web. Jim decides to include a hyperlink to a competitor's Web site.

 Using an Excel query to retrieve data from the Web

By using Microsoft Query from Excel, you can get data from the Web that you can bring into your workbooks, and then organize and manipulate it with Excel spreadsheet and graphics tools. See Figure N-2. Jim uses a query to get stock information about one of MediaLoft's competitors.

Toolbar allows users to manipulate worksheet data and format in browser

FIGURE N-1: Interactive worksheet in Web browser

Adding a worksheet total in Internet Explorer

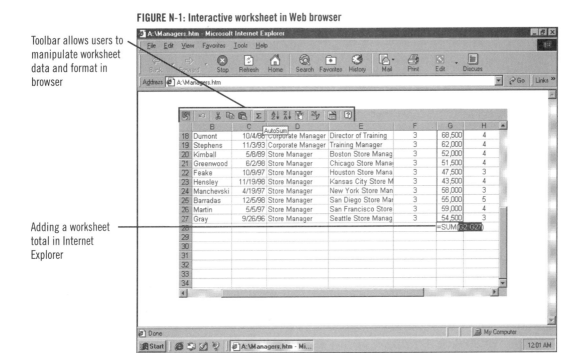

Excel workbook contains stock data imported from the World Wide Web

FIGURE N-2: Retrieving data from the World Wide Web using a Web query

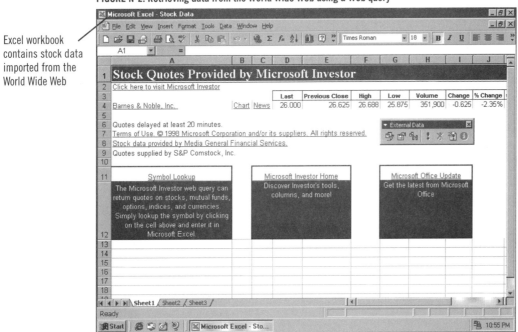

Excel 2000

Setting Up a Shared Workbook

You can make an Excel file a **shared workbook** so that several users can open and modify it at the same time. This is very useful for workbooks that you want others to review on a network server. The workbook is equally accessible to all users who have access to that location on the network. When you share a workbook, you can have Excel keep a list of all changes to the workbook, called a **change history**, that you can view and print at any time. Users must have Excel 97 or later to modify the workbook. Scenario> Jim makes his workbook containing customer and sales data a shared workbook. He will later put it on a network server and ask for feedback from selected corporate staff and store managers before using the information in a presentation at the next corporate staff meeting.

QuickTip

To return personalized toolbars and menus to their default state, click Tools on the menu bar, click Customize, click the Options tab in the Customize dialog box, click Reset my usage data to restore the default settings, click Yes, click Close, then close the Drawing toolbar if it is displayed.

1. Open the workbook titled **EX N-1**, then save it as **Sales Info**

The workbook with the sales information opens. It contains three worksheets. The first is the chart of café pastry sales for the first quarter, the second contains the worksheet and map of pastry sales by state, and the third contains a listing of sales for selected stores and sales representatives for the last four quarters.

2. Click **Tools** on the menu bar, then click **Share Workbook**

The Share Workbook dialog box opens, similar to Figure N-3.

3. If necessary, click the **Editing** tab

The lower part of the dialog box lists the names of people who are currently using the workbook. You are the only user, so your name (or the name of the person entered as the machine user) appears, along with the date and time.

QuickTip

You can remove users from the list by clicking their names and clicking Remove User.

4. Click to select the check box next to **Allow changes by more than one user at the same time**, then click **OK**

A dialog box appears, asking if you want to save the workbook. This will resave it as a shared workbook.

QuickTip

You can easily return the workbook to unshared status. Click Tools, click Share Workbook, and on the Editing tab click to deselect the Allow changes… option.

5. Click **OK**

Excel saves the file as a shared workbook. The toolbar now reads Sales Info [Shared]. See Figure N-4. This version replaces the unshared version.

FIGURE N-3: Share Workbook dialog box

Select this option to allow more than one person to use the workbook at the same time

If the workbook is already shared, people currently using the workbook are listed here

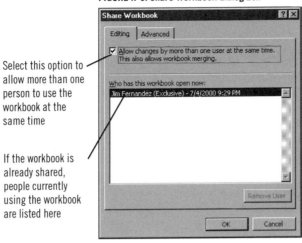

FIGURE N-4: Shared workbook

Title bar indicates workbook is shared

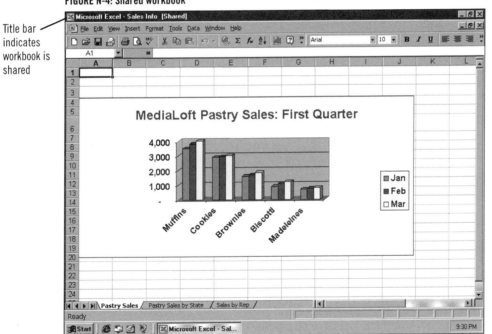

Excel 2000

Tracking Changes in a Shared Workbook

When you share workbooks, it is often helpful to **track** modifications, or identify who made which changes. If you disagree with any of the changes, you can reject them. When the Excel change tracking feature is activated, changes are highlighted in a different color for each user. Each change is identified with the user name and date. In addition to highlighting changes, Excel keeps track of all changes in a **change history**, a list of all changes that you can place on a separate worksheet so you can review them all at once. Scenario▶ Jim sets up the shared Sales Info workbook so that all future changes will be tracked. He then opens another workbook that has been on the server and reviews the changes and the change history.

Steps 1234

1. Click **Tools** on the menu bar, point to **Track Changes**, click **Highlight Changes**
   The Highlight Changes dialog box opens, allowing you to turn on change tracking, to specify which changes to highlight, and to display changes on the screen or save the change history in a separate worksheet.

2. Click to select **Track changes while editing**, remove check marks from all other boxes except for Highlight changes on screen, compare your screen to Figure N-5, click **OK**, then click **OK** in the dialog box that informs you that you have yet to make changes
   To track all changes, you can leave the When, Who, and Where check boxes blank.

3. Click the **Pastry Sales by State tab**, then change the sales figure for Texas to **133,000**
   A border with a small triangle in the upper-left corner appears around the figure you changed.

4. After you enter the change, move the **mouse pointer** over the cell you just changed, but do not click
   A screen tip appears with your name, the date, the time, and a phrase describing the change. See Figure N-6. Cells that other users change will appear in different colors.

5. Save and close the workbook
   Alice Wegman and Maria Abbott have made changes to a version of this workbook.

6. Open the workbook **EX N-2** and save it as **Sales Info Edits**

7. Click **Tools** on the menu bar, point to **Track Changes**, click **Highlight Changes**, in the Highlight Changes dialog box click the **When** check box to deselect it, click to select **List changes on a new sheet**, then click **OK**
   The History tab appears, as shown in Figure N-7, with a record of each change in the form of a filtered list. Notice that you could, for example, click the Who list arrow in row 1 and show a list of Maria Abbott's changes only.

8. Examine the three sheets, holding the pointer over each change, then click the **History sheet tab**

9. Put your name in the History sheet footer, preview and print the History sheet on one page, then save the workbook, which closes the History worksheet, and close the workbook
   The change history prints, showing who has made which changes to the workbook.

FIGURE N-5: Highlight changes dialog box

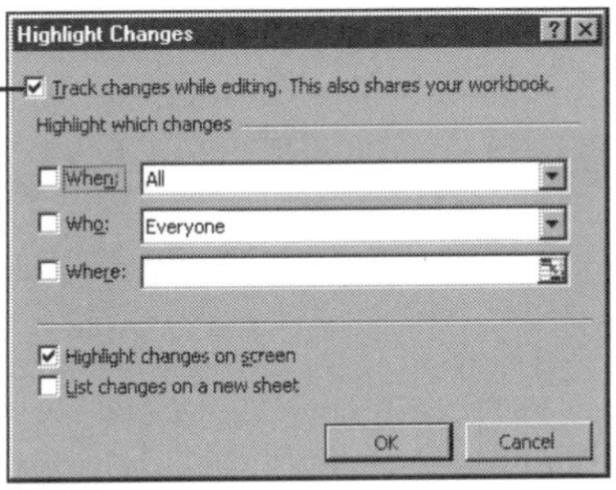

Click here so that all changes will be visible on the worksheet

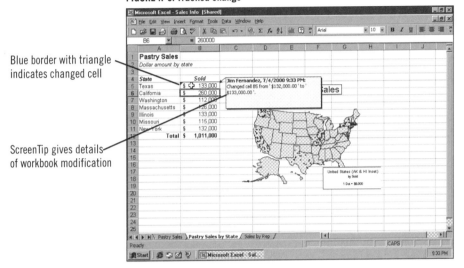

FIGURE N-6: Tracked change

Blue border with triangle indicates changed cell

ScreenTip gives details of workbook modification

FIGURE N-7: History sheet tab with change history

Details of each change listed here

Two users made changes to this worksheet

Click any list arrow to filter changes

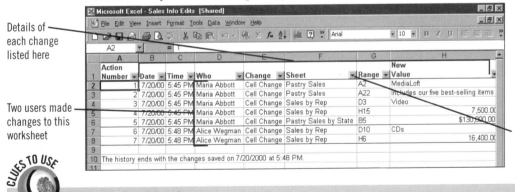

CLUES TO USE

Merging workbooks

Instead of putting the shared workbook on a server, you may want to distribute copies to your reviewers, perhaps via e-mail. Once everyone has entered their changes, you can merge the changed copies into one workbook that will contain all the changes. Each copy you distribute must be designated as shared, and the Change History feature must be activated. Once you get the changed copies back, open your master copy of the workbook, click Tools on the menu bar, click Merge Workbooks, then save when prompted. The Select Files to Merge Into Current Workbook dialog box opens. Click the name of the workbook you want to merge, then click OK. Repeat for all shared workbooks. It's important that you specify that each copy of the shared workbook keep a change history from the date you copy them to the merge date. In the Advanced tab in the Share Workbooks dialog box, set Keep change history for a large number, such as 1,000 days.

Applying and Removing Passwords

When you place a shared workbook on a server, you may want to use a password so that only certain people will be able to open it or make changes to it. If you do assign a password, it's very important that you write it down and keep it in a secure place where you can access it, in case you forget it. *If you lose your password, you will not be able to open or change the workbook.* Remember also that all passwords are case sensitive, so you must type them exactly as you want users to type them, with the same spacing and upper- and lowercase letters. For example, if your password to open a workbook is Stardot, and a user enters stardot, star dot, or StarDot, the workbook will not open. **Scenario** Jim wants to put the Sales Info 2 workbook on a server, so he decides to save a copy with two passwords: one that users will need to open it, and another to make changes to it.

Steps

1. Open the workbook **EX N-1**, click **File** on the menu bar, then click **Save As**

2. In the Save As dialog box, click **Tools**, then click **General Options**
   The Save Options dialog box opens, with two password boxes: one to open the workbook, and one to allow changes to the workbook, similar to Figure N-8.

3. In the Password to open box, type **Saturn**
   Be sure to type the capital S and the rest of the letters lowercase. This is the password users will have to type to open the workbook. Whenever you type passwords, they appear as asterisks (***) so that no one nearby will be able to see them.

4. Press **[Tab]**, then in the Password to modify box type **Atlas**, compare your screen to Figure N-8, then click **OK**
   This is the password users will have to type to make changes to the workbook. A dialog box asks you to verify the password by re-entering it.

5. In the first Confirm Password dialog box, type **Saturn**, then click **OK;** in the second Confirm Password dialog box, type **Atlas**, click **OK**, edit the workbook name so it reads **Sales Info PW**, then click **Save** and close the workbook

6. Reopen the workbook **Sales Info PW**, enter the password **Saturn** when prompted in order to open the workbook as shown in Figure N-9, click **OK**, then type **Atlas** to obtain write access and click **OK**

7. In the Pastry Sales by State worksheet, click cell A-14 and enter **One-year totals**
   You have confirmed that you can make changes to the workbook.

8. Save and close the workbook

FIGURE N-8: Save options dialog box

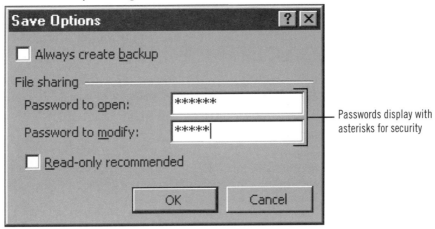

Passwords display with asterisks for security

FIGURE N-9: Password entry prompt

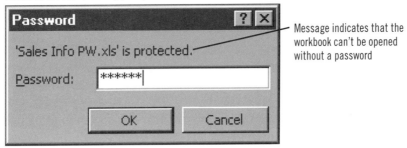

Message indicates that the workbook can't be opened without a password

Removing passwords

You must know a workbook's password in order to change or delete it. Open the workbook, click File on the menu bar, then click Save As. In the Save As dialog box, click Tools, then click General Options. Double-click the symbols for the existing passwords in the Password to open or Password to modify boxes, and press [Delete]. Change the filename if you wish, then click Save.

Creating an Interactive Worksheet for an Intranet or the Web

You can save an entire workbook in HTML format for users to view. But you can also save part of a workbook—a worksheet, chart, or PivotTable—in HTML format and make it interactive. You cannot save an entire workbook in interactive format. To work with interactive data, users must have installed Internet Explorer version 4.01 or later as well as the Office Web Components. Anyone with Office 2000 will have these. Users do not need to have Excel. **Scenario** Jim decides to save the Pastry Sales by State sheet as an interactive Web page.

Steps 1 2 3 4

QuickTip
Internet Explorer 4.01 or later must be your default browser or you will not be able to use interactive features.

1. Open **EX N-1**, save it as **Sales Info 2**, then click the **Pastry Sales by State sheet**

2. Click **File** on the menu bar, click **Save as Web Page**, then click **Publish**
   The Publish as Web Page dialog box opens.

3. Click the **Choose list arrow** and choose **Items on Pastry Sales by State**, then under Viewing options click to select **Add interactivity with**

4. In the Publish as section, click **Change** and type **Pastry Sales by State**, click **OK**, click **Browse**, make sure your project disk name appears as the Save in location, type the filename **Pastry Sales Web**, then click **OK**

QuickTip
See the Microsoft Excel Help topic "Limitations of putting interactive data on a Web page" for more information about which features might not work or might appear differently on your Web page.

5. If necessary, click to select **Open published Web page in browser** at the bottom of the dialog box, click **Publish**, then maximize your browser window
   After a pause, Internet Explorer opens the HTML version of your data. See Figure N-10. Notice that only the worksheet appears, not the map.

6. Change the Sold number for Washington in cell B7 to **115,000**, press **Enter**, and observe the total update automatically to 1,013,000
   You know the interactive feature is working. Changes you make to the HTML file in your browser remain in effect until you close your browser.

7. Select the range **A5:B11**, click the **Sort Ascending button** 🔼 on the toolbar above the worksheet, then click **State**
   The data is sorted in a new order according to state name.

8. Select the range **A4:B11**, click the **AutoFilter button** 🔽 , click the **State list arrow**, click the **Total check mark** to remove it, click **OK**, then click the **Property Toolbox button** 📋
   The total is no longer visible on the worksheet. The Spreadsheet Property Toolbox opens and should look similar to that shown in Figure N-11.

9. Click the **Fill Color list arrow** 🎨▾ after Cell format, click the **light green color** in the bottom row, then click the Spreadsheet **Property Toolbox close button** ❌ and click outside the selected range
   The range fills with the light green color.

10. Enter your name in any worksheet cell, click **File** on the menu bar, click **Print**, click **OK**, then close your browser

FIGURE N-10: Pastry Sales worksheet as Web page in Internet Explorer

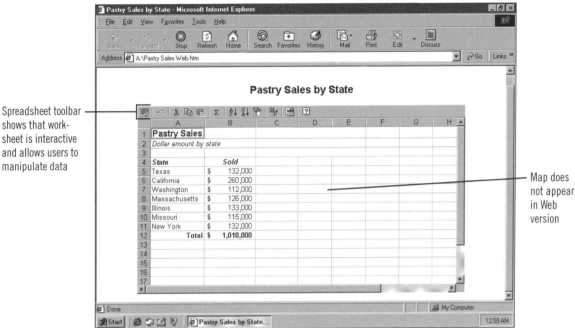

Spreadsheet toolbar shows that work-sheet is interactive and allows users to manipulate data

Map does not appear in Web version

FIGURE N-11: Spreadsheet Property Toolbox

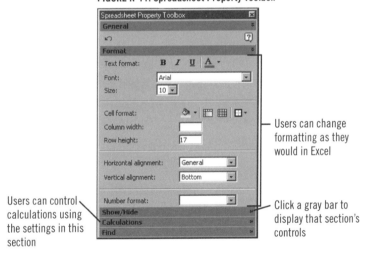

Users can control calculations using the settings in this section

Users can change formatting as they would in Excel

Click a gray bar to display that section's controls

Managing HTML files on an intranet or Web site

Once you save your Excel file or item in HTML format, determine the best location for saving your file: an HTTP site, an FTP (File Transfer Protocol) site, or a network server. Check with your system administrator or Internet Service Provider (ISP) to see how your files should be organized—whether they should all be in one folder, whether graphics and other supporting files should be in a separate folder, and the like.

Excel 2000

Creating an Interactive PivotTable for an Intranet or the Web

Not only can you create interactive worksheets that users can modify in their Web browsers, but you can also create interactive PivotTables that users can analyze by dragging fields to get different views of the data. An interactive PivotTable for the Web is called a **PivotTable list**. Users cannot enter new values to the list, but they can filter and sort data, add calculations, and rearrange data to get a different perspective on the information. As the PivotTable list creator, you have complete control over what information is included from the source data, which could be an Excel worksheet, a PivotTable, or external data (for example, an Access database). You can include only selected columns of information if you wish. You can also include charts with your PivotTable data. As with spreadsheets you publish in HTML format, users view PivotTable lists in their browsers, and changes they make to them are retained for only that browser session. The HTML file remains in its original form. <mark>Scenario</mark> Jim has compiled some sales information about sales representatives at selected stores for the last four quarters. He saves it as a PivotTable list so he and selected corporate staff and store managers can review it using their Web browsers.

Steps

QuickTip

As with saving spreadsheets in interactive format, you need Office Web Tools and Internet Explorer 4.01 or later to create and use PivotTable lists.

1. In the **Sales Info 2** workbook, click the **Sales by Rep tab**
   Jim will create the PivotTable list directly from the data rather then creating an Excel PivotTable first.

2. Click **File** on the menu bar, click **Save as Web Page**, then click **Publish**

3. Click the **Choose list arrow**, click **Items on Sales by Rep**, then in the Choose list make sure **Sheet All contents of Sales by Rep** is selected
   This will select all the items on the selected PivotTable sheet.

4. Under Viewing options, click **Add interactivity with**, click the **Add interactivity with list arrow**, and click **PivotTable functionality**
   PivotTable functionality will give users the option to move list items around on the PivotTable list as they would move data items on a PivotTable in Excel.

5. Click **Browse**, type **Sales Info PT List**, make sure your Project Disk is selected, click **OK**, make sure **Open published web page in browser** is checked, and compare your screen to Figure N-12

QuickTip

To retain the PivotTable in its original state, click the Address box containing the URL and press [Return]

6. Click **Publish**, then maximize the Internet Explorer window if necessary
   The new PivotTable list opens in Internet Explorer. Its layout looks similar to a PivotTable report in Excel, with row and column fields and field drop-down arrows. As with an Excel PivotTable, you can change the layout to view the data in different ways. In this case, however, there is no PivotTable toolbar; you simply drag the field headings to the desired drop areas.

7. Drag the **Store field** to the Row area, then drag the **Department field** to the Column area
   The layout of the PivotTable list changes, and you now see the data rearranged by region, department, and store. See Figure N-13.

8. Click **File** on the menu bar, click **Print**, then close your browser

FIGURE N-12: Publish as Web Page dialog box

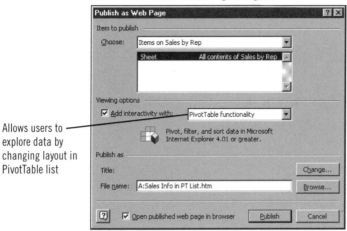

Allows users to explore data by changing layout in PivotTable list

FIGURE N-13: PivotTable list with new layout in Internet Explorer

User drags fields to drop areas to explore data relationships

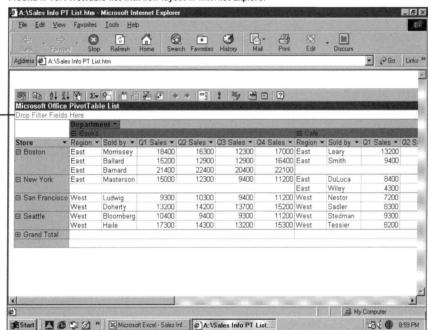

Adding fields to a PivotTable list using the Web browser

You can add filter, data, or detail fields to the PivotTable list to display data. On the toolbar above the PivotTable list, click the Field List button ▤. In the PivotTable Field List dialog box locate the name of the field you want to add. Click the field, and in the lower-right corner of the box, click the area list arrow, then click the section to which you want to add the field: Filter Area, Data Area, or Detail Data. If Add to is not available, the PivotTable creator may have restricted access to it.

Creating Hyperlinks between Excel Files and the Web

In addition to using hyperlinks to connect related Excel files, you can also create hyperlinks between files created in other Windows programs. You can even use hyperlinks to move between Excel files and information stored on the Web. Every Web page is identified by a unique address called a **Uniform Resource Locator (URL)**. You create a hyperlink to a Web page in the same way you create a hyperlink to another Excel file—by specifying the location of the Web page (its URL) in the Link to File or URL text box in the Insert Hyperlink dialog box. You enter a URL for an intranet site or a site on the World Wide Web using the same method. **Scenario** Jim decides that users of the Pastry Sales worksheet would find it helpful to view competitive information. He decides to include a hyperlink to the URL of one of MediaLoft's competitors, Barnes and Noble, which is also a café bookstore.

Steps

1. Activate the **Pastry Sales worksheet**, click cell **A2**, type **Barnes and Noble**, then click the **Enter button** ☑ on the Formula bar

Trouble?

If this button does not appear on your Standard toolbar, click the More Buttons button ⁇ to view it.

2. Click the **Insert Hyperlink button** 🔗 on the Standard toolbar
   The Insert Hyperlink dialog box opens. This is where you specify the target for the hyperlink, the Barnes and Noble Web site, by entering its URL in the Link to file or URL section of the Insert Hyperlink dialog box.

QuickTip

Make sure the URL address appears in the text box exactly as shown in Figure N-14. Every Web page URL begins with "http://". This acronym stands for HyperText Transfer Protocol, the method all intranet and Web page data use to travel over the Internet to your computer.

3. Under Link to, click **Existing File or Web Page**, click in the Type the file or Web page name text box, and type the URL for the Barnes and Noble Web site: **http://www.barnesandnoble.com**
   Your completed Insert Hyperlink dialog box should match Figure N-14. The program will automatically add a slash after the URL, as shown in Figure N-14, if you return to the dialog box and enter a Web address that you've entered previously.

4. Click **OK**
   The Barnes and Noble text is blue and underlined, indicating that it is a hyperlink. You should always test new hyperlinks to make sure they link to the correct destination. To test this hyperlink, you must have a modem, a Web browser installed on your computer, and access to an Internet Service Provider (ISP).

5. Click the **Barnes and Noble** hyperlink in cell A2
   After a moment, the Web browser installed on your computer starts and displays the Barnes and Noble Web page in your browser window.

6. If necessary, click the **Maximize button** ▢ on the browser title bar to maximize the browser window

7. Click **File** on the menu bar, click **Print**, click **OK**, then click the **Back button** ⇐ on the Web toolbar
   Now that you know the hyperlink works correctly, you return to the Sales Info 2 worksheet.

8. Save and close the workbook, then if necessary close your browser, but stay connected to the Internet

FIGURE N-14: Insert Hyperlink dialog box

URL for Barnes and
Noble Web site

Previously visited
Web sites are
listed here

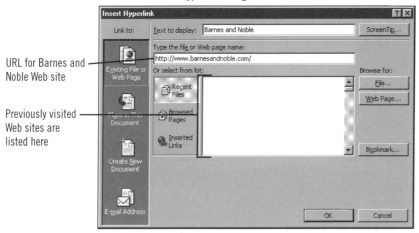

FIGURE N-15: Barnes and Noble Web site in Internet Explorer

URL appears
here

Your screen
contents may
differ because
Web pages
are revised
frequently

CLUES TO USE

Using hyperlinks to navigate large worksheets

Previously, when you needed to locate and view different sections of a particularly large worksheet, you used the scroll bars, or, if there were range names associated with the different worksheet sections, the name box. You can also use hyperlinks to more easily navigate a large worksheet. To insert a hyperlink that targets a cell or a range of cells at another location in the worksheet or another sheet in the workbook, click the cell where you want the hyperlink to appear, then click the Insert Hyperlink button on the Standard toolbar. In the Insert Hyperlink dialog box, click Place in This Document. Enter the cell address or range name of the hyperlink target in the Type the cell reference text box, or select a sheet or a defined name from the list box below it, then click OK.

Running Queries to Retrieve Data on the Web

Often you'll want to access information on the Web or the Internet to incorporate into an Excel worksheet. Using Excel, you can obtain data from a Web, Internet, or intranet site by running a **Web query**. You can then save the information as an Excel workbook and manipulate it in any way you choose. **Scenario** As part of a special project for Leilani Ho, Jim needs to obtain stock information on MediaLoft's competitors. He will run a Web query to obtain the most current stock information from the World Wide Web.

1. Open a new workbook, then save it as **Stock Data**

2. Click **Data** on the menu bar, point to **Get External Data**, then click **Run Saved Query**
   The Run Query dialog box opens, similar to Figure N-16. This is where you select the Web query you want to run from a list of predefined queries.

3. Click **Microsoft Investor Stock Quotes**, then click **Get Data**
   The Returning External Data to Microsoft Excel dialog box opens. This is where you specify the location to place the incoming data.

4. Make sure the **Existing worksheet option button** is selected, then click **OK**
   The Enter Parameter Value dialog box opens, prompting you to enter a stock symbol. The stock symbol for Barnes and Noble is BKS.

Trouble?

If you don't have a modem and access to the Web through an ISP, check with your instructor or technical support person. If your ISP's connection dialog box opens, follow your standard procedure for getting online, then continue with Step 6.

5. Type **BKS**, then click **OK**
   Your Internet Service Provider connects to the Web. The Microsoft Investor stock quote for Barnes and Noble appears on the screen. The External Data toolbar also appears, as shown in Figure N-17. Now you have the stock information that Jim can use to research one of MediaLoft's competitor's stock values.

6. Click **File** on the menu bar, click **Print**, then click **Chartlink** on the stock quote page
   A chart appears, showing the stock price and company income for the last year, similar to Figure N-18.

7. Print the chart, close your browser, disconnect from the Internet, save and close the workbook, then exit Excel and your browser

Finding stock symbols

If you want to check on a stock but don't know its symbol, click the Symbol Lookup hyperlink on the Stock Data worksheet. You may need to download the Microsoft Investor software, which takes about five minutes.

FIGURE N-16: Run Query dialog box

Predefined queries ————— from Microsoft

Use this query to
get up-to-date
stock information

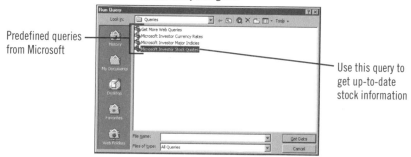

FIGURE N-17: Stock quote in Stock Data worksheet

Stock name

Click here to view ———
chart of this stock's
performance in the
last year

Click here to find ———
stock symbols for
other stocks

Stock information for
Barnes and Noble (your
screen will display
updated information)

External Data toolbar

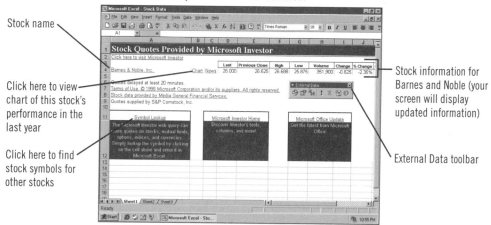

FIGURE N-18: Stock chart for Barnes and Noble

Stock name and time
period covered are
listed here

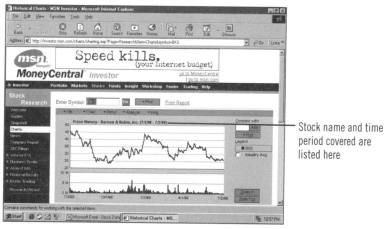

Creating a new query to retrieve Web page data

To retrieve data from a particular Web page on a regular basis, it's easiest to create a customized Web query. Click Data on the menu bar, point to Get External Data, then click New Web Query. In the New Web Query dialog box, click Browse Web to start your browser, go to the Web page from which you want to retrieve data, click the Web page, then return to the dialog box; the address of the Web page will appear in the address text box. Specify which part of the Web page you want to retrieve (for example, only the tables) and how much formatting you want to keep. Click Save Query to save the query for future use with the Run Saved Query command. Then click OK. Specify the location in the worksheet where you want the data, then click OK. The data from the Web page appears in the open Excel worksheet.

Excel 2000

Practice

► Concepts Review

Label each of the elements shown in Figure N-19

FIGURE N-19

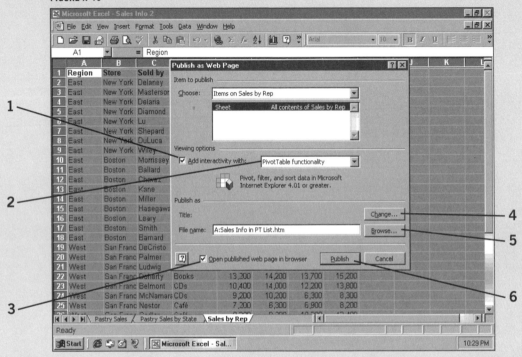

Match each item with the statement that describes it.

7. Web query
8. Change history
9. Shared workbook
10. Interactive worksheet or PivotTable
11. URL

a. A unique address on the World Wide Web
b. Used by many people on a network
c. Can be manipulated using a Web browser
d. Starts the installed Web browser to search the WWW
e. A record of edits others have made to a worksheet

12. A _____ is a list of recipients to whom you are sending a workbook sequentially.
    a. PivotTable
    b. Hypertext document
    c. Routing slip
    d. Shared workbook

13. Which of the following can be saved in HTML format, placed on a server, and then manipulated on an intranet or Internet using a Web browser?
    a. A worksheet
    b. A PivotTable
    c. A workbook
    d. a and b only

14. Which of the following allows you to obtain data from a Web or intranet site?
    a. Web Wizard
    b. PivotTable
    c. Data query
    d. Web query

15. A shared workbook is a workbook that
    a. Has hyperlinks to the Web.
    b. Is on the World Wide Web.
    c. Several people can use at the same time.
    d. Requires a password to open.

16. In an interactive worksheet or PivotTable,
    a. You can make changes and they are saved to the HTML file.
    b. You can make changes but they are not saved to the HTML file.
    c. You can change formatting but not perform calculations.
    d. You can perform calculations but not change formatting.

▶ Skills Review

1. **Set up a shared workbook**
    a. Open the file EX N-3 and save it as Ad Campaigns.
    b. Set up the workbook so that more than one person can use it at one time.
    c. On the Advanced tab, specify that the change history should be maintained for 1,000 days.

2. **Track changes in a shared workbook**
    a. Specify that all changes should be highlighted. Changes should be both highlighted on the screen and listed in a new sheet.
    b. In the Ads Q1 All Stores worksheet, change the Billboards totals to $600 for each month.
    c. Save the file.
    d. Display and print the History sheet. (If the History worksheet does not appear, reopen the Highlight Changes dialog box and reselect the options for All and List changes on a new sheet.)
    e. Save and close the workbook.

3. Apply and remove passwords

   a. Open the file EX N-3, open the Save As dialog box, then open the General Options dialog box.

   b. Set the password to open as Marsten and the password to modify as Spring.

   c. Resave the password-protected file as Ad Campaigns PW.

   d. Close the workbook.

   e. Reopen the workbook and verify that you can change it, using passwords where necessary.

4. Create an interactive worksheet for an intranet or the Web.

   a. Save the Ads Q1 All Stores worksheet as an interactive Web page, with spreadsheet functionality.

   b. Set the title bar to read Ad Campaign Forecast, automatically preview it in Internet Explorer, if that is your Web browser, and save it to your Project Disk using the filename Ad Campaigns. If you use a different Web browser, don't use the automatic preview option.

   c. If you can open the HTML file in Internet Explorer, do so.

   d. In Internet Explorer, add totals for each month in B11:D11, then add a grand total to cell E11.

   e. In F3, enter a formula that calculates the percentage newspaper ads are of the grand total. (*Hint:* You will need to type in the formula instead of clicking cells, and use the Property Toolbox to change the number format to a percent.)

   f. Use the Property Toolbox to fill the range B11:E11 with yellow.

   g. Sort the list in ascending order by ad type. You might need to reenter the percentage formula.

   h. Print the worksheet from Internet Explorer, then close Internet Explorer.

5. Create an interactive PivotTable for an intranet or the Web.

   a. In the Ad Campaigns PW workbook, save the worksheet Ad Detail as an interactive PivotTable with PivotTable functionality. Make the title Ad Forecast 4 Stores, and save it as Ads4Stores. Open the file in Internet Explorer.

   b. Drag fields to analyze the data by Region, Ad Piece, Store, and Department.

   c. Print the page showing changed data.

6. Create Hyperlinks between Excel files and the Web.

   a. On the Ads Q1 All Stores worksheet, enter the text "American Ad Foundation" and make it a hyperlink to the American Ad Foundation at http://www.aaf.org in cell A13.

   b. Test the hyperlink and print the Web page.

   c. Save and close the workbook.

7. Run queries to retrieve data on the Web.

   a. Open a new workbook and save it as Stock Quotes.

   b. Use the Run Saved Query command to locate Microsoft Investor Major Indices.

   c. Specify that you want to return the data to cell A1 of the current worksheet.

   d. After the stock quotes appear, click one of the stock indices listed and print the results.

   e. Display a chart for one of the indices, then print the chart. (*Hint:* If you are prompted to download MSN Money Central and you are unable to download software at your site, continue with step f.)

   f. Preview and print the Stock Quotes sheet, then save and close the workbook.

   g. Open a new workbook and save it as MediaLoft Products.

   h. Create a new Web query that retrieves the following page from the MediaLoft intranet site: www.course.com/illustrated/MediaLoft/Product.html. Import the entire page with full HTML formatting, and save the query as MediaLoft Products on your project disk.

   i. Test the hyperlinks on the imported Web page, use the Back arrow to return to the workbook, then save and close the workbook.

▶ Visual Workshop

Create the interactive Web page shown in Figure N-20. Use Excel to create the company name, product listing, and the sales figures for each quarter, all in black text. Save and print the worksheet. Save the worksheet in interactive HTML format, using the title bar text shown. Use Internet Explorer to obtain totals for each quarter and to apply formatting to totals, column headings, and the company name. (*Hint:* If you have any trouble with AutoSum, try formatting the figures using the Number format.) Print the HTML worksheet with your modifications applied.

FIGURE N-20

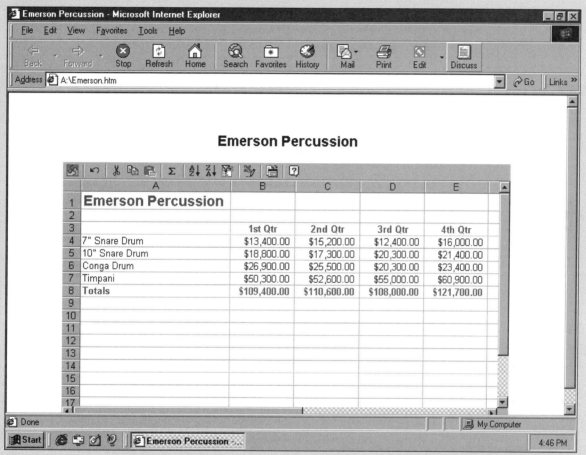

Excel 2000

Unit
O

Gaining
Control over Your Work

Objectives

- ► **Find files**
- ► **Audit a worksheet**
- ► **Outline a worksheet**
- ► **Control worksheet calculations**
- ► **Create custom AutoFill lists**
- ► **Customize Excel**
- ► **Add a comment to a cell**
- ► **Save a workbook as a template**

Excel includes numerous tools and options designed to help you work as efficiently as possible. In this unit, you will learn how to use some of these elements to find errors and hide unnecessary detail. You'll also find out how to eliminate repetitive typing chores, save calculation time when using a large worksheet, and customize basic Excel features. Finally, you'll learn how to document your workbook and save it in a format that makes it easy to reuse. **Scenario** MediaLoft's assistant controller, Lisa Wong, routinely asks Jim Fernandez to help with a variety of spreadsheet-related tasks. The numerous options available in Excel help Jim perform his work quickly and efficiently.

Finding Files

The Open dialog box in Excel contains powerful searching tools that make it easy for you to find files. You can search for a file in several ways, such as by name or according to specific text located within a particular file. **Scenario** Recently, Jim created a workbook that tracks the number of overtime hours worked in each MediaLoft store. He can't remember the exact name of the file, so he searches for it by the first few letters of the file name.

Steps

1. **Start Excel, then click the Open button** 📂 **on the Standard toolbar**
   At the top of the Open dialog box, there are two menus: the Views menu (represented by the Views icon ⊞▾) and the Tools menu. The Views menu controls the amount of information displayed about each file and folder. See Table O-1 for a description of Views menu selections. The amount of detail currently on your screen depends on the view option that you clicked the last time you opened this dialog box. The Tools menu helps you find, delete, and print files, as well as perform other file management tasks. First you'll display files so they match the figures in this lesson.

QuickTip

You can cycle through the four available views by clicking the Views button repeatedly.

2. **Click the Views list arrow** ⊞▾, **click each of the views to observe the results, then click Details**
   Your files display with the file name, size, type, and date modified.

3. **Click Tools, then click Find**
   The Find dialog box opens, similar to Figure O-1. You can find files by specifying one or more criteria, or conditions that must be met, to find your file. For example, you can specify that Excel should find only files that have the word "Inventory" in the file name and that were created after 6/15/2000. The criteria list in the "Find files that match these criteria" list is already set to find only Excel files. You'll specify another criterion. Jim thinks his file name starts with the prefix EX O but he's not sure of the number.

QuickTip

You can also search for text within Excel files. For example, if you know your worksheet contains the text "Overtime hours", you can specify Contents under property, and then specify the appropriate "include" condition and value. To use this feature you may need to install the Find Fast utility from your Office 2000 CD.

4. **In the Define more criteria area, under Property, select File name if necessary, then under Condition select includes if necessary**

5. **Click in the Value box, then type EX O***
   Be sure you type the letter "O" and not a zero. Because you know only the first few letters of the file name, you'll use the wildcard symbol * (an asterisk) to substitute for the remaining unknown characters. Next, you need to specify where you want Excel to search for the file. This saves you time if you have access to several disks and you want to limit the search to one or two of them.

6. **Click the Look in list arrow, click the drive that contains your Project Disk, then click the Search subfolders check box to select it**

Trouble?

If Excel doesn't find the files you're looking for, you may have typed zero instead of the letter "O" or you may not have selected the Search subfolders check box. Repeat the steps from Step 4, being sure to use the letter "O".

7. **Click Find Now, then click Yes to add your search criterion to the criteria list**
   After a moment, Excel displays five files that begin with "EX O", along with detailed information about the files. See Figure O-2. You can check to see if the criterion was added.

8. **Click Tools, then click Find**
   The criterion "Filename **begins with** EX O." appears in the criteria list.

9. **Click Cancel, double-click the file EX O-1 in the Open dialog box, then save the workbook as Overtime Hours**

FIGURE O-1: Find dialog box

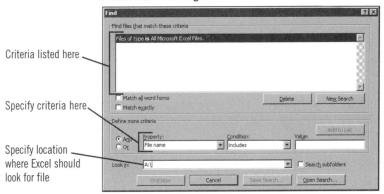

Criteria listed here

Specify criteria here

Specify location where Excel should look for file

FIGURE O-2: Search results

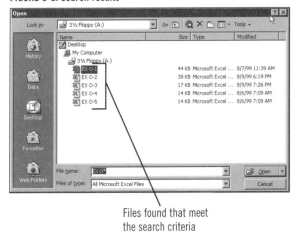

Files found that meet the search criteria

FIGURE O-3: Properties dialog box

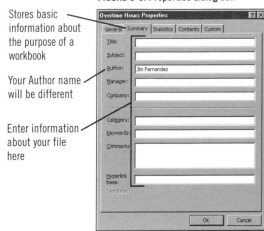

Stores basic information about the purpose of a workbook

Your Author name will be different

Enter information about your file here

TABLE O-1: Views menu selections

button	name	description
	List	Displays file and folder names
	Details	Displays file and folder names, along with the file type and the date last modified
	Properties	Displays information about the highlighted file, such as subject and keywords
	Preview	Displays the upper-left corner of the first sheet in a workbook
Arrange Icons	Arrange icons	Lets you rearrange your file icons by name, type, size, and date

CLUES TO USE

File properties

Excel automatically tracks specific file properties, such as author name, file size, and file type, and displays them when you display file details. You can also enter additional file properties, such as a descriptive title or a subject. Right-click the file in the Open dialog box, click Properties to open the [Filename]

Properties dialog box, click the Summary tab, then add any information you want. See Figure O-3. To search for a file by a specific property, in the Open dialog box, click Tools, then click Find. In the Find dialog box select Text or property in the Property list, then enter the property text in the Value box.

Excel 2000

Auditing a Worksheet

The Excel auditing feature helps you track errors and determine worksheet logic—that is, how a worksheet is set up. Because errors and faulty logic can be introduced at any stage of worksheet development, it is important to include auditing as part of your workbook-building process. Scenario Jim audits the worksheet that tracks the number of overtime hours at each store to verify the accuracy of the year-end totals. Before beginning the auditing process, Jim adds a vertical pane to the window so he can view the first and last columns of the worksheet at the same time.

1. Drag the **vertical split box** (the small box to the right of the horizontal scroll arrow) to the left until the vertical window pane divider is situated between columns A and B, then scroll the worksheet to the right until columns P through S are visible in the right pane
See Figure O-4.

Trouble?
If the Auditing toolbar blocks your view of the worksheet, drag it to another place on the worksheet.

2. Click **Tools** on the menu bar, point to **Auditing**, then click **Show Auditing Toolbar**
You use the buttons on the Auditing toolbar, shown in Figure O-5, to identify any errors in your worksheet. Notice the #DIV/0! error in cell S6. These symbols indicate a **divide-by-zero error**, which occurs when you divide a value by zero. The Trace Error button on the Auditing toolbar helps locate the source of this problem.

3. Click cell **S6**, then click the **Trace Error button** ⬦ on the Auditing toolbar
The formula bar reads =R6/$R$16, indicating that the value in cell R6 will be divided by the value in cell R16. Tracer arrows, or **tracers**, point from cells that might have caused the error to the active cell containing the error, as shown in Figure O-5. The tracers extend from cells R6 and R16 to cell S6. Note that cell R6 contains a value, whereas cell R16 is blank. In Excel formulas, blank cells have a value of zero. That means the value in cell R6 cannot be divided by the value in cell R16 (zero) because division by zero is impossible. To correct the error, you must edit the formula so that it references cell R15, the grand total of overtime hours, not R16.

4. Press **[F2]** to switch to Edit mode, edit the formula to read **=R6/$R$15**, then click the **Enter button** ☑ on the formula bar
The error message and trace arrows disappear, and the formula produces the correct result, 9%, in cell S6. Next, notice that the total for the Boston store in cell R5 is unusually high compared with the totals of the other stores. You can investigate this value by tracing the cell's precedents—the cells on which cell R5 depends.

QuickTip
To find cells with formulas that refer to a specific cell, click the cell, then click the Trace Dependents button ▣ on the Auditing toolbar.

5. Click cell **R5**, click the **Trace Precedents button** ▣ on the Auditing toolbar, then scroll left until you identify the tracer's starting point
The tracer arrow runs between cells B5 and R5, indicating that the formula in cell R5 reflects the quarterly *and* monthly totals of overtime hours. Because both the quarterly totals and monthly totals are summed in this formula, the resulting figure is twice what it should be. Only the quarterly totals should be reflected in cell R5.

Trouble?
If the AutoSum button does not appear on your Standard toolbar, click the More Buttons button ▣ to view it.

6. If necessary, click cell **R5**, click the **AutoSum button** Σ on the Standard toolbar, then press **[Enter]**
The tracer arrow disappears, the formula changes to include only the quarterly totals, and the correct result, 490, appears in cell R5. Correcting the formula in cell R5 also adjusts the Grand Total percentage in cell S5 to 13%. Now that all the errors in the worksheet have been identified and corrected, you are finished auditing.

QuickTip
You can also double-click the split to remove it.

7. Click **Window** on the menu bar, click **Remove Split**, then close the Auditing toolbar and save the workbook

FIGURE O-4: Worksheet ready for auditing

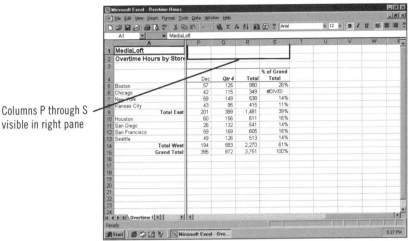

Columns P through S
visible in right pane

FIGURE O-5: Worksheet with traced error

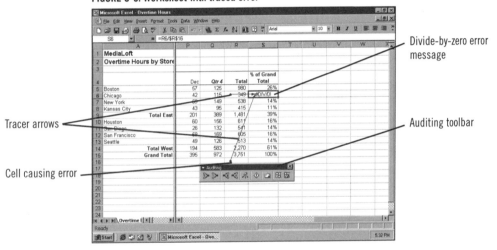

Divide-by-zero error
message

Tracer arrows

Auditing toolbar

Cell causing error

Circular references

A cell with a **circular reference** contains a formula that refers to its own cell location. If you accidentally enter a formula with a circular reference, a warning box will open, alerting you to the problem, and the Circular Reference toolbar appears. Click OK to open a Help window explaining how to find the circular reference using the Circular Reference toolbar. In simple formulas, a circular reference is easy to spot. To correct it, simply edit the formula to remove any reference to the cell where the formula is located.

Hiding and displaying toolbars

You display the Auditing toolbar using the Tools menu, however, to display other toolbars, right-click the Standard or Formatting toolbar, then click the name of the toolbar you want to display. To hide the toolbar, right-click it and select its name from the pop-up menu.

Outlining a Worksheet

Excel 2000

The Excel Outline command displays a worksheet with buttons that allow you to adjust the display of the worksheet to show only the critical rows and columns. For outlining to function properly, worksheet formulas must point consistently in the same direction: Summary rows, such as subtotal rows, must be located below related data, whereas summary columns, such as grand total columns, must be located to the right of related data. (If you're not sure which way your formulas point, click the Trace Precedents button on the Auditing toolbar.) **Scenario** Jim needs to give Lisa Wong, the MediaLoft assistant controller, the updated year-end totals. To emphasize the subtotals for both East and West regions, as well as the grand total of overtime hours, he decides to outline the worksheet first.

1. If necessary, press **[Ctrl][Home]** to display the upper-left corner of the worksheet

2. Click **Data** on the menu bar, point to **Group and Outline**, then click **Auto Outline**
   The worksheet is displayed in Outline view, as shown in Figure O-6. There are several ways to change the amount of detail in an outlined worksheet, but the easiest is by using the Column Level and Row Level buttons, which hide a varying amount of detail. The Row Level 1 button hides everything in the worksheet except the most important row or rows—in this case, the Grand Total row.

3. Click the **Row Level 1 button** ▢ 1
   This selection doesn't display enough information, so you'll try the Row Level 2 button, which hides everything except the second most important rows—in this case, the subtotal rows and the Grand Total row.

4. Click the **Row Level 2 button** ▢ 2
   Now you can see the rows you want. Next, you'll display only the columns you choose—in this case, the Qtr 1–Qtr 4 columns, the Total column, and the % of Grand Total column. Like the Row Level 2 button, the Column Level 2 button displays the Grand Total column, along with its corresponding subtotals.

5. Click the **Column Level 2 button** ▢ 2
   The quarterly totals appear and the monthly figures are no longer visible. Jim needs to give a printed copy of the worksheet outline to Lisa.

6. Place your name in the worksheet footer, then print the worksheet
   Your printed worksheet should look like the one shown in Figure O-7. You're finished using the outlining feature.

7. Click the **Row Level 3 button** ▢ 3, then click the **Column Level 3 button** ▢ 3
   The monthly figures for each store reappear.

8. Click **Data** on the menu bar, point to **Group and Outline**, then click **Clear Outline**

FIGURE O-6: Worksheet in Outline view

Column Level buttons

Row Level 1 button

Row Level buttons

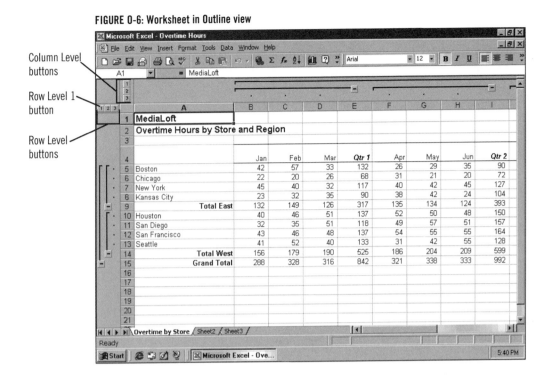

FIGURE O-7: Printed worksheet outline

Overtime by Store

Subtotal rows

Total row

Outline automatically includes title from the upper-left corner of the worksheet

MediaLoft
Overtime Hours by Store and Region

	Qtr 1	Qtr 2	Qtr 3	Qtr 4	Total	% of Grand Total
Total East	317	393	382	389	1,481	39%
Total West	525	599	563	600	2,287	61%
Grand Total	842	992	945	989	3,768	100%

Total columns

Subtotal columns

Jim Fernandez   Page 1

Excel 2000

Controlling Worksheet Calculations

Whenever you change a value in a cell, Excel automatically recalculates all the formulas in the worksheet based on that cell. This automatic calculation is efficient until you create a worksheet so large that the recalculation process slows down data entry and screen updating. Worksheets with many formulas, data tables, or functions may also recalculate slowly. In these cases, you might want to selectively determine if and when you want Excel to perform calculations automatically. You do this by applying the manual calculation option. Once you change the calculation mode to manual, the manual mode is applied to all open worksheets. **Scenario** Because Jim knows that using specific Excel calculation options can help make worksheet building more efficient, he decides to change from automatic to manual calculation.

1. Click Tools on the menu bar, click Options, then click the Calculation tab
The Calculation tab of the Options dialog box opens, as shown in Figure O-8.

QuickTip

To automatically recalculate all worksheet formulas except one- and two-input data tables, under Calculation, click Automatic except tables.

2. Under Calculation, click the Manual option button
The Recalculate before save box automatically becomes active and contains a checkmark when you select the Manual option. Because the workbook will not recalculate until you save or close and reopen the workbook, make sure to recalculate your worksheet before you print and after you make changes.

3. Click OK
Jim just received word that the December total for the San Francisco store is incorrect. You'll adjust the entry in cell P12 accordingly.

4. Click cell B5, click Window on the menu bar, click Freeze Panes, then scroll right to bring columns P through S into view

5. Click cell P12, type 76, then click the Enter button ☑ **on the formula bar**
See Figure O-9. Notice that the formula results in the worksheet are *not* updated. (For example, the percentage in cell S12 is still 16%.) The word "Calculate" appears in the status bar to indicate that a specific value in the worksheet did indeed change and must be recalculated. You can press [F9] at any time to calculate all the open worksheets manually or [Shift][F9] to calculate just the active worksheet.

QuickTip

If a worksheet formula is linked to a worksheet that you have not recalculated and you update that link, you will see a message informing you of the situation. To update the link using the current value, click OK. To use the previous value, click Cancel.

6. Press [Shift][F9], then save the workbook
See Figure O-10. The percentage in cell S12 is now 17% instead of 16%. The other formulas in the worksheet affected by the value in cell P12 changed as well. Because this is a relatively small worksheet that recalculates quickly, you will return to automatic calculation.

7. Click Tools on the menu bar, click Options if necessary, click the Calculation tab if necessary, under Calculation click the Automatic option button, then click OK
Now any additional changes you make to the worksheet will again be recalculated automatically.

FIGURE O-8: Calculation tab of the Options dialog box

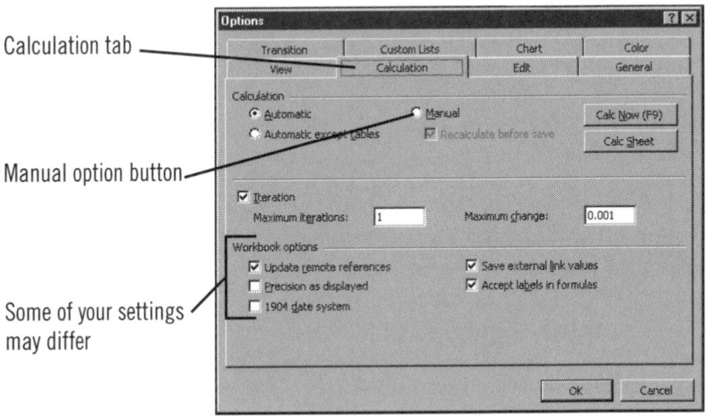

Calculation tab ——

Manual option button ——

Some of your settings
may differ ——

FIGURE O-9: Worksheet in manual calculation mode

Value still needs
to be updated ——

Changed value ——

Indicates that work-
sheet needs to be
recalculated ——

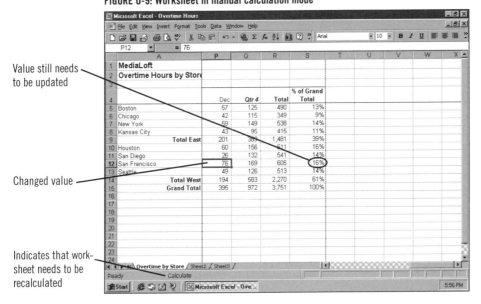

FIGURE O-10: Worksheet with updated values

Updated values ——

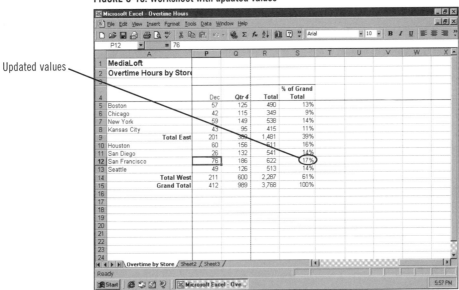

Excel 2000

Creating Custom AutoFill Lists

Whenever you need to type a list of words regularly, you can save time by creating a custom AutoFill list. Then you need only to enter the first value in a blank cell and drag the AutoFill handle. Excel will enter the rest of the information for you automatically. Figure O-11 shows some examples of AutoFill lists. **Scenario** Jim often has to repeatedly enter MediaLoft store names and regional total labels in various worksheets. He decides to create an AutoFill list to save time in performing this task. He begins by selecting the names and total labels in the worksheet.

Steps

1. Select the range **A5:A15**

Trouble?

If a list of store names already appears in the Custom lists box, the person using the computer before you forgot to delete it. Click the list, click [Delete], and proceed with Step 3. You cannot delete the four default lists for days and months.

2. Click **Tools** on the menu bar, click **Options**, then click the **Custom Lists** tab
See Figure O-12. The Custom Lists tab shows the existing AutoFill lists. The Import list from cells box contains the range you selected in Step 1.

3. Click **Import**
The list of names is highlighted in the Custom lists box and displays in the List entries box. Jim wants to test the custom AutoFill list by placing it in a blank worksheet.

4. Click **OK**, click the **Sheet2 tab**, then type **Boston** in cell A1

5. Position the pointer over the AutoFill handle in the lower-right corner of cell A1
Notice that the pointer changes to +, as shown in Figure O-13.

QuickTip

You also can drag the AutoFill handle down or to the right to repeat the AutoFill in other rows or columns.

6. Click and drag the pointer down to cell **A11**, then release the mouse button
The highlighted range now contains the custom list of store names and total rows you created. Now that you've finished creating and applying your custom AutoFill list, you need to delete it from the Options dialog box in case others will be using your computer to complete the lesson. If no one else will be using the computer, skip Step 7 and proceed to the next lesson.

7. Click **Tools** on the menu bar, click **Options** if necessary, click the **Custom Lists tab**, click the list of store and region names in the Custom lists box, click **Delete**, click **OK** to confirm the deletion, then click **OK** again

8. Save the workbook

FIGURE O-11: Sample AutoFill list

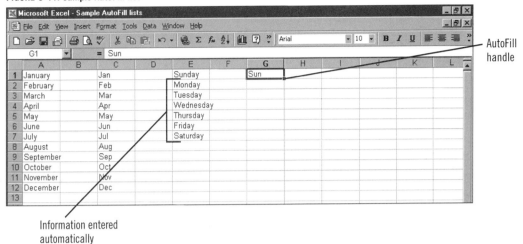

AutoFill handle

Information entered automatically

FIGURE O-12: Custom Lists tab

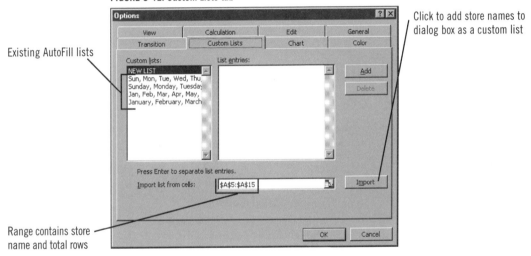

Click to add store names to dialog box as a custom list

Existing AutoFill lists

Range contains store name and total rows

FIGURE O-13: Applying a custom AutoFill list

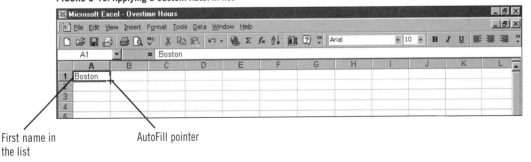

First name in the list

AutoFill pointer

Customizing Excel

The Excel default settings for editing and viewing the worksheet are designed with user convenience in mind. You may find, however, that a particular setting doesn't always fit your needs (for example, where the cell selector moves after you press [Enter]). The eight tabs of the Options dialog box allow you to customize Excel to suit your work habits and needs. You've already used the Calculation tab to switch to manual calculation and the Custom Lists tab to create your own AutoFill list. The most commonly used functions of the Options dialog box tabs are explained in more detail in Table O-2. It's especially important not to permanently change any other General tab settings if you're sharing a computer. **Scenario** Jim is curious about how he can customize Excel to allow him to work more efficiently. He decides to use a blank workbook to explore some of the features of Excel accessed through the Options dialog box.

Steps 1234

1. Click the **New button** on the Standard toolbar, click **Tools** on the menu bar, click **Options**, then click the **Edit tab**

   In some worksheets, it's more convenient to have the cell selector automatically move right one cell, rather than down one cell, after you press [Enter].

2. Click the **Direction list arrow**, then click **Right**

   See Figure O-14. Now when you press [Enter] the selector will move to the right. You can enter detailed information (or properties) to document your workbook in the Properties dialog box. This documentation may be useful to co-workers because it allows them to read a summary of your workbook without actually having to open it; they can right-click the file in the Open dialog box, then click Properties.

3. Click the **General tab**, then click the **Prompt for workbook properties check box**

   Now, when you save a workbook, Excel will open a dialog box asking you to enter file properties. Finally, Jim thinks the workbook would look better without gridlines.

4. Click the **View tab**, then under Window options click the **Gridlines check box** to deselect it

   This setting, as well as the others under "Window options", affects only the active worksheet. Next you'll check the results of your new workbook settings.

5. Click **OK**, type **Accounts Receivable** in cell A1, then press **[Enter]**

   The information in your new worksheet is displayed without any gridlines. In addition, the cell selector moved to the right of cell A1 when you pressed [Enter]. Next, as you save the workbook, you'll enter some information in the Properties dialog box.

6. Save the workbook as **Accounts** to your Project Disk, in the Accounts Properties dialog box click the **Summary tab** if necessary, then in the Comments text box type **Sample workbook used to practice customizing Excel**

   See Figure O-15.

7. Click **OK**

   Now that you're finished exploring the Options dialog box, you need to reestablish the original Excel settings. You don't need to adjust the Gridlines setting because that change applied only to the active worksheet.

8. Click **Tools** on the menu bar, click **Options**, click the **Edit tab**, click the **Direction list arrow**, click **Down**, click the **General tab**, click the **Prompt for workbook properties check box** to deselect it, click **OK**, then close the workbook

   The Overtime Hours workbook reappears.

FIGURE O-14: Edit tab in the Options dialog box

Some of your settings may differ

Updated setting moves cell selector right after you press [Enter]

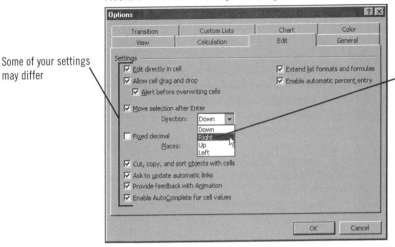

FIGURE O-15: Properties dialog box

Your information will differ

Description of the workbook

Click to enable workbook preview in Open dialog box

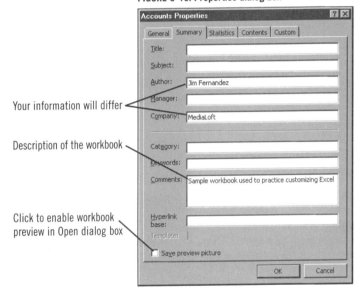

TABLE O-2: Options dialog box tabs

tab	description
Calculation	Controls how the worksheet is calculated; choices include automatic versus manual
Chart	Controls how empty cells are treated in a chart and whether chart tips are displayed
Color	Allows you to copy a customized color palette from one workbook to another
Custom Lists	Allows you to add or delete custom AutoFill lists
Edit	Controls the direction in which the cell selector moves after you press [Enter] and the ability to edit directly in cells
General	Controls the option to display the Properties dialog box after saving a workbook, the number of sheets in a new workbook, and the drive and folder used in the Save dialog box by default; User name is also listed here
Transition	Provides options useful for users familiar with Lotus 1-2-3
View	Controls the visibility of the formula bar, status bar, gridlines, row and column headers, and scroll bars; also controls the option to display formulas in a worksheet

Excel 2000

Adding a Comment to a Cell

Whenever you'll be sharing a workbook with others, it's a good idea to **document**, or make notes about, basic assumptions, complicated formulas, or questionable data. By reading your documentation, a co-worker can quickly become familiar with your workbook. The easiest way to document a workbook is to use **cell comments**, which are notes you've written about your workbook that appear when you place the pointer over a cell. When you sort or copy and paste cells, any comments in them will move to the new location. In PivotTable reports, however, the comments stay in the original cell locations. [Scenario] Jim thinks one of the figures in the worksheet may be incorrect. He decides to add a comment for Lisa, pointing out the possible error.

Steps

1. Click the **Overtime by Store sheet tab**, then right-click cell **P11**

QuickTip

You can also insert a comment by clicking the New Comment button on the Auditing or Reviewing toolbar.

2. Click **Insert Comment** on the pop-up menu

The Comment box opens, as shown in Figure O-16. Notice that Excel automatically includes the user name at the beginning of the comment. The user name data was collected from information previously entered in the General tab of the Options dialog box. Notice the white sizing handles on the border of the Comment box. You use these handles to change the size of the box by dragging.

3. Type **Is this figure correct? It looks low to me**.

Notice how the text automatically wraps to the next line as necessary.

4. Click outside the Comment box

A red triangle appears in the upper-right corner of cell P11, indicating that a comment is attached to the cell. People who use your worksheet can easily display comments.

QuickTip

To edit an existing comment, select the cell to which the comment is attached, click Insert on the menu bar, then click Edit Comment. To copy only comments, copy the cell contents, right-click the destination cell, select Paste Special, then click Comments.

5. Place the pointer over cell P11

The comment appears next to the cell. When you move the pointer outside of cell P11, the comment disappears. The worksheet is now finished and ready for printing. You'll print the worksheet in landscape orientation on one page. On a second printed page, you print only the cell comment along with its associated cell reference.

6. Click **File** on the menu bar, click **Page Setup**, click the **Page tab** if necessary, under Orientation click the **Landscape option button**, under Scaling click the **Fit to option button**, click the **Sheet tab**, under Print click the **Comments list arrow**, click **At end of sheet**, click the **Row and column headings check box** to select it, click **Print**, then click **OK**

Excel prints two pages.

7. Save the workbook

FIGURE O-16: Comment box

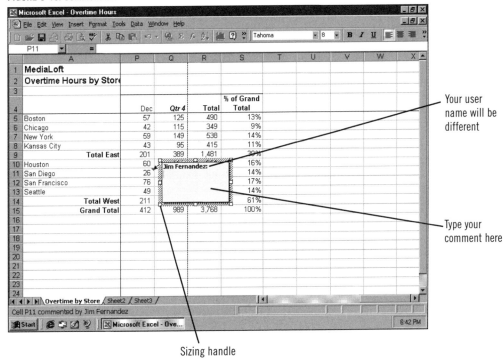

Your user name will be different

Type your comment here

Sizing handle

Preview and print multiple worksheets

To preview and print multiple worksheets, press and hold down [Ctrl] and click the tabs for the sheets you want to print, then click the Preview or Print button.

In Page Preview, the multiple worksheets will appear as separate pages in the Preview window, which you can display by clicking Next and Previous.

Saving a Workbook as a Template

A **template** is a workbook that contains text (such as column and row labels), formulas, macros, and formatting you use repeatedly. Once you save a workbook as a template, it provides a model for creating a new workbook without your having to reenter standard data. Excel provides several templates on the Spreadsheet Solutions tab of the New dialog box. In most cases, though, you'll probably want to create your own template from a worksheet you use regularly. When you save a file as a template, the original workbook remains unchanged. `Scenario` Jim plans to use the same formulas, titles, frozen panes, and row and column labels from the Overtime Hours worksheet for subsequent yearly worksheets. He will delete the extra sheets, the comments, and the data for each month, then save the workbook as a template.

1. Click the **Sheet2 tab**, press **[Ctrl]**, click the **Sheet3 tab**, right-click the **Sheet3 tab**, click **Delete**, then click **OK**

2. Right-click cell **P11**, then click **Delete Comment**
   Now that you've removed the extra sheets and the comment, you'll delete the data on overtime hours. You'll leave the formulas in rows 9, 14, and 15, and in columns E, I, M, Q, R, and S, however, so that another user can simply begin entering data without having to re-create the formulas.

Trouble?

If you accidentally delete a formula, insert a copy from the appropriate adjoining cell or click the Undo button and repeat Step 3.

3. Press **[Ctrl]**, select the ranges **B5:D8**, **B10:D13**, **F5:H8**, **F10:H13**, **J5:L8**, **J10:L13**, **N5:P8**, **N10:P13**, press **[Delete]**, then click anywhere to deselect the ranges
   See Figure O-17. The hyphens in the subtotal and total rows and columns indicate that the current value of these cells is zero. The divide by zero error messages in column S are only temporary and will disappear as soon as you open the template, save it as a workbook, and begin to enter next year's data. To make subsequent template use easier, it's best to have the first data entry cell selected when you save it.

4. Scroll left to bring columns B through G into view, then click cell **B5**

5. Click **File**, click **Save As**, click the **Save as type list arrow**, then click **Template (.xlt)**
   Excel adds the .xlt extension to the file name (although you will not see it if your file extensions are turned off) and automatically switches to the Templates folder, as shown in Figure O-18. If you are using a computer on a network, you may not have permission to save to the Templates folder. You'll save your template to your Project Disk instead.

6. Click the **Save in list arrow**, click the drive and folder containing your Project Disk, click **Save**, close the workbook, then exit Excel
   Jim would save the template to one of his template folders. Next year, when he needs to compile the information for overtime hours, he can simply open a document based on the Overtime Hours template and begin entering data. When this new work is saved for the first time, Excel will automatically save the template as a regular workbook. The original template will remain intact.

FIGURE O-17: Preparing the template

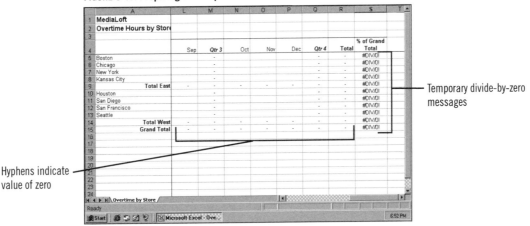

Temporary divide-by-zero messages

Hyphens indicate value of zero

FIGURE O-18: Saving a template

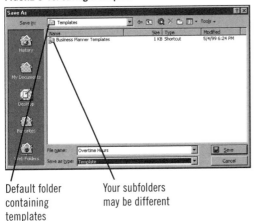

Default folder containing templates

Your subfolders may be different

FIGURE O-19: New dialog box

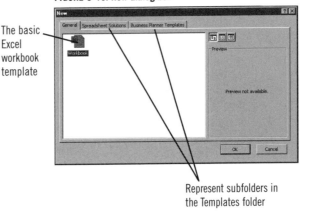

The basic Excel workbook template

Represent subfolders in the Templates folder

CLUES TO USE

Storing, applying, and modifying templates

If you're using your own computer, you may want to save your templates in one of the Templates subfolders, such as the one shown in Figure O-18. Then you can quickly open a document based on your template (that is, apply a template to a document) from the New dialog box by clicking File, clicking New, then selecting the template.

The New dialog box contains tabs containing icons for workbook templates, as shown in Figure O-19. The Spreadsheet Solutions tab in the New dialog box contains several ready-made templates you can use for business-related tasks, such as creating invoices or purchase orders. The other tabs in the New dialog

box depend on which subfolders of the Templates folder you used to save your templates. For instance, if you saved a template named "Personnel" in the Other Documents subfolder, then you would see an Other Documents tab in the New dialog box, with the Personnel template as an option. To open a document based on this template, you would click it, then click OK.

To edit a template, you must use the Open command to open the template itself, change it, then save it under the same name. The changes will be applied only to new documents you create; it does not change documents you've already created using the template.

Practice

► Concepts Review

Label each element of the Excel screen shown in Figure O-20.

FIGURE O-20

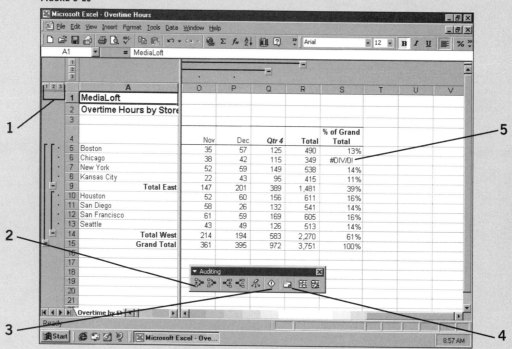

Match each term with the statement that describes it.

a. **Outlining a worksheet**

b. **Options dialog box**

c. **Auditing toolbar**

d. **Find dialog box**

e. **Circular reference**

f. **[Shift][F9]**

g. **AutoFill**

h. **Comment**

6. Contains settings for customizing Excel

7. Note that appears when you place the pointer over a cell

8. Occurs in a formula that refers to its own cell location

9. Calculates the worksheet manually

10. Automatically enters a list in a worksheet

11. Used to track errors and determine worksheet logic

12. A powerful searching tool that makes it easy to locate files

13. Allows you to display the most important columns and rows

Select the best answer from the list of choices.

14. **When searching for a file, which of these characters can substitute for unknown characters in a file name?**
    a. !
    b. &
    c. *
    d. #

15. **You can search for a file by**
    a. Property.
    b. Text within the file.
    c. Name.
    d. All of the above.

16. **The _____ button locates the cells used in the active cell's formula.**
    a. Validation Circle
    b. Trace Antecedents
    c. Function
    d. Trace Precedents

17. **The _____ automatically hides everything in the worksheet except the most important row or rows.**
    a. Outline feature
    b. Row Level 1 button
    c. Trace Precedents button
    d. Column Level 1 button

18. **To create a custom AutoFill list you should first**
    a. Select the list in the worksheet.
    b. Click the AutoFill tab in the Edit dialog box.
    c. Drag the AutoFill handle.
    d. Press [Shift][F9].

19. **The _____ tab in the Options dialog box controls whether the Properties dialog box is displayed when you save a workbook.**
    a. General
    b. Edit
    c. Properties
    d. View

▶ Skills Review

1. Find files.
a. In the Open dialog box, locate the drive that contains your Project Disk, and, if necessary, the folder where you store your Project Files.
b. If necessary, display detailed information about each file.
c. Display the files' properties.
d. Display only filenames.
e. Search for all files that begin with EX O, adding the search criterion to the criteria list.
f. Open the workbook EX O-2.
g. Save the workbook as "Cafe Budget".

2. Audit a worksheet.
a. Display the Auditing toolbar and drag it to the bottom of the worksheet.
b. Select cell E10, then use the New Comment button on the Auditing toolbar to add the comment "Does this include temporary holiday staff?" Close the Comments box, then use the pointer to redisplay the comment.
c. Select cell B10, then use the Trace Dependents button to locate all the cells that depend on this cell. (*Hint:* Click the button three times.)
d. Clear the arrows from the worksheet using the Remove All Arrows button on the Auditing toolbar.
e. Select cell B19, use the Trace Precedents button on the Auditing toolbar to find the cells on which that figure is based, then correct the formula in cell B19.
f. Select cell G6, trace the error it contains, then correct the formula.
g. Hide the Auditing toolbar, then save the workbook.
h. Practice opening and hiding the Picture toolbar.

3. Outline a worksheet.
a. Display the worksheet in outline view.
b. Use the Row Level buttons to display only the most important rows in the budget.
c. Use the Row Level buttons to display the second most important rows in the budget.
d. Add your name to the footer, then print the outlined worksheet in Landscape orientation.
e. Use the Row Level buttons to display all the rows in the budget.
f. Clear the outline from the worksheet.

4. Control worksheet calculations.
a. Open the Options dialog box and switch to manual calculation.
b. Change the figure in cell B6 to 30000.
c. Recalculate the worksheet manually using the appropriate key combination.
d. Turn off manual calculation and save the workbook.

5. Create a custom AutoFill list.
a. Select the range A4:A19.
b. Open the Custom Lists tab in the Options dialog box. Delete any custom lists except the four default day and month lists.
c. Import the selected text into the dialog box.
d. Close the dialog box.
e. On Sheet2, enter "Income" in cell A1.
f. Drag the fill handle to cell A15.

g. Select cell A1 again, and drag its fill handle to cell O1.

h. Open the Options dialog box again, and delete the list you just created.

i. Save the workbook.

6. Customize Excel.

a. Open the Options dialog box.

b. In the Edit tab, change the direction of the cell selector to "Up".

c. In the General tab, indicate that you want the Properties dialog box to appear when you save a workbook for the first time.

d. In the View tab, turn off the worksheet gridlines.

e. Close the dialog box and return to Sheet2, which is now displayed without gridlines.

f. Click the Budget tab, and notice that this worksheet is displayed with gridlines.

g. Open a new workbook.

h. Type your name in cell C5, then press Enter. Check to make sure the cell selector moves up.

i. Save the workbook to your Project Disk as "Customizing Excel", adding your name if necessary, and the comment "Sample workbook" to the Properties dialog box, then close the workbook.

j. Open the Options dialog box and change the cell selector direction back to "Down". Then turn off the Prompt for workbook properties option and close the Options dialog box.

7. Add a comment to a cell.

a. In the Budget sheet, select cell E12.

b. Open the Comment box by using the Comment command on the Insert menu.

c. Type "Does this include TV and radio spots, or only newspaper and magazine advertising? It is very important to include these."

d. Drag the resize handles on the borders of the Comment box until you can see the entire note.

e. Click anywhere outside the Comment box to close it.

f. Display the comment, and check it for errors.

g. Edit the comment in cell E12 so it ends after the word "spots", with a question mark at the end.

h. Delete the comment you added earlier in cell E10.

i. Print the worksheet and your comment in landscape orientation.

j. Change the orientation of Sheet2 to landscape and fit it to one page.

k. Preview and print both the Budget worksheet and Sheet2 at the same time.

l. Save the workbook.

8. Save a workbook as a template.

a. Delete Sheet2 and Sheet3.

b. Delete the comment in cell E12.

c. Delete the budget data for all four quarters. Leave the worksheet formulas intact.

d. Save the workbook to your Project Disk as a template, using the filename Budget Template.

e. Select cell B4 and close the template.

f. Copy the template into your Business Planner directory. (If you do not have access to the Business Planner directory, skip to Step 1.)

g. Open a document based on the template using the New command on the File menu.

h. Enter your own data for all four quarters and in every budget category.

i. Save the workbook as Cafe Budget 2.

j. Open the template using the Open command on the File menu, reformat it any way you wish, then save it.

k. Delete the copy of the template from the Business Planner directory.

l. Print and close the workbook, then exit Excel.

Visual Workshop

Open the workbook titled EX O-5, then click Cancel to close the dialog box warning you of a circular reference. Save the workbook as "City Zoo Animal Count" to your Project Disk. Use the auditing techniques you have learned so far to correct any errors so that the worksheet entries and formulas match Figure O-21. Make sure to include the cell comment in cell F11. Add your name to the footer, then preview and print the worksheet and comment in landscape orientation, showing row and column headings. In addition to printing the worksheet, also print the worksheet formulas on a separate sheet, showing row and column headings.

FIGURE O-21

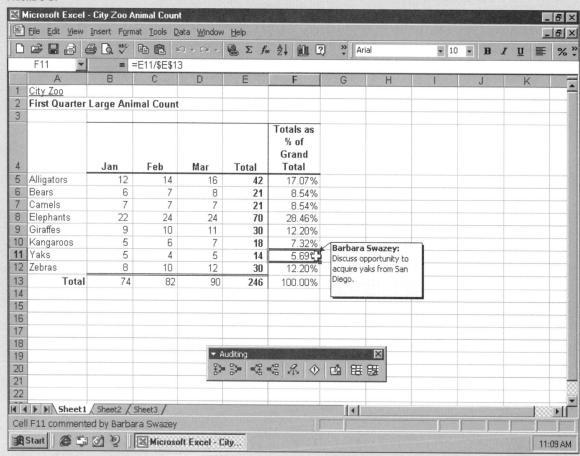

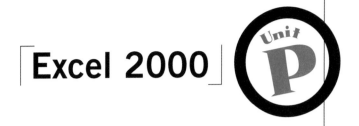

Programming
with Excel

Objectives

- ► **View VBA code**
- ► **Analyze VBA code**
- ► **Write VBA code**
- ► **Add a conditional statement**
- ► **Prompt the user for data**
- ► **Debug a macro**
- ► **Create a main procedure**
- ► **Run a main procedure**

All Excel macros are written in a programming language called Visual Basic for Applications or, simply, **VBA**. When you create a macro with the Excel macro recorder, the recorder writes the required VBA instructions for you. You can also create an Excel macro by entering the appropriate VBA instructions manually. The sequence of VBA statements contained in a macro is called a **procedure**. In this unit, you will view and analyze existing VBA code. Then you will write some VBA code on your own. You will learn how to add a conditional statement to a procedure, as well as how to prompt the user for information while the macro is running. You will also find out how to locate any errors, or bugs, in a macro. Finally, you will combine several macros into one. **Scenario** Alice Wegman, MediaLoft's marketing manager, has asked Jim Fernandez to create five macros to automate some of the division's time-consuming tasks.

Excel 2000

Viewing VBA Code

Before you can write Excel macro procedures, you must become familiar with the VBA (Visual Basic for Applications) programming language. A common method of learning any programming language is to view existing code. To view VBA, you open the Visual Basic Editor, which contains a Project window, a Properties window, and a Code window. The VBA code for macro procedures appears in the Code window. The first line of a procedure, called the **procedure header**, defines the procedure's type, name, and arguments. Items displayed in blue are **keywords**, which are words recognized as part of the VBA programming language. **Comments**, which are notes explaining the code, are shown in green, and the remaining code is shown in black. You use the Editor to view or edit an existing macro procedure as well as to create a new macro procedure. Scenario Each week, MediaLoft receives a text file from the KHOT radio station containing information about weekly radio ads. Alice has already imported the text file into a worksheet but still needs to format it. Jim has begun work on a macro to automate the process of formatting this imported text file.

Steps

Trouble?

If the Virus warning dialog box shown in Figure P-1 appears, click Enable Macros. If a macro information dialog box opens informing you that Visual Basic macro modules are now edited in the Visual Basic Editor, click OK, then continue with Step 2.

1. Open the workbook titled **EX P-1**, save it as **KHOT Procedures**, then reset personalized toolbars and menus to their default state
   The KHOT Procedures workbook displays a blank worksheet. It is in this workbook that you will create and store all the procedures for this lesson.

2. Click **Tools** on the menu bar, point to **Macro**, then click **Macros**
   The Macro dialog box appears with the FormatFile macro procedure selected in the list box.

3. Click **Edit**
   The Visual Basic Editor opens and displays the FormatFile procedure in the Code window. See Figure P-2.

QuickTip

If you only see the Code window, click Tools on the menu bar, click Options, click the Docking tab, and make sure the Project Explorer and Properties options are selected.

4. Make sure both the Visual Basic window and the Code window are maximized to match Figure P-2. If the Properties or Project Explorer window is not displayed, click the **Properties Window button** 🖼️, then click the **Project Explorer button** 📇 on the toolbar

5. Examine the top three lines of comments and the first line of code beginning with Sub FormatFile ( )
   Notice that the different parts of the procedure appear in various colors. The third line of comments explains that the keyboard shortcut for this macro procedure is Ctrl+F. The keyword *Sub* in the procedure header indicates that this is a **Sub procedure**, or a series of Visual Basic statements that perform an action but do not return a value. In the next lesson, you will analyze the procedure code to see what each line does.

FIGURE P-1: Virus warning dialog box

Click here to open
workbook with the
ability to run macros

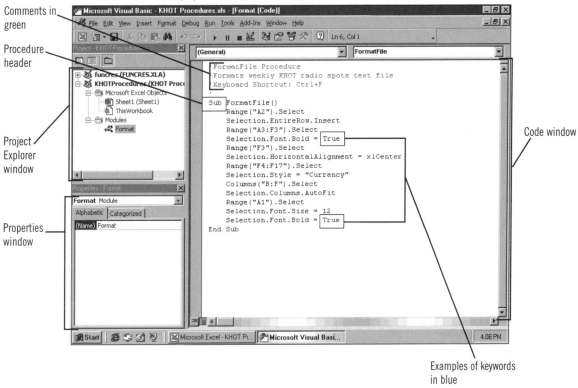

FIGURE P-2: Procedure displayed in the Visual Basic Editor

Comments in
green

Procedure
header

Project
Explorer
window

Properties
window

Code window

Examples of keywords
in blue

Understanding the Visual Basic Editor

A **module** is the Visual Basic equivalent of a worksheet. In it, you store macro procedures, just as you store data in worksheets. Modules, in turn, are stored in workbooks (or **projects**), along with worksheets. You view and edit modules in the Visual Basic Editor, which is made up of three windows, the Project Explorer (also called the Project window), the Code window, and the Properties window. The **Project Explorer** displays a list of all open projects (or workbooks) and the worksheets

and modules they contain. To view the procedures stored in a module, you must first select the module in the Project Explorer (just as you would select a file in the Windows Explorer). The **Code window** then displays the selected module's procedures. The **Properties window** displays a list of characteristics (or **properties**) associated with the module. A newly inserted module has only one property, its name.

Excel 2000

Analyzing VBA Code

You can learn a lot about the VBA language simply by analyzing the code generated by the Excel macro recorder. The more VBA code you analyze, the easier it will be for you to write your own programming code. **Scenario** Before writing any new procedures, Jim analyzes the procedure he's already written, then opens a worksheet to which he wants to apply the formatting macro and runs the macro.

Steps 1 2 3 4

1. **With the FormatFile procedure still displayed in the Code window, examine the next four lines of code, beginning with Range("A2").Select**

   See Figure P-3. Every element of Excel, including a range, is considered an **object**. A **range object** represents a cell or a range of cells. The statement *Range("A2").Select* selects the range object cell A2. Notice that several times in the procedure a line of code (or **statement**) selects a range, and then subsequent lines act on that selection. The next statement, *Selection.EntireRow.Insert*, inserts a row above the selection, which is currently cell A2. The next two lines of code select range A3:F3 and apply bold formatting to that selection. In VBA terminology, whether bold formatting is enabled is a value of an object's Bold property. A **property** is an attribute of an object that defines one of the object's characteristics (such as size) or an aspect of its behavior (such as whether it is enabled). The properties of an object are listed in the Properties window. To change the characteristics of an object, you simply change the values of its properties. For example, to apply bold formatting to a selected range, you assign the value True to the range's Bold property. To remove bold formatting, assign the value False.

2. **Examine the remaining lines of code, beginning with Range ("F3").Select**

   The next two statements select the range object cell F3 and center its contents, then the following two statements select the F4:F17 range object and format it as currency. Column objects B through F are then selected and their widths set to AutoFit. Finally, the range object cell A1 is selected, its font size is changed to 12, and its Bold property is set to True. The last line, *End Sub*, indicates the end of the Sub procedure and is also referred to as the **procedure footer**.

3. **Click the View Microsoft Excel button ▦ on the Visual Basic Editor Standard toolbar to return to Excel**

   The macro is stored in the KHOT Procedures workbook. This way Jim can use it repeatedly each week after he receives that week's data. You will open the workbook containing data for January 1–7 and run the macro to format that data. You must leave the KHOT Procedures workbook open to use the macro stored there.

4. **Open the workbook titled EX P-2, maximize if necessary, then save it as KHOT Advertising Jan 1-7**

   This is the workbook containing data you want to format.

5. **Press [Ctrl][F] to run the procedure**

   The FormatFile procedure formats the text, as shown in Figure P-4.

6. **Place your name in the worksheet footer, print the worksheet, then save the workbook**

   Now that you've successfully viewed and analyzed code and run the macro, you will learn how to write your own code.

FIGURE P-3: VBA code for the FormatFile procedure

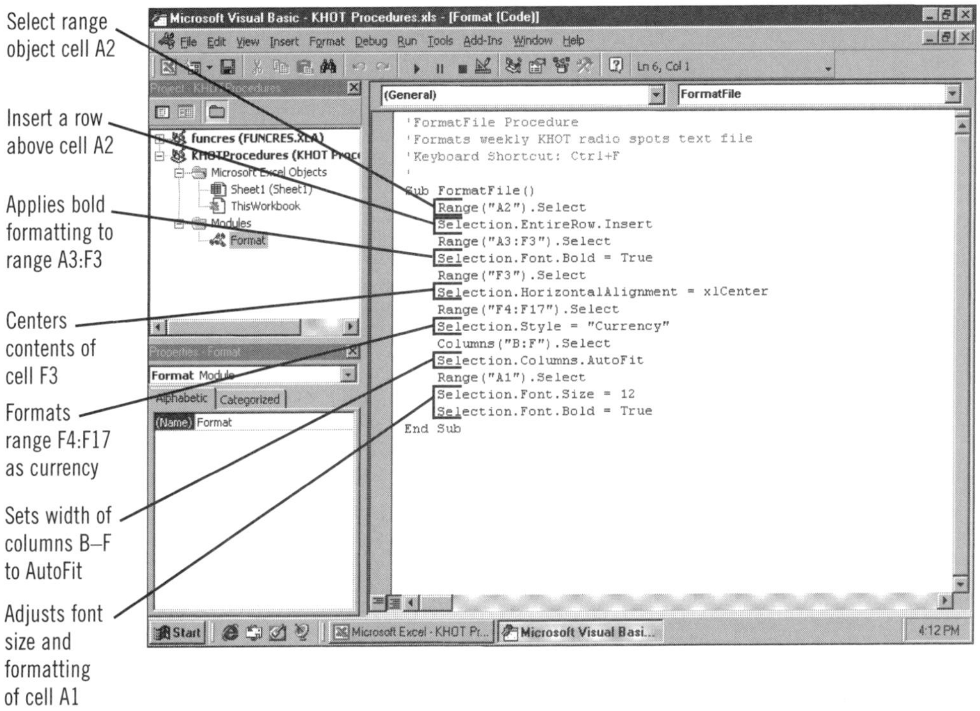

Select range
object cell A2

Insert a row
above cell A2

Applies bold
formatting to
range A3:F3

Centers
contents of
cell F3

Formats
range F4:F17
as currency

Sets width of
columns B–F
to AutoFit

Adjusts font
size and
formatting
of cell A1

```
'FormatFile Procedure
'Formats weekly KHOT radio spots text file
'Keyboard Shortcut: Ctrl+F
'
Sub FormatFile()
    Range("A2").Select
    Selection.EntireRow.Insert
    Range("A3:F3").Select
    Selection.Font.Bold = True
    Range("F3").Select
    Selection.HorizontalAlignment = xlCenter
    Range("F4:F17").Select
    Selection.Style = "Currency"
    Columns("B:F").Select
    Selection.Columns.AutoFit
    Range("A1").Select
    Selection.Font.Size = 12
    Selection.Font.Bold = True
End Sub
```

FIGURE P-4: Worksheet formatted using FormatFile procedure

Formatted
title

Row inserted

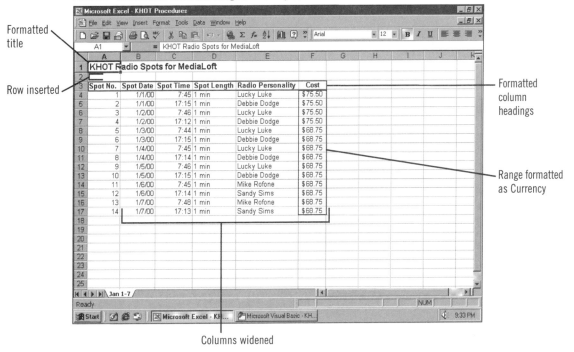

Formatted
column
headings

Range formatted
as Currency

Columns widened

Excel 2000

Writing VBA Code

To write your own code, you first need to open the Visual Basic Editor and add a module to the workbook. You can then begin entering the procedure code. In the first few lines of a procedure, you typically include comments indicating the name of the procedure, a brief description of the procedure, and shortcut keys, if applicable. When writing Visual Basic code for Excel, you must follow the formatting rules, or **syntax**, of the VBA programming language exactly. Even an extra space or a period could cause a procedure to fail. It is important to review the procedure based on the code you've written before you actually run it. ► Scenario ► Each week, Alice asks Jim to total the cost of the radio ads. Jim decides to write a procedure that will automate this routine task.

Trouble?

If the Code window is empty, verify that the workbook that contains your procedures (KHOT Procedures) is open.

1. **With the Jan 1-7 worksheet still displayed, click Tools on the menu bar, point to Macro, then click Visual Basic Editor**
   Two projects are displayed in the Project Explorer window, KHOT Procedures and KHOT Advertising Jan 1-7. KHOT Procedures is the active project; the Visual Basic title bar confirms this. The FormatFile procedure is again displayed in the Visual Basic Editor.

2. **Click the Modules folder in the KHOT Procedures project**
   You will store all of the procedures in the KHOT Procedures project.

3. **Click Insert on the Visual Basic Editor menu bar, then click Module**
   A new, blank module, with the default name Module1, is inserted in the KHOT Procedures workbook.

QuickTip

As you type, you may see lists of words in dropdown menus. For now, just continue to type.

4. **Click (Name) in the Properties window, type Total, then press [Enter]**
   This changes the default name to a more descriptive one. The module name ("Total") should not be the same as the procedure name (which will be "AddTotal"). Look at the code shown in Figure P-5. Notice that comments begin with an opening apostrophe and that the lines of code under "Sub AddTotal ( )" have been indented using the Tab key. When you enter the code in the next step, after you type *Sub AddTotal( )* (the procedure header) and press [Enter], the Visual Basic Editor will automatically enter *End Sub* (the procedure footer) in the Code window.

5. **Click in the Code window, then type the procedure code exactly as shown in Figure P-5**
   The lines that begin with *ActiveCell.Formula* insert the information enclosed in quotation marks into the active cell. For example, *ActiveCell.Formula = "Weekly Total:"* inserts the words "Weekly Total:" into cell E18, the active cell. The *With* clause near the bottom of the procedure is used to repeat several operations on the same object.

6. **Compare the procedure code you entered in the Code window with Figure P-5; if necessary, make any corrections; then click the Save KHOT Procedures.xls button** 🖫 **on the Visual Basic Editor Standard toolbar**

7. **Click the View Microsoft Excel button** 🖾 **on the Visual Basic Editor Standard toolbar, use the Windows menu to display the KHOT Advertising Jan 1-7 workbook, click Tools on the Excel menu bar, point to Macro, then click Macros**
   The Macro dialog box opens. This is where you select the macro procedure you want to run. Notice that the names of the macros have two parts. The first part ('KHOT Procedures.xls'!) indicates the workbook where the macro is stored. The second part (AddTotal or FormatFile) is the name of the procedure, taken from the procedure header.

Trouble?

If an error message appears, click Debug. Click the Reset button ▪ on the Visual Basic Editor Standard toolbar to leave debug mode, correct the error by referring to Figure P-5, then repeat Steps 6–8.

8. **Click 'KHOT Procedures.xls'!AddTotal if necessary, then click Run**
   The AddTotal procedure inserts and formats the ad expenditure total in cell F18, as shown in Figure P-6.

9. **Save the workbook**

FIGURE P-5: VBA code for the AddTotal procedure

Save KHOT Procedures button

Comments begin with apostrophes

Press [Tab] to indent lines

New module name

With clause repeats several operations on the same object

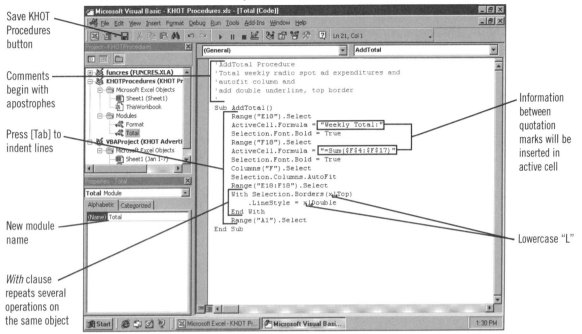

Information between quotation marks will be inserted in active cell

Lowercase "L"

FIGURE P-6: Worksheet after running the AddTotal procedure

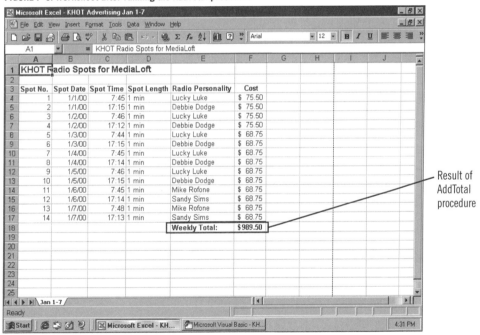

Result of AddTotal procedure

CLUES TO USE

Entering code

To assist you in entering the macro code, the Editor often displays a list of words that can be used in the macro statement. Typically, the list appears after you press the . (period). To include a word from the list in the macro statement, select the word in the list, then press [Tab]. For example, to enter the *Range("E12").Select* instruction, type *Range(" E12")*, then press the . (period). Type *s* to select the Select command in the list, then press [Tab] to enter the word "Select" in the macro statement.

Adding a Conditional Statement

Sometimes, you may want a procedure to take an action based on a certain condition or set of conditions. For example, *if* a salesperson's performance rating is a 5 (top rating), *then* calculate a 10% bonus; otherwise (*else*), there is no bonus. One way of adding this type of conditional statement in Visual Basic is by using an **If...Then...Else statement**. The syntax for this statement is: "If *condition* Then *statements* Else [*elsestatements*]." The brackets indicate that the Else part of the statement is optional. **Scenario** Alice wants to find out if the amount spent on radio ads stays within or exceeds the $1,000 budgeted amount. Jim will use Excel to add a conditional statement that indicates this information. He starts by returning to the Visual Basic Editor and inserting a new module in the KHOT Procedures workbook.

Steps 1 2 3 4

1. With the Jan 1-7 worksheet still displayed, click **Tools** on the menu bar, point to **Macro**, click **Visual Basic Editor**, verify that KHOT Procedures is the active project in the Project Explorer window, click **Insert** on the Visual Basic Editor menu bar, then click **Module**

   A new, blank module is inserted in the KHOT Procedures workbook.

2. In the Properties window click **(Name)**, then type **Budget**

3. Click in the Code window, then type the code exactly as shown in Figure P-7

   Notice the additional comment lines (in green) in the middle of the code. These extra lines help explain the procedure.

   QuickTip

   The If...Then...Else statement is similar to Excel's IF function.

4. Compare the procedure you entered with Figure P-7; if necessary, make any corrections; then click the **Save KHOT Procedures.xls button** 🖫 on the Visual Basic Editor Standard toolbar

5. Click the **View Microsoft Excel button** 🔣 on the Visual Basic Editor toolbar; click **Tools** on the menu bar; point to **Macro**; click **Macros**; in the Macro dialog box, click **'KHOT Procedures.xls'!BudgetStatus**; then click **Run**

   The BudgetStatus procedure indicates the status—within budget—as shown in Figure P-8.

6. Save your work

FIGURE P-7: VBA code for the BudgetStatus procedure

Elements of the
If...Then...Else
statement
appear in blue

Module name

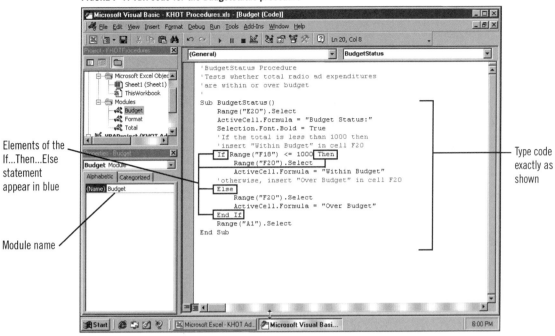

Type code
exactly as
shown

FIGURE P-8: Result of running BudgetStatus procedure

Indicates status
of ad budget

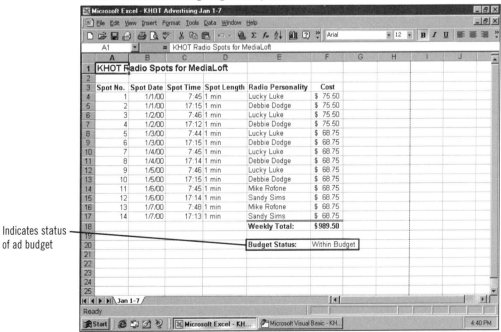

Excel 2000

Prompting the User for Data

When automating routine tasks, you sometimes need to pause a macro to allow user input. You use VBA's InputBox function to display a dialog box that prompts the user for information. A **function** is a predefined procedure that returns a value; in this case the value returned is the information the user enters. The required elements of an InputBox function are as follows: *object*.InputBox("*prompt*"), where "*prompt*" is the message that appears in the dialog box. For a detailed description of the InputBox function, use the Visual Basic Editor's Help menu. **Scenario** Jim decides to create a procedure that will insert the user's name in the left footer area of the workbook. He'll use the InputBox function to display a dialog box in which the user can enter his or her name.

Steps 1 2 3 4

1. With the Jan 1-7 worksheet still displayed, click **Tools** on the menu bar, point to **Macro**, click **Visual Basic Editor**, click **Insert** on the Visual Basic Editor menu bar, then click **Module**

   A new, blank module is inserted in the KHOT Procedures workbook.

2. In the Properties window, click **(Name)**, then type **Footer**

QuickTip

To enlarge your Code window, place the mouse pointer on the left border of the Code window until it turns into ◄┃►, then drag the border to the left until the Code window is the desired size.

3. Click in the Code window, then type the procedure code exactly as shown in Figure P-9

   Like the Budget procedure, this procedure also contains comments that explain the code. The first part of the code, *Dim LeftFooterText As String,* **declares**, or defines, *LeftFooterText* as a text string variable. In Visual Basic, a **variable** is a slot in memory in which you can temporarily store one item of information. Dim statements are used to declare variables and must be entered in the following format: Dim *variablename* As *datatype*. The datatype here is "string." In this case, you plan to store the information received from the input box in the temporary memory slot called LeftFooterText. Then you can place this text in the left footer area. The remaining statements in the procedure are explained in the comment line directly above each statement.

4. Review your code for errors, make any changes if necessary, then click the **Save KHOT Procedures.xls button** 🖫 on the Visual Basic Editor Standard toolbar

QuickTip

If your macro doesn't run correctly, it may contain a spelling or syntax error. You'll learn how to correct such macro errors in the next lesson.

5. Click the **View Microsoft Excel button** 🖾 on the Visual Basic Editor toolbar, click **Tools** on the menu bar, point to **Macro**, click **Macros**, in the Macro dialog box click **'KHOT Procedures.xls'!FooterInput**, then click **Run**

   The procedure begins, and a dialog box generated by the InputBox function appears, prompting you to enter your name. See Figure P-10.

6. With the cursor in the text box, type your name, then click **OK**

7. Click the **Print Preview button** 🔍 on the Standard toolbar

   Although the customized footer is inserted on the sheet, notice that, due to an error, your name does *not* appear in the left section of the footer. In the next lesson, you will learn how to step through a procedure's code, line by line. This will help you locate the error in the Footer procedure.

8. Click **Close**

   This closes the Print Preview window and returns you to the Jan 1-7 worksheet.

FIGURE P-9: VBA code for the FooterInput procedure

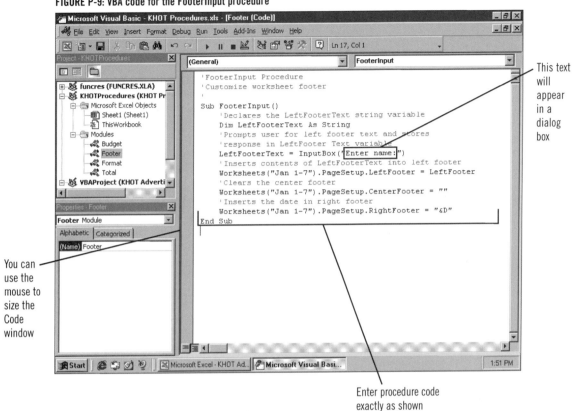

This text will appear in a dialog box

You can use the mouse to size the Code window

Enter procedure code exactly as shown

FIGURE P-10: InputBox function's dialog box

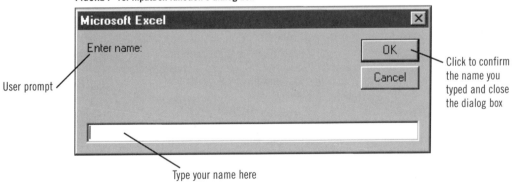

User prompt

Type your name here

Click to confirm the name you typed and close the dialog box

Debugging a Macro

When a macro procedure does not run properly, it can be due to an error, referred to as a **bug**, in the code. To assist you in finding the bug(s) in a procedure, you can use the Visual Basic Editor to step through the procedure's code, one line at a time. When you locate the error (bug), you can then correct, or **debug**, it. Scenario Jim decides to debug the macro procedure to find out why it failed to insert his name in the worksheet's footer.

Steps

1. **With the KHOT Advertising Jan 1-7 workbook still displayed, click Tools on the menu bar; point to Macro; click Macros; in the Macro dialog box, click 'KHOT Procedures.xls'!FooterInput; then click Step Into**

   The Visual Basic Editor appears with the statement selector positioned on the first statement of the procedure. See Figure P-11.

2. **Press [F8] to step through the code**

   The statement selector skips over the comments and the line of code beginning with Dim. The Dim statement indicates that the procedure will store your name in a variable named LeftFooterText. Because Dim is a declaration of a variable and not a procedure statement, the statement selector skips it and moves to the line containing the InputBox function.

3. **Press [F8] again; with the cursor in the text box in the InputBox function dialog box, type your name, then click OK**

   The Visual Basic Editor reappears. The statement selector is now positioned on the statement that reads *Worksheets ("Jan 1-7").PageSetup.LeftFooter = LeftFooter*. This statement inserts your name (which you just typed in the Input Box) in the left section of the footer. This is the instruction that does not appear to be working correctly.

4. **If necessary, scroll right until the end of the LeftFooter instruction is visible, then place the mouse pointer I on LeftFooter, as shown in Figure P-12**

   The last part of the InputBox function should be the variable (LeftFooterText) where the procedure stored your name. Rather than containing your name, however, the variable at the end of the procedure is empty. That's because the InputBox function assigned your name to the LeftFooterText variable, not to the LeftFooter variable. Before you can correct this bug, you need to turn off the Step Into feature.

5. **Click the Reset button ▪ on the Visual Basic Editor Standard toolbar to turn off the Step Into feature, click at the end of the statement, then type Text**

   The revised statement now reads *Worksheets("Jan 1-7").PageSetup.LeftFooter = LeftFooterText*.

6. **Click the Save KHOT Procedures.xls button 🖫 on the Visual Basic Editor Standard toolbar, then click the View Microsoft Excel button 🖾 on the Visual Basic Editor toolbar**

7. **Click Tools on the menu bar, point to Macro, click Macros; in the Macro dialog box, click 'KHOT Procedures.xls'!FooterInput; click Run to rerun the procedure; when prompted, type your name; then click OK**

8. **Click the Print Preview button 🔍 on the Standard toolbar**

   Your name now appears in the bottom-left section of the footer.

9. **Click Close, save the workbook, then print your work**

FIGURE P-11: Statement selector positioned on first procedure statement

Statement selector

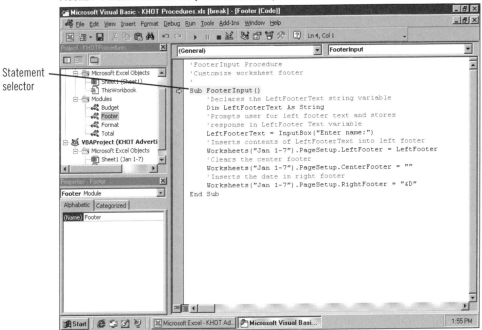

FIGURE P-12: Value contained in LeftFooter variable

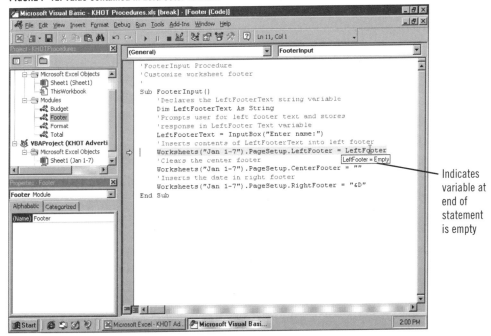

Indicates variable at end of statement is empty

Creating a Main Procedure

When you routinely need to run several macros one after another, you can save time by combining them into one procedure. The resulting procedure, which processes (or runs) multiple procedures in sequence, is referred to as the **main procedure**. To create a main procedure, you type a Call statement for each procedure you want to run. The syntax of the Call statement is Call *procedurename*, where *procedurename* is the name of the procedure you want to run. Scenario To avoid having to run his macros one after another every month, Jim decides to create a main procedure that will run (or call) each of the procedures in the KHOT Procedures workbook in sequence.

Steps

1. With the Jan 1-7 worksheet displayed, click **Tools** on the menu bar, point to **Macro**, then click **Visual Basic Editor**

2. Verify that KHOT Procedures is the active project, Click **Insert** on the menu bar, then click **Module**
   A new, blank module is inserted in the KHOT Procedures workbook.

3. In the Properties window, click **(Name)**, then type **MainProc**

4. In the Code window, enter the procedure code exactly as shown in Figure P-13

5. Compare your main procedure code with Figure P-13, correct any errors if necessary, then click the **Save KHOT Procedures.xls button** on the Visual Basic Editor Standard toolbar
   To test the new main procedure you need an unformatted version of the KHOT radio spot workbook.

6. Click the **View Microsoft Excel button** on the Visual Basic Editor Standard toolbar, then close the KHOT Advertising Jan 1-7 workbook, saving your changes
   The KHOT Procedures workbook remains open.

7. Open the workbook titled EX P-2, then save it as **KHOT Advertising Jan 1-7 Version 2**
   In the next lesson, you'll run the main procedure.

FIGURE P-13: VBA code for the MainProcedure procedure

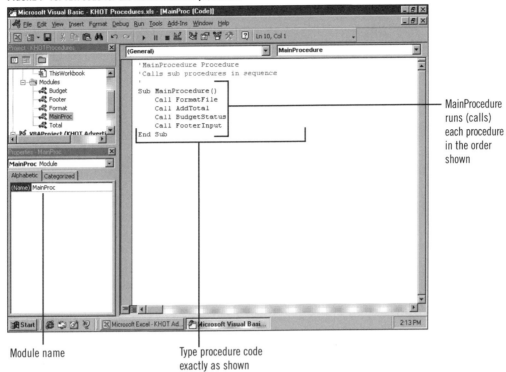

Module name

Type procedure code
exactly as shown

MainProcedure
runs (calls)
each procedure
in the order
shown

Running a Main Procedure

Running a main procedure allows you to instantly run several macros in sequence. You can run a main procedure just as you would any other macro procedure—by selecting it in the Macro dialog box, then clicking Run. **Scenario** Jim has finished creating his main procedure and is now ready to run it. If the main procedure works correctly, it should format the worksheet, insert a budget status message, insert the ad expenditure total, and add Jim's name to the worksheet footer.

Steps

1. **With the Jan 1-7 Version 2 worksheet displayed, click Tools on the menu bar, point to Macro, and click Macros; in the Macro dialog box click 'KHOT Procedures.xls'! MainProcedure; click Run; when prompted type your name, then click OK**
   The MainProcedure runs the FormatFile, AddTotal, BudgetStatus, and FooterInput procedures in sequence. See Figure P-14. You can see the results of the FormatFile, AddTotal, and BudgetStatus procedures in the worksheet window. To view the results of the FooterInput procedure, you need to switch to the Preview window.

2. **Click the Print Preview button [icon] on the Standard toolbar, verify that your name appears in the left footer area, then click Close**
   You could print each procedure separately, but it's faster to print all the procedures in the workbook at one time.

3. **Click Tools on the menu bar, point to Macro, then click Visual Basic Editor**

4. **In the Project Explorer window, double-click each procedure and add a comment line after the procedure name that reads "Written by [your name]"**

5. **Click File on the Visual Basic Editor menu bar, then click Print**
   The Print - KHOTProcedures dialog box opens, as shown in Figure P-15. Collectively, all procedures in a workbook are known as a project, as mentioned earlier in the unit.

6. **In the Print - KHOTProcedures dialog box, select the Current Project option button if necessary, then click OK**
   Each procedure prints on a separate page.

7. **Click the View Microsoft Excel button [icon] on the Visual Basic Editor Standard toolbar**

8. **Save the workbook and close it, close the KHOT Procedures workbook, then exit Excel**

FIGURE P-14: Result of running MainProcedure procedure

Click to verify that footer has been added

Formatting added to worksheet

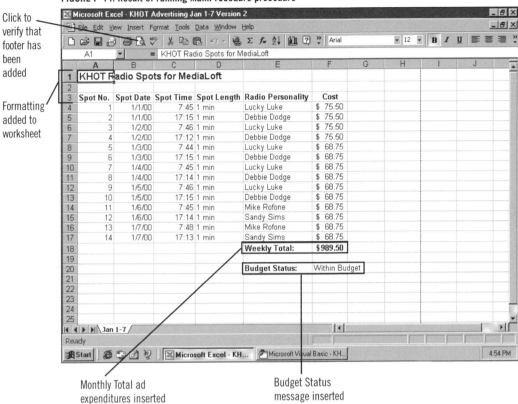

Monthly Total ad expenditures inserted

Budget Status message inserted

FIGURE P-15: Printing the macro procedures

Current Project option button

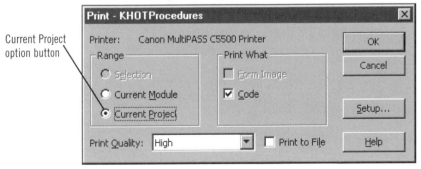

Practice

► Concepts Review

Label each element of the Visual Basic Editor screen shown in Figure P-16.

FIGURE P-16

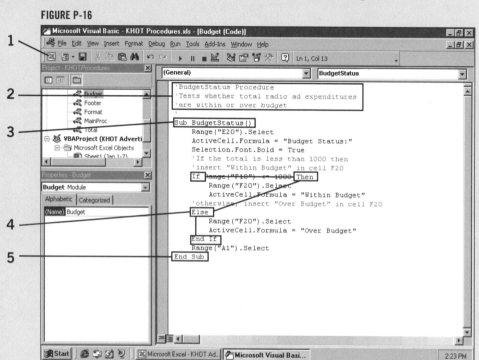

Match each term with the statement that describes it.

6. Sub procedure   a. A series of statements that perform an action but don't return a value
7. Procedure   b. A procedure that returns a value
8. Keywords   c. Words that are recognized as part of the programming language
9. Function   d. Another term for a macro in Visual Basic for Applications (VBA)
10. Comments   e. Descriptive text used to explain parts of a procedure

Select the best answer from the list of choices.

11. **You enter the statements of a macro in**
    a. The Code window of the Visual Basic Editor.
    b. Any blank worksheet.
    c. The Properties window of the Visual Basic Editor.
    d. The Macro dialog box.
12. **What must you keep in mind when typing VBA code?**
    a. The different parts of the code will appear in different colors.
    b. You can edit your code just as you would text in a word processor.
    c. Typographical errors can cause your procedures to fail.
    d. All of the above.
13. **If your macro doesn't run correctly, you should**
    a. Close the workbook and start over with a new macro.
    b. Select the macro in the Macro dialog box, click Step Into, and then debug the macro.
    c. Debug the macro in the worksheet window.
    d. Create an If . . . Then . . . Else statement.

▶ Skills Review

1. **View and analyze VBA code.**
    a. Open the workbook titled EX P-3, then save it as "Mission Medical Inc".
    b. Review the unformatted worksheet named Sheet1.
    c. Open the Visual Basic Editor.
    d. Select the ListFormat module.
    e. Insert comments in the List Format code describing what action you think each line of code will perform.
       (*Hint:* One of the statements will sort the list alphabetically by customer name.)
    f. Run the FormatList macro.
    g. Compare the results with the code and your comments.
    h. Save the workbook.
2. **Write VBA code.**
    a. Open Visual Basic Editor and insert a new module named "Total".
    b. Enter the Code exactly as shown in Figure P-17.
    c. Run the SalesTotal macro.
    d. Save the workbook.

FIGURE P-17

```
'SalesTotal Procedure
'Totals monthly sales
Sub SalesTotal()
 Range("F17").Select
 ActiveCell.Formula = "=SUM($F$2:$F$16)"
 Selection.Font.Bold = True
 With Selection.Borders(xlTop)
  .LineStyle = xlSingle
 End With
 Range("A1").Select
End Sub
```

3. Add a conditional statement.

a. Open Visual Basic Editor and insert a new module named "Goal".

b. Enter the procedure exactly as shown in Figure P-18.

c. Run the SalesGoal macro. If the procedure returns the message "Missed goal", the procedure worked as planned.

d. Save the workbook.

FIGURE P-18

```
'SalesGoal Procedure
'Tests whether sales goal was met
'
Sub SalesGoal()
  'If the total is >= 225000, then insert "Met Goal"
  'in cell G17
  If Range("F17") >= 225000 Then
   Range("G17").Select
   ActiveCell.Formula = "Met goal"
  'otherwise, insert "Missed goal" in cell G17
  Else
   Range("G17").Select
   ActiveCell.Formula = "Missed goal"
  End If
End Sub
```

4. Prompt the user for data.

a. Open Visual Basic Editor and insert a new module named "Header".

b. Enter the procedure exactly as shown in Figure P-19.

c. Run the HeaderFooter macro. When you encounter a runtime error, click End.

d. Save the workbook.

FIGURE P-19

```
'HeaderFooter Procedure
'Procedure to customize the header and footer
'
Sub HeaderFooter()
  'Inserts the filename in the header
  Worksheets("Sheet1").PageSetup.CenterHeader = "&F"
  'Declares the variable LeftFooterText as a string
  Dim LeftFooterText As String
  'Prompts user for left footer text
  LeftFooter = InputBox("Enter your full name:")
  'Inserts response into left footer
  Workbooks("Sheet1").PageSetup.LeftFooter = LeftFooterText
  Workbooks("Sheet1").PageSetup.CenterFooter = ""
  Workbooks("Sheet1").PageSetup.RightFooter = "&D"
End Sub
```

5. Debug a macro.

a. Run the HeaderFooter macro. When you encounter a runtime error, click Debug.

b. The statement selector is positioned on the incorrect procedure statement:

Workbooks("Sheet1").PageSetup.LeftFooter = LeftFooterText.

(*Hint:* Note that Workbooks, instead of Worksheets, was entered in the statement.)

c. Change *Workbooks* in the incorrect line of code to *Worksheets*. Do the same in the two following lines of code.

d. Rerun the HeaderFooter procedure.

e. Check the header and footer. Notice that the procedure does not display your name in the left section of the footer.

f. Use the Step Into feature to find the error in the code and then correct it. Make sure you leave Debugger mode by clicking the Reset button.

g. Rerun the HeaderFooter procedure.

h. Verify that your name now appears in the left section of the footer.

i. Save the workbook.

6. Create and run a main procedure.

a. Return to the Visual Basic Editor, insert a new module, and name it "MainProc".

b. Enter comments that give the procedure's name (MainProcedure), and explain its purpose.

c. Enter the following procedure header: *Sub MainProcedure ().*

d. Enter four Call statements that will run the FormatList, SalesTotal, SalesGoal, and HeaderFooter procedures in sequence.

e. Save the procedure and return to Excel.

f. Open the EX P-3 workbook, then save it as Medical Mission Inc Version 2.

g. Run the MainProcedure procedure. (*Hint:* In the Macro dialog box, the macro procedures you created will now have *'Medical Mission Inc.xls'!* as part of their names. That's because the macros are stored in the Medical Mission Inc workbook, and not in the Medical Mission Inc Version 2 workbook.)

h. Save the Medical Mission Inc Version 2 workbook, print the worksheet, then close the workbook.

i. Print the current project's code.

j. Return to Excel and close any open workbooks.

▶ Visual Workshop

Open the workbook titled EX P-5 and save it as "Big Time Audio". Create a macro procedure that will format the work-sheet as shown in Figure P-20.

FIGURE P-20

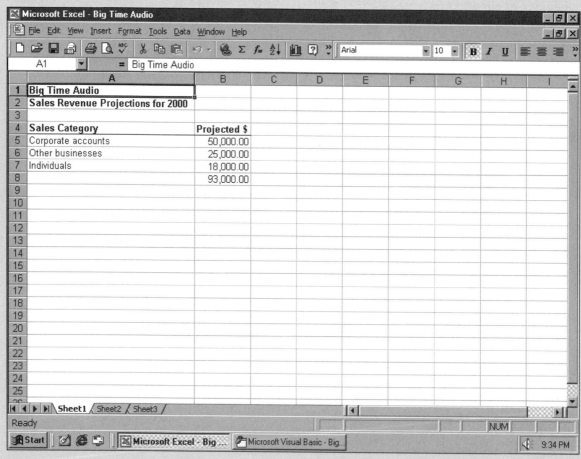

Excel 2000

Glossary

3-D references A reference that uses values on other sheets or workbooks, effectively creating another dimension to a workbook.

Absolute reference A cell reference that contains a dollar sign before the column letter and/or row number to indicate the absolute, or fixed, contents of specific cells. For example, the formula $A$1+$B$1 calculates only the sum of these specific cells no matter where the formula is copied in the workbook.

Active cell The current location of the cell pointer.

Address The location of a specific cell or range expressed by the coordinates of column and row; for example, A1.

Alignment The horizontal placement of cell contents; for example, left, center, or right.

Analyze To manipulate data, such as a list, with Excel or another tool.

Anchors Cells listed in a range address. For example, in the formula =SUM(A1:A15), A1 and A15 are anchors.

Area chart A line chart in which each area is given a solid color or pattern to emphasize the relationship between the pieces of charted information.

Arguments Information a function needs to create the answer. In an expression, multiple arguments are separated by commas. All of the arguments are enclosed in parentheses; for example, =SUM(A1:B1).

Arithmetic operator A symbol used in a formula, such as + or -, / or *, to perform mathematical operations.

ASCII file A text file that contains data but no formatting; instead of being divided into columns, ASCII file data are separated, or delimited, by tabs or commas.

Attribute The styling features such as bold, italics, and underlining that can be applied to cell contents.

AutoComplete A feature that automatically completes labels entered in adjoining cells in a column.

AutoFill A feature that creates a series of text or numbers when a range is selected using the fill handle.

AutoFit A feature that automatically adjusts the width of a column to accommodate its widest entry when the boundary to the right of the column selector is double-clicked.

AutoFormat Preset schemes that can be applied to format a range instantly. Excel comes with 16 AutoFormats that include colors, fonts, and numeric formatting.

AutoSum A feature that automatically creates totals using the AutoSum button.

Background color The color applied to the background of a cell.

Backsolving A problem-solving method in which you specify a solution and then find the input value that produces the answer you want; sometimes described as a what-if analysis in reverse.

Bar chart A chart that shows information as a series of (horizontal) bars.

Border The edge of a selected area of a worksheet. Lines and color can be applied to borders.

Bug In programming, an error that causes a procedure to run incorrectly.

Cancel button The X in the formula bar; it removes information from the formula bar and restores the previous cell entry.

Cell The intersection of a column and row in a worksheet.

Cell address The unique location identified by intersecting column and row coordinates.

Cell comments Notes you've written about a workbook that appear when you place the pointer over a cell.

Cell pointer A highlighted rectangle around a cell that indicates the active cell.

Cell reference The address or name that identifies a cell's position in a worksheet; it consists of a letter that identifies the cell's column and a number that identifies its row; for example, cell B3. Cell references in worksheets can be used in formulas and are relative or absolute.

Change history A worksheet containing a list of changes made to a shared workbook.

Changing cells In what-if analysis, cells that contain the values that change in order to produce multiple sets of results.

Chart A graphic representation of information from a worksheet. Types include 2-D and 3-D column, bar, pie, area, and line charts.

Chart sheet A separate sheet that contains a chart linked to worksheet data.

Chart title The name assigned to a chart.

Chart Wizard A series of dialog boxes that helps create or modify a chart.

Check box A square box in a dialog box that can be clicked to turn an option on or off.

Clear A command on the Edit menu used to erase a cell's contents, formatting, or both.

Clipboard A temporary storage area for cut or copied items that are available for pasting. See *Office Clipboard*.

Clipboard toolbar A toolbar that shows the contents of the Office Clipboard; contains buttons for copying and pasting items to and from the Office Clipboard.

Close A command that closes the file so you can no longer work with it, but keeps Excel open so that you can continue to work on other workbooks.

Code window In the Visual Basic Editor, the window that displays the selected module's procedures, written in the Visual Basic programming language.

Column chart The default chart type in Excel that displays information as a series of (vertical) columns.

Column selector button The gray box containing the letter above the column.

Comments In a Visual Basic procedure, notes that explain the purpose of the macro or procedure; they are preceded by a single apostrophe and appear in green on a color monitor.

Conditional format The format of a cell based on its value or the outcome of a formula.

Conditional formula A formula that makes calculations based on stated conditions, such as calculating a rebate based on a purchase amount.

Consolidate To add together values on multiple worksheets and display the result on another worksheet.

Control menu box A box in the upper-left corner of a window used to resize or close a window.

Copy A command that copies the content of selected cells and places it on the Clipboard.

Criteria range A cell range containing one row of labels (usually a copy of column labels) and at least one additional row underneath it that contains the criteria you want to match.

Custom chart type A specially formatted Excel chart.

Cut A command that removes the cell contents from the selected area of a worksheet and places them on the Clipboard.

Data entry area The unlocked portion of a worksheet where users are able to enter and change data.

Data form In an Excel list (or database), a dialog box that displays one record at a time.

Data label Descriptive text that appears above a data marker in a chart.

Data map An Excel chart that shows information plotted on a map with symbols representing data points.

Data marker A graphical representation of a data point, such as a bar or column.

Data point Individual piece of data plotted in a chart.

Data series The selected range in a worksheet that Excel converts into a graphic and displays as a chart.

Data table A range of cells that shows the resulting values when one or more input values are varied in a formula; when one input value is changed, the table is called a one-input data table, and when two input values are changed, it is called a two-input data table.

Database An organized collection of related information. In Excel, a database is called a list.

Debug In programming, to correct an error in code.

Declare In the Visual Basic programming language, to define a text string as a variable.

Delete A command that removes cell contents from a worksheet.

Dependent cell A cell, usually containing a formula, whose value changes depending on the values in the input cells. For example, a payment formula or function that depends on an input cell containing changing interest rates is a dependent cell.

Destination program In a data exchange, the program that will receive the data.

Dialog box A window that opens when more information is needed to carry out a command.

Divide-by-zero error An Excel worksheet error that occurs when a formula attempts to divide a value by zero.

Document To make notes about basic worksheet assumptions, complex formulas, or questionable data.

Dummy column/row Blank column or row included at the end of a range that enables a formula to adjust when columns or rows are added or deleted.

Dynamic page breaks In a larger workbook, horizontal or vertical dashed lines that represent the place where pages print separately. They also adjust automatically when you insert or delete rows or columns, or change column widths or row heights.

Edit A change made to the contents of a cell or worksheet.

Electronic spreadsheet A computer program that performs calculations on data and organizes information into worksheets. A worksheet is divided into columns and rows, which form individual cells.

Embedding Inserting a copy of data into a destination document; you can double-click the embedded object to modify it using the tools of the source program.

Enter button The check mark in the formula bar used to confirm an entry.

Exploding pie slice A slice of a pie chart that has been pulled away from the whole pie to add emphasis.

External reference indicator The exclamation point (!) used in a formula to indicate that a referenced cell is outside the active sheet.

Extract To place a copy of a filtered list in a range you specify in the Advanced Filter dialog box.

Field In a list (an Excel database), a column that describes a characteristic about records, such as first name or city.

Field name A column label that describes a field.

Fill color Cell background color.

Fill Down A command that duplicates the contents of the selected cells in the range selected below the cell pointer.

Fill handle A small square in the lower-right corner of the active cell used to copy cell contents.

Fill Right A command that duplicates the contents of the selected cells in the range selected to the right of the cell pointer.

Filter To hide data in an Excel list that does not meet specified criteria.

Find A command used to locate information the user specifies.

Floating toolbar A toolbar within its own window that is not anchored along an edge of the worksheet.

Font The typeface or design of a set of characters (letters, numbers, symbols, and punctuation marks).

Footer Information that prints at the bottom of each printed page; on screen, a footer is visible only in Print Preview. To add a footer, use the Header and Footer command on the View menu.

Format The appearance of text and numbers, including color, font, attributes, borders, and shading. See also *Number format.*

Format Painter A feature used to copy the formatting applied to one set of text or in one cell to another.

Formula A set of instructions used to perform numeric calculations (adding, multiplying, averaging, etc.).

Formula bar The area below the menu bar and above the Excel workspace where you enter and edit data in a worksheet cell. The formula bar becomes active when you start typing or editing cell data. It includes the Enter button and the Cancel button.

Freeze To hold in place selected columns or rows when scrolling in a worksheet that is divided in panes. See also *panes.*

Function A special, predefined formula that provides a shortcut for a commonly used calculation; for example, AVERAGE. In the Visual Basic programming language, a predefined procedure that returns a value.

Goal cell In backsolving, a cell containing a formula in which you can substitute values to find a specific value, or goal.

Gridlines Horizontal and/or vertical lines within a chart that make the chart easier to read.

Header Information that prints at the top of each printed page; on screen, a header is visible only in Print Preview. To add a header, use the Header and Footer command on the View menu.

Hide To make rows, columns, formulas, or sheets invisible to workbook users.

HTML Hypertext Markup Language, the format of pages that a Web browser such as Internet Explorer or Netscape Navigator can read.

Hyperlink An object (a filename, a word, a phrase, or a graphic) in a worksheet that, when you click it, will display another worksheet, called the target.

If...Then...Else statement In the Visual Basic programming language, a conditional statement that directs Excel to perform specified actions under certain conditions; its syntax is "If *condition* Then *statements* Else [*elsestatements*]."

Input Information that produces desired results in a worksheet.

Input cells Spreadsheet cells that contain data instead of formulas and that act as input to a what-if analysis; input values often change to produce different results. Examples include interest rates, prices, or other data.

Insertion point Blinking I-beam that appears in the formula bar during entry and editing.

Interactive Describes a worksheet saved as an HTML document and posted to an intranet or Web site that allows users to manipulate data using their browsers.

Internet A large computer network made up of smaller networks and computers.

Intranet An internal network site used by a particular group of people who work together.

Keywords In a macro procedure, words that are recognized as part of the Visual Basic programming language.

Label Descriptive text or other information that identifies the rows and columns of a worksheet. Labels are not included in calculations.

Label prefix A character that identifies an entry as a label and controls the way it appears in the cell.

Landscape orientation A print setting that positions the worksheet on the page so the page is wider than it is tall.

Legend A key explaining how information is represented by colors or patterns in a chart.

Line chart A graph of data that is mapped by a series of lines. Line charts show changes in data or categories of data over time and can be used to document trends.

Linking The dynamic referencing of data in other workbooks, so that when data in the other workbooks is changed, the references in the current workbook are automatically updated.

List The Excel term for a database, an organized collection of related information.

Lock To secure a row, column, or sheet so that data there cannot be changed.

Logical test The first part of an IF function; if the logical test is true, then the second part of the function is applied, and if it is false, then the third part of the function is applied. In the function IF(Balance>1,000,Rate*0.05,0), the 5% rate is applied to balances over $1,000.

Macro A set of instructions, or code, that performs tasks in the order you specify.

Main procedure A procedure containing several macros that run sequentially.

Mixed reference Formula containing both a relative and an absolute reference.

Mode indicator A box located at the lower-left corner of the status bar that informs you of the program's status. For example, when Excel is performing a task, the word "Wait" appears.

Model A worksheet used to produce a what-if analysis that acts as the basis for multiple outcomes.

Module In Visual Basic, a module is stored in a workbook and contains macro procedures.

More Buttons button A button you click on a toolbar to view toolbar buttons that are not currently visible.

Mouse pointer A symbol that indicates the current location of the mouse on the desktop. The mouse pointer changes its shape at times; for example, when you insert data, select a range, position a chart, change the size of a window, or select a topic in Help.

Moving border The dashed line that appears around a cell or range that is copied to the Clipboard.

Name box The left-most area in the formula bar that shows the cell reference or name of the active cell. For example, A1 refers to cell A1 of the active worksheet. You can also get a list of names in a workbook using the Name list arrow.

Named range A range of cells given a meaningful name; it retains its name when moved and can be referenced in a formula.

Number format A format applied to values to express numeric concepts, such as currency, date, and percentage.

Object A chart or graphic image that can be moved and resized and contains handles when selected. In object linking and embedding (OLE), the data to be exchanged between another document or program.

Object Linking and Embedding (OLE) A Microsoft Windows technology that allows you to transfer data from one document and program to another using embedding or linking.

Office Assistant An animated character that appears to offer tips, answer questions, and provide access to the program's Help system.

Office Clipboard A temporary storage area shared by all Office programs that can be used to cut, copy, and paste multiple items within and between Office programs. The Office Clipboard can hold up to 12 items collected from any Office program. See also *Clipboard toolbar*.

One-input data table A range of cells that shows resulting values when one input value in a formula is changed.

Open A command that retrieves a workbook from a disk and displays it on the screen.

Order of precedence The order in which Excel calculates parts of a formula: (1) exponents, (2) multiplication and division, and (3) addition and subtraction.

Output The end result of a worksheet.

Page field In a PivotTable or a PivotChart report, a field area that lets you view data as if it is stacked in pages, effectively adding a third dimension to the data analysis.

Panes Sections into which you can divide a worksheet when you want to work on separate parts of the worksheet at the same time; one pane freezes, or remains in place, while you scroll in another pane until you see the desired information.

Paste A command that moves information on the Clipboard to a new location. Excel pastes the formula, rather than the result, unless the Paste Special command is used.

Paste Function A series of dialog boxes that lists and describes all Excel functions and assists the user in function creation.

Pie chart A circular chart that represents data as slices of pie. A pie chart is useful for showing the relationship of parts to a whole; pie slices can be extracted for emphasis. See also *Exploding pie slice*.

PivotChart report An Excel feature that lets you summarize worksheet data in the form of a chart in which you can rearrange, or "pivot," parts of the chart structure to explore new data relationships.

PivotTable list An interactive PivotTable on a Web or intranet site that lets users explore data relationships using their browsers.

PivotTable report An Excel feature that allows you to summarize worksheet data in the form of a table in which you can rearrange, or "pivot," parts of the table structure to explore new data relationships; also called a PivotTable.

Plot area The area of a chart that contains the chart itself, its axes, and the legend.

Point A unit of measure used for fonts and row height. One inch equals 72 points.

Pointing method Specifying formula cell references by selecting the desired cell with your mouse instead of typing its cell reference; this eliminates typing errors.

Portrait orientation A print setting that positions the worksheet on the page so the page is taller than it is wide.

Precedence Algebraic rules that Excel uses to determine the order of calculations in a formula with more than one operator.

Procedure A sequence of Visual Basic statements contained in a macro that accomplishes a specific task.

Procedure footer In Visual Basic, the last line of a Sub procedure.

Procedure header The first line in a Visual Basic procedure.

Print Preview A command you can use to view the worksheet as it will look when printed.

Print title In a list that spans more than one page, the field names that print at the top of every printed page.

Program Task-oriented software (such as Excel or Word) that enables you to perform a certain type of task, such as data calculation or word processing.

Programs menu The Windows 95/98 Start menu that lists all available programs on your computer.

Project In the Visual Basic Editor, the equivalent of a workbook; a project contains Visual Basic modules.

Project Explorer In the Visual Basic Editor, a window that lists all open projects (or workbooks) and the worksheets and modules they contain.

Properties In the Visual Basic Editor, the characteristics associated with a module.

Properties window In the Visual Basic Editor, the window that displays a list of characteristics, or properties, associated with a module.

Range A selected group of adjacent cells.

Range format A format applied to a selected range in a worksheet.

Range object In Visual Basic, an object that represents a cell or a range of cells.

Record In a list (an Excel database), data about an object or a person.

Refresh To update a PivotTable so it reflects changes to the underlying data.

Relative cell reference A type of cell reference used to indicate a relative position in the worksheet. It allows you to copy and move formulas from one area to another of the same dimensions. Excel automatically changes the column and row numbers to reflect the new position.

Replace A command used to find one set of criteria and replace it with new information.

Reset usage data An option that returns personalized toolbars and menus to their default settings.

Route To send an e-mail attachment sequentially to each user in a list, who then forwards it to the next user on the list.

Routing slip A list of e-mail users who are to receive an e-mail attachment.

Row height The vertical dimension of a cell.

Row selector button The gray box containing the number to the left of the row.

Save A command used to permanently store your workbook and any changes you make to a file on a disk. The first time you save a workbook you must give it a filename.

Save As A command used to create a duplicate of the current workbook with a new filename. Used the first time you save a workbook.

Scenario A set of values you use to forecast results; the Excel Scenario Manager lets you store different scenarios.

Scenario summary An Excel table that compiles data from various scenarios so that you can view the scenario results next to each other for easy comparison.

Search criterion The specification for data that you want to find in an Excel list, such as "Denver" or "is greater than 1000."

Selection handles Small boxes appearing along the corners and sides of charts and graphic images that are used for moving and resizing.

Series of labels Pre-programmed series, such as days of the week and months of the year. They are formed by typing the first word of the series, then dragging the fill handle to the desired cell.

Shared workbook An Excel workbook that several users can open and modify.

Sheet Another term used for a *worksheet*.

Sheet tab A description at the bottom of each worksheet that identifies it in a workbook. In an open workbook, move to a worksheet by clicking its sheet tab. Also known as *Worksheet tab*.

Sheet tab scrolling buttons Buttons that enable you to move among sheets within a workbook.

Sort keys Criteria on which a sort, or a reordering of data, is based.

Source list The list on which a PivotTable is based.

Source program In a data exchange, the program used to create the data you are embedding or linking.

Spell check A command that attempts to match all text in a worksheet with the words in the dictionary.

standard chart type A commonly used column, bar, pie, or area chart in the Excel program; each type has several variations. For example, a column chart variation is the Columns with Depth.

Start To open a software program so you can use it.

Statement In Visual Basic, a line of code.

Status bar The bar at the bottom of the Excel window that provides information about various keys, commands, and processes.

Sub procedure A series of Visual Basic statements that perform an action but do not return a value.

Summary function In a PivotTable, a function that determines the type of calculation applied to the PivotTable data, such as SUM or COUNT.

Syntax In the Visual Basic programming language, the formatting rules that must be followed so that the macro will run correctly.

Table In an Access database, a list of data.

Target The location that a hyperlink displays after you click it.

Target cell In what-if analysis (specifically, in Excel Solver), the cell containing the formula.

Template A workbook containing text, formulas, macros, and formatting you use repeatedly; when you create a new document, you can open a document based on the template workbook. The new document will automatically contain the formatting, text, formulas, and macros in the template.

Text annotations Labels added to a chart to draw attention to a particular area.

Text color The color applied to the text within a cell.

Tick marks Notations of a scale of measure on a chart axis.

Title bar The bar at the top of the window that indicates the program name and the name of the current worksheet.

Toggle button A button that turns a feature on and off.

Toolbar A bar that contains buttons that give you quick access to the most frequently used commands.

Tracers In Excel worksheet auditing, arrows that point from cells that might have caused an error to the active cell containing an error.

Track To identify and keep a record of who makes which changes to a workbook.

Two-input data table A range of cells that shows resulting values when two input values in a formula are changed.

Truncate To shorten the display of a cell based on the width of a cell.

Uniform Resource Locator (URL) A unique address for a location on the World Wide Web; www.course.com is an example.

Values Numbers, formulas, or functions used in calculations.

Variable In the Visual Basic programming language, a slot in memory in which you can temporarily store an item of information; variables are often declared in Dim statements such as Dim variablename As datatype.

View A set of display or print settings that you can name and save for access at another time. You can save multiple views of a worksheet.

Visual Basic for Applications (VBA) A programming language used to create macros in Excel.

Web query An Excel feature that lets you obtain data from a Web, Internet, or intranet site and places it in an Excel workbook for analysis.

What-if analysis A decision-making feature in which data is changed and automatically recalculated.

Wildcard A special symbol you use in defining search criteria in the data form or Replace dialog box. The most common types of wildcards are the question mark (?), which stands for any single character, and the asterisk (*), which represents any group of characters.

Window A rectangular area of a screen where you view and work on a worksheet.

Workbook A collection of related worksheets contained within a single file.

Worksheet An electronic spreadsheet containing 256 columns by 65,536 rows.

Worksheet tab See *Sheet tab*.

Worksheet window The worksheet area in which data is entered.

World Wide Web A structure of documents, called pages, connected electronically over a large computer network called the Internet.

X-axis The horizontal line in a chart.

X-axis label A label describing the x-axis of a chart.

Y-axis The vertical line in a chart.

Y-axis label A label describing the y-axis of a chart.

Zoom A feature that enables you to focus on a larger or smaller part of the worksheet in Print Preview.

Index

special characters

' (apostrophe)
   indicating numbers as text with, EXCEL H-2,
      EXCEL H-4
* (asterisk) wildcard, EXCEL O-2
   in custom filters, EXCEL I-4
$ (dollar sign), identifying absolute cell references
      with, EXCEL B-16
= (equal sign), indicating formulas, EXCEL B-6,
      EXCEL E-2
! (exclamation point), external reference indicator,
      EXCEL F-6
? (question mark) wildcard, EXCEL H-9
   in custom filters, EXCEL I-4
symbols, column width and, EXCEL C-8

▶A

absolute cell references, EXCEL E-8
   copying formulas with, EXCEL B-16–17
   defined, EXCEL B-12
   identifying, EXCEL B-16
   for named ranges, EXCEL B-17
   using, EXCEL B-12–13
Access tables
   converting lists to, EXCEL M-16–17
Active Sheet(s) option button, EXCEL A-12
Add Constraint dialog box, EXCEL K-14
Add Report dialog box, EXCEL K-7
Add Scenario dialog box, EXCEL K-4–5
Advanced Filter dialog box, EXCEL I-6–7, EXCEL I-8
advanced filters
   creating, EXCEL I-6–7
   criteria range for, EXCEL I-6–7, EXCEL I-8–9
   extracting list data with, EXCEL I-8–9
alignment
   defined, EXCEL C-6
   of labels, EXCEL A-10, EXCEL C-6–7
   setting, EXCEL E-17
   of text in cells, EXCEL J-14–15
   of text in charts, EXCEL-D-12
   of values, EXCEL A-10
analysis, of list data, EXCEL I-1–17
   Advanced Filter for, EXCEL I-6–7

   AutoFilter for, EXCEL I-2–3
   custom filters for, EXCEL I-4–5
   data validation for list entries, EXCEL I-14–15
   extracting list data, EXCEL I-8–9
   looking up specific values, EXCEL I-12–13
   subtotals for, EXCEL I-10–11
   summarizing list data, EXCEL I-14–15
And condition
   in custom filters, EXCEL I-5
annotating charts, EXCEL D-14–15
Answer Report, EXCEL K-16–17
apostrophe (')
   indicating numbers as text with, EXCEL H-2,
      EXCEL H-4
   prefacing code comments with, EXCEL G-9
applications. See programs; specific programs
area charts, EXCEL D-3, EXCEL D-9
arguments
   defined, EXCEL E-6
   in functions, EXCEL B-8–9
arithmetic operators, EXCEL B-6
Arrange icons view, EXCEL O-3
Arrow button, EXCEL D-14
arrow keys
   navigating worksheet with, EXCEL A-11
arrows
   adding to charts, EXCEL D-14
ascending order sorts, EXCEL H-12–13, EXCEL H-14
ASCII files, EXCEL M-2
Assign Macro dialog box, EXCEL G-14
asterisk (*) wildcard, EXCEL O-2
   in custom filters, EXCEL I-4
attachments
   e-mailing workbooks as, EXCEL F-17
attributes
   conditional formatting, EXCEL C-14–15
   defined, EXCEL C-6
   of labels, EXCEL C-6–7
Auditing toolbar, EXCEL O-4–5
auditing worksheets, EXCEL O-4–5
AutoCalculate, EXCEL E-7
AutoFill, EXCEL O-10–11
AutoFilter, EXCEL I-2–3

AutoFilter button, EXCEL N-10
AutoFit, EXCEL C-8
AutoFit Selection, EXCEL C-9, EXCEL H-4
AutoFormat, EXCEL C-7
   formatting PivotTables with, EXCEL L-12–13
   removing from PivotTables, EXCEL L-13
AutoShape, EXCEL D-14
AutoSum function, EXCEL B-8, EXCEL E-6-7,
      EXCEL M-6, EXCEL O-4
AVERAGE function, EXCEL B-8, EXCEL B-9,
      EXCEL E-13, EXCEL L-6
   creating subtotals with, EXCEL I-10
axes, for charts
   formatting, EXCEL J-6–7

▶B

backsolving, EXCEL K-12–13
[Backspace] key
   correcting errors with, EXCEL A-10
bar charts, EXCEL D-3, EXCEL D-8–9
Between conditional formatting option, EXCEL C-15
blank lines
   inserting in macro code, EXCEL G-9
Bold button, EXCEL C-6
border buttons, EXCEL C-12, EXCEL C-13
borders
   for field names, EXCEL H-4
   in worksheets, EXCEL C-12–13
bugs
   in macros, EXCEL P-12–13
built-in custom chart types, EXCEL J-2–3

▶C

calculations
   with AutoCalculate, EXCEL E-7
   controlling, EXCEL O-8–9
   dates in, EXCEL E-8–9
   future value, with FV function, EXCEL E-15
   generating multiple totals with AutoSum,

Index

EXCEL E-6—7
payment, with PMT function, EXCEL E-14—15
Calculation tab
of Options dialog box, EXCEL O-8, EXCEL O-13
Call statement, EXCEL P-14
Cancel button, EXCEL B-4
case
matching, in searches, EXCEL H-8—9
Category Axis Title, EXCEL D-12
Category (x) axis, EXCEL J-6—7
cell address, EXCEL A-6
cell comments, EXCEL O-14—15
cell entries
copying, EXCEL B-10—11
editing, EXCEL B-4—5
moving, EXCEL B-10—11
cell names. *See* named cells
cell pointer, EXCEL A-6
returning to cell A1, EXCEL F-2
cell references
absolute, EXCEL B-12—13, EXCEL E-8
copied formulas and, EXCEL E-8
defined, EXCEL B-6, EXCEL B-12
mixed, EXCEL B-12
relative, EXCEL B-12—13, EXCEL B-14-15
cells
active, EXCEL A-6
applying colors, patterns, and borders to,
EXCEL C-12—13
defined, EXCEL A-6
deleting, EXCEL E-11
deleting contents of, EXCEL G-6
deleting formatting of, EXCEL G-6
filling with sequential text, EXCEL B-15
formatting, EXCEL C-2-3
hiding, EXCEL F-8-9
inserting, EXCEL E-11
locking, EXCEL F-8-9
moving border, EXCEL B-6
protecting, EXCEL F-8-9
ranges of, EXCEL A-10, EXCEL B-4—5
rotating text within, EXCEL J-14—15
unlocking/relocking, EXCEL F-9
Center button, EXCEL C-6
change history
for shared workbooks, EXCEL N-4, EXCEL N-6—7
changing cells
in what-if analysis, EXCEL K-4, EXCEL K-14—15

chart axis
formatting, EXCEL J-6—7
chart labels
rotating, EXCEL J-15
Chart Objects list box, EXCEL D-6, EXCEL D-7
Chart Options dialog box, EXCEL D-10—11,
EXCEL D-12—13, EXCEL J-8—9
charts, EXCEL A-2, EXCEL D-1—17, EXCEL J-1—17
adding data table to, EXCEL J-8—9
annotating, EXCEL D-14—15
creating, EXCEL D-4—5
drawing on, EXCEL D-14—15
editing, EXCEL D-8—9
embedding into PowerPoint slides, EXCEL M-14—15
enhancing, EXCEL D-12—13
formatting, EXCEL D-10—11
identifying objects in, EXCEL D-7
legends for, EXCEL J-5
moving, EXCEL D-6—7
planning, EXCEL D-2—3
previewing, EXCEL D-16—17
printing, EXCEL D-16—17
resizing, EXCEL D-6—7
rotating, EXCEL D-8, EXCEL J-10—11
uses of, EXCEL D-1
Word Art in, EXCEL J-12—13
chart sheets, EXCEL D-4
Chart Source Data dialog box, EXCEL D-4
Chart tab
of Options dialog box, EXCEL O-13
Chart toolbar, EXCEL D-6—7, EXCEL J-2, EXCEL J-15
buttons, EXCEL D-10
docking, EXCEL D-6
chart type buttons, EXCEL D-9
chart types
area, EXCEL D-3, EXCEL D-9
bar, EXCEL D-3, EXCEL D-8—9, EXCEL D-9
changing, EXCEL D-8—9
column, EXCEL D-3, EXCEL D-8—9
commonly used, EXCEL D-3
custom, EXCEL J-2—3
doughnut, EXCEL D-9
line, EXCEL D-3, EXCEL D-9
pie, EXCEL D-3, EXCEL D-9, EXCEL D-15
radar, EXCEL D-9
selecting, EXCEL D-2
standard, EXCEL J-2
3-D, EXCEL D-8, EXCEL D-9

3-D area, EXCEL D-9
3-D bar, EXCEL D—9
3-D column, EXCEL D-9
3-D cone, EXCEL D-9
3-D cylinder, EXCEL D-9
3-D line, EXCEL D-9
3-D pie, EXCEL D-9
3-D surface, EXCEL D-9
user-defined, EXCEL J-3
XY (scatter), EXCEL D-3, EXCEL D-9
Chart Wizard button, EXCEL D-4
on PivotTable toolbar, EXCEL L-7
Chart Wizard dialog box, EXCEL J-2—3
circular references, EXCEL O-5
Circular Reference toolbar, EXCEL O-5
Clipboard, EXCEL B-10—11
Clippit, EXCEL A-14
Code window
in Project Explorer, EXCEL P-3
in Visual Basic Editor, EXCEL P-6
Col_index_num
for VLOOKUP function, EXCEL I-12
Collapse dialog box, EXCEL B-8, EXCEL B-9,
EXCEL E-12
color
in worksheets, EXCEL C-12—13
Color tab
of Options dialog box, EXCEL O-13
column charts, EXCEL D-3, EXCEL D-8—9, EXCEL D-9
three-dimensional, EXCEL D-8
Column command, EXCEL C-8
column delimited files, EXCEL M-3
column fields
in PivotTables and PivotCharts, EXCEL L-15
column headings
printing, EXCEL H-16
Column Hide command, EXCEL C-9
column labels
improving appearance of, EXCEL H-12
sorting and, EXCEL H-12
columns
deleting, EXCEL C-10—11
dummy, EXCEL C-11
freezing, EXCEL F-2—3
hiding/unhiding, EXCEL F-9
inserting, EXCEL C-10—11
Column Standard Width command, EXCEL C-8,
EXCEL C-9

Columns with Depth chart, EXCEL J-2–3
Column Unhide command, EXCEL C-9
column width
    adjusting, EXCEL C-8–9
    adjusting for field names, EXCEL H-4
    restoring defaults, EXCEL C-8, EXCEL C-9
Column Width command, EXCEL C-8–9
Column Width dialog box, EXCEL C-8
combination charts, EXCEL D-3
Comma style, EXCEL C-2
Comment box, EXCEL O-14–15
comments
    adding to cells, EXCEL O-14–15
    adding to macro code, EXCEL G-9
    in VBA code, EXCEL P-2
comparison operators, EXCEL E-11
conditional formatting, EXCEL C-14–15
    deleting, EXCEL C-15
    options, EXCEL C-15
Conditional Formatting dialog box, EXCEL C-14–15
conditional formulas
    building with IF function, EXCEL E-10–11
    defined, EXCEL E-10
Confirm Password dialog box, EXCEL N-8
consolidating data
    with 3-D references, EXCEL F-6–7
    with linking, EXCEL F-7
Convert to Access dialog box, EXCEL M-16
Copy button, EXCEL B-10, EXCEL B-14,
copying
    active worksheet, EXCEL F-4
    cell entries, EXCEL B-10–11
    formulas, EXCEL E-2–3, EXCEL E-8–9
    formulas, with absolute cell references,
        EXCEL B-16–17
    formulas, with relative cell references,
        EXCEL B-14–15
    list data, to another location, EXCEL I-8–9
    named ranges, EXCEL B-17
    with Paste Special command, EXCEL E-3
    worksheets, EXCEL B-19
copy pointer, EXCEL B-3
Copy to another location option
    for extracting list data, EXCEL I-8–9
COUNTA function, EXCEL E-12–13
COUNT function, EXCEL B-9, EXCEL E-12–13,

EXCEL L-6
    creating subtotals with, EXCEL I-10
criteria
    for deleting records, EXCEL H-10–11
    for finding records, EXCEL H-8–9, EXCEL I-2
Criteria data form, EXCEL H-8–9
criteria range
    for advanced filters, EXCEL I-6–7, EXCEL I-8–9
    defining in Advanced Filter dialog box, EXCEL I-9
crosshair pointer, EXCEL J-16
cross (normal) pointer, EXCEL B-3
CSV (comma separated values) files, EXCEL M-3
Currency style, EXCEL C-2–3
custom AutoFill lists, EXCEL O-10–11
Custom AutoFilter dialog box, EXCEL I-3–4
Custom Buttons
    for Macros toolbar, EXCEL G-16–17
custom chart types
    creating, EXCEL J-3
    selecting, EXCEL J-2–3
    sizing handles for, EXCEL J-2
custom filters
    creating, EXCEL I-3–4
custom formats
    for numbers and dates, EXCEL E-9
customization, of Excel, EXCEL O-12–13
Customize dialog box, EXCEL G-16–17
    restoring defaults with, EXCEL A-7, EXCEL A-8
Custom Lists tab, EXCEL O-10–11
    of Options dialog box, EXCEL O-13
custom sort order, EXCEL H-15
custom views
    saving, EXCEL F-10–11
Custom Views dialog box, EXCEL F-10–11
custom Web queries, EXCEL N-17

▶ D

data
    consolidating, with 3-D references, EXCEL F-6–7
    deleting, EXCEL O-16
    exporting, EXCEL M-7
    illustrating in charts, EXCEL D-2
    recalculation of, EXCEL A-2
    sharing with others, EXCEL A-2

databases
    defined, EXCEL H-1 (See also lists)
    vs. lists, EXCEL H-3
database tables
    importing, EXCEL M-6–7
data entry
    computer vs. manual systems, EXCEL A-2
data entry area
    locking cells outside of, EXCEL F-8
data exchange, EXCEL M-1–17
    converting lists to Access tables, EXCEL M-16–17
    destination program for, EXCEL M-2
    determining goal of, EXCEL M-2
    embedding Excel charts into PowerPoint slides,
        EXCEL M-14–15
    embedding worksheets, EXCEL M-10–11
    importable files, EXCEL M-3
    importing database tables, EXCEL M-6–7
    importing text files, EXCEL M-4–5
    inserting graphic files in worksheets, EXCEL M-8–9
    linking worksheets to another program,
        EXCEL M-12–13
    planning, EXCEL M-2–3
    source program for, EXCEL M-2
data form
    adding records to lists with, EXCEL H-6–7
data format, EXCEL C-2
data input values
    for what-if analysis, EXCEL K-2–3
data labels, EXCEL J-4
data maps, EXCEL J-16–17
data markers, on charts, EXCEL D-2
data points, on charts, EXCEL D-2
data series
    customizing, EXCEL J-4–5
    defined, EXCEL J-4
    formatting, for charts, EXCEL D-10–11
data tables
    adding to charts, EXCEL J-8–9
    one-input, EXCEL K-8–9
    projecting figures with, EXCEL K-8–9
    two-input, EXCEL K-10–11
data validation
    for list entries, EXCEL I-16–17
DATE function, EXCEL E-8
dates

Index

in calculations, EXCEL E-8–9
custom formats, EXCEL E-9
functions, EXCEL E-8–9
dBase files, EXCEL M-3
DCOUNTA function, EXCEL I-14–15
DD-MM-YY format, EXCEL C-2
debugging
macros, EXCEL P-12–13
declarations
in VBA code, EXCEL P-10
default settings, Windows A-2
defaults
column width, EXCEL C-8, EXCEL C-9
customizing settings, EXCEL O-12–13
macros names, EXCEL G-4
menus, EXCEL A-7, EXCEL E-2
restoring with Customize dialog box, EXCEL A-7, EXCEL A-8
toolbars, EXCEL A-7, EXCEL D-4, EXCEL E-2
Define Name dialog box, EXCEL B-5
Delete button, EXCEL H-10–11
Delete Conditional Format dialog box, EXCEL C-15
Delete dialog box, EXCEL E-11
[Delete] key
correcting errors with, EXCEL A-10
deleting
cells, EXCEL E-11
conditional formatting, EXCEL C-15
data, EXCEL O-16
macros, EXCEL G-6
ranges, EXCEL H-10
records, EXCEL H-10–11
rows and columns, EXCEL C-10–11
worksheets, EXCEL B-18, EXCEL F-4–5
delimiters
in text files, EXCEL M-4
dependent cells
defined, EXCEL K-2–3
descending order sorts, EXCEL H-12, EXCEL H-14
destination program
defined, EXCEL M-2
details
showing or hiding in outlines, EXCEL I-11
Details view, EXCEL O-3
diagonal resizing pointer, EXCEL D-7
dictionary (spell checker)
modifying, EXCEL C-16

DIF (Data Interchange Format) files, EXCEL M-3
Dim statements
using, EXCEL P-12
in VBA code, EXCEL P-10
displaying formula contents, EXCEL E-16–17
divide by zero messages, EXCEL O-16
documentation
of workbook assumptions, EXCEL O-14–15
dollar sign ($)
identifying absolute cell references with, EXCEL B-16
doughnut charts, EXCEL D-9
drag-and-drop
copying information with, EXCEL B-10–11
drawing
on charts, EXCEL D-14–15
Drawing toolbar, EXCEL D-14, EXCEL J-12
drawn objects
charts as, EXCEL D-6
draw pointer, EXCEL D-7
Drop Page Fields, EXCEL L-8
drop shadows
surrounding chart titles, EXCEL D-12
DSUM function, EXCEL I-14–15
dummy columns, EXCEL C-11
dummy rows, EXCEL C-11
dynamic page breaks, EXCEL F-12

► E

editing
cell entries, EXCEL B-4–5
charts, EXCEL D-8–9
Edit mode
changing to, EXCEL B-4
correcting errors in, EXCEL A-10
Edit tab
of Options dialog box, EXCEL O-13
Edit Text Object dialog box, EXCEL J-16–17
Edit WordArt Text dialog box, EXCEL J-12–13
electronic spreadsheets. See also worksheets
defined, EXCEL A-2
e-mail
sending workbooks via, EXCEL F-17
embedded objects, EXCEL M-2–3
embedding

charts into slides, EXCEL M-14–15
defined, EXCEL M-2–3
objects in worksheets, EXCEL B-11
vs. pasting, EXCEL M-10
worksheets, EXCEL M-10–11
Enter Parameter Value dialog box, EXCEL N-16
Entire workbook option button, EXCEL B-18
entry order sorts, EXCEL H-12
equal sign (=)
indicating formulas, EXCEL B-6, EXCEL E-2
Equal to conditional formatting option, EXCEL C-15
Excel 2000
advantages of, EXCEL A-2
exiting, EXCEL A-16–17
Help system, EXCEL A-14–15
starting, EXCEL A-4–5
Excel Chart Wizard, EXCEL D-4–5
Excel 4.0/5.0/7.0 files, EXCEL M-3
Excel Macro Recorder
recording macros with, EXCEL G-4–5, EXCEL G-8
Excel Query Wizard, EXCEL M-6
Excel window. See worksheet window
exclamation point (!)
external reference indicator, EXCEL F-6
exiting
Excel 2000, EXCEL A-16–17
Expand dialog box, EXCEL B-8
exploded pie charts, EXCEL D-15
exporting data, EXCEL M-7
External Data toolbar, EXCEL N-16
external reference indicator, EXCEL F-6
extracting list data, EXCEL I-8–9
extract range
defining in Advanced Filter dialog box, EXCEL I-9

► F

field names
adjusting column widths for, EXCEL H-4
borders for, EXCEL H-4
defined, EXCEL H-2
guidelines for, EXCEL H-5
planning, EXCEL H-2
fields
defined, EXCEL H-2
planning, EXCEL H-2

sorting lists by, EXCEL H-12–13
Field Settings button
  on PivotTable toolbar, EXCEL L-7
file formats
  importable, EXCEL M-3
file properties
  tracking, EXCEL O-3
  ASCII, EXCEL M-2
  column delimited, EXCEL M-3
  finding, EXCEL O-2–3,
  HTML, EXCEL F-16–17, EXCEL M-9, EXCEL N-10–11
  hyperlinks between, EXCEL F-14–15
  importable, EXCEL M-3
  importing, EXCEL M-4–5, EXCEL M-9
  inserting graphic files in worksheets, EXCEL M-8–9
  posting to Web, EXCEL F-16
  saving as HTML files, EXCEL F-16–17
  sharing, EXCEL N-2–3
fill handle pointer, EXCEL B-3
fill handles
  copying formulas with, EXCEL B-14–15
Fill Right method, EXCEL B-14
Fill Series command, EXCEL B-15
filtering
  with advanced filters, EXCEL I-6–7
  with custom filters, EXCEL I-3–4
  defined, EXCEL I-2
  with page fields, EXCEL L-8–9
  using AutoFilter, EXCEL I-2–3
Find dialog box, EXCEL O-2–3
finding
  files, EXCEL O-2–3
  records in lists, EXCEL H-8–9
  text, EXCEL F-2
  with wildcards, EXCEL H-9
fonts,
  in charts, EXCEL D-12
  conditional formatting, EXCEL C-14–15
  defined, EXCEL C-4
  formatting, EXCEL C-4–5
  types of, EXCEL C-5
font size
  defined, EXCEL C-4
  formatting, EXCEL C-4–5
  row height and, EXCEL C-8
footers
  specifying, EXCEL F-5
Formal Report button

on PivotTable toolbar, EXCEL L-7
Format Axis dialog box, EXCEL J-6
Format button, EXCEL D-12
Format Cells dialog box, EXCEL C-2–3, EXCEL C-4–5,
  EXCEL C-12–13, EXCEL C-14, EXCEL E-9,
  EXCEL K-8, EXCEL K-10
  Alignment tab, EXCEL J-14–15
Format Chart Title dialog box, EXCEL D-12
Format Column commands, EXCEL C-8–9
Format Data Series dialog box, EXCEL D-10–11,
  EXCEL J-4–5
Format Painter, EXCEL C-3, EXCEL C-14
formatting, Windows B-2
  chart axis, EXCEL J-6–7
  charts, EXCEL D-10–11
  chart titles, EXCEL D-12
  clearing, EXCEL C-6
  conditional, EXCEL C-14–15
  custom, for numbers and dates, EXCEL E-9
  data series, EXCEL J-4–5
  defined, EXCEL C-2
  deleting, EXCEL G-6
  fonts and font sizes, EXCEL C-4–5
  legends, EXCEL J-5
  numbers, EXCEL C-2–3, EXCEL H-2
  predefined, EXCEL C-7
  shortcuts, EXCEL C-6
  values, EXCEL C-2–3
  worksheets, EXCEL C-1–17
Formatting toolbar, EXCEL H-4
  changing fonts and font sizes with, EXCEL C-4
  defined, EXCEL A-6
  restoring defaults, EXCEL A-7
formula bar
  defined, EXCEL A-6
  editing cell entries in, EXCEL B-4–5
  formulas with names in, EXCEL E-4–5
Formula Palette, EXCEL E-13
formula prefix (equal sign), EXCEL B-8
formulas
  absolute cell references in, EXCEL B-12,
    EXCEL B-16–17
  conditional, EXCEL E-10–11
  copying, EXCEL E-2–3, EXCEL E-8–9
  copying, with absolute cell references,
    EXCEL B-16–17
  copying, with relative cell references,
    EXCEL B-14–15

defined, EXCEL B-6
  displaying contents of, EXCEL E-16–17
  editing with Formula Palette, EXCEL E-13
  entering, EXCEL B-6–7
  entering with Formula Palette, EXCEL E-13
  hiding/unhiding, EXCEL F-8–9
  inserting and deleting rows and columns,
    EXCEL C-10
  order of precedence in, EXCEL B-6
  pointing method for, EXCEL B-6
  precedence rules, EXCEL E-2
  printing contents of, EXCEL E-16–17
  relative cell references in, EXCEL B-12,
    EXCEL B-14–15
  with several operators, EXCEL E-2–3
  using names in, EXCEL E-4–5
Freeze panes command, EXCEL F-2
freezing
  rows and columns, EXCEL F-2–3
functions, EXCEL B-7–8
  arguments for, EXCEL B-8
  date, EXCEL E-8–9
  defined, EXCEL B-7
  entering, EXCEL E-6
  frequently used, EXCEL B-9
  most recently used, EXCEL B-8
  statistical, EXCEL E-12–13
  in VBA code, EXCEL P-10–11
future value, EXCEL E-15
FV function, EXCEL E-15

▶G

General tab
  of Options dialog box, EXCEL O-13
GETPIVOTDATA function, EXCEL L-16–17
goal cells, EXCEL K-12
Goal Seek, EXCEL K-1, EXCEL K-12–13
Goal Seek dialog box, EXCEL K-12–13
Go To command, EXCEL E-2
graphics
  as hyperlinks, EXCEL M-8
  inserting, EXCEL F-15
  inserting in worksheets, EXCEL M-8–9
Greater than conditional formatting option,
  EXCEL C-15
Greater than or equal to conditional formatting option,

Index

EXCEL C-15
gridlines
  on charts, EXCEL D-10
  printing, EXCEL H-16
grouping
  creating subtotals using, EXCEL I-10—11

►H

headers
  specifying, EXCEL F-5
Help, EXCEL A-14—15
Help feature, Windows A-16—17
Hide Detail button
  on PivotTable toolbar, EXCEL L-7
Hide Details button, EXCEL I-11
hiding
  formulas, EXCEL F-8—9
  worksheets areas, EXCEL F-7—8
Highlight Changes dialog box, EXCEL N-6—7
HLOOKUP function, EXCEL I-13
Horizontal Lookup function. See HLOOKUP function
horizontal resizing pointer, EXCEL D-7
HTML files
  importing data from, EXCEL M-9
  saving Excel files as, EXCEL F-16—17,
    EXCEL N-10—11
HTML round tripping, EXCEL M-9
hyperlinks
  creating between Excel files, EXCEL F-14—15
  creating to Web URLs, EXCEL N-14—15
  graphics as, EXCEL M-8
  navigating large worksheets with, EXCEL N-15
Hypertext Markup Language. See HTML files

►I

I-beam pointer, EXCEL B-3, EXCEL D-7
If ... Then ... Else statement
  in VBA code, EXCEL P-8—9
IF function
  building conditional formulas with, EXCEL E-10—11
importable file formats, EXCEL M-3
importing
  database tables, EXCEL M-6—7

data from HTML files, EXCEL M-9
  methods, EXCEL M-5
  text files, EXCEL M-4—5
Import Spreadsheet Wizard dialog boxes,
  EXCEL M-16—17
Increase Decimal button, EXCEL C-2
indenting
  labels, EXCEL H-12
InputBox function, EXCEL P-10—11
input cells, EXCEL K-2—3
input values
  in one-input data tables, EXCEL K-8
  in two-input data tables, EXCEL K-10—11
Insert ClipArt window, EXCEL F-15
Insert dialog box, EXCEL C-10—11, EXCEL E-11
Insert Hyperlink dialog box, EXCEL F-14—15,
  EXCEL N-14—15
inserting
  blank lines, in macro code, EXCEL G-9
  cells, EXCEL E-11
  columns, EXCEL C-10—11
  pictures, EXCEL F-15
  rows, EXCEL C-10—11
  worksheets, EXCEL F-4—5
insertion point, EXCEL B-4,
Insert Object command, EXCEL M-9
Insert Object dialog box, EXCEL M-10—11, EXCEL M-14
Insert Picture dialog box, EXCEL M-8—9
interactive PivotTables
  creating for intranet or Web, EXCEL N-12—13
  publishing on intranet or Web, EXCEL N-2—3
interactive worksheets
  creating for intranet or Web, EXCEL N-10—11
  publishing on intranet or the Web, EXCEL N-2—3
  viewing interactive PivotTables in, EXCEL N-12—13
  viewing interactive worksheets in, EXCEL N-10—11
intranets, EXCEL F-16
  creating interactive PivotTables for, EXCEL N-12—13
  creating interactive workbooks for, EXCEL N-10—11
  managing HTML files on, EXCEL N-11
  publishing interactive workbooks and PivotTables to,
    EXCEL N-2—3
Italics button, EXCEL C-6

►K

keywords
  in VBA, EXCEL P-2

►L

Label Ranges dialog box, EXCEL E-4
labels. See also column labels
  alignment of, EXCEL A-10, EXCEL C-6—7
  attributes of, EXCEL C-6—7
  defined, EXCEL A-10
  entering, EXCEL A-10—11
  entering numbers as, EXCEL A-10
  truncated, EXCEL A-10
landscape orientation, EXCEL E-16—17
  printing charts in, EXCEL D-16—17
  printing worksheets in, EXCEL H-16
legends
  inserting, formatting, and removing, EXCEL J-5
  for maps, EXCEL J-16—17
Less than conditional formatting option, EXCEL C-15
Less than or equal to conditional formatting option,
  EXCEL C-15
line charts, EXCEL D-3, EXCEL D-9
Line Style button, EXCEL M-8
linked objects, EXCEL M-2—3
linking
  consolidating data with, EXCEL F-7
  defined, EXCEL M-2—3
  worksheets to another program, EXCEL M-12—13
links
  managing, EXCEL M-13
Links dialog box, EXCEL M-13
list data
  analyzing, EXCEL I-1—17
  analyzing with Advanced Filter, EXCEL I-6—7
  analyzing with AutoFilter, EXCEL I-2—3
  analyzing with custom filters, EXCEL I-4—5
  data validation for list entries, EXCEL I-14—15
  extracting, EXCEL I-8—9
  looking up specific values, EXCEL I-12—13
  subtotals for, EXCEL I-10—11
  summarizing list data, EXCEL I-14—15
lists, EXCEL H-1—17
  adding records with data form, EXCEL H-6—7
  converting to Access tables, EXCEL M-16—17
  creating, EXCEL H-4—5

custom AutoFill, EXCEL O-10—11

databases *vs.*, EXCEL H-3

defined, EXCEL H-1

finding records in, EXCEL H-8—9

maintaining quality of information in, EXCEL H-5

number formatting for, EXCEL H-2

PivotTable, EXCEL N-12—13

planning, EXCEL H-2—3

printing, EXCEL H-16—17

row and column content guidelines, EXCEL H-3

size and location guidelines, EXCEL H-3

sorting, by multiple fields, EXCEL H-14—15

sorting by one field, EXCEL H-12—13

List view, EXCEL O-3

Locked check box, EXCEL F-8

locking selected cells, EXCEL F-8—9

logical conditions

in custom filters, EXCEL I-5

logical operators

conditional formatting and, EXCEL C-14—15

logical tests, EXCEL E-10

Lotus 1-2-3 files, EXCEL M-3

▶M

Macro dialog box, EXCEL P-2, EXCEL P-16

macros, EXCEL G-1—17, EXCEL P-1

adding as menu items, EXCEL G-14—15

adding blank lines to, EXCEL G-9

adding comments to code, EXCEL G-9

creating main procedure, EXCEL P-14—15

creating toolbars for, EXCEL G-16—17

debugging, EXCEL P-12—13

default names for, EXCEL G-4

defined, EXCEL G-1

deleting, EXCEL G-6

descriptions of, EXCEL G-2—3

disabling, EXCEL G-3

editing, EXCEL G-8—9

enabling, EXCEL G-3

naming, EXCEL G-2

Personal Macro Workbook, EXCEL G-12—13

planning, EXCEL G-2—3

recording, EXCEL G-4—5

running, EXCEL G-6—7

running main procedure, EXCEL P-16—17

shortcut keys for, EXCEL G-10—11

stopping, while running, EXCEL G-6

storing, EXCEL G-2, EXCEL G-8

uses of, EXCEL G-1

viruses and, EXCEL G-3

main procedures

creating, EXCEL P-14—15

running, EXCEL P-16—17

Major Gridlines checkbox, EXCEL D-10

manual recalculation, EXCEL O-8—9

mapping data, EXCEL J-16—17

margin lines

displaying in Print Preview window, EXCEL D-16

margins

setting, EXCEL E-17

Match case box, EXCEL H-8—9

MAX function, EXCEL B-9, EXCEL E-12—13

creating subtotals with, EXCEL I-10

menu(s). *See also specific menus*

adding macros to, EXCEL G-14—15

restoring defaults to, EXCEL A-7, EXCEL E-2

Merge and Center button, EXCEL C-6

merging

scenarios, EXCEL K-4

workbooks, EXCEL N-7

Microsoft Clip Gallery, EXCEL F-15

Microsoft Investor, EXCEL N-16

Microsoft Investor Stock Quotes, EXCEL N-16—17

Microsoft Map Control dialog box, EXCEL J-16—17

MIN function, EXCEL B-9, EXCEL E-12—13

creating subtotals with, EXCEL I-10

Minor Gridlines check box, EXCEL D-10

mixed cell references, EXCEL B-12

mode indicator, EXCEL B-4

models. *See also* what-if analysis

what-if analysis as, EXCEL K-2

modules

storing macros in, EXCEL G-8

in Visual Basic, EXCEL P-3

More Buttons button, EXCEL A-6, EXCEL A-7

move chart pointer, EXCEL D-7

move pointer, EXCEL B-3

moving

cell entries, EXCEL B-10—11

charts, EXCEL D-6—7

named ranges, EXCEL B-17

worksheets, EXCEL B-18—19

moving border, EXCEL B-6

Multiple Maps Available dialog box, EXCEL J-16

▶N

name box, EXCEL A-6

named cells

in formulas, EXCEL E-4—5

named ranges

absolute references for, EXCEL B-17

copying, EXCEL B-17

in formulas, EXCEL E-4—5

moving, EXCEL B-17

range names, EXCEL B-5

named worksheets, EXCEL B-18—19

names

producing list of, EXCEL E-5

navigating worksheets, EXCEL A-11

with hyperlinks, EXCEL F-14, EXCEL N-14—15

New Database Query, EXCEL M-6

New dialog box

Spreadsheet Solutions tab, EXCEL O-17

New Toolbar dialog box, EXCEL G-16—17

normal (cross) pointer, EXCEL B-3

Not between conditional formatting option, EXCEL C-15

Not equal to conditional formatting option, EXCEL C-15

NOW function, EXCEL E-8

numbers

custom formats, EXCEL E-9

entering as labels, EXCEL A-10

formatting, EXCEL C-2—3, EXCEL H-2

▶O

object linking and embedding (OLE), EXCEL M-2

objects

charts as, EXCEL D-6

defined, EXCEL M-2

embedding, EXCEL B-11

identifying in charts, EXCEL D-7

moving, EXCEL D-6

resizing, EXCEL D-6

in VBA code, EXCEL P-4

Index

Office Assistant, EXCEL A-14–15
Office Assistant dialog box, EXCEL A-14
Office Clipboard, EXCEL B-10–11
OLE, EXCEL M-2
one-input data tables, EXCEL K-8–9
Open command, EXCEL O-17
Open dialog box, EXCEL A-8–9, EXCEL M-4,
    EXCEL O-2
operators
    multiple, in formulas, EXCEL E-2–3
    precedence and, EXCEL E-2
Options dialog box
    Calculation tab, EXCEL O-8
    customizing Excel with, EXCEL O-12–13
Or condition
    in custom filters, EXCEL I-5
    for extracting list data, EXCEL I-8
order of precedence
    in formulas, EXCEL B-6, EXCEL E-2
Outline command, EXCEL O-6
outlines
    creating subtotals using, EXCEL I-10–11
    showing or hiding details in, EXCEL I-11
    of worksheets, EXCEL O-6–7

▶ P

Page Break command, EXCEL F-12
Page Break Preview, EXCEL F-13, EXCEL H-17
page breaks, EXCEL F-12–13
    dynamic, EXCEL F-12
    horizontal, EXCEL F-12–13
    vertical, EXCEL F-12
page fields
    for analyzing three-dimensional data, EXCEL L-8–9
    in PivotTables and PivotCharts, EXCEL L-15
page numbering, EXCEL F-12–13
Page Setup dialog box, EXCEL D-16–17
    Sheet tab, EXCEL H-16–17
Page Setup options, EXCEL E-16–17
panes,
    defined, EXCEL F-2
    splitting vertically, EXCEL O-4–5
    splitting worksheets in, EXCEL F-3
parentheses
    formulas using, EXCEL E-2
password entry prompt, EXCEL N-8–9

passwords
    applying, EXCEL N-8–9
    removing, EXCEL N-9
Paste button, EXCEL B-14,
Paste command, EXCEL B-10
    embedding vs., EXCEL M-10
Paste function button, EXCEL I-12
Paste Function dialog box, EXCEL B-8, EXCEL B-9,
    EXCEL L-16
Paste Special command, EXCEL B-11, EXCEL E-3
patterns
    using in worksheets, EXCEL C-12–13
payments
    calculating with PMT function, EXCEL E-14–15
Pencil button, Windows B-5
Percent style, EXCEL C-2, EXCEL E-4
Personal Macro Workbook, EXCEL G-1, EXCEL G-12–13
perspective
    of 3-D charts, EXCEL J-10–11
Picture menu, EXCEL M-8–9
Picture options, EXCEL M-8
pictures. See also Graphics
    inserting, EXCEL F-15
pie charts, EXCEL D-3, EXCEL D-9
    exploding slice, EXCEL D-15
PivotChart reports, EXCEL L-1
    creating, EXCEL L-14–15
PivotChart Wizard dialog box, EXCEL L-4
PivotTable and PivotChart Wizard, EXCEL L-14–15
PivotTable dialog box, EXCEL L-6
PivotTable Field dialog box, EXCEL L-6, EXCEL L-12
PivotTable Field List dialog box, EXCEL N-13
PivotTable lists
    adding fields to, using Web browser, EXCEL N-13
    defined, EXCEL N-12
    publishing to the Web, EXCEL N-12–13
PivotTable Menu button
    on PivotTable toolbar, EXCEL L-7
PivotTable reports, EXCEL L-1
    analyzing three-dimensional data with,
        EXCEL L-8–9
    changing structure and format of, EXCEL L-12–13
    creating, EXCEL L-4–5
    creating PivotChart tables from, EXCEL L-14–15
    planning and designing, EXCEL L-2–3
    summary function of, EXCEL L-6–7
    updating, EXCEL L-10–11
PivotTables, EXCEL L-1–17

determining location of, EXCEL L-2
determining purpose of, EXCEL L-2
features of, EXCEL L-1
GETPIVOTDATA function, EXCEL L-16–17
interactive, creating for intranet or Web,
    EXCEL N-12–13
interactive, publishing on intranet or the Web,
    EXCEL N-2–3
uses of, EXCEL L-1
PivotTable toolbar, EXCEL L-14
    buttons, EXCEL L-7
PivotTable Wizard button
    on PivotTable toolbar, EXCEL L-7
PivotTable Wizard dialog box, EXCEL L-4–5
PivotTable Wizard Layout dialog box, EXCEL L-12–13
plot area, EXCEL J-6
PMT function, EXCEL E-14–15
pointers
    cell, EXCEL A-6, EXCEL F-2
    commonly used, EXCEL B-3, EXCEL D-7
    copy, EXCEL B-3
    cross (normal), EXCEL B-3
    diagonal resizing, EXCEL D-7
    draw, EXCEL D-7
    fill handle, EXCEL B-3
    horizontal resizing, EXCEL D-7
    I-beam, EXCEL B-3, EXCEL D-7
    move, EXCEL B-3
    move chart, EXCEL D-7
    vertical resizing, EXCEL D-7
    Zoom, EXCEL E-16
pointing method
    for entering formulas, EXCEL B-6
points,
    defined, EXCEL C-4
    row height in, EXCEL C-8
Portrait option, EXCEL E-16–17
posting files to the Web, EXCEL F-16
PowerPoint slides
    embedding Excel charts into, EXCEL M-14–15
precedence, order of, EXCEL E-2
previewing
    charts, EXCEL D-16–17
    multiple worksheets, EXCEL O-15
    worksheets, EXCEL A-12–13, EXCEL B-18
Preview view, EXCEL O-3
primary keys, EXCEL M-16
print areas

clearing, EXCEL H-17

setting, EXCEL H-17

Print dialog box, EXCEL A-12–13, EXCEL H-17

printing

charts, EXCEL D-16–17

formula contents, EXCEL E-16–17

landscape orientation, EXCEL D-16–17

lists, EXCEL H-16–17

more than one worksheet, EXCEL H-16

multiple ranges, EXCEL H-16

multiple worksheets, EXCEL O-15

selected areas of worksheets, EXCEL H-16–17

setting margins and alignment for, EXCEL E-17

worksheets, EXCEL A-12–13

Print Preview, EXCEL E-16–17, EXCEL G-14,
EXCEL H-16–17

for charts, EXCEL D-16–17

for page breaks, EXCEL F-13

for worksheets, EXCEL A-12–13

Zoom in, EXCEL A-12

print title, EXCEL H-16

PRN files, EXCEL M-3

procedure footers, EXCEL P-4

procedure headers, EXCEL P-2

procedures

defined, EXCEL P-1

main, EXCEL P-14–15, EXCEL P-16–17

PRODUCT function, EXCEL L-6

programming, EXCEL P-1–17

Programs list, EXCEL A-4–5

Project Explorer

in Visual Basic, EXCEL P-3

Project Explorer button, EXCEL P-2

Project Explorer window, EXCEL P-16

projects

in Visual Basic, EXCEL P-3

prompts

in VBA code, EXCEL P-10–11

properties, Windows A-12

associated with modules, EXCEL P-3

in VBA code, EXCEL P-4

Properties dialog box, EXCEL O-3, EXCEL O-12–13

Properties view, EXCEL O-3

Properties window

in Project Explorer, EXCEL P-3

Properties Window button, EXCEL P-2

Property Toolbox button, EXCEL N-10

protection, of worksheets areas, EXCEL F-8–9

Protection tab, EXCEL F-8–9

Publish as Web Page dialog box, EXCEL N-10,
EXCEL N-12–13

▶**Q**

Quattro/Quattro Pro, EXCEL M-3

queries

retrieving data from Web with, EXCEL N-2–3,
EXCEL N-16–17

question mark (?) wildcard, EXCEL H-9

in custom filters, EXCEL I-4

▶**R**

radar charts, EXCEL D-9

range address, EXCEL B-5

range finder, EXCEL B-16

range names. *See* named ranges

range objects

in VBA code, EXCEL P-4

ranges

defined, EXCEL A-10, EXCEL B-5

deleting, EXCEL H-10

formatting, EXCEL C-2–3

printing multiple, EXCEL H-16

working with, EXCEL B-4–5

recalculation

computer *vs.* manual systems, EXCEL A-2

controlling, EXCEL O-8–9

recording macros, EXCEL G-4–5

Record Macro dialog box, EXCEL G-4–5,
EXCEL G-10–11, EXCEL G-12–13

records

defined, EXCEL H-2

deleting, EXCEL H-10–11

finding in lists, EXCEL H-8–9

restoring, EXCEL H-11

retrieving, with AutoFilter, EXCEL I-2–3

Redisplay Dialog Box button, EXCEL E-12

references. *See also* absolute cell references; relative
cell references

circular, EXCEL O-5

creating, EXCEL F-6

external reference indicators, EXCEL F-6

3-D, EXCEL F-6–7

Refresh Data button

on PivotTable toolbar, EXCEL L-7

Refresh Data command, EXCEL L-10–11

refreshing PivotTables, EXCEL L-7, EXCEL L-10–11

relative cell references

copying formulas with, EXCEL B-14–15

defined, EXCEL B-12

using, EXCEL B-12–13

Relative Reference button, EXCEL G-10–11

Replace All option, EXCEL H-8–9

Replace dialog box, EXCEL H-8–9

Replace option, EXCEL H-8–9

Report Manager, EXCEL F-10, EXCEL K-7

reports

creating with Report Manager, EXCEL K-7

PivotChart, EXCEL L-1

PivotTable, EXCEL L-1, EXCEL L-2–13

resizing charts, EXCEL D-6–7

restoring records, EXCEL H-11

restricted cells

entering data in, EXCEL I-16–17

Result cells box, EXCEL K-6

Returning External Data to Microsoft Excel dialog box,
EXCEL N-16

rotating chart labels, EXCEL J-15

rotating charts, EXCEL D-8, EXCEL J-10–11

rotating labels, EXCEL H-12

rotating text, EXCEL J-14–15

round tripping, HTML, EXCEL M-9

row fields

in PivotTables and PivotCharts, EXCEL L-15

row headings

printing, EXCEL H-16

Row Height command, EXCEL C-8

Row_index_num

for HLOOKUP function, EXCEL I-13

rows

deleting, EXCEL C-10–11

dummy, EXCEL C-11

freezing, EXCEL F-2–3

hiding/unhiding, EXCEL F-9

inserting, EXCEL C-10–11

Index

specifying height of, EXCEL C-8
running macros, EXCEL G-6—7
Run Query dialog box, EXCEL N-16

►S

Sample box
  in Chart Wizard dialog box, EXCEL J-2—3
Save As command
  creating new workbook with, EXCEL A-8—9
  importing data with, EXCEL M-6—7
Save As dialog box, EXCEL F-16—17,
  creating folder in, EXCEL F-16
Save command, EXCEL A-8
Save Options dialog box, EXCEL N-8—9
saving
  custom views, EXCEL F-10—11
  as HTML files, EXCEL F-16—17
  workbooks, EXCEL A-8—9
scatter (XY) charts, EXCEL D-3, EXCEL D-9
Scenario Manager, EXCEL K-1
  tracking what-if analysis with, EXCEL K-4—5
Scenario Manager dialog box, EXCEL K-4, EXCEL K-6
scenarios
  creating, EXCEL K-4—5
  defined, EXCEL K-4
  merging, EXCEL K-4
scenario summaries, EXCEL K-6—7
Scenario Summary dialog box, EXCEL K-6—7
Scenario Values dialog box, EXCEL K-4—5
ScreenTips, EXCEL A-14,
  tracking changes to shared workbooks with,
    EXCEL N-6—7
search criteria. See criteria
searches. See finding
section handles
  for charts, EXCEL D-4
selections, of worksheets
  printing, EXCEL E-17
sequential text
  filling cells with, EXCEL B-15
Series (y) axis, EXCEL J-7
shared workbooks, EXCEL N-2
  applying and removing passwords, EXCEL N-8—9
  change history for, EXCEL N-4
  defined, EXCEL N-4
  issues, EXCEL N-2—3

setting up, EXCEL N-4—5
  tracking changes in, EXCEL N-6—7
Share Workbook dialog box, EXCEL N-4—5
sheet tabs, EXCEL A-6
sheet tab scrolling buttons, EXCEL A-6, EXCEL B-18
shortcut keys, for macros, EXCEL G-10—11
shortcuts
  formatting, EXCEL C-6
Show Detail button
  on PivotTable toolbar, EXCEL L-7
Show Details button, EXCEL I-11
Show/Hide Fields button
  on PivotTable toolbar, EXCEL L-7
sizing handles
  for custom charts, EXCEL J-2
slides
  embedding Excel charts into, EXCEL M-14—15
Solver, EXCEL K-1
  setting up complex what-if analyses with,
    EXCEL K-14—15
Solver Parameters dialog box, EXCEL K-14—15,
  EXCEL K-16
Solver Results dialog box, EXCEL K-16—17
sort buttons, EXCEL H-12
Sort command, EXCEL H-12
Sort Descending button, EXCEL M-6
Sort dialog box, EXCEL H-14—15
sorting
  ascending order, EXCEL H-12—13, EXCEL H-14
  custom sort order, EXCEL H-15
  descending order, EXCEL H-12, EXCEL H-14
  entry order, EXCEL H-12
  lists, by multiple fields, EXCEL H-14—15
  lists, by one field, EXCEL H-12—13
sort keys, EXCEL H-14—15
source list
  updating, EXCEL L-10—11
source programs, EXCEL M-2
space delimited files, EXCEL M-3
spell checking, EXCEL C-16—17
Spelling dialog box, EXCEL C-16—17
splitting worksheets, EXCEL F-3
Spreadsheet Property Toolbox, EXCEL N-10—11
spreadsheets. See worksheets
Spreadsheet Solutions tab
  in New dialog box, EXCEL O-17
standard chart types, EXCEL J-2

Standard toolbar
  defined, EXCEL A-6
  restoring defaults, EXCEL A-7
Start button,
Start menu, EXCEL A-5
statements
  in VBA code, EXCEL P-4
statistical functions, EXCEL E-12—13
status bar, EXCEL A-6
stock symbols, EXCEL N-16
Stop Recording button, EXCEL G-4—5
Stop Recording toolbar, EXCEL G-4—5, EXCEL G-10—11
strings
  in VBA code, EXCEL P-10
Style dialog box, EXCEL E-4
styles
  applying, EXCEL E-4
  defined, EXCEL E-4
  defining own, EXCEL E-4
Sub procedures, EXCEL P-2
subtotals
  creating using functions, EXCEL I-10
  creating with grouping, EXCEL I-10—11
  creating with outlines, EXCEL I-10—11
Subtotals dialog box, EXCEL I-10—11
SUM function, EXCEL B-8, EXCEL B-9, EXCEL E-13,
  EXCEL L-6
  creating subtotals with, EXCEL I-10
  entering with AutoSum button, EXCEL E-6—7
summarizing list data, EXCEL I-14—15
summary function
  of PivotTables, EXCEL L-6—7
summary rows and columns
  outlining and, EXCEL O-6—7
SYLK files, EXCEL M-3
Symbol Lookup hyperlink, EXCEL N-16
syntax
  of VBA code, EXCEL P-5, EXCEL P-8

►T

Tab delimited files, EXCEL M-3
Table dialog box, EXCEL K-8—9, EXCEL K-10—11
tables. See Access tables; database tables; data
  tables; PivotTables
target cells
  in what-if analysis, EXCEL K-14—15

targets
hyperlinks to, EXCEL F-14–15
templates
applying, EXCEL O-17
creating workbooks with, EXCEL G-5
defined, EXCEL O-16
modifying, EXCEL O-17
saving workbooks as, EXCEL O-16–17
storing, EXCEL O-17
Templates folder, EXCEL O-16–17
text
alignment in charts, EXCEL D-12
color of, EXCEL C-12–13
rotating, EXCEL J-14–15
sequential, filling cells with, EXCEL B-15
text annotations
adding to charts, EXCEL D-14–15
repositioning, EXCEL D-15
Text box button, EXCEL D-14
text files
delimiters in, EXCEL M-4
importing, EXCEL M-4–5
Text Import Wizard dialog boxes, EXCEL M-4–5
three-dimensional data
analyzing, EXCEL L-8–9
three-dimensional (3-D) charts
rotating, EXCEL D-8, EXCEL J-10–11
types of, EXCEL D-9
3-D references, EXCEL F-6–7
3-D View dialog box, EXCEL J-10–11
tick marks, EXCEL D-2
title bar, EXCEL A-6,
titles
for charts, EXCEL D-12–13
printing, EXCEL H-16
for x- and y-axis, EXCEL D-12–13
TODAY function, EXCEL E-8
toolbars,
Auditing, EXCEL O-4–5
Chart, EXCEL D-6–7,
EXCEL D-10, EXCEL J-2, EXCEL J-15
Circular Reference, EXCEL O-5
creating for macros, EXCEL G-16–17
defined, EXCEL A-6
Drawing, EXCEL D-14, EXCEL J-12

External Data, EXCEL N-16
Formatting, EXCEL A-6, EXCEL A-7, EXCEL C-4,
EXCEL H-4
hiding and displaying, EXCEL O-5
PivotTable, EXCEL L-7, EXCEL L-14
restoring defaults, EXCEL A-7, EXCEL D-4,
EXCEL E-2
Standard, EXCEL A-6, EXCEL A-7
Stop Recording, EXCEL G-4–5, EXCEL G-10–11
Visual Basic Editor Standard, EXCEL P-16
Visual Basic Standard, EXCEL P-6
Top 10 AutoFilter dialog box, EXCEL I-2
tracer arrows, EXCEL O-4–5
trackballs, Windows A-5
tracking changes
in shared workbooks, EXCEL N-4, EXCEL N-6–7
Transition tab
of Options dialog box, EXCEL O-13
truncated labels, EXCEL A-10
two-input data tables, EXCEL K-10–11
TXT files, EXCEL M-3

▶U

Underline button, EXCEL C-6
Undo button, EXCEL B-4
Undo command
restoring deleted records with, EXCEL H-11
Unfreeze panes command, EXCEL F-2
Uniform Resource Locators (URLs)
creating hyperlinks to, EXCEL N-14–15
User-defined chart types, EXCEL J-3

▶V

validation, of data. See data validation
Value Axis Title, EXCEL D-12
values
alignment of, EXCEL A-10
defined, EXCEL A-10
entering, EXCEL A-10–11
formatting, EXCEL C-2–3
looking up in a list, EXCEL I-12–13
Value (y) axis, EXCEL J-6–7

Value (z) axis, EXCEL J-7
variables
in VBA code, EXCEL P-10
VBA, EXCEL P-1
VBA code
adding conditional statements in, EXCEL P-8–9
analyzing, EXCEL P-4–5
creating main procedures, EXCEL P-14–15
defined, EXCEL P-1
functions in, EXCEL P-10–11
prompting the user for data, EXCEL P-10–11
running main procedures, EXCEL P-16–17
syntax of, EXCEL P-5
viewing, EXCEL P-2–3
writing, EXCEL P-5–6
Vertical Lookup function. See VLOOKUP function
vertical resizing pointer, EXCEL D-7
vertical split box, EXCEL O-4
views
custom, saving, EXCEL F-10–11
View tab
of Options dialog box, EXCEL O-13
viruses
macros and, EXCEL G-3
Virus warning dialog box, EXCEL P-2, EXCEL P-3
Visual Basic Applications. See VBA
Visual Basic Editor, EXCEL P-2–3
adding conditional statements in, EXCEL P-8–9
code-writing aids in, EXCEL P-6
debugging macros in, EXCEL P-12–13
writing VBA code in, EXCEL P-5–6
Visual Basic Editor Standard toolbar, EXCEL P-16
Visual Basic Standard toolbar, EXCEL P-6
VLOOKUP dialog box, EXCEL I-12–13
VLOOKUP function, EXCEL I-12–13

▶W

Web. See World Wide Web
Web browsers
adding fields to PivotTable lists with, EXCEL N-13
viewing interactive PivotTables in, EXCEL N-12–13
viewing interactive worksheets in, EXCEL N-10–11
Web Page Preview, EXCEL F-16–17
what-if analysis, EXCEL K-1–17

Index

complex, Solver for, EXCEL K-14—17

copying formulas with absolute cell references for, EXCEL B-16—17

data tables for, EXCEL K-8—9

defined, EXCEL A-2, EXCEL K-1

defining, EXCEL K-2—3

generating scenarios summary, EXCEL K-6—7

generating Solver Answer Report, EXCEL K-16—17

Goal Seek for, EXCEL K-12—13

tracking with Scenario Manager, EXCEL K-4—5

two-input data tables for, EXCEL K-10—11

wildcards

finding files with, EXCEL O-2

for searches, EXCEL H-8—9

WKS files, EXCEL M-3

Word Art

in charts, EXCEL J-12—13

WordPad,

linking worksheets to, EXCEL M-12—13

workbooks, EXCEL F-1—17

applying and removing passwords, EXCEL N-8—9

closing, EXCEL A-16—17

consolidating data from, with linking, EXCEL F-7

creating, by modifying existing workbook, EXCEL A-8—9

creating hyperlinks between, EXCEL F-14—15

creating with templates, EXCEL G-5

defined, EXCEL A-6

deleting worksheets from, EXCEL F-4—5

distributing to others, EXCEL N-2

documenting, with comments, EXCEL O-14—15

inserting pictures in, EXCEL F-15

inserting worksheets in, EXCEL F-4—5

merging, EXCEL N-7

opening, EXCEL A-8—9

protecting, EXCEL F-9

saving, EXCEL A-8—9

saving as a template, EXCEL O-16—17

saving as HTML documents, EXCEL F-16—17

saving text files as, EXCEL M-4—5

sending via e-mail, EXCEL F-17

on server, controlling access to, EXCEL N-2

setting up, EXCEL N-4—5

shared, EXCEL N-2

specifying headers and footers for, EXCEL F-5

tracking changes in, EXCEL N-6—7

using range names in, EXCEL B-5

worksheet logic, EXCEL O-4

Worksheet menu bar

adding macros to, EXCEL G-14—15

worksheets

auditing, EXCEL O-4—5

borders in, EXCEL C-12—13

calculations for, EXCEL B-2

color in, EXCEL C-12—13

common business uses for, EXCEL A-3

computer vs. manual systems, EXCEL A-2—3

conditional formatting, EXCEL C-14—15

copying, EXCEL B-19, EXCEL F-4

creating, EXCEL A-2, EXCEL B-2—3

defined, EXCEL A-2

deleting, EXCEL B-18, EXCEL F-4—5

embedding, EXCEL M-10—11

embedding objects in, EXCEL B-11

enhancing, EXCEL J-1

formatting, EXCEL C-1—17

hiding areas of, EXCEL F-8—9

inserting, EXCEL F-4—5

inserting graphic into, EXCEL M-8—9

interactive, creating for intranet or Web, EXCEL N-10—11

interactive, publishing on intranet or the Web, EXCEL N-2—3

linking to another program, EXCEL M-12—13

moving, EXCEL B-18—19

moving among, EXCEL B-18

multiple, previewing and printing, EXCEL O-15

naming, EXCEL B-18—19

navigating, EXCEL A-11

navigating with hyperlinks, EXCEL F-14, EXCEL N-15

outlining, EXCEL O-6—7

page breaks and page numbering, EXCEL F-12—13

patterns in, EXCEL C-12—13

planning and designing, EXCEL B-2—3

predefined formats, EXCEL C-7

previewing, EXCEL A-12—13, EXCEL B-18

printing, EXCEL A-12—13, EXCEL H-16—17

printing more than one, EXCEL H-16

printing selected areas of, EXCEL E-17, EXCEL H-16—17

protecting areas of, EXCEL F-8—9

publishing on intranet or the Web, EXCEL N-2—3

recalculating, EXCEL O-8—9

saving as HTML documents, EXCEL F-16—17

spell checking, EXCEL C-16—17

splitting into multiple panes, EXCEL F-3

title for, EXCEL B-2

worksheet window

defined, EXCEL A-6

viewing, EXCEL A-6—7

workspaces, EXCEL F-11

World Wide Web,

creating interactive PivotTables for, EXCEL N-12—13

creating interactive workbooks for, EXCEL N-10—11

customized queries on, EXCEL N-17

managing HTML files on, EXCEL N-11

preparing workbooks for publishing on, EXCEL F-14—17

publishing interactive workbooks and PivotTables to, EXCEL N-2—3

running queries on, EXCEL N-2—3, EXCEL N-16—17

Wrap Text, EXCEL H-4

▶ X

x-axis, EXCEL D-2

creating titles for, EXCEL D-12—13

XLM files, EXCEL M-3

.xlt extension, EXCEL O-16

XLT files, EXCEL M-3

XY (scatter) charts, EXCEL D-3, EXCEL D-9

▶ Y

y-axis, EXCEL D-2

creating titles for, EXCEL D-12—13

▶ Z

Zoom

in Print Preview, EXCEL A-12

Zoom box, EXCEL F-10

Zoom pointer, EXCEL E-16

What's On The CD-ROM

The **MOUS Excel 2000 Prep**'s companion CD-ROM contains elements specifically selected to enhance the usefulness of this book, including:

► Projects designed to reinforce concepts learned from the book

► Solutions for the Concepts Review questions found at the end of each chapter in the book

System Requirements
Software:

► Your operating system must be Windows 95, 98, NT4, or higher.

► Microsoft Excel 2000 is needed to complete the projects included in this book. (The software is not provided on this CD-ROM.)

Hardware:

► An Intel (or equivalent) Pentium 100MHz processor is the minimum platform required.

► 32MB of RAM is the minimum requirement.